Sports, Convention, and Entertainment Facilities

David C. Petersen

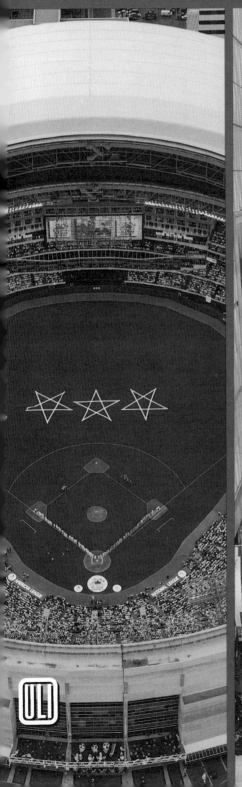

Urban Land
Institute

ABOUT ULI– THE URBAN LAND INSTITUTE

ULI–the Urban Land Institute is a nonprofit education and research institute that is supported and directed by its members. Its mission is to provide responsible leadership in the use of land in order to enhance the total environment.

ULI sponsors educational programs and forums to encourage an open international exchange of ideas and sharing of experience; initiates research that anticipates emerging land use trends and issues and proposes creative solutions based on this research; provides advisory services; and publishes a wide variety of materials to disseminate information on land use and development.

Established in 1936, the Institute today has some 13,000 members and associates from more than 50 countries representing the entire spectrum of the land use and development disciplines. They include developers, builders, property owners, investors, architects, public officials, planners, real estate brokers, appraisers, attorneys, engineers, financiers, academics, students, and librarians. ULI members contribute to higher standards of land use by sharing their knowledge and experience. The Institute has long been recognized as one of America's most respected and widely quoted sources of objective information on urban planning, growth, and development.

Richard M. Rosan
Executive Vice President

PROJECT STAFF

Rachelle L. Levitt
Senior Vice President
Research, Education, and Publications

Frank H. Spink, Jr.
Vice President/Publisher
Project Director

Nancy H. Stewart
Managing Editor

Ann Lenny
Manuscript Editor

Helene Redmond
HYR Graphics
Book Design and Layout

Kim Rusch
Graphics

Diann Stanley-Austin
Production Manager

Recommended bibliographic listing:

Petersen, David C. *Sports, Convention, and Entertainment Facilities.* Washington, D.C.: ULI–the Urban Land Institute, 1996.

ULI Catalog Number: S04
International Standard Book Number: 0-87420-781-9
Library of Congress Catalog Card Number: 95-62037

Copyright 1996 by ULI–the Urban Land Institute
1025 Thomas Jefferson Street, N.W.
Washington, D.C. 20007-5201

ABOUT THE AUTHOR

Real estate economic research, financial analysis, and city planning have occupied David Petersen for 30 years. In a diversity of roles, he has analyzed a broad spectrum of land uses and building types. Following his graduation from San Jose State University, where he received his degree in economics with distinction and honors, he was employed by a Wall Street investment banking firm to conduct credit analysis of local and state government securities. He then managed urban economic planning and real estate market studies for Booz, Allen, Hamilton, also in New York City. In 1972, he became the first executive director of Lexington Center Corporation and coordinated the development of its arena/theater/convention center/hotel/retail complex, which opened in 1976. He now serves as managing director of the Price Waterhouse Sports, Convention, and Entertainment Facilities Group.

He has presented the results of his research and analysis of development trends and issues to various organizations, including the Annual Stadium Managers Seminar; International City/County Managers Associa-tion Annual Conference; European Incentive, Business Travel, and Meetings Conference; International Association of Auditorium Managers; International Convention Center Conference; Association Internationale des Palais de Congrès; Japan National Tourist Organization; Society of Business Writers; and others. His articles have been published in *Facility Manager; Conferences, Exhibitions & Incentives; Urban Land; Amusement Business; Convene; Practicing Planner; Meetings and Conventions; Agent and Manager;* and *Tradeshow Week*. He has also been quoted in periodicals such as the *New York Times, Governing, Atlantic Monthly, Barrons,* the *Wall Street Journal,* and the *Washington Post.*

Petersen has conducted economic studies for 29 of the 74 case-study facilities in this book and personally inspected almost all of them. He has provided services to 34 major league teams and venues, and his clients have included center owners, management firms, franchise owners, and developers in most major North American destinations, as well as the Asia-Pacific region, Europe, Australia, and the Caribbean.

REVIEW COMMITTEE

As the manuscript for a ULI book nears completion, a manuscript review committee is formed under the aegis of the ULI Research Committee responsible for oversight of the subject area of the book. For *Sports, Convention, and Entertainment Facilities*, this was a challenge as the book covers so many types of venues, each with its own unique characteristics. And, in addition to the facility itself, ULI is always concerned about the broader land use aspects of major land use elements as they affect the community with regard to traffic, environmental, and economic impacts. The review committee for *Sports, Convention, and Entertainment Facilities* is listed below. Committee members read and commented on the substance of the manuscript, in terms both of accuracy and completeness. These comments were then considered by the author in making revisions or adding materials. As is always the case, the review committee was most helpful.

Frank H. Spink
ULI Vice President/Publisher

REVIEWERS

William R. Eager
President
TDA Inc.
Seattle, Washington

Michael F. Kelly
Chairman
Madison Marquette Realty Services, Ltd.
Minneapolis, Minnesota

Ruben A. Roca
Vice President and Director
Research and Site Strategy
The Rouse Company
Columbia, Maryland

Ron Roberts
Executive Director
Cincinnati Business Committee
Cincinnati, Ohio

David A. Sherf
Senior Vice President, Development
Doubletree Hotels Corporation
Phoenix, Arizona

Janet Marie Smith
Vice President, Sports Facilities
Turner Properties
Atlanta, Georgia

ACKNOWLEDGMENTS

I would like to express my gratitude to the Price Waterhouse partners who support the national and international scope of our sports, convention, and entertainment facilities group. Developing this practice in a single location has enabled us to recruit and train a highly specialized staff of professionals, maintain extensive databases, develop more reliable analytical techniques, and obtain important economic research and financial planning assignments that would not have been possible if we had been limited by local or even regional boundaries. Consequently, the geographic scope of this practice has enabled our group to conduct major assignments in nearly every metropolitan market in the United States and in many foreign countries.

These economic evaluations for new and expanding centers involve an extensive (and exhaustive) amount of travel, nearly every week. The unique characteristics of each community and the diverse priorities of project sponsors require long hours of touring sites, conferring with prospective tenants, data gathering, discussing key issues with local civic and business leaders, and performing other on-location analysis. These assignments are typically time-sensitive (six to 12 weeks) and are completed for a fixed fee.

Providing objective recommendations and functioning as a viable enterprise require our staff to possess an extraordinary level of discipline, ethics, dedication, and esprit de corps. It is with deep appreciation that I extend my thanks to Karel Estes, Teresa Reiss, and Nilgün Kamp, who have assisted in assembling the project data and preparing narrative descriptions for the case studies in this book, and to my colleague Rob Canton for his valuable insights and constant support. For the past five years, Sandra Gerenski has worked diligently to edit our reports and to design and produce effective and attractive graphics that ensure the readability and reliability of our written products. Her intelligence, creativity, and dedication have enabled us to meet many short deadlines, to complete the always unexpected requests for additional services, and to keep smiling.

The planning and development process requires the collaborative efforts of many professional disciplines. I must also acknowledge the important contributions, insights, and ideas shared with me by venue managers, architects, urban designers/planners, developers, builders, concessionaires, attorneys, and owners over the past 30 years. For their special help and extra efforts on this book, I wish to acknowledge my indebtedness to Janet Marie Smith, Tom Ventulett, Ron Labinski, and Dan Graveline.

Most important, I must thank my wife, Eileen, for her support and encouragement in these endeavors.

David C. Petersen
Price Waterhouse LLP
Tampa, Florida

CONTENTS

CHAPTER 9. ECONOMIC IMPACTS: FISCAL BENEFITS VERSUS DEBT AND NET OPERATING COSTS . .

CHAPTER 10. FINANCING AND FUNDING

PART II: U.S. CASE STUDIES 109

AMPHITHEATERS 110

ARENAS 134

CONVENTION CENTERS 176

STADIUMS 222

PART I
SPORTS, CONVENTION, AND ENTERTAINMENT FACILITIES

Chapter 1

INTRODUCTION

struggling to divest themselves of their heavy deficits? How do location, design, and management affect the financial success of these enterprises?

These issues are the focus of this book.

It is important to understand the similarities and differences among arenas, stadiums, amphitheaters, and convention centers: what they have in common and how they perform different functions and serve unrelated industries. It is also helpful to understand some of the terminology used in describing these facilities and, in the process, to avoid some of the confusion that arises from such terms as "civic center" and "coliseum." This chapter will deal with these topics and will preview the organization of the book as a whole.

THE FACILITY TYPES: SIMILARITIES AND DIFFERENCES

Arenas, stadiums, and amphitheaters, with their oval, bowl, or boomerang shapes for spectator seating, obviously differ in appearance from the rectangular boxes en-

Today, the construction of nearly all public assembly facilities is financed by local and state governments. Economic or community improvement is the most frequent motive for the facilities' development. They hold little interest for the private real estate developer because most facilities are publicly owned and subsidized. And they often baffle the public sector, which typically knows little about dealing with the peculiar issues they involve. Most facilities lose money, they frequently generate controversy or become political liabilities, and they do not fit neatly into the traditional purposes of local governments, as do city halls, water plants, fire stations, and public works. Unlike these and other "essential" public facilities (to provide for citizens' safety and welfare), assembly facilities are not always considered the business of government. Not surprisingly, their most vocal advocates are sports franchise owners, concert promoters, and hotel managers.

Although it is difficult, if not impossible, to identify an ancient city that did not have a public market, *agora*, lyceum, forum, stadium, arena, or amphitheater, most modern cities still debate their value and cost-effectiveness. And yet, as Figure 1-1 shows, an increasing number of convention centers and spectator facilities are being built each year—almost always through projects sponsored by local and state governments, encouraged by local business leaders, and suspected by everyone else.

In rare instances, private developers successfully develop and operate assembly facilities. Why and how? Why are some cities and counties incurring significant debt to have such buildings constructed, while others are

The current state of the art: America West Arena, Phoenix, Arizona.

Figure 1-1

RECENT CONSTRUCTION OF PUBLIC ASSEMBLY FACILITIES

Year Built	Convention Centers[1]	Major League Arenas	Major League Stadiums	Amphitheaters	Total
1985	5	3	1	1	10
1986	5	–	1	2	8
1987	5	–	2	3	10
1988	2	5	5	3	15
1989	2	1	1	1	5
1990	4	1	1	3	9
1991	1	1	1	3	6
1992	1	1	2	–	4
1993	3	3	3	3	12
1994	–	3	2	1	6
1995[2]	2	5	3	1	11
Total	30	23	22	21	96

[1]New centers with more than 100,000 square feet of exhibition space.
[2]Includes facilities under construction.

closing convention centers and exhibition halls. Similarities among all these types, however, are more subtle. In terms of their financial operations, most convention centers and spectator facilities are subsidized. Because most incur operating losses, only a few contribute any operating surplus to debt service or depreciation costs. Accordingly, nearly all are owned by local or state governments or their agencies. Within a community, they are one-of-a-kind buildings. Unlike office buildings, retail centers, hotels, school facilities, or residential developments, few communities have more than one hockey arena, one football stadium, or one convention center. And most cities and towns have no major assembly centers. Only the largest localities have all types.

Arenas, stadiums, and amphitheaters are developed in the largest metropolitan areas to accommodate major league football, baseball, and hockey, basketball games, and/or popular music concerts. In the first half of the 20th century, most of these buildings were developed, owned, and operated by entrepreneurs or owners of professional sports teams.

SPORTS FACILITIES

In 1986, the owner of the Miami Dolphins NFL (National Football League) team developed a privately financed stadium just north of Miami. More recently, in 1992, the owners of the Chicago Bulls and the Blackhawks financed the development of the United Arena in Chicago. The Pine Knob Amphitheater outside Detroit and the Palace (arena) at Auburn Hills also were privately financed, by the owners of the Detroit Pistons. Nevertheless, most sports facilities are publicly financed, and their operations are subsidized to enable local communities or states to attract or retain a professional sports team. Cities build such facilities for many reasons: to be known as a "major league city" and to receive the attendant free advertising; to lure industry and national or regional office headquarters, whose executives prize a major league team in their community as a benefit for their employees and for the entertainment of clients. Cities that worked feverishly to obtain major league franchises in the 1960s are now contemplating or have already constructed domed stadiums. To such a community, the "dome" will ensure its status as a first-tier city in the 21st century.

Public development/ownership of major league sports facilities outnumbers private ownership by 61 to 22, a pattern that can be seen in Figure 1-2. At one time, nearly all baseball stadiums were privately owned. With facility replacements and franchise relocations, the public sector has assumed responsibility for new facility ownership.

Many professional football teams played in baseball stadiums as the sport emerged in the late 1930s and

Figure 1-2

OWNERSHIP OF MAJOR LEAGUE U.S. STADIUMS AND ARENAS

City	Stadiums		Arenas	
	Baseball (MLB)	Football (NFL)	Basketball (NBA)	Hockey (NHL)
Anaheim	Public	–	–	Public
Atlanta	Public	Public	Private	–
Baltimore	Public	–	–	–
Boston/Foxboro	Private	Private	Private	Private
Buffalo	–	Public	–	Public
Charlotte	–	Public	Public	–
Chicago	Public/Private	Public	Private	Private
Cincinnati	Public	Public	–	–
Cleveland	Private	Public	Public	–
Dallas/Irving/Arlington	Public	Private	Public	Public
Denver	Public	Public	Public	Public
Detroit/Pontiac/Auburn Hills	Public	Public	Private	Public
East Rutherford	–	Public	Public	Public
Hartford	–	–	–	Public
Houston	Private	Private	Public	–
Indianapolis	–	Public	Public	–
Jacksonville	–	Public	–	–
Kansas City	Public	Public	–	–
Los Angeles/Inglewood	Private	–	Public/Private	Private
Miami	Private	Private	Public	Public
Milwaukee/Green Bay	Public	Public	Private	–
Minneapolis	Public	Public	Private	–
New Orleans	–	Public	–	–
New York	Public (2)	–	Private	Private
Oakland	Public	Public	Public	–
Orlando	–	–	Public	–
Philadelphia	Public	Public	Private	Private
Phoenix	Public	Public	Public	–
Pittsburgh	Public	Public	–	Public
Portland, Oregon	–	–	Private	–
Sacramento	–	–	Private	–
St. Louis	Public	Public	–	Public
Salt Lake City	–	–	Private	–
San Antonio	–	–	Public	–
San Diego	Public	Public	–	–
San Francisco	Public	Public	–	–
San Jose	–	–	–	Public
Seattle	Public	Public	Public	–
Tampa/St. Petersburg	Public	Public	–	Public
Uniondale, New York	–	–	–	Public
Washington, D.C.	–	Public	Private[1]	Private[1]

[1]Landover, Maryland.

4

1940s. New football and multipurpose stadiums were publicly financed in the 1950s and 1960s, when local governments perceived—as they had with professional baseball—the public benefit to be derived from retaining or enhancing their professional football franchises. Similarly, an older sport, professional ice hockey, originally was played in privately owned ice arenas. As these facilities grew older and as basketball matured as a professional sport, local governments built new, multipurpose hockey/basketball arenas.

THEATRICAL AND CONCERT VENUES

Open-air amphitheaters are among the most prevalent and most elegant structures in ancient, notably Greek and Roman, cities. Many are in current use for plays, concerts, and civic ceremonies. The popular musician Sting, for instance, performed to a sold-out audience in the 25,000-seat (and 2,000-year-old) amphitheater in Ephesus (Efes, Turkey) in June 1993.

Amphitheater development in the 20th century was sporadic until the 1980s. Many were noted as the summer homes of major city symphony orchestras that offered pops concerts from June through September. Such venues included Blossom Music Center (Cleveland Symphony), Wolf Trap Farm Park for the Performing Arts (National Symphony), Chastain Park (Atlanta Symphony), and Riverbend Music Center (Cincinnati Symphony). Some amphitheaters have been developed in natural geological bowl formations, such as Red Rocks Amphitheater, near Denver.

The recent surge in amphitheater development has reflected a major shift in the preferences of both audiences and performers from arenas to amphitheaters. This shift has been fueled by negative as well as positive forces. The number of indoor arenas, especially those with NHL and NBA (National Hockey League and National Basketball Association) teams as anchor tenants, continued to multiply from the 1960s through the 1990s, distributing 16,000- to 20,000-seat venues among nearly all "top 50" metropolitan markets.

During the 1980s, the most popular touring acts, such as rock music groups, reduced the number and length of their tours. This change caused increased competition for the shrinking number of acts among the large supply of arenas and meant lower profit margins for concert promoters and the owners of arenas. While production costs and transportation expenses of shows continued to rise, the overhead cost per performance rose dramatically. This set of circumstances has pushed booking agents and concert promoters to seek lower-cost locations offering higher margins.

The trend away from arenas to outdoor venues was furthered by the trend toward the aging of concert audiences. With some justification, members of the demographic bubble of baby boomers may believe that they invented outdoor rock concerts. In any case, these audiences have shown that they prefer the ambience of an outdoor setting in which to enjoy their (now) middle-aged, if not middle-of-the-road, performers.

Over the past 20 years of amphitheater development, local governments have paid for an increasing portion of the land and construction costs, rather than accept the loss of outdoor concert activity to a neighboring community. More and more touring groups are equipped or booked exclusively for outdoor-only venues. The decline in indoor concert activity has been simultaneous with the rise in the numbers of events held at outdoor venues. The motive for attracting nonresident spending or retaining local resident spending (taxes) produces competition among rival communities in a metropolitan area to construct an amphitheater. This same competition fuels bidding wars to attract a major league franchise team by offering attractive terms for occupying a new stadium or arena, or, not infrequently, to steal a professional sports franchise from a neighboring community.

REASONS FOR DEVELOPMENT

A community's hospitality industry and/or its advocates of central-city revitalization are the vested interests or stakeholders most likely to promote the development of a convention center to increase out-of-town visitors' spending in their community. Compared with tourists, delegates to conventions and trade shows stay longer in most destinations and spend more per day. Figure 1-3 estimates the expenditure patterns of various types of special-event or leisure-oriented visitors. A successful convention center and exhibition hall generates additional hotel occupancy, retail sales, and restaurant sales. If a facility is built in the heart of a city, it augments the types of businesses (specialty shops, restaurants, and hotels) that attract first-class office-space developers, theaters, and—it is hoped—new residents to the downtown. Thus, a convention center can help establish the downtown as an entertainment center and, possibly, a more diverse or cosmopolitan environment.

In the 20 years following the end of World War II, explosive growth took place outside cities' cores. This growth was soon followed by the suburbanization of retail trade, by the development of perimeter office centers ("edge cities"), and occasionally by the relocation outside the center city of other, traditionally downtown anchors:

Figure 1-3

DIRECT ECONOMIC IMPACT PER TYPE OF VISITOR: ILLUSTRATIVE EXAMPLES

	Type of Visitor						
	Fair/ Exposition	Professional Sports	Concert/ Cultural	Independent Tourist	Tour-Bus Tourist	Convention Delegate	Super Bowl
Average Expenditure per Day	$24 (or less)	$36 (or less)	$42 (or less)	$60	$96	$114	$252
Percent Requiring Overnight Accommodations	5–10% (or less)	5–10% (or less)	5–10% (or less)	50–80%	70–80%	80–95%	90%
Weighted Average Length of Stay (days)	NA	NA	NA	5.0	3.0	3.5	5.3
Total Direct Economic Impact per Visitor	$24 (or less)	$36 (or less)	$42 (or less)	$300	$288	$400	$1,335
Relative Degree of Impact through *New* Dollar Generation	Low	Low	Low	High	High	High	High

NA means Not Applicable.

Sources: Florida State Fairground representatives; University of Washington Educational Assessment Center and Tampa Bay Buccaneers representative; The Cultural Policy Institute, 1980; Florida Division of Tourism, 1983, and Medallion Travel; National Tour Bus Association; International Association of Convention and Visitors Bureaus; *Super Bowl XVIII: Economic Impact on the Tampa Bay Area;* Price Waterhouse LLP.

governmental, judicial, or financial services. The federal government responded with urban renewal programs whose local administrators recognized convention centers, arenas, and stadiums as attractive reuse opportunities for the large tracts of land that had been vacated when blighted and functionally obsolete buildings in the inner cities had been demolished.

Often, the forces at work to acquire, demolish, and clear physically deteriorated buildings were more powerful than the market demand for redevelopment of the newly cleared land. The demand for the reuse of land in the central city, however, was often insufficient to overcome the negative image of the land's earlier condition or of the area's other locational disadvantages (lack of schools, modern hotels, convenience-type shopping facilities, and other facilities). As downtowns in most cities lost their position as regional retailing centers, the development of arenas, stadiums, and convention centers was viewed as a means for downtowns to claim a new reason for being: to function as entertainment centers. In other words, arenas and stadiums (originally built and paid for by team owners) and convention centers (built for large exhibitions and assemblies in a few large markets) were now promoted, constructed, and operated by dozens of local governments, large and not so large, for

two reasons: to stimulate the revitalization of the central city and to foster the diversity of pedestrian-oriented uses, on which stable and growing urban ecosystems must depend.

Because so many facilities had been constructed for this reason—as public works projects or catalysts for economic development—they were not expected to operate at a profit. The private sector found it increasingly difficult to develop and finance them, or even to continue to operate them, because the relatively lower rents established by the new public sector buildings were insufficient to generate the cash flow needed to pay operating costs, mortgage payments, taxes, and a profit to equity investors. With so many cities competing for a fixed number of major league franchises in spectator sports, team owners discovered that they no longer needed to assume the additional financial burden of becoming their teams' landlords.

Today, many of the most bottom line–oriented managers of public assembly facilities talk about offering free rent to attract events that increase hotel occupancy during the slow season of the year. Or they discuss renting arenas for free because they will make a profit on concessions, event services, and parking on nights when the arenas would otherwise be unoccupied.

The inability or unwillingness of owners to set economic rents for convention centers has resulted from: (1) a need to increase occupancies for hotels, (2) the overbuilding of convention facilities in many secondary markets and generic destinations, and (3) an inability to influence the supply of trade shows. Many exhibition halls in Europe are privately owned, with the same parties also owning many, if not most, of the trade and consumer shows that occupy them. Thus, these owners control to a large extent their buildings' occupancy while also receiving the profits from ownership of the shows, in addition to food sales, parking, and so on. This ownership pattern has not developed in the United States (except among merchandise marts) because local and state governments had built nearly all of the exhibition halls in advance of their need by the private companies that created the shows.

One more characteristic distinguishes the development of convention centers, stadiums, arenas, and amphitheaters from that of other types of real estate. Local and state government operators of these facilities often have had no previous experience in their construction, marketing, and management. As a result, many public assembly facilities may create larger financial burdens for their owners and require more tax revenues because they have been improperly designed, built in the wrong location, or inadequately marketed. Other centers are handicapped by inadequate space or are difficult to market because of their locations. Again, their owners may have had noble intentions in reducing construction costs or in finding less expensive sites. The results show too often, however, that these economies have proven penny-wise and pound-foolish.

TERMINOLOGY

The confusion caused by the names given to different types of facilities can best be seen by looking at the various types of buildings to which the term "coliseum" has been applied. A coliseum—like its progenitor, the Roman Colosseum—traditionally is an outdoor or open stadium. "Coliseum" properly describes the open stadium in Los Angeles that hosted the 1932 and 1984 Olympic games. It also has been used to describe the New York Coliseum, which was an exhibition hall, and many arenas throughout the country. Similarly, the term "civic center" has been used variously to describe an arena, a convention center, an auditorium, or the area around city hall. Much of this confusion arises from marketers of facilities, who decide what name will best "sell" the venue.

The largest association of managers of public assembly facilities—the International Association of Auditorium Managers (IAAM)—has debated for more than two decades alternative names for its organization. The majority of IAAM members are managers of arenas, stadiums, and convention centers, not auditoriums (though an NHL team currently plays in a 17,000-seat arena called "the Auditorium"). Until a more precise or less abstract term can be found, the phrase "public assembly facilities" will have to refer to the types of buildings that are the subject of this book. In the definitions that follow, the terms "coliseum" and "civic center" are omitted. Theaters, trade centers, and merchandise marts are also excluded from this book. They are defined in this chapter, however, to differentiate them from arenas, amphitheaters, auditoriums, and convention centers.

THEATERS

Enclosed performing arts venues accommodate audiences ranging in size from 300 to 3,500 in fixed seats, which are arranged in an arc of less than 90 degrees on a sloped floor with sightlines directed to a permanent stage behind a proscenium arch. A multistory space above the stage, known as the fly loft, is required for operas, Broadway musicals, and other dramatic presentations that need to change ("fly") numerous sets rapidly between scenes. A touring Broadway company will require as many as 40 to 60 different sets or scenes to be hung (flown) on lir

Not just a convention center, the San Diego Convention Center has six lighted championship tennis courts, a pro shop, and an exercise facility located on its rooftop and operated by the adjacent Marriott hotel and marina.

(rigging) above the stage. These touring Broadway shows typically need 2,500 to 3,500 seats to generate enough income to pay for their production costs plus the on-the-road transportation costs and living expenses of cast and crew. In contrast, a community theater or repertory theater may find 300 to 500 seats more than adequate to provide the intimacy and to attract the size of audience needed for its artistic and financial success.

A symphony orchestra playing in a multipurpose theater with a fly loft must have an acoustical shell to direct the sound to the audience; otherwise, the sound is lost in the space above and beside the stage (the wings). Similarly, a ballet company requires a dance-floor overlay to cover the top of a multipurpose theater stage to provide the resilience, or spring, that the dancers need. Therefore, to meet the various needs of its diverse groups of users, a multipurpose theater will often contain a portable acoustical shell, a portable dance-floor overlay, and an orchestra pit and may be able to reconfigure the audience seating area (the house) from as many as 2,500 seats to as few as 500. Some large cities, on the other hand, have been able to obtain the financial resources to develop and operate a multitheater complex. Such complexes include the Kennedy Center in Washington, D.C., the Lincoln Center in New York City, and the Los Angeles Music Center. Each theater is designed to meet the needs of specific users: symphony orchestras, musical theater, opera, ballet, repertory theater, cinema, or chamber music ensembles.

Auditoriums

Auditoriums are characterized by a flat floor that enables them to function as small arenas, exhibition halls, and theaters. They often have a fixed stage at one end with permanent, horseshoe-shaped seating that directs the sightlines to the center of the flat floor. Generally, portable seating on risers is set up on the floor for a proscenium-stage event or for a center-floor event, such as a boxing match. The portable seats in the center of the floor can be removed to accommodate a basketball game, circus, or 25,000 to 30,000 square feet of exhibits or of a "flat-show" event. These types of buildings often had fixed seating in a balcony or second tier, which was also horseshoe-shaped, to view a stage at the end of the first floor.

Auditoriums were popular from the 1920s through the late 1940s, with most communities having their own municipal or veterans' memorial auditoriums. In recent decades, though, these structures have been replaced by single-purpose theaters, arenas, and exhibition halls. It is more common today for communities that need a multi-purpose building to construct a 75,000- to 100,000-square-

foot exhibition hall (without a balcony to restrict ceiling height, or a permanent stage) and to provide it with portable (telescopic) seating for 7,000 to 8,000. Seating can be stored flat against the walls when it is not in use for a spectator event. Venues with horseshoe-shaped balcony, flat floor, and fixed end-stage are now relics.

Arenas

The arena is a flat-floor facility with 8,000 to 22,000 fixed seats configured in an oval shape on one or more tiers or levels. Arenas of fewer than 10,000 seats generally have all seats on one tier and a single, mid-level concourse for circulation, concessions, toilets, and entry lobby. Arenas with more than 10,000 seats provide seating on at least two levels, typically reached from one or more concourses that divide the tiers of seating. Sightlines for the audience in an arena are nearly always designed for events played or performed in an area the size of a hockey floor because hockey requires the largest playing area of all the events that these arenas typically host. Major touring circuses and ice shows, indoor soccer, and arena football are all designed for this floor size and configuration. To accommodate the sightlines for a regulation horse show ring, like the original Freedom Hall in Louisville, Kentucky, seats must be located at a greater distance than they are from the edge of a hockey floor and at a much greater distance than from a basketball floor. Freedom Hall was remodeled (floor lowered and tiered seating extended) to obtain the favor of its basketball fans. And a second, special-purpose arena has been built nearby to serve the needs of horse shows. Optimal sightlines for the edges of a basketball floor obscure the visibility of important portions of the floor during a hockey game.

Premium seating, including box suites and club seating, is frequently provided on the main concourse or middle level, between the upper and lower tiers of seating. This location brings the most expensive seats closer to the action on the court than did the old "sky-boxes." Appropriately named, skyboxes were added in the only space available, above the last row of seats—sometimes above the rafters—and consequently farthest from the court or ice.

Stadiums and Ballparks

A stadium is characterized by seating and sightlines designed for viewing a baseball or football game. Major league baseball parks, or ballparks, contain 40,000 to 50,000 seats. Ideally, most baseball seating is arranged in a boomerang shape behind home plate and parallel to the "power alleys" along the first- and third-base lines.

The rectangular or oval football stadium can hold 65,000 to 100,000 seats; the NFL currently requires 70,000 seats for a Super Bowl game.

Multipurpose (baseball/football) facilities, popular in the 1960s, and domed facilities, developed in the 1970s and 1980s, have provided some additional event opportunities and substantially changed the financial operating characteristics of these venues, compared with those of traditional single-purpose stadiums. In the same way, an arena designed to accommodate a horse show ring compromises the sightlines for basketball, and a stadium that provides sightlines for a regulation, 400-meter oval running track requires seating to be placed farther from the football field of play than is acceptable to most franchise owners. A generic stadium configuration to facilitate spectator seating for baseball and football is criticized for not providing acceptable sightlines or angles of view for either sport. Enough seats for football is too many for baseball.

The most recent innovation in stadium design is seen in the Olympic stadium in Atlanta. The field and seating configuration and the design for permanent reconfiguration will enable the 85,000-seat track-and-field stadium to be converted into a 50,000-seat, state-of-the-art ballpark after the closing ceremonies for the 1996 summer games.

Walnut Creek Amphitheatre, Raleigh, North Carolina, has ranked among the ten most successful amphitheaters in the country each year since its opening in 1991.

DOMED AND RETRACTABLE-ROOF STADIUMS

The increasing number of these facilities in North America, from one in 1965 to 13 in 1995, is providing a circuit on which new events can develop, such as indoor stadium-only concert tours. The facilities are becoming a necessity for such established events as the quadrennial U.S. national political conventions or the annual NCAA Final Four basketball tournament. This trend may motivate communities to develop enclosed stadiums for reasons other than weather conditions.

AMPHITHEATERS

Nearly half of these outdoor concert venues, serving audiences of 15,000 to 20,000, have been developed in the past 15 years. A modern amphitheater accommodates about 40 percent of the audience in fixed seats under a permanent roof (no walls), while the remainder of the attendees are provided with a sloped lawn on which to stand, sit, or lie. Hartford, Connecticut, and Camden, New Jersey, have built prototype venues that enable the fixed seating area to be enclosed completely, thereby providing an indoor concert venue for the colder seasons. In addition to offering the obvious benefits of year-round operations, this innovation creates an entirely new size-type of live-performance venue: the 3,000- to 7,000-seat concert theater. At present, the Fox Theaters in Atlanta and Detroit, the Universal Theater in Los Angeles, the Paramount (formerly the Felt Forum) at Madison Square Garden, and Radio City Music Hall in New York City are the largest indoor concert venues ("megatheaters") in the 4,500- to 6,000-seat range.

Price Waterhouse's *Annual Amphitheater Report* publishes the operating characteristics of major amphitheaters by geographic region of the United States. In 1995, these facilities averaged 34 popular music concerts during their three- to four-month seasons, and those venues that hosted their local symphony or philharmonic summer pops concerts averaged 13 performances of orchestral music. According to the report, most newer facilities provide premium seating in the most desirable locations, often called "box seats," for rent by the season. The fixed price includes tickets (for the number of seats in the box) to all events and usually one or more reserved, preferred parking spaces. Currently, local governmental units are paying approximately two-thirds of amphitheater development costs. The private developer-operator providing the balance of construction costs is usually a company specializing in concert promotion (e.g., PACE, Cellar Door, Nederlander, and so on).

Specialized facilities like the Kentucky Horse Park, Lexington, Kentucky, build on a unique characteristic of the community or region they serve.

Jim Durham

NEW "MEGATHEATER"

The development of a circuit of 5,000- to 8,000-seat musical concert venues in major markets is being driven by forces that emerged between 1985 and 1995:

- The increased use of arenas for sporting events and family shows, which are booked in advance of concerts, reduces the number of good dates—such as Friday and Saturday nights—available for concerts.
- Older audiences, which are increasing in importance as the population ages, prefer the sightlines, acoustics, and interior finishes of a theater-type environment. The hike from an arena's parking lot, the concrete surfaces, 90-foot ceilings, poor acoustics, and patrons jostling each other for ballpark-style food on crowded concourses do not enhance a dressy event.
- Performing artists who attract more discriminating audiences (jazz, middle-of-the-road, and variety acts) often prefer the acoustics, the more intimate setting, or the theatrical-cathartic experience that is possible only with the connection between audience and performer provided by a smaller venue. Artists may elect to play two sell-out performances at 7,000 seats rather than one performance in a 14,000-seat house for the same fee.
- Many popular acts are financially successful with 5,000 to 7,000 attendees and are unable to draw the

larger arena audiences required to avoid the unsettling effects (on audience and performers) of half-empty houses.
- Developing amphitheaters with the capability of enclosing the fixed seating area may be a cost-effective means of creating "megatheaters."

SOCCER STADIUMS

The new, outdoor professional soccer leagues that are currently organizing themselves require their host communities to provide stadiums seating 25,000 to 30,000. Many analysts believe that previous efforts to sustain outdoor professional soccer leagues failed because they never *appeared* to be successful. Though they may have been financially profitable, if they only filled one-third of their seats in the 60,000- to 80,000-seat stadiums, the crowds appeared meager. This is analogous to the all-too-common history of successful restaurants that failed after they expanded or of professional sports teams unable to sell season tickets in a larger venue because fans believed the stadium was so large that day-of-the-game seats would always be available in preferred locations. This theory suggests that a stadium for the new U.S. professional soccer league would be sized more appropriately at 25,000 to 30,000 seats.

SPECIAL-EVENT FACILITIES

Tennis stadiums, horse racetracks, motor speedways, horse show arenas, and velodromes (steeply banked bicycle racetracks) are all examples of special-event or single-purpose facilities. Because they are few in number, they are not described in the narrative section of this book. However, examples have been included in the case studies section.

EXHIBITION HALLS

An exhibition hall may contain 50,000 to over 1 million square feet of contiguous flat-floor space with a 25- to 35-foot-high ceiling. The space is typically larger than that of the local hotel's largest ballroom or exhibit facilities. The total contiguous area of an exhibition hall located in the center city is often limited by the number of city blocks that can be assembled (how many streets can be closed) to provide contiguous floor space on grade. Hence, halls are often located next to rivers, lakes, or rail lines at the edge of a central core.

Multilevel exhibition halls are successfully marketed in only a few of the most popular destinations in the world, such as Boston and Hong Kong. In the United States, exhibition halls almost always form part of convention centers. In Canada and Europe, they are often freestanding, and in Europe, they are referred to as trade fairs.

CONVENTION CENTERS

A convention center contains one or more exhibition halls and a large number of meeting or "breakout" rooms. Total meeting-room and ballroom space is typically one-third to one-half the size of the center's exhibition space. Space is usually provided for a kitchen, separate ballroom, or banquet hall and, occasionally, for a theater-style assembly center. Entry lobbies are usually sized to accommodate attendee registration. Interior lobbies, for entry to ballrooms or banquet halls, often serve as prefunction areas and are sized to host receptions or cocktail parties for guests before a banquet, ball, or assembly event.

Convention centers host trade shows, public or consumer shows, conventions, religious or political conferences, receptions, dances, banquets, and other large assemblies. Meeting-room space or ballroom space is often described in terms of the number of people it can accommodate for different events: a banquet-style event requires approximately 12 square feet per person, a reception or cocktail party–type event needs five square feet per person, and a classroom-style event runs seven square feet per person.

CONGRESS CENTERS

Conventions in Europe are called congresses. Exhibitions are traditionally held in separate, often remote trade fair buildings because many members of professional associations believe that the commercialism of an exhibition detracts from the dignity of their events. Most congress centers do not have special-purpose or dedicated exhibit space. Because European centers host more diplomatic and plenary sessions than are held in North America, they usually contain one or more fixed-seat theaters. Consequently, many congress centers also host cultural events in their elegant theater-style halls. As associations and their members in Europe discover the substantial revenues to be realized by conducting trade shows or exhibitions concurrently with their meetings so as to lower conference registration fees, existing congress centers are adding exhibit halls, and new centers are being built that include them.

CONFERENCE CENTERS

According to the International Association of Conference Centers (IACC), conference centers typically consist of guest rooms located next to or near the center, though some centers are in fact nonresidential. Conference centers differ from full-service or "convention" hotels and convention centers in that they are designed primarily for more intimate seminars and top-level strategic planning sessions, typically serving groups of fewer than 75 people and offering a limited number of guest rooms separate from the conference and leisure areas.

The biggest differences between conference centers and convention centers are the size of the group served (typically smaller in conference centers) and the level of service provided (typically higher in conference centers). Further, conference centers offer a higher ratio of meeting space to guest rooms and provide upscale furnishings (i.e., upholstered ergonomic chairs), high-tech audiovisual equipment, skilled conference planning staff, and other amenities that maximize the effectiveness of the seminars and other intensive, high-value meetings that they host. Conference centers and their guest rooms are nearly always privately owned, as compared with convention centers, which are primarily owned by public agencies or governmental entities. As well, convention center ownership is separate from and/or unrelated to hotel ownership.

TRADE CENTERS

A trade center is usually a special-purpose office building oriented toward a specific group of users with a common interest in international trade. Tenants are engaged in the sale, service, regulation, or transportation of goods for import or export, as are customs agents, insurance brokers, freight forwarders, banks, trading companies, and the like. The buildings are designed as offices and bear no relationship to the facilities designed for public assembly that are described in this book. Trade centers often purchase franchises for their areas, granting them exclusive use of the name "World Trade Center" in their territory or metropolitan area.

MERCHANDISE MARTS

A merchandise mart, often confused with a trade center or exhibition hall, is typically a mid- or high-rise building with offices and permanent showrooms for consumer product displays and a modest amount of permanent exhibit space (30,000 to 50,000 square feet) on the ground floor. The ceilings in the exhibit area are usually lower in a mart than in an exhibition hall or convention center. While these buildings do not compete directly with convention centers and exhibition halls, cities that have no merchandise marts in their regions often host a large number of merchandise mart–type events in their convention centers or exhibition halls. Merchandise mart tenants generally fall into one or more of four consumer-oriented industry groupings: gifts, apparel, furniture, and home interiors (carpets, accessories, and so on). More recently, in Atlanta and Dallas, computers and software represent a new grouping.

Outside the United States, some world trade centers, as in Taipei and Seoul, include permanent exhibits of their countries' major exports. These buildings look like merchandise marts and foster the confusion among trade centers, trade marts, and trade shows. Outside the United States, trade centers are typically government-owned, while in the United States, they are privately owned.

MULTIPURPOSE CENTERS

In smaller or less affluent cities, multipurpose centers have been developed to host a wide variety of exhibition, meeting, and spectator events. The multipurpose center may be referred to as a convention, civic, or community center and typically consists of a large, rectangular flat-floor space to accommodate exhibitions, public shows, and mart-type events. With portable or telescopic seating in place, they can also host spectator events. In the resort area of Daytona Beach, Florida, for example, tourists create high occupancy rates for the area's hotels and motels for about six months

annually, discouraging most hotels from "blocking" rooms for conventions during those months. The multipurpose Ocean Center is ideally designed to remain in an arena or consumer-show configuration during these peak periods of tourist occupancy and then to attract conventions during the "shoulder," or lower-occupancy, seasons.

TYPES OF EVENTS

CONVENTIONS

Conventions are large gatherings hosted by professional associations or social organizations that are held in hotels or convention centers. These meetings may take place annually or more often and are attended by association members and invited guests. A convention can consist of a single assembly or plenary session and/or a number of concurrent meetings or "breakout" sessions. Conventions often include trade shows (exhibits) to display and demonstrate products and services unique to their businesses or professions. Admission to the exhibitions may be open to nonmembers, who must purchase a ticket to view the exhibits.

Conventions with and without exhibits are considered high-economic-impact events because attendees normally stay two to four days and nights in the host city. In addition to spending money at hotels, attendees purchase other goods and services from restaurants, retail shops, local attractions, and transportation services.

TRADE SHOWS

Trade shows are attended by persons engaged in commercial activities and belonging to a trade association rather than to a professional association. Consequently, attendees are more interested in seeing the display and demonstration of products than in going to seminars or lectures for the exchange of ideas or information. Historically, trade shows required little or no meeting-room space. But as they offer increasing numbers of lectures and training sessions during their exhibitions to attract larger audiences, trade shows are becoming less distinguishable from conventions.

Trade shows, known as trade fairs in Europe, are often held in the same part of the country as that in which their activities or members are concentrated, and often in the same venue each year. The latter kind of trade show, known as nonambulatory or nonrotational, includes such types as a regular jewelry show in New York City, a display of textile mill equipment in Atlanta, and a show

The National Indoor Arena in Birmingham, England, is a sports/entertainment facility designed for maximum flexibility. In its first year of operation, 18 different sports were presented, along with rock concerts and opera performances.

of petroleum drilling supplies in Houston. Compared with conventions, however, trade shows tend to draw greater numbers of attendees whose average stay is shorter. Participants often travel to the exhibition to see a specific type of product of interest to them and then leave. Although a trade-show exhibition may run five days, the average attendee may stay only one or two nights.

Convention and trade-show markets are further distinguished by the fact that trade shows often draw more of their attendees from the local metropolitan area or region because the industry may be headquartered in the geographic area that is home to the trade-show facility.

International conventions and trade shows make up a category that is somewhat misleading within the framework of the U.S. meetings market. The "international" classification is largely derived from the name of the association sponsoring the event, but various studies indicate that foreign attendees account for only 2 to 12 percent of the delegates to meetings of U.S.–headquartered international associations. For this reason, the attendance at international conventions and trade shows held in the United States is predominantly national in scope. The events are distinguished from international conventions or "congresses" in Europe, where the majority of attendees reside outside the host nation and where simultaneous, multilingual interpretation of speakers is therefore a common requirement.

A more relevant distinction would involve the mix of attendees from different continents: "intercontinental" meetings. So few of these are held each year, however, that they have not yet been given their own event classi-

fication. Few, if any, international congresses hosted in Europe are headquartered outside Europe.

National conventions and trade shows are major meetings of organizations whose attendees reside throughout the nation. Regional conventions and trade shows, on the other hand, may be either (1) gatherings of the members of a national association residing within a subregion of a nation, or (2) gatherings of the members of a regional organization that includes two or more states.

State conventions and trade shows are gatherings of the members of a state association or other type of organization whose membership is limited to persons residing in a single state. And district or local conventions and trade shows involve gatherings of local chapters of state, regional, national, or international groups whose activities or memberships are entirely contained within a locality or area within a state.

MERCHANDISE MART EVENTS

Although merchandise mart–type events essentially are trade shows, they differ in that a high percentage of attendees are buyers for retail stores. Their length of stay is usually limited to the time it takes to see new product lines and to place orders. There may be few, if any, meetings or seminars. These events typically generate less revenue for the local economy than do trade shows. Retail merchandise shows are open only to specific product buyers for a given category of retail merchants, such as women's shoe stores.

CONSUMER SHOWS

Consumer shows are ticketed events open to the public. They are exhibitions of consumer retail products for display and sale to attendees. Examples include boat, auto, recreational vehicle, antique, and home and garden shows. They take place in convention centers and, depending on the size, location, and type of merchandise sold, usually attract mostly local residents. The largest of these shows, such as the Miami Boat Show, will fill a community's hotel rooms for the duration of the event. Smaller shows—for example, those exhibiting coins or baseball cards—may not attract any overnight attendees.

Because local dealers display and sell their products at consumer shows, their trade associations claim, justifiably, that there will be an economic loss to the locality if the show is not held, even if few overnight visitors are expected. After all, local residents might otherwise attend the same type of show in a neighboring region and buy products from out-of-town dealers rather than from their local dealers. The validity of this argument depends on the participation by local dealers in the show and on the proximity of the show to an alternative venue in a nearby city. Hence, this logic may be more valid for boat and car shows than for shows featuring other types of merchandise (rattan furniture or tropical plants), which may consist 100 percent of nonlocal dealers.

OTHER EVENTS

Other events commonly hosted at public assembly facilities include festivals, concerts, sporting events, banquets, and business meetings. The types and sizes of these events are determined by the local and regional economy and by the availability of other assembly, exhibition, and entertainment facilities in the community.

ORGANIZATION OF THIS BOOK

The first six chapters of this book explain how successful public assembly facilities are sized, planned, located, and designed. Chapters 7 through 10 describe their management and financial operations, the economic benefits to the community, and financing and funding options. Part

Two provides detailed descriptions of individual projects, all located in the United States, within each type of facility. Part Three provides international examples, with their sometimes different characteristics. A total of more than 70 convention centers, arenas, stadiums, amphitheaters, and single-purpose facilities have been selected—about ten to 15 of each facility type. Most of these centers were selected because they represent some distinctive and/or important achievements in their location, design, management, financing, use, or impact. Other projects have been selected to illustrate certain physical or operational characteristics that may be unique to their geographic locations (e.g., Asia), to their primary users (e.g., minor league or college teams), or to the economic characteristics of their communities. Communities are classified as (1) international "gateway" cities or major destinations (more than 20,000 hotel rooms in the metropolitan area); (2) "national" cities (10,000 to 20,000 hotel rooms); and (3) "regional" cities (fewer than 10,000 hotel rooms in the metropolitan area).

Each center studied in the book is described in terms of its size, development history, financing, and use. Diagrams, maps, and photographs depict layouts, site plans, or local settings. Most important, each case study illustrates the benefit to be obtained, or lessons learned, from the facility's development and operation.

Chapter 2

DETERMINING THE NEED

The forces influencing the construction or development of convention, sports, and entertainment centers (supply) should be distinguished from those causing changes in their use (demand). The popularity, prosperity, or population size of a market area will influence the occupancy or financial success of its assembly centers. Other forces, many noneconomic, will either cause or prevent their construction: team-owner motives, available sites, civic leadership, voter perceptions, and local political conditions. Because the supply of these types of centers is frequently determined by nonmarket forces, it is essential to consider seriously and to evaluate these forces in each local situation. Although these factors are usually difficult and elusive to discern, they will, more often than not, determine the ultimate success or failure of a center.

Certain fundamental economic forces influence all types of real estate development. For example, the fact that the supply of convention center space may be outpacing nationwide demand does not mean that all regional or local markets are overbuilt. Consequently, while overbuilding may be quantified on a national scale, many centers in strong markets will be forced to turn away business because their space is inadequate or insufficient to meet the demands of many potential space users in that specific market. In popular destinations, a center's high occupancy rates cause scheduling or booking conflicts because two or more groups want the same date.

In professional sports, major league franchises consider relocation for the same reasons that expansion teams are attracted to new markets. They are offered a large, affluent, or rapidly growing market-area population, low rent, or generous shares of the revenues from premium seats, concessions, advertising, and so on. While the fact of a team's relocation does not necessarily represent a growth in national demand, it frequently represents a geographic shift of demand resulting from the physical or functional obsolescence of facilities. And such obsolete venues may have been built as recently as the 1970s. Within the past decade, St. Petersburg, Indianapolis, Orlando, and St. Louis have built major league facilities to lure franchises. All four cities have been successful in signing a permanent tenant.

As smaller communities grow, they perceive the need to host professional sports and major entertainment events. To serve this need, they develop multipurpose arenas and minor league facilities ranging from 10,000 to 15,000 seats (see Figure 2-1). Residents of these growing communities seek some of the amenities enjoyed in large metropolitan areas. For example, they would like to eliminate the hour-and-a-half to two-hour drive to a larger community to take their small children to see an ice show or circus, and most families do not want their teenagers driving that distance to attend a concert.

The size of a new or expanded sports facility or convention center is normally determined by a community's economic and locational characteristics. Because there are so many variations of these traditional criteria and because the relative weighting of their importance differs in each situation, the results from using a checklist or formula might be misleading. A community's

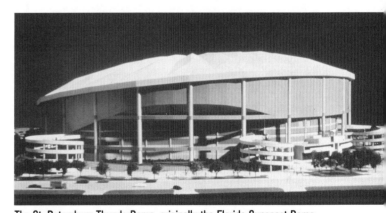

The St. Petersburg ThunderDome, originally the Florida Suncoast Dome, was built to attract major league baseball. It became the ThunderDome in August 1993, when the Tampa Bay Storm arena football league and the Tampa Bay Lightning National Hockey League teams began playing in the facility.

Figure 2-1

Minor league baseball facilities

ROB CANTON

BALLPARKS

In recent years, minor league baseball has become an increasingly popular investment for localities interested in owning a professional baseball franchise but unwilling or unable to pay the $100 million+ expansion fees of major league baseball, as well as for communities that want the recreational amenity of professional baseball but lack the market demographics and corporate support to attract a major league franchise. The "affordability" of minor league baseball may be evidenced by the value of recent transactions: $5 million to $10 million for a Class AAA franchise, $3 million to $5 million for a Class AA franchise, and $2 million to $3 million for a Class A franchise. The development costs associated with minor league parks, due primarily to their smaller size, fewer amenities, and lower level of "finish," are significantly lower than the costs for major league facilities. A typical range of development costs for a minor league park may be $10 million to $20 million, while their major league counterparts generally cost ten times that amount.

Significant growth has taken place in the development of minor league baseball stadiums. These include spring training facilities for major league baseball, which typically play a dual role as minor league parks after spring training. As well, they include stadiums built specifically for their respective minor league franchises. Figure 2-1a lists the minor league ballparks constructed since 1985. As illustrated, over the past 11 years, NAPBL (National Association of Professional Baseball Leagues) stadiums have been constructed in 68 communities

Figure 2-1a

Minor league ballpark construction since 1985

City	Year Built	City	Year Built	City	Year Built	City	Year Built
Richmond, VA	1985	Sarasota, FL	1989	Wilmington, DE	1993	Appleton, WI	1995
Osceola, FL	1985	Boise, ID	1989	Hickory, NC	1993	Auburn, NY	1995
Huntsville, AL	1985	Charlotte, NC	1990	Fort Wayne, IN	1993	Augusta, GA	1995
Shreveport, LA	1985	El Paso, TX	1990	Norfolk, VA	1993	Durham, NC	1995
Port Charlotte, FL	1987	Dunedin, FL	1990	Ottawa, Ontario	1993	Edmonton, Alberta	1995
Fayetteville, NC	1987	Kane County, IL	1991	Yakima, WA	1993	Erie, PA	1995
Harrisburg, PA	1987	High Desert, CA	1991	Bowie, MD	1994	Kannapolis, NC	1995
Buffalo, NY	1988	Frederick, MD	1991	Fishkill, NY	1994	Kingsport, TN	1995
Colorado Springs, CO	1988	Zebulon, NC	1991	Grand Rapids, MI	1994	Norwich, CT	1995
South Bend, IN	1988	Binghamton, NY	1992	Lake Elsinore, CA	1994	Salem, VA	1995
Augusta, GA	1988	Des Moines, IA	1992	New Haven, CT	1994	Charleston, SC	1995
Birmingham, AL	1988	Fort Myers, FL	1992	Portland, ME	1994	Indianapolis, IN	1995
Port St. Lucie, FL	1988	Scottsdale, AZ	1992	Salt Lake City, UT	1994	Lansing, MI	1995
Princeton, WV	1988	Albany, GA	1993	San Antonio, TX	1994	Rochester, NY	1995
Rockford, IL	1988	Danville, VA	1993	Sussex County, NJ	1994	San Bernardino, CA	1995
Scranton, PA	1989	Rancho Cucamonga, CA	1993	Trenton, NJ	1994	Syracuse, NY	1995
Canton, OH	1989			Melbourne, FL	1994	Tampa, FL	1995
London, Ontario	1989						

Source: National Association of Professional Baseball Leagues.

Figure 2-1b

ANNUAL BALLPARK CONSTRUCTION

Source: National Association of Professional Baseball Leagues.

throughout the United States and Canada, with 48 parks built in the 1990s. Figure 2-1b illustrates this annual trend. Note that Figure 2-1b does not include spring training facilities that do not also host a minor league team.

As noted, the past two years have seen the most dramatic growth in the development of minor league facilities, with 11 and 17 parks developed in 1994 and 1995, respectively. This recent increase in facility development may be due, in part, to the new stadium standards handed down by the NAPBL, the governing body for minor league baseball. In 1990, the NAPBL developed and presented its *Facility Standards and Compliance Inspection Procedures* as a combination of recommendations and minimum requirements for all new minor league facilities with a construction starting date of January 1, 1991, or later. As of that date, all existing facilities had a deadline of April 1, 1994, to meet certain playing-field and other team-facility standards.

A primary directive of the new standards addressed the capacity, type, and arrangement of seating in all facilities. Recommended minimum seating capacities included 10,000 seats for Class AAA stadiums, 6,000 seats for Class AA, 4,000 seats for Class A, and 2,500 seats for short-season A/rookie stadiums.

In an attempt to enhance the professional atmosphere of minor league ballparks, the NAPBL requires each facility to provide its choice of two or three separate "grades" of seating, such as general admission, reserved, or box seating. In no event can more than 90 percent of the total seating capacity be general admission. The recommended seating distribution for facilities with two grades of seating consists of 75 percent general admission and 25 percent reserved or box seats. For three grades of seating, the recommended distribution is 50 percent general admission and 25 percent each for reserved and box seating.

In addition to seating capacities and configurations, other standards addressed the following issues:

- Public facilities (restrooms, ramps, and other arrangements for handicapped access, drinking fountains, telephones).
- Concession stands.
- Miscellaneous public space (club, restaurant, recreation areas).
- Ticket windows and entry lobbies.
- Security and first aid considerations.
- Parking and street access.
- Sound system and scoreboard.
- Media facilities.
- Administrative areas.
- Team facilities (locker rooms, field, storage, training areas, and so on).
- Playing field (dimensions, surface, equipment, lighting, and the like).
- Maintenance.

MARKETING

While a major league baseball team is generally supported by a fan base that may encompass several cities, counties, and even states, a minor league club typically relies heavily on the local market area for support. In many communities, this reliance results in the need for minor league franchises to compete directly with other local options to capture local residents' entertainment dollars. This competition may include amateur sports events (high-school and college), concerts, local movie theaters, and other attractions. Local competition has generated some unusual marketing approaches used by franchises to attract fans. In addition to promoting affordability and a family-friendly atmosphere, clubs have used promotions such as:

- Free concerts after the games.
- Fireworks/laser shows.
- "Car-a-night" giveaways.
- Money-back guarantees.
- Carnival atmosphere (clowns, jugglers, magicians, face painting).
- Free haircuts in the stands.

Minor league stadiums, unlike most major league venues, often serve as multipurpose facilities, hosting such events on nongame days as concerts, festivals, high-school and college baseball, celebrity softball and baseball, theatrical presentations, and symphonies.

FINANCING

In recent years, minor league stadium developments have been funded through a variety of sources. As with major league venues, these sources often involve traditional local government participation, in the form of debt issuance supported by local taxes or contributions of land, infrastructure, and other assets. Private sector participation takes the form of equity contributions and a pledge of a percentage of team or facility revenue from gate receipts, food and beverage sales, parking, suites, and advertising.

Several recently developed stadiums were funded primarily by the public sector. These included the $16 million Class AAA facility developed in 1993 for the Norfolk (Virginia) Tides, which has been funded primarily through the city's general obligation bonds; the $17 million Rancho Cucamonga (California) Quakes Sports complex, a Class A facility constructed in 1993 and funded by tax increment financing; and the $9.3 million Class AAA Scottsdale (Arizona) Stadium, developed in 1991 and financed mainly through the city of Scottsdale's general obligation bonds.

An example of public/private participation in the 1994 development of a minor league stadium in Texas was San Antonio's Nelson Wolff Municipal Stadium (Class AA). Of the estimated $10 million development cost, approximately $6.5 million was provided by city-issued certificates of obligation, subject to annual appropriations; $700,000, land contribution; $500,000, team contribution; and $250,000, San Antonio Sports Foundation contribution.

Another example of a public/private effort was the $25.4 million Class AAA MacArthur Stadium, home of the Syracuse (New York) Chiefs. MacArthur Stadium, built in 1995, was a joint development involving the state of New York, Onondaga County, the Syracuse Chiefs, and the Toronto Blue Jays. Funding was provided in the form of a $16 million UDC grant, $6.4 million in team contributions, and $3 million in county general obligation bonds.

Rob Canton is comanager with David Petersen of the Price Waterhouse Sports, Convention, and Entertainment Group.

ability to capture the required attendance levels or occupancy for its facilities is often influenced by a unique characteristic of its home team, by local traditions, or by the town's attractiveness to tourists. The feasibility of public assembly facilities, unlike that of traditional real estate developments, is rarely measured by operating profits.

Various analytical techniques have been developed that enable the public assembly venue planner to measure market demand, estimate future use or occupancy, and determine optimal size. Although any one of these methods for measuring demand might by itself provide an accurate result, relying on the same method in different situations is not dependable. In fact, multiple techniques must be employed to achieve an acceptable level of reliability. The most accurate result can be obtained from evaluating the various results of these techniques and considering their unique strengths and weaknesses, given the specific setting and conditions.

AN ADEQUATE FACILITY TO SERVE EXISTING ACTIVITIES

The demand for entertainment events, as measured by the number of events and audience size, is primarily determined by population size within the market area. An 8,000-seat arena may have accommodated the requirements of touring family shows, sporting events, and entertainment groups in the 1960s, but if later population growth now requires multiple performances, the venue will be considered undersized, and the same event, returning, may have to play another center in the same region, even in a smaller city, with a 15,000-seat capacity. Future attendance and number of events can be readily determined for a sports team that consistently sells out its tickets and has a long waiting list for season's tickets.

A convention center with a 100,000-square-foot exhibition hall will begin to lose important repeat customers that have outgrown the space and will have to turn away potential new customers because of the building's size limitations. In the case of simultaneous events, the facility will probably be unable to offer dates to schedule additional groups during the most desirable time periods. The larger share of lost business often remains unknown to the center's management because potential users requiring larger space usually know the center's limited size and, consequently, never contact the management. A "lost business" or "turnaway" report is typically not recorded each time that a center's limitations result in lost business. Therefore, the community loses to its competitors a share of the market to which it is otherwise entitled and is unable to achieve attendance commensurate with its resources or attractiveness.

In all of these situations, historical records and surveys of past, current, and potential users may point to needed additions and future use of an expanded or new facility. Obviously, it is important for building management and the local convention and visitors' bureau (CVB) to maintain detailed records of previous years' activities, conduct exit interviews, and maintain turnaway/lost business reports.

A NEW BUILDING AS A CATALYST

The most common rationale for a government subsidy of a new public assembly facility is to make something else happen. If this is the motive, the building's secondary purpose is often expected to be to attract events or to serve current user needs. The primary motive for developing the facility may be to attract a large hotel or mixed-use development, to provide downtown merchants with additional visitors or customers, or to retain or lure a professional sports franchise. In other words, the combined benefits from all the anticipated consequences, primary and secondary, of the building's development will be evaluated to determine its feasibility. Unlike privately sponsored real estate projects, a public assembly facility is usually not judged feasible or infeasible based on its cash flow or profitability.

The publicity and big-league image that a community receives by winning an NFL franchise are widely believed to justify a public subsidy for a 70,000-seat

The new Olympic stadium for the Atlanta games is under construction in the foreground. Following the games, it will be modified to become the new home of the Atlanta Braves, and the Atlanta–Fulton County Stadium will be torn down for parking. But the footprint of the old field will remain in a ghost outline on the surface of the new parking lot and in part of the foundation walls, left as a permanent monument.

stadium that may be used by its primary tenant for only 11 or 12 professional football games annually. In a typical year, however, the team's games may be broadcast on 300 to 400 local television stations across the nation and on 100 to 200 regional radio stations. The team's scores, draft picks, star players' personal behavior, and other team- or player-related events may be reported by major wire services and printed in dozens of major metropolitan newspapers. New business locations and expansions may be influenced by the recreational amenity, name recognition, and major league image of the city provided by the team.

The community may obligate itself to substantial financial subsidies over 30 years to obtain the qualitative, unquantifiable, or intangible benefits, or "warm fuzzies," of becoming a big-league city. Certainly, emerging cities (such as Atlanta in the 1960s, Tampa in the 1970s, or Charlotte in the 1980s) are more likely to employ this image-boosting strategy than are older, larger cities that already may host four or five professional sports franchises. Many major cities assume that their prestige or importance as international destinations does not depend on their affiliation with professional sports. These considerations may cause a potential facility sponsor or advocate to request a needs analysis rather than a feasibility study.

Substantial economic and tax benefits derive from a facility that attracts overnight and other nonresident attendees to its conventions and trade shows. The attendee's average daily expenditures and length of stay are well documented for different types of events in various sizes of cities. These spending estimates, which are published by the International Association of Convention and Visitors Bureaus, also include expenditures by exhibitors, association executives, and exhibition-service (exhibit set-up or decoration) companies associated with an event. More recently, facility owners have sponsored studies that measure the extent to which convention or trade-show attendees engage in pre- or postconvention tours or more lengthy vacations in local communities or regions. These statistics make it easier to quantify all the sales, employment, and taxes generated by facility visitors through their spending outside the hall or city hosting the event.

Normally, the feasibility of a convention center is determined by the extent to which the taxes received by state and local governments (from the spending by event attendees) exceed the government expenditures required to pay the facility's annual debt service and operating costs. Unfortunately, many of the local and state government units that receive the largest shares of these tax revenues do not support the centers in proportion to these revenues. Nevertheless, the new, net, or incremental ra-

tio of tax revenue to tax expense (net operating cost and debt service) is a logical basis for determining the justification for expanding an existing convention center or the feasibility of building a new one.

ESTIMATING FUTURE USE OR OCCUPANCY

Market researchers have employed various analytical techniques or methods to provide estimates of future use or occupancy for a proposed center. As previously stated, the most reliable estimate can be obtained when several methods are employed simultaneously.

THE PARABLE OF THE PRUDENT NAVIGATOR

Illustrating this point is a notice printed on navigational charts published by the United States Defense Mapping Agency. Printed in bold type and purple ink, it reads as follows: "Warning: The prudent mariner will not rely solely on any single aid to navigation, especially floating aids. . . ." It is likewise advisable to caution the prudent market research analyst not to rely on any single method or research task to estimate future use. As when a physician diagnoses a patient's illness by conducting a range of examinations, tests, and inquiries, the more research techniques that are employed, the more reliable is the result, assuming that the tests are designed logically, conducted accurately, and known to be predictive.

The logic and accuracy of the analysis must be verifiable by any intelligent businessperson without expertise or earlier training in this type of research. The reliability of the analysis does not depend on "black-box" procedures, obscure terminology, or esoteric information. There is nothing abstruse about these procedures or the sources of data on which they depend. All assumptions must be reasonable, plausible, logical, and substantiated or documented by credible and reliable sources. The methodology for preparing estimates for a proposed venture demands the same care, accuracy, and audit trail expected in preparing financial statements for ongoing enterprises.

HISTORICAL TRENDS

If the purpose of the planned facility or expansion is to improve the operation of an existing activity or event, such as a convention or sporting event, then the records of past attendance, types of events, numbers of performances, occupancy, and residences of attendees are usually obtainable. Information is normally available that describes these centers' current and future scheduled activities. These are typically the most reliable data and methods for estimating occupancy or use for a proposed facility or for competing venues that accommodate existing activities occurring in the area. The new venue may be larger, include modern design features or equipment, or occupy a new location. In evaluating past attendance at the event, factors or conditions must be considered that may have induced or constrained any growth or decline in occupancy. The cause or causes, which might be unrelated to the proposed changes to the size or location of the center, might include:

- Contractual obligations that may expire in the near term.
- Abnormal or unseasonable weather: hurricanes, floods, blizzards.
- Unusual social, political, or economic circumstances: strikes, civil disturbances, prolonged economic recession, or high unemployment.
- Extraordinary team performance, as shown in best or worst win-loss records.
- One-of-a-kind or infrequent events, such as a season of Olympic games, a World Bank meeting, a Super Bowl, an ambulatory "mega"-convention or trade show, a world's fair, or other special occurrence.

Clearly, the analyst will evaluate historical activity to identify patterns such as long-term or emerging trends and concurrent changes in related economic activities or demographic statistics. The most common related activities are concomitant changes in:

- Convention attendance and hotel rooms in the market area.
- Hotel room demand and Class A office-space occupancy.
- Importance or length of event, and market-area drive-time radii.
- Market-area population and total attendance.
- Specialty retail space or high-fashion stores, and attendees' retail spending figures.
- Game attendance figures and team performance record.
- Total attendance per venue in the market, and the number of competing venues.
- Box or suite rental income, and the number of businesses with 500 or more employees.

Many such relationships exist, some with a high percentage of correlation and others that may appear unrelated except when judged in combination with other specific events or economic activities. Some of these

relationships have been assessed by using computer-based regression analysis to yield information that is highly accurate when predicting future occupancy or attendance, given a fixed set of circumstances.

The accuracy of these methods of quantitative analysis obviously depends on the availability of comparable, often proprietary time-series data from reliable sources for a statistically representative cross section of cases. Such models have been employed to estimate several important operating characteristics for venues, such as ranges of major league baseball attendance or exhibition-hall occupancy.

The reliability of these estimates depends entirely on the reasonableness of other key assumptions in the analysis, usually including the stability of local economic conditions, future development of support facilities, future development of competing facilities, booking policy, and team performance. If assumptions about these or other conditions or circumstances are reasonable, realistic, and supportable, then the reliability of the resulting estimate is much greater than that of estimates based on assumptions that are aggressive, unprecedented, infeasible, or illogical.

USER SURVEYS

The statistical reliability of surveys is influenced by the survey sample size, the method of soliciting responses (telephone versus mail), direct or firsthand knowledge of the person interviewed, the phrasing or wording of questions, open- versus closed-ended question style, the order in which questions are asked, and whether the requested information pertains to an action or choice that has already been made or to a future choice or action, that is, to speculative behavior.

Conclusions drawn from responses to user surveys must be carefully considered. Valuable qualitative information can be obtained from users about their past experiences and their preferences relative to specific experiences. For example, a suggested question might require the respondent to "Name the past three centers that your organization has rented for an annual meeting that you have attended; rank these three, from best to worst, according to or in terms of. . . ." And, if the duration of the same event held in each center was the same, "What was the attendance and average length of stay for attendees at each center?" Surprisingly, much of the information obtained from these opinion surveys about future behavior, site selection criteria, or the use of a new destination or center is not supported by the characteristics of destinations or centers that respondents have previously selected. In other words, responses do not always reflect actual behavior.

Finally, it is essential to understand the numerous types of market segments and the characteristics of a center's location or destination before preparing a survey questionnaire or interpreting its results. For example, Boston and San Francisco have demonstrated extraordinary success in attracting groups associated with the medical profession. Of the hundreds of such organizations, an undersampling of one segment of professional associations in one destination may represent an oversampling of the same segment in another destination.

OPERATIONAL CHARACTERISTICS OF SIMILAR CENTERS IN COMPARABLE MARKETS

Information on operational characteristics can be helpful in estimating reasonable limits or ranges for occupancy, based on similar data for centers in markets with comparable economic and demographic traits. This knowledge is especially useful when evaluating future operations for an activity or type of center that is new to a particular market. The analyst must, again, be cautioned about the importance of selecting reasonable key assumptions and of understanding conditions that may be unique to a market but that appear to be comparable in other relevant aspects.

For example, an intangible factor may be the most important determinant of market demand, that is, of the number of events and attendance at, say, motor speedways. That intangible factor may be far more important than economic and demographic characteristics. Certainly, many communities that offer regional market-area demographic characteristics that may exceed Daytona Beach's could never expect to outdraw the Daytona International Speedway without first attaining the substantial reputations of the major events held at Daytona Beach and, after 1960, at the International Speedway throughout most of the 20th century. In contrast to a stadium selected to host a Super Bowl, the reputation and image of a motor speedway is less portable than the event. The drawing power of the Daytona Speedway's heritage may take 20 or 30 years to achieve at another location.

Characteristics of the local economy and resident population are more relevant for analysis of sports and entertainment market demand than for determining support for convention facilities. Successful convention centers are measured by their ability to attract nonresident attendees. Consequently, comparable characteristics have more to do with the attractiveness of the destination and its physical (manmade and natural) characteristics than with its local population.

Market-area characteristics relevant for identifying comparable sports and entertainment markets include:

- Population of the local television market area.
- Population of the area within one-half-hour and one-hour drive time.
- Age and income stratification of the population.
- Diversity of the economy.
- Employment and population growth rates.
- Enrollment at a major local university.
- Location of a large population on a military base.
- Seasonal climate conditions.
- Popularity of the event or sport in the region.

Relevant characteristics for evaluating the comparability of destinations for convention centers include:

- Hotel room supply, quality, and pricing.
- Restaurant and retail sales.
- Air service.
- Interstate highway access.
- State capital location.
- Primary tourist attractions.
- Seasonal weather conditions.
- Hotel occupancy by season and business mix.
- Dominant industry or employment specialization.
- Proximity of a concentration of occupied office space.

Next to an analysis of historical activity or trends, an analysis of comparable facilities is often the most reliable type of assessment. Certainly, for a destination without an existing convention center, an understanding of the operational characteristics of centers in comparable destinations will be highly useful. Nevertheless, like the prudent mariner, the prudent market analyst will not rely on any one analytical technique.

The task of identifying comparable communities always leaves the analyst with a renewed appreciation for the extraordinary extent to which every city is unique. People tend to generalize about various types of cities or regions. Given objective scrutiny, however, comparable cities' many significant differences become apparent. The large extent to which each city reveals itself to differ from all others is always a great discovery.

INDUSTRY GROWTH

Is attendance at NFL games or at the 20 top trade shows growing faster than the rate of increase in the population? Is occupancy of exhibit space or attendance at amphitheaters in the 20 top markets declining? Does this mean that trade shows have lost their effectiveness as a medium for marketing new products? Is the popularity of MTV causing a loss of interest in live concerts? Which organization provides the most reliable data on convention attendance: the International Association of Convention and Visitors Bureaus (IACVB), the American Society of Association Executives (ASAE), the *Successful Meetings* Data Bank, *Tradeshow Week*, *Meetings and Conventions* magazine, or the International Association of Exposition Managers (IAEM)? Should growth in the convention market be measured by the total number of events, annual attendance, event days, or attendee room-nights? In determining need, answers to questions like these must be found, as they relate to the venue type being contemplated.

ARENAS AND STADIUMS

Arena and stadium attendance levels and their varieties of events will be determined not only by the size and affluence of the population residing within the market area, but also by the competitive facilities in the market area and region and by the current supply of available events.

The market area for sports facilities is usually defined by the area covered by the local media: television, radio, and newspapers. Broadcast media refer to this market as the dominant market area, or DMA. Unlike the metropolitan statistical area (MSA) or the larger metropolitan area measured by a regional planning agency, chamber of commerce, or others, the DMA tells a concert promoter, team owner, or marketing director for a family show how many people can be effectively and economically reached through the major local broadcast outlets.

Population characteristics—age, employment, and income—are often discussed. Only in the poorest regions of the country, however, has it been documented that these characteristics influence attendance. When they do, age and employment status are less important than income. Arenas in areas affected by economic recessions and dislocations often enjoy greater occupancy and higher attendance during economic downturns than in times of economic prosperity. This may be true for the same reason that motion picture attendance was unusually high during the Great Depression: people seek escape from the drabness of their own impoverished conditions.

In smaller communities, the presence of a large university or military base will tend to increase effective audience size and will do so more than the permanent or civilian population would seem to indicate. Similarly, a big band–type act will draw better in a retirement community than in a suburban area with a younger-than-median-age population.

The most reliable tools for estimating demand for facilities are surveys of event promoters, reviews of sports league attendance records, and evaluations of the mix of events and attendance at competitive facilities in the same market area and in comparably sized metropolitan areas.

Demand for sports venues is influenced by long-term growth or decline in league attendance. These trends can be measured, and it is possible to estimate the probable increase in teams or league expansions based on changes in league attendance and the growth in the number of major television markets.

CONVENTION AND CONGRESS CENTERS

Several sources report the increase in convention and trade-show activity. Reports from different sources vary because each source relies on a different database. For instance, the IACVB reports statistics it receives from convention bureaus in member cities; the Trade Show Bureau reports data supplied by trade-show owners and producers; and the ASAE bases its reports on information from association executives. Each major type of event, such as professional association conventions, is further segmented, say, into religious associations, medical meetings, and many other professional groupings. Each of these subgroups can be further segmented into users who can be accommodated only in convention centers, compared with those who will consider only a hotel, a resort hotel, or other accommodation. Consequently, it is not uncommon, for example, for attendance at medical meetings to increase during a period when the number of persons attending trade shows serving the electronics industry is decreasing.

The same subgroup of associations over the same time period may also evidence divergent trends among such factors as event attendance, total hotel room-nights, length of stay, number of meetings, national meetings versus regional meetings, number of exhibitors, and total occupied exhibit space.

Given these inconsistencies in trends and the major differences among types of events and data sources, it is not advisable to draw conclusions about the characteristics of demand for a convention center in a specific location based on industry trends.

AMPHITHEATERS

Recent years have seen a significant increase in the number of amphitheaters in the United States, with more than 20 amphitheaters built in the past ten years alone.

Red Rocks Amphitheatre outside Denver was conceived in the 1920s but not completed until 1941. It has a singularly dramatic site and remains a model for natural amphitheater design.

Currently, more than 60 amphitheaters are in operation for a portion of each calendar year. The rapid increase in the number of amphitheaters is directly correlated with the decline in concert activity at most U.S. arenas, and growth in the development of these venues appears to be continuing unabated.

Amphitheaters will go on causing substantial decreases in arena concert events—50 percent or more—in most areas where the two venue types share the same audience. Because the significant financial loss that has affected arena operations has occurred during a period (1989 to the present) when arena owners (mostly city governments) are staggering from major reductions in their tax bases, it is important to consider what the future may hold.

Amphitheaters, specifically the newer venues operated, owned, or booked exclusively by concert promoters, have replaced indoor arenas as the venue of choice among most touring acts during the late spring, summer, and early fall seasons. The proliferation of outdoor amphitheaters in recent years is due to a change in music industry economics, as well as to a change in market demographics. Today, promoters are finding it more profitable to develop (mostly as a joint venture with local government) and to operate their own facilities instead of renting them. By operating their own venues, promoters retain the profits from concessions, parking, advertising, and other revenues normally received by arenas. This ensures that promoters keep all the "upside" profits from a successful show when they already assume most of the "downside" risks of loss. Obviously, amphitheaters are less costly to operate than enclosed arenas and far less costly to build.

In regard to changing demographics, many industry analyses point to the growing strength of the middle-aged baby boom market. This Woodstock generation, weaned on rock-and-roll, has rediscovered its affinity for live music and has begun attending events at outdoor amphitheaters to regain the experience of a live concert.

Amphitheater growth is expected to continue, with both private and public money used to finance development. According to the 1994 annual Price Waterhouse industry survey, 38 percent of amphitheaters were financed with private funds, while 62 percent were financed publicly.

Reliance on private and public funding to develop amphitheaters likely will continue because of increased competition among concert promoters to build a larger circuit and among cities to attract performers to their facilities and localities. Rather than resist this competitive threat, many local governments, which own the arenas that will suffer financial loss from new amphitheaters, have joined forces with concert promoters such as PACE, Cellar Door, and Nederlander to ensure that new venues keep concert ticket sales and other sales on their tax rolls. A cursory glance at the top 25 metropolitan markets (DMAs) reveals which markets are candidates for the next amphitheater (see Figure 2-2). The table lists one of the most successful amphitheaters in the country, Pine Knob near Detroit, which was acquired, renovated, and is aggressively run (79 events in 1995) by the private company that also owns the Palace at Auburn Hills and the NBA Pistons.

No boom continues indefinitely, and amphitheaters will be no exception. Some markets are not sufficiently large or affluent to produce the audiences and ticket sales required to attract most touring shows. Average attendance in 1993 was almost 9,000, and the more popular acts may require a minimum of 12,000 or more to keep their operators, promoters, and venue owners in the black after all expenses are paid.

The recent market dominance of amphitheaters is an instance of market segmentation. Unmet demand existed among concertgoers for venues that presented their favorite performers in a setting totally different from an

Figure 2-2

U.S. AMPHITHEATERS OF MORE THAN 10,000 CAPACITY IN DMAs[1] OF OVER 2 MILLION POPULATION

DMA Rank	DMA	DMA Population (millions)	City	State	Amphitheater	Capacity
1	New York City	18.8	Wantagh	NY	Jones Beach Theatre	10,400
			Holmdel	NJ	Garden State Arts Center	10,802
2	Los Angeles	15.2	Devore	CA	Glen Helen Blockbuster Pavilion	65,000
			Irvine	CA	Irvine Meadows Amphitheatre	15,000
			Los Angeles	CA	Hollywood Bowl	17,965
			Costa Mesa	CA	Pacific Amphitheatre	18,861
3	Chicago	8.7	Tinley Park	IL	World Music Theatre	28,000
			Highland Park	IL	Ravinia Festival	18,500
			Hoffman Estates	IL	Poplar Creek Music Theatre	20,000
			East Troy	IL	Alpine Valley Music Theatre	40,000
4	Philadelphia	7.3	Philadelphia	PA	Mann Music Center	15,000
5	San Francisco/ San Jose	6.3	Santa Clara	CA	Redwood Amphitheatre	10,000
			Mountain View	CA	Shoreline Amphitheatre	20,000
6	Boston	5.7	Mansfield	MA	Great Woods	20,000
7	Washington, D.C.	5.1		DC	None	
8	Dallas/Fort Worth	4.9	Dallas	TX	Starplex Amphitheatre	20,000
9	Detroit	4.7	Auburn Hills	MI	Pine Knob Music Theatre	15,253
10	Houston	4.4	The Woodlands	TX	Cynthia Woods Mitchell Pavilion	10,000
11	Atlanta	4.2	Atlanta	GA	Lakewood Amphitheatre	18,920
12	Cleveland	3.8	Cuyahoga Falls	OH	Blossom Music Center	18,781
13	Seattle	3.8		WA	None	
14	Minneapolis/St. Paul	3.7		MN	None	
15	Miami	3.4		FL	None	
16	Tampa/St. Petersburg	3.3		FL	None	
17	Sacramento	3.1	Sacramento	CA	Cal Expo Amphitheatre	14,000
18	Phoenix	3.0	Phoenix	AZ	Blockbuster Desert Sky Pavilion	19,807
19	St. Louis	3.0	Maryland Heights	MO	Riverport Amphitheatre	20,000
20	Pittsburgh	2.9	Burgettstown	PA	Star Lake Amphitheatre	22,631
21	Denver	2.9	Englewood	CO	Fiddlers Green Amphitheatre	17,916
22	San Diego	2.7		CA	None	
23	Baltimore	2.6	Columbia	MD	Merriweather Post Pavilion	15,290
25	Orlando	2.5		FL	None	

[1]Dominant market areas.
Source: Price Waterhouse LLP.

arena. There was also an insufficient supply of touring performers because most markets could not support 30 to 40 performances, promoter costs, and indoor arena costs. And there was the unmet need among concert promoters to reduce the risks (high fixed-minimum rents, event advertising, and event staff costs) of an unsuccessful show and to increase their shares of the profits from a sellout. The amphitheater satisfied these needs.

Is there another new venue type on the horizon? Will amphitheaters be replaced by another, perhaps more threatening species? The author believes that the answer is yes. In 1994 and 1995, a rare occurrence took place, a simultaneous invention. In Lenox, Massachusetts, Tanglewood opened Seiji Ozawa Hall, a venue that offers artists and audiences both an amphitheater and an enclosed, formal theater. The amphitheater has the classic lawn seating configuration, while the theater features interior ambience, climate control, and high-quality acoustics.

Almost concurrently, PACE began construction of the city of Camden's theater/amphitheater, and Hartford approved development of the Connecticut Center for the Performing Arts. These 7,500- to 8,000-seat enclosed venues are designed to open the back wall, making them convertible and transformable to accommodate additional outdoor audience capacities of 25,000 to 30,000 under the stars. Indeed, this project type is the answer for those who pondered the possible use of 7,000 to 8,000 fixed amphitheater seats, often under a roof or canopy, during the winter months and for those who considered the advantages of a 5,000- to 8,000-seat theater-type musical concert venue.

Again, changing demographics have provided performers and promoters with a mid-sized concert venue that affords performers larger gross ticket sales and more intimate rapport with audiences; offers fans more elegant interiors than arena concourses and better acoustics than are achievable with 90-foot ceilings; and provides promoters and venue owners with the benefits of an amphitheater combined with a potential market from October through April.

Only time will tell whether this new supply of venues will foster a new demand outside the markets with 10 million+ population in Los Angeles and New York. Time has proven that people will always enjoy live performances, indoors or outdoors. When Sting performed in Ephesus, the audience enjoyed his music in a 24,000-seat venue built in the third century B.C., and the same stars came out to create the same enchantment as they did 2,300 years ago.

Any estimates of touring concert performers in a particular market should consider national trends in the number of touring groups by type and size of venue, length of tours, and number of performances. These trends are influenced by forces such as changes in the economics of the recording industry, as well as by other, perhaps less obvious, trends.

Market share

Market share analysis is an excellent test of the reasonableness of occupancy or attendance estimates for convention centers or sports and entertainment venues. If, for example, all amphitheaters within a given market size host 25 to 35 concerts per year, it would be reasonable to accept an estimate of 31 events per year, as determined by other analytical techniques such as promoter interviews and historic activity. On the other hand, if no convention center ever exceeded 8 percent of the total occupied square foot-days of all the convention and trade-show events in primary venues in the largest markets, an estimate of 15 percent market share should be considered unreliable.

Support facilities and services

Convention attendance is most highly correlated with or dependent on three variables within a market area: hotel rooms, air service, and population (when population is a surrogate for specialty retail shops and restaurants). If this sounds like a quantitative method to measure a qualitative attribute (i.e., attractiveness), well, it is. A destination's attractiveness can be measured by the number of airline passengers or hotel room-nights it generates. The number of things to do, restaurants, and retail shops is influenced by the number of visitors but also, most important, by the size of the resident population. Nevertheless, decisions are still made, mistakenly, to build or expand centers based solely on estimates of market capture related to the size of the center, without regard to the availability of rooms to accommodate the delegates being attracted. Remember, for nearly all types of real estate development, supply does not beget demand.

The relative under- or oversizing of a center can almost always be determined by assessing its comparative share of visitor support or hospitality facilities and services.

The size of the hotel room supply for a destination (MSA), or the room supply found within a two- or three-block radius of its convention center, is the single most important determinant or gauge of its marketability. It is logical, therefore, to consider future growth in the room supply. Estimates of future growth may be based on hotel rooms under construction; lodging facilities that are planned, announced, or rumored; and/or historic and future trends.

In addition, the likelihood or reliability of any anticipated growth should consider special circumstances such as nonrecurrent growth, the availability and suitability of new rooms, and economic viability. Bear in mind that "nonrecurrent growth" may result from a one-time event such as the legalization of gambling in a locality. The room supply in Biloxi, Mississippi, may have doubled during the five-year period of 1988 to 1993, but

Connection via an extension of the Riverwalk provides attendees at San Antonio's Henry B. Gonzalez Convention Center, currently slated for a major expansion, with excellent pedestrian access from most of the major hotels in the downtown.

it is unlikely to continue to increase by the same amount in the subsequent five- or even 15-year period.

Availability and suitability of new hotel rooms is contingent on owner/manager booking policy and the market orientation of a property. Certain properties will not block more than 20 percent of their rooms for conventions because of lower room rates or the shorter length of stay of convention attendees, compared with other sources of business such as tourists and corporate travelers. Other types of properties (e.g., 100-room limited-service and economy motels) often will not block rooms at all, or their rooms are not suitable for some groups.

Insufficient economic viability in an existing room supply is currently the most significant obstacle to new development. Economic viability must be differentiated from what might be called "statutory viability" and "subsidized viability." An existing hotel may appear to be economically viable because its cash flow is sufficient to cover operating expenses, pay debt service and other fixed costs, and generate an acceptable return on equity or investment. True economic viability, however, is determined by the ability of the property's cash flow to pay all operating costs, expenses, and debt service on current (replacement) construction costs and interest rates for a new hotel, that is, on "replacement-level cash flow."

Many, if not most, major convention-center hotels with more than 400 rooms are satisfying their financial obligations because of mortgage reductions or legislatively enacted fiscal incentives intended to induce development. The tax laws of the 1980s providing for accelerated depreciation and historic preservation tax credits may have created statutory feasibility or viability. As a result of federal fiscal policy, local inducements, or unique local deal structuring, noneconomic conditions have meant financial feasibility that would otherwise not have existed for a property or investment. Similarly, various government programs at the local, state, or federal levels have provided for below-market-interest loans, grants, property tax exemptions or abatements, free sites or parking facilities, and other such inducements without which a property would not be financially viable.

The recent (1989–1992) volume of hotel mortgage defaults led to substantial writedowns in loan values as mortgages were sold by one lender to another until a low enough mortgage value was obtained to enable debt payments to be paid from the hotel's net cash flow. The converse of this phenomenon was the value writeups caused by secondary financing in the 1980s, when owners withdrew their equity from projects through refinancing. Such refinancings were often based on values created by anticipated increases in cash flows that were projected by appraisals. These higher cash flows were based on assumed increases in future demand or trends in inflation rates.

It is always surprising to discover that there are successful businesspersons who have sincere expectations of new hotel development simply because the existing hotel/motel inventory is achieving high occupancy rates with substantially less than replacement-cost cash flows. In fact, the determination of true, or nonstatutory, economic viability typically includes an analysis of market demand, competitive supply, determinants of growth for each demand segment, and other forces influencing prices, operating and construction costs, and absorption. This work traditionally requires quantitative analysis of demographic statistics, political economics, economic geography, and real estate. Determination of statutory value is often predicated on skillful deal structuring and on an understanding of tax law, accounting policies, and their creative applications to obtaining values unrelated to market forces.

MARKET RANKING

The success of various types of sports and entertainment venues may be predicted, given the absolute size or relative size ranking of their market areas. At this time, for instance, nearly all of the top 35 market areas in the United States contain at least one amphitheater. The probability for success in the 13th-largest market would seem good, but it would not be as good for a venue proposed in the 74th-largest market.

SITE LOCATION AND SURROUNDINGS, PRESENT AND FUTURE

As mentioned earlier, proximity to a large concentration of high-quality hotel rooms is nearly always a requirement for a successful convention center. After evaluating nearby hotel rooms' availability, quality, and rates, a project sponsor would be prudent to evaluate the future strength of the demand for these rooms. If 70 percent of their occupancy depends on nearby, occupied Class A office space, is the area continuing to capture office development? In other words, a strategy to develop a successful convention center must include a plan to capture new office development.

Surrounding environment, as perceived by visitors and local residents, is essential to the marketability of a public assembly venue. Concerns about personal safety will influence meeting planners in *not* selecting destinations and fans in *not* attending events. Again, the community's commitment to preserving or enhancing the future quality of the venue's vicinity is essential to con-

sider when planning a center that may take two years to plan and design, two years to build, and three years to achieve stabilized operations. From this perspective, it is clear that the success of the center will depend on surrounding economic conditions and on the physical/social environment ten years from today, not as they may exist today. How stable and secure, or volatile, are conditions today? How stable were they over the past ten years? And in what direction are the trends leading?

MANAGEMENT AND MARKETING

The single most important factor influencing the financial performance of an arena, stadium, or convention center is management. Aggressive and effective management will book extra events; build a cheerful and positive attitude among employees, customers, performers, and others; maintain the building so that it offers a clean and attractive appearance; and effectively market the building to potential users and their customers.

Unhappily, although management is the most important element in a building's success, it is also the most neglected. For this reason, it is important to understand as much as possible about the owner's specific plans to manage the facility: procedures to recruit and qualifications for management, operating policies and procedures, salary and wage scales, and so forth. If the owner is indifferent to these issues, the analysis should anticipate a wider (downward) range of occupancy and income. (This matter is discussed in greater detail in Chapter 7.)

EVENT CHARACTERISTICS

Recently developed, computer-based models permit forecasting attendance at professional basketball and major league baseball games. Given team quality, market-area population, and other relevant factors, attendance can be predicted with reasonable accuracy, that is, within 5 to 10 percent. This is important information when a facility is dependent on its anchor tenant for 50 to 80 percent of its annual attendance.

The variety and number of touring sports events, concerts, and family shows will vary substantially from year to year. Obviously, the number of contemporary musical concert performances for any one building or market will be determined by the total number of groups on tour and the length of their tours.

By properly identifying and evaluating the critical factors influencing attendance and occupancy and by employing the appropriate quantitative methodology, the facility planner will be able to predict with a high level of reliability the range of events, attendance, and number of performances for the arena or stadium in a stabilized year of operation. Through these same techniques and estimates of population growth, future changes in occupancy can also be predicted (see Figures 2-3 and 2-4).

This type of analysis can accurately reveal the appropriate size and type of building for a successful center. Although market research indicates the ability of a superstar's performance in a given location to attract 25,000 fans, if all other events draw 12,000 to 15,000 attendees and modest growth is anticipated over a five- to ten-year period, an arena with 16,000 to 17,000 seats—not 25,000 seats—should be developed.

Figure 2-3

PROPOSED ARENA: ESTIMATED USE (illustrative example)

Event	Without National Basketball Association (NBA) Team Franchise			With National Basketball Association (NBA) Team Franchise		
	Number of Events	Average Attendance	Total Attendance	Number of Events	Average Attendance	Total Attendance
Professional Sports						
NBA Regular Season	0	0	0	41	13,000	533,000
NBA Exhibition	0	0	0	2	10,000	20,000
Major Indoor Soccer League (MISL) Regular Season	28	9,000	252,000	28	9,000	252,000
Wrestling	6	13,000	78,000	5	13,000	65,000
Boxing	5	13,000	65,000	3	13,000	39,000
Tennis	6	8,000	48,000	4	8,000	32,000
Other	5	10,000	50,000	3	10,000	30,000
Amateur Sports						
College Basketball	5	10,000	50,000	4	10,000	40,000
High-School Sports	7	6,000	42,000	5	6,000	30,000
Other	6	8,000	48,000	4	8,000	32,000
Concerts						
Top Performers	15	16,000	240,000	13	16,000	208,000
Middle-of-the-Road	12	12,000	144,000	10	12,000	120,000
Other	8	8,000	64,000	6	8,000	48,000
Family Events						
Ice Shows	12	7,000	84,000	12	7,000	84,000
Circuses	14	10,000	140,000	14	10,000	140,000
Other Family Events	15	11,500	172,500	13	11,500	149,500
Flat Shows						
Consumer Shows	4	15,000	60,000	3	15,000	45,000
Graduations/Meetings Miscellaneous	5	12,000	60,000	3	12,000	36,000
Total	153		1,597,500	173		1,903,500

Source: Price Waterhouse LLP.

Figure 2-4

PROPOSED DOMED STADIUM: ESTIMATED USE (illustrative example)

	Multipurpose		Baseball		Football	
	Performances or Event Days	Total Paid Attendance	Performances or Event Days	Total Paid Attendance	Performances or Event Days	Total Paid Attendance
Capacity	[65,000–70,000]		[50,000–55,000]		[65,000–70,000]	
Event						
Professional Sports						
Baseball	81	1,612,000	81	1,612,000	0	
Football	10	618,000	0	0	10	618,000
Amateur Sports						
Football						
Georgia Tech	6	200,000	0	0	6	200,000
Peach Bowl	1	45,000	0	0	1	45,000
Freedom Bowl	1	20,000	0	0	1	20,000
Basketball						
Georgia Tech	0	0	0	0	0	0
Concerts	7	190,000	4	900,000	7	190,000
Family Events	6	120,000	0	0	6	120,000
Trade Shows[1]	24	NA	24	NA	24	NA
Consumer Shows[1]	36	45,000	36	45,000	36	45,000
Conventions[1]	0	0	0	0	7	NA
Total	172	2,850,000	145	2,557,000	98	1,238,000

NA means Not Applicable.
[1]Event days include move-in/move-out days.
Source: Price Waterhouse LLP.

SITE AND BUILDING CHARACTERISTICS AFFECTING A CENTER'S MARKETABILITY

While an open stadium often can be cost-effectively expanded, an enclosed arena cannot. Whereas there have been numerous instances in which a second deck or end-zone seating has been added to a stadium, there has been no instance in which an arena's roof has been raised to provide more seats in a cost-effective manner. Although expansion may be less expensive than building a new, larger facility, the additional cost has not been justified by the estimated revenue from extra events.

In contrast to sports facilities, though, a convention center's market area is usually national, regional, or state-wide in scope. The local market, as defined for convention facilities, is relevant only for measuring the demand for consumer shows and other events that draw from the local resident population. The size and future use of a convention center can be determined through:
- Surveys of meeting planners, association executives, and trade-show producers.
- An evaluation of use characteristics of comparable facilities in communities with similar convention-center resources, (e.g., hotel rooms, metropolitan-area population, airline service, and contiguous exhibit space).

- A comparison of the city's convention attendance performance with its ranking according to its resources.
- An evaluation of a reasonable market share, as determined by the growth in exhibit-space requirements and attendance for those conventions and trade shows that the facility is sized to capture. A comparison with the market shares of cities with comparable convention resource ranking should then follow.

For Price Waterhouse's *Convention and Congress Center Annual Report,* occupancy data are collected annually from all primary convention centers in markets with over 20,000 rooms and from nearly all centers in markets with 10,000 to 20,000 rooms. The total exhibition-space occupancy can then be determined for major users of these types of facilities as follows: Take the square feet of exhibit space used for each event, multiply it by the number of event days (including move-in/-out days), and the result will be the number of occupied square foot-days. Then, divide this figure by the available square foot-days—the total exhibit space in the building multiplied by 365—to arrive at total effective occupancy.

The results of this research over the past several years have determined that the maximum practical exhibit-space occupancy for trade shows and conventions with exhibits is approximately 70 percent. This practical maximum is due to the inability to schedule successive convention and trade-show events back to back, resulting in many one- to five-day dead periods between these types of events. Exhibition-space occupancy is used to gauge a convention center's performance because, in North America, the use of meeting rooms often is granted free of charge in proportion to the total exhibit space rented. (For example, if a group rents 50 percent of total exhibit space, it frequently is given the use of up to 50 percent of the meeting rooms without charge.) Figure 2-5 shows the average occupancy for convention and trade show–type events for various-sized buildings in the three major regions (time zones) of North America.

The results of research over the past ten years indicate that occupancy characteristics for convention centers vary widely by region and size of facility. In reality, regional variations reflect a preference for selected cities within a region rather than for the region itself: Las Vegas, San Diego, Anaheim, and San Francisco enjoy high occupancies when compared with facilities in other regions with few tourist-oriented cities.

Historically, trade shows or trade association events have used exhibit space almost exclusively; that is, they have had few or no meetings, food functions, or assemblies. By contrast, conventions of professional associations have used most or all of a center's meeting rooms,

A white-tablecloth restaurant at Jacob's Field in Cleveland, a dramatic alternative to the hot dog with mustard and relish.

ballrooms, and assembly halls and have had few and, by comparison, smaller exhibit-space needs. In recent years, however, trade associations have scheduled more meetings—seminars—and food functions to increase attendance, and conventions have discovered the financial benefits of hosting large trade shows in conjunction with their meetings. Today, without knowing the name of an event's sponsor, it is often impossible to differentiate a convention from a trade show by the space assigned for its meeting/exhibit use. Clearly, however, the demand for convention facilities outside hotels is a function of both the amount of exhibition space and meeting rooms needed. As shown in Figure 2-6, the market may be quantified roughly by size of attendance and trade-show size characteristics.

Many forecasts of demand are based on so-called "market shares" analysis. Although understanding the rotational patterns of state, regional, and national groups is helpful, it is not a reliable basis for projecting the occupancy of a building because locational factors influence market capture more than the current distribution of market segments—whether national, regional, or state.

Figure 2-5

CONVENTION AND TRADE-SHOW OCCUPANCY, BY MARKET SIZE AND REGION

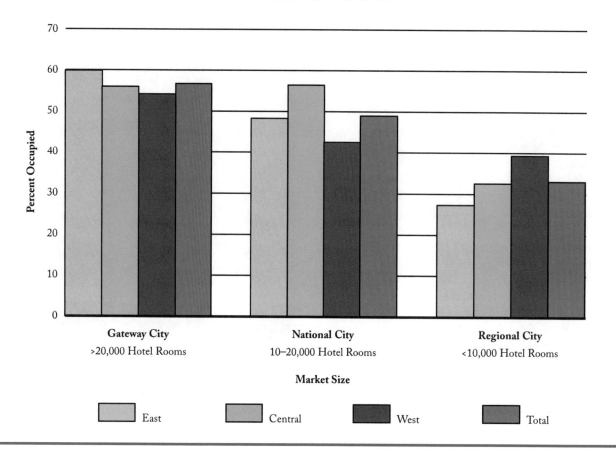

Therefore, market shares analysis must be secondary to consideration of the site's location characteristics.

New construction of convention facilities is mandated as much by growth in demand as it is by the functional obsolescence of older buildings. The characteristics of the new facility will be shaped by an analysis of the demand. Meeting planners and trade-show producers are becoming more sophisticated and more specific in defining their facility requirements. It is not enough for a facility to provide meeting rooms of a given size; the interior finishes of the rooms must meet high standards, offer appropriate ceiling heights, make available a variety of lighting types and levels of illumination, and, ideally, provide separate corridors for service access. The number of rooms required in the headquarters hotel and other ancillary needs are also carefully specified.

In other words, it is not possible to determine market share by a count of meetings by size, origin, and rotational pattern and then to divide by the number of competitive facilities. All the facilities in the competitive supply are not equally or even approximately competitive. The occupancy of one building may exceed by four or five times that of another building with similar dimensions in a comparably sized community in the same region. The determinants of market demand are more numerous and complex for convention centers than for arenas or stadiums. Notable are the stratification and segmentation of user groups, whose needs are as complex and dissimilar as are the communities competing for their business. Again, no single analytical technique adequately quantifies future use.

In second- and third-tier cities, the convention center or civic center will function more frequently as a multipurpose or community center. The major convention users will be regional, state-based, or sometimes industry-specialized organizations. A smaller city's building will attract public or consumer shows, boat shows, car shows, home and garden shows, retail buyer or merchandize mart–type shows, and so on. The dominant category of users may be local civic and social groups or

Figure 2-6

GRAPHIC SUMMARY OF CONVENTION-CENTER MARKET: NATIONAL MEETINGS (illustrative example)

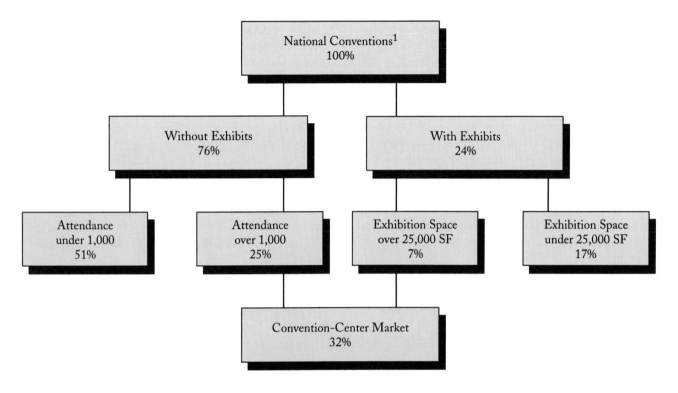

[1]Based on a sample of 489 national conventions held in the southeastern region of the United States.
Sources: International Association of Convention and Visitors Bureaus; Price Waterhouse LLP.

fraternal groups, with events including high-school graduations, political rallies, religious crusades and revivals, local concerts, amateur athletic contests, and the like. While attendees at these events will be locally based and thus will generate minimal economic impact, the proper sizing and pricing of facilities for local use can result in financial operations that break even.

OPTIMIZING THE SIZE

More frequently than might be expected, the client's charge to the architect is, "Build all that my budget will fund" or "Get all that you can fit onto this site that can be functionally competitive." In other words, the planner must grapple with how much market will fit the fixed size of "the box" or will fit on a tight site, rather than with how big the center should be to fit market demand requirements. Convention centers in San Francisco and Boston are examples of such an approach.

As mentioned earlier, the appropriate size for an arena can easily be determined from the market's size or from the anchor tenant's requirements. Determining the size of a convention center, however, presents more problems. If an increase in size is needed, it often responds to the demands of two or more groups for simultaneous use, i.e., for the same time period, rather than to the needs of larger groups using the entire hall. An ideal booking policy for a 300,000-square-foot exhibit space would have Group 1 in session, with its show occupying 100,000 square feet; Group 2 moving in its 100,000-square-foot show; and Group 3 moving out. This arrangement would be preferable to one large group's using the entire 300,000-square-foot hall with a three-day move-in period (no room demand), a five-day show with peak in-hotel demand displacing other hotel business, and a two- to three-day move-out period (no hotel/retail/restaurant demand).

Popular destinations such as New York, San Francisco, and Chicago can fill more space in their facilities than they can afford to build or than they have land available at the right location to build. Third-tier cities will struggle to balance their business communities' goals of generating economic impact (i.e., new visitor spending) against the demands of local groups (which are often willing to pay higher rent) to use the hall for civic, social, sports, and entertainment events. These lower-economic-impact events are sometimes referred to as SMERF-type events: social, military (active or reunions), educational (and other public employees limited to "government" rates), religious, and fraternal.

Sizing facilities in fast-growing second-tier cities is the most challenging task because each increment of 100,000 square feet affords increased opportunities for adding events during the peak demand season(s). Consequently, the optimal building program will yield maximum delegates per square foot or minimum cost (in annual debt service and operating costs) per delegate. At some point, additional space will yield diminishing returns, meaning that the optimal size has been exceeded. Although adding more building space almost always results in more or larger events and more attendees, the added investment in more space produces a smaller increase on return.

Future growth needs usually are determined by growth in the hotel room supply and occur in three- to five-year increments, or cycles. These long-term requirements should be accommodated through land banking, not through additional space. It is not cost-effective to build and operate underused space in anticipation of growth in hotel room supply in years seven through ten. Conversely, a center should not become site-bound, or landlocked.

There are, of course, exceptions to this rule. Seattle, for example, is better off to have built as much as it could build on the site it created (by bridging the interstate that bisects its central core). Seattle's alternative was to abandon its best site in favor of a location outside the CBD with more land but too remote from hotels and retail/restaurant establishments. Later, if demand emerges, the city can build a second, larger facility outside the CBD to satisfy the needs of trade associations and exhibitions, which do not require large hotel room supplies nearby.

The building program determined by market research for a new arena or stadium will be expressed in terms of numbers of seats and their configuration. A

James F. Housel

To maintain a central location and still offer an adequately sized facility, the Washington State Convention and Trade Center in Seattle straddles Interstate 5.

Figure 2-7

RECOMMENDED CONVENTION-CENTER BUILDING PROGRAM (illustrative example)

Building Component	Area in Square Feet
Exhibition Hall	200,000
Meeting Rooms	70,000
Auditorium (5,000 seats)	45,000
Multipurpose Ballroom	40,000
Lobby and Prefunction Areas	104,000
Support Areas	122,000
Kitchen	21,000
Office Space	5,000
Total	607,000

convention center will be planned in terms of the amount and configuration of exhibition space (ceiling height, utility mix, column spacing, floor loads); the number, size, and locations of prefunction areas; meeting-room characteristics (size, divisibility, aspect ratio, interior finishes, and so on); and any single-purpose banquet and assembly space needed. The architect, potential user groups, and space planner will refine the specifications for these areas and for circulation, "back-of-house" needs, mechanical areas, lobbies, storage, offices, and other types of "nonrentable" space. The total building area will be specified, together with the footprint or exterior dimensions of the building. Figure 2-7 illustrates an optimal convention-center building program, given its projected use.

It is essential to specify the building location, space program, layout, and performance specifications in estimating market demand or future use. The single most important reason that buildings are unsuccessful, aside from their site and destination characteristics, is the assumption by the market analyst that the client will design an efficient, marketable, and competitive building. Usually, this is not a reliable assumption.

NEEDS ANALYSIS FOR SPECTATOR FACILITIES OUTSIDE NORTH AMERICA

Countries outside the North American continent have not developed as extensive a network of professional hockey and basketball leagues and, consequently, have not developed the large network of 15,000- to 20,000-seat arenas that has been possible in the United States

and Canada to support the touring concert industry. Some multipurpose arena–type venues of various sizes and configurations are now being developed, but it is still too early to predict the future expansion of arena sports or concert demand without the clear emergence of sports leagues or other dominant user groups.

Stadiums, of course, have been developed throughout Europe, South America, Asia, and the Middle East to support FIFA football (soccer) leagues. Like stadiums in North America, they are primarily used by their home teams, with only three to five concert events per year.

Convention centers in the Asia-Pacific region have developed rapidly in the past two decades. Major new centers have been opened or are under construction in most Asia-Pacific capital cities. They function in much the same way as North American centers, with a combination of professional association conventions and trade association events. Intercontinental rotation of events in Asia-Pacific, European, South and North American centers is extremely rare. If a European or U.S. trade show is expected to succeed in Asia, its producer or a competitor will start an Asian version of the show rather than move the European or U.S. event from its existing circuit.

Convention centers in Europe are called congress centers, as "congress" is the European term for "convention." Unlike centers in the United States and Asia-Pacific nations, trade association events are held in separate fairground-type facilities called trade fairs. Historically, professional associations in Europe, as in the United States, did not promote large exhibitions in conjunction with their professional association congresses. The trend to host conventions with exhibitions or trade shows was accelerated in the United States by the early governmental subsidization of trade fair facilities and availability of ample exhibit space in the multipurpose (trade association and professional association) centers. But this did not occur as easily in Europe because groups soliciting exhibitors owned their own trade fair centers or did not have access to larger purpose-built space to accommodate exhibitors. Accordingly, exhibitors at trade shows promoted by congresses erected their stands in hallways, lobbies, and banquet rooms.

Many newer congress centers have purpose-built exhibit areas (Birmingham), multipurpose halls (Berlin, Vienna), or adjacent trade fair facilities (Nice/Acropolis). Nevertheless, there is still a resistance on the part of most European congress organizers and association members to host commercial exhibitions "under the same roof" at these meetings. Suffice it to say that European centers are more likely to serve performing arts events—with their multiplicity of grand theater–type halls with

The needs analysis for an international facility like the Singapore Convention and Exhibition Centre, a part of the giant Suntec City Development at Marina Centre, will differ from that for a less strategic site.

fixed seats on sloped floors for plenary and other large assemblies—rather than trade shows.

Europe's numerous, elegant, fixed-seat assembly venues, which exist in a range of sizes, are adaptable or designed also to accommodate the local community's symphony, ballet, opera, and dramatic performances. Except for a few centers like Boston and Atlanta, fixed-seat auditoriums have been relatively unavailable in U.S. centers; Houston, however, followed Atlanta in developing a highly flexible, fixed-seat auditorium. Orlando is doing likewise. In the future, we expect that U.S. convention centers will be more likely to develop fixed-seat assembly facilities, and European congress centers will be less likely to include large (i.e., over 300,000-square-foot) exhibit halls. This, as explained further, is the result of the facilities' locational characteristics and site limitations.

In listing the primary differences between U.S. and European centers, it is instructive to recognize that most of the U.S. centers that are most attractive to professional associations—Boston, Washington, D.C., Cincinnati, and San Francisco—are, like their counterparts in Europe, located in the very center and heart of

a city and are unable to expand. Their limited contiguous exhibit space—100,000 square feet to 230,000 square feet—does not prevent them from achieving practical maximum occupancy and the highest ratios of room-night demand to attendees and per square feet of building space. It may be most advantageous for destinations like these to develop separate trade fair–type facilities at less-developed locations on the edges of their center cities, like those provided in Europe, rather than try to accommodate the ever-increasing demands for more space by more show managers of trade associations. Indeed, the most successful venues for trade shows in the United States are not in the city centers. Facilities in Atlanta, New York, Orlando, New Orleans, Chicago, Dallas, Las Vegas, and Anaheim are all located on the edge of or outside the center city. Trying to accommodate the needs of two divergent groups in one building in our largest urban areas may not be a cost-effective practice over the next decade or two. Serious plans are pending for more fixed-seat/sloped-floor auditoriums for convention centers in center cities. Similarly, plans are being made, e.g., in Boston, for purpose-built trade-show halls that will be located beyond the existing downtowns.

South and Central America and Africa have mostly smaller centers, but only South American capitals are seriously discussing major U.S.–type centers. Plans for new centers are proposed in Mexico, Bolivia, Venezuela, and Brazil, to name a few places. To date, however, no network has emerged that is capable of supporting large ambulatory convention or trade fair events in either South and Central America or Africa.

Unlike in North America, the presence of a dozen or more large, industrialized nation-states on a single continent, as in Europe, has produced many annual, international governmental/financial conferences that are held in congress centers. These events are, by comparison, rare occasions in U.S. centers. Indeed, most major European congresses are truly international in delegate origin and composition and require extensive arrangements for simultaneous interpretation of all proceedings. This requirement works to limit the number of breakout sessions and encourages more plenary sessions. Arrangements that are unusual in the United States are considered routine in Europe: following strict security procedures, observing proper dress codes, maintaining international protocol and etiquette, and providing many elaborate meal functions, receptions, formal gatherings, and welcoming speeches by political and business leaders.

ESTIMATING USE FOR THE RECOMMENDED BUILDING PROGRAM

It should be more apparent at the end of this chapter than it was at the beginning that there is no precise definition of feasibility and no single formula that all stakeholders would agree is appropriate. Accordingly, the market research analyst is usually well advised not to present a recommended size of facility. As an example, it is more appropriate and useful for the prospective owner, sponsor, or manager of a convention center to understand the building program as a plan that best accomplishes the primary objective(s): the lowest cost per delegate-day, generating the most room-nights per square foot, the best fit for the site, accommodation of specific event(s), and/or finance-ability with the estimated tax revenue pledged to the amortization of the development costs.

Similarly, the most appropriately or optimally sized arena or stadium may be the one that meets the demands of the franchise owner, pleases the university team coach/athletic director, or elicits the enthusiastic support of civic leaders and voters. Occasionally, the client will decide that the size of the center should be limited by the debt it can support as determined by the sum of its annual debt service and net operating cost, which should be less than the annual new tax revenue it generates. More often, some other criterion is identified as the measure of feasibility.

Again, every effort should be made to encourage the facility owner to define feasibility and to specify management and booking policy (i.e., priority of scheduling certain events versus other, less desirable events), the marketing program and budget, site location requirements, and building program/design concept. Ironically, owners often fail to understand the relationship between these issues and the center's future use or occupancy, which many intelligent business and civic leaders still believe is simply market-driven. That is, many project sponsors do not appreciate the significant impact of a building's design, location, and management on its marketability.

The next chapter will provide a more in-depth discussion of the methods and criteria for evaluating sites, site location, and site acquisition issues and procedures.

Chapter 3

PLANNING THE PROJECT: CONCEPT TO GROUNDBREAKING

A major project without a strong constituency is much like a child without parents. It may be successful, but without one or more strong individuals' ego involvement, the odds against its success are greater. Accordingly, the first step in planning any major project is to identify and measure the extent of support for it. Without enthusiastic, dedicated stakeholders or an influential constituency, the proposed center will likely flounder after high public expectations have been raised by media hype and after much time and money have been spent in the economic analysis or preliminary design studies.

ADVOCATES AND SPONSORS

The primary advocates of public assembly facilities are usually elected government officials, although they are not the centers' prime financial beneficiaries or largest single user group. An arena or stadium should be a significant entertainment or recreational amenity for the entire community and should enhance the attractiveness of the area for existing businesses and for people who may be considering locating their residences or companies in the community. Thus, they would most likely receive the support and leadership of civic officials and chambers of commerce, as well as those of the hotel, airline, restaurant, and retail shop owners who stand to benefit from increased visitor spending.

Because owners of professional team franchises currently are in a buyers' market and have many communities competing for their venue selections, they are not likely to take a strong, upfront, advocacy position and risk appearing to be greedy. If the local community leaders will not build new or expand existing venues for their teams, other communities are often eager to do so, usually with more attractive financial incentives.

Financing, building, and operating a public assembly facility is a major, long-term task requiring tenacious and concentrated commitment. If the most logical constituencies or largest prospective beneficiaries are not motivated to sponsor the proposed center early in the planning process, the project should be mothballed until some later date, by which time the most likely stakeholders will have recognized and appreciated its benefits enough to risk their credibility on its success. Conversely, a strong, dedicated advocacy group will usually ensure that the project is well planned, properly located, and professionally managed.

The first step in the planning process is to identify and organize the leadership/advocacy group. The second step is to identify the organizations that will be responsible for the planning, site selection, design, financing, and operation of the facility. Ideally, the same organization will function as leader/advocate and assume responsibility for all predevelopment planning. In this way, each step will be planned and conducted with the level of diligence expected of an organization that will one day be responsible for the project's operation, maintenance, and financial success.

To the extent that separate organizations perform planning and operations, the following events are almost certain to occur:

- The planners will not evaluate the project in sufficient detail to consider the later needs of operation, such as adequate parking, service access, or special lighting requirements.
- The lure of lower "first costs" may lead center planners to opt for an inferior location (cheaper land) or for inadequate equipment or interior finishes that have higher lifecycle costs.
- Financing may not include funding for the reserve accounts needed to replace carpeting or seats or to remodel in the near or mid-term.

- The site that is easiest to purchase or assemble may be chosen, but its less favorable location may reduce center marketability or economic benefit. For instance, the site may be remote from retail shops or restaurants.
- Adequate land area for future expansion needs may not be acquired.
- The budget for furniture and equipment may be inadequate to purchase the items needed to serve important user groups, to minimize labor costs, or to maximize event revenue.
- Management staff may be selected who will lack the experience, skills, and motivation needed to minimize operating costs and to satisfy user requirements and expectations.

Many a worthwhile project has floundered because a successful transition was not made from one project sponsor (e.g., the project planner) to the next (the builder or operator), even when the project's owner was part of the same entity as its operator (e.g., another department of the same city). And this type of project is notorious for a flurry of finger pointing among various sponsors when operations go awry.

The third step in the planning process is twofold: to identify the primary user groups and to prioritize the objectives of the center. A mission statement is essential for a multipurpose building or complex. The board of directors or project sponsors must understand and support the goals and objectives of the center before they can provide the direction and guidance needed by center architects, management, and financial planners.

It is important for them to understand the multipurpose intentions for the facility and the degree to which one user will dominate the design and use of the facility for other purposes. If, for example, a major league owner objects to any other activity than baseball on the stadium turf, it is unrealistic to expect revenue from concert events. Similarly, if event booking for a university's multipurpose arena is controlled by the athletic director, the arena is unlikely to host events attracting nonstudent participants or audiences.

Consumer shows and conventions with trade shows compete for dates in a convention center. Consumer shows generate more income for the center and are often favored by its owner, while conventions generate more hotel room demand and restaurant patrons. Clearly, booking priorities must be established and implemented with an effective policy and procedures. The issue is often more complex as it relates to the use of other facilities in the community that are essential to the success of the center but that have other owners and objectives. These other facilities might include a hotel, major attraction, or

Groundbreaking ceremony for the new MCI Center arena, Washington, D.C., which will be the new home for the Washington Wizards, formerly the Bullets, and for the Washington Capitols hockey team.

theater. For example, an adjacent theater can be reserved for the local symphony, a touring Broadway show, the plenary session of the convention, a high-school graduation, a travel club's film series, or a recital by Miss Jones's Academy of Baton and Tap Dance (coincidentally, Miss Jones is the mayor's sister-in-law). If the "ideal" package of facilities is essential, their availability should be assured.

Each user group will have a greater or lesser economic impact on the community, the CBD, and the center, and each will be perceived to serve the taxpayers' needs to a greater or lesser extent. If the construction budget for a convention center and theater complex must be reduced, for instance, the architect may do one or more of the following:
- Reduce the number of seats in the theater and thus the associated building size.
- Eliminate the theater's fly loft.
- Eliminate the service corridors behind the meeting rooms in the convention center.
- Put columns on 90-foot centers instead of specifying a clear-span roof structure for the exhibit hall.
- Suggest that the caterer pay for kitchen equipment and installations.

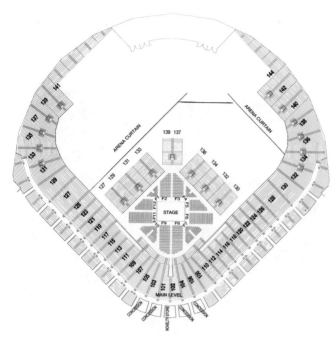

At the ThunderDome in Tampa/St. Petersburg, an arena curtain converts a baseball stadium into a concert venue.

In each case, one interest is sacrificed to another. Each alternative cost-reduction option will have a different effect on income. Similarly, an arena cannot have ideal sightlines for basketball, hockey, and horse shows. An oval stadium is designed to accommodate either a running track or an NFL franchise, not both. The design will be guided by the primary tenant.

Neither the architect nor the operations manager should be expected to make decisions affecting the center's ability to accomplish intended objectives. Likewise, both during the planning stages and throughout the operational period, the board of directors must consist of representatives of the various constituencies and interest groups that the center is expected to serve.

Ideally, the sponsorship/planning group should, from its beginning, be empowered to plan, build, finance, own, and operate the facility. Its board of directors should be composed of multipartisan and multidisciplinary business and professional leaders and persons recognized for their accomplishments in other challenging and important endeavors. Generally speaking, persons who have achieved success in other major enterprises will commit themselves and will persevere to achieve success in projects with which they are identified. They will give generously of their limited time and, if necessary, "cash in a chip" or trade in a personal IOU to benefit the project when the need arises. The project's sponsor group should therefore be selected carefully from, and limited

to, the strongest and most influential community and business leaders.

Many projects without strong market support have achieved extraordinary success because their development and operations were managed by strong leaders. Conversely, many projects that have had strong market demand, ideal sites, and readily available funding have failed because leadership was inept, weak, uncommitted, or limited in its interests to one type of event or user.

PREPARING THE PLAN

Many useful models for planning, budgeting, and progress monitoring are available, among them the critical path method and others. Whichever model is chosen, however, the major factors are time, tasks, responsible agents, costs, and milestone events scheduled at specific points. These events may recognize the completion of a major task or the initiation or continuation of a task that is dependent on a decision. Every plan should specify in sufficient detail all tasks that must be done, who will do each task, how much time it will take, what it will cost, and when progress reports, quality tests, and decisions will be made. A realistic planning budget and time frame can then be prepared, and project management with quality controls put in place.

Most developers/construction managers today use one of the many computer-based planning/scheduling models, which allow them to modify or update the schedule and budget readily, as well as to provide detailed routines to demonstrate the interrelationship and sequencing of tasks. This latter feature will show how a delay or cost variance in one task will affect later tasks, overall completion time, and total project costs.

Typically, many technical consultant specialists are employed to assume responsibility for such functions as analysis of geotechnical-subsurface site conditions, estimates of number and type of events, building design, traffic and parking analysis, landscape planning, roof structure engineering, management and operations planning, marketing program, financial operations forecasting, financing planning/underwriting, and many others. For each of these specialists, separate firms or subcontractors must be identified, the scope of services defined, selection criteria defined and contracts prepared, budgets negotiated, and a reporting process and schedule agreed upon.

Finding the specialists who will deliver high-quality service or a reliable product on time is not easy. Specialists' backgrounds and track records should be carefully studied and verified. The credibility of a project can be substantially influenced by the credibility of these firms and individuals, for what these out-of-town experts' and specialists' past clients say about their work is more important than the abilities they, their likable "face men," or their attractive brochures claim on their behalf.

Although most or all of the costs for preconstruction planning can be reimbursed from the development financing, it is often hard to find the upfront dollars to engage qualified professionals to evaluate a project's objectives and resources and to prepare reliable plans. Nevertheless, a realistic and comprehensive preconstruction budget must be completed and fully funded if the project is to progress on schedule, retain creditability, and achieve its goals. Funds are sometimes borrowed from private banks or businesses, but most often the investment in predevelopment planning is obtained from local or state government sources.

IMPLEMENTING THE PLAN

- "Plan your work, then work your plan" is a shibboleth more difficult to follow than this easily turned phrase would suggest. Although a project's sponsors may give unstintingly of their time, typically no one individual will have enough time to devote to the day-to-day im-

plementation of the plan. A full-time, experienced, and resourceful project manager must be hired. The role of the project manager will include:

- Day-to-day supervision and monitoring of the plan's progress.
- Identification and ranking of specialists for the sponsoring board's approval.
- Preparation of the agenda for board meetings. Also, in states that require board meetings to be open to the press, the project manager should meet with all board members individually before a board meeting. The point is to avoid public disclosure of differing opinions about matters that may be seen as controversial, open to misrepresentation, or even falsified. In serving their own interests by reporting or misreporting on open board meetings, today's "infotainment" media sometimes damage the reputations or question the integrity of staff or board members.
- Conduct of public relations and preparation of press releases.
- Briefing of various community groups on the progress of the project and preparation of presentations for board members to give to such groups.
- Provision of a liaison, as needed, to related groups.
- Performance of any other tasks necessary to keep the project on track.

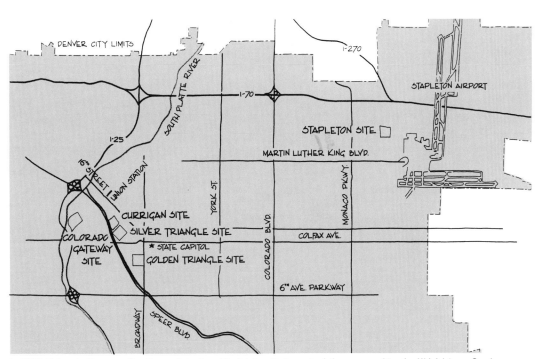

In 1987, Colorado Governor Roy Romer introduced legislation that required the sponsorship of a ULI Advisory Services panel, which recommended the Silver Triangle site in the Denver CBD—one of five alternative site and design proposals under contention for the development of the Colorado Convention Center.

The critical position of project manager (or clerk of the works) must be filled before the permanent, full-time operating staff are hired. This person or firm should effectively coordinate many professional disciplines—legal, financial, design, marketing, and others—and prevent the objectives of one discipline from dominating or eclipsing the effectiveness of the other disciplines.

ALTERNATIVE DEVELOPMENT OPTIONS

As far as possible, the plan should provide for contingencies. The successful business plan will integrate the building design, operations, marketing, and financing plans. Identifying and evaluating various what-if scenarios will often lead to alternative contingency plans. The ideal or optimal plan will be pursued until it is implemented or derailed, but, if at all possible, alternative or fallback plans should be ready.

If less than 100 percent of the required funding is obtainable, should the project be phased, reconfigured, or downsized? If site assembly is blocked, can another site be identified? If a professional sports franchise cannot be obtained, can another anchor tenant be found? If the entire building program for the convention center cannot be funded, can multipurpose or "swing" space be developed? Contingency plans to take care of such problems will avoid delays in development.

Sometimes, a thorough evaluation of alternative development scenarios will reveal a plan that is preferable to or more cost-effective than the initial one. Often, however, it will reveal options that compromise a center's marketability or capacity to such a degree that the project becomes dysfunctional, that is, unable to accomplish the objectives for which it was intended. Examples of such compromises are:

- A convention center that had to be developed below grade to accommodate a local interest group, which insisted that the site be used as a park.
- A stadium design change that ended up saving less money than the reduction in value of some of the seats, which had to be reduced in price because their sightline was obstructed.
- A convention center's site that was chosen for its lower cost but that was too distant from hotels to attract many associations.

Certainly, centers can be successful even if built below grade. Structural changes have reduced costs without obscuring the field of play, and alternative sites have been acquired that have provided locations acceptable to users. But care must be taken to ensure that a compromise is feasible, not fatal. Better to abandon the project than to render it dysfunctional by adopting a crippling compromise.

Chapter 4

SITE SELECTION AND ACQUISITION

The three most important factors to consider in selecting a site for a convention, sports, or entertainment facility are those that affect attendance, income, and occupancy. In other words, location, location, location.

Attendance and occupancy are measures of a center's marketability. Maximizing attendance for a spectator venue will be most affected by its proximity to potential attendees, to transportation, and to available parking. A convention center's occupancy by professional associations, and the amount of attendee spending generated by it, are most influenced by its nearness to support facilities: hotels, restaurants, retail shops, entertainment establishments, and local attractions. Its occupancy by trade associations is determined by the population of its metropolitan area and by its level of air service. Because the site location will have a major influence on both attendance and occupancy, the use of convention, sports, and entertainment facilities cannot be estimated reliably without first identifying the location or at least the locational characteristics required for the site.

SELECTION CRITERIA

SIZE, VISIBILITY, AND SCALE

The minimum size for a facility's site will be determined by the footprint of the building (which is expressed in its exterior dimensions), service access needs, required on-site parking, zoning regulations, area reserved for future expansion or related facilities, and requirements for setbacks and circulation.

Single-story convention centers, with 30-foot-high ceilings and 15-foot-deep trusses in their exhibit halls, are often the same height as five- to six-story commercial office buildings. Arenas usually provide 100 to 150+ feet to the bottom of their 20- to 30-foot-deep roof trusses. And the vertical dimensions of stadiums are even higher. These typically high and long, blank walls present design challenges to architects working with downtown sites. Sloped sites often give the designer a chance to hide the massive structure by tucking one side of it into an excavated portion of the site, thereby obtaining a more human scale for attendees approaching the entrance, creating pedestrian plazas, and keeping the massive scale of the structure more in harmony with nearby building facades.

The Georgia World Congress Center in Atlanta is an excellent example of exploiting the development opportunities of a two-level sloped site. In contrast, San Francisco—the city of hills—chose a flat site, then opted to place Moscone Convention Center underground to minimize the unattractive visual impact on the center's surroundings. This design decision proved to be expensive, limiting truck access and requiring even costlier construction in the limited area available for expansion under a street and below the water table.

An important civic structure should be set on a prominent, highly visible spot. It is readily understandable why the architect's skills are stretched to the limits to accomplish the many, usually conflicting, design objectives for these bulky (and balky) building types. These structures ought to be prominent on the urban horizon to celebrate civic pride, to symbolize the 21st century, or simply to justify a $250 million investment. At the

The Pyramid in Memphis is located in the heart of the city on the Mississippi River waterfront.

Oriole Park at Camden Yards is a powerful engine driving the revitalization of Baltimore's Inner Harbor area. Plans are underway to add a new stadium to house the to-be-renamed Cleveland Browns franchise.

same time, as friendly neighbors on a city block, the buildings need to blend in.

Their marketability often depends on how close they are to existing reservoirs of parking, regional mass transit, hotel rooms, retail shops, and restaurants. Simple. They should be in the center of the city. At the same time, their functional efficiency requires enormous building mass, height, and space to accommodate a 22-acre exhibit-hall floor plate, peak vehicle access, 50 truck docks, and semi–truck tractor-trailer marshaling and queuing. Simple. These buildings should be sited in exurban areas, behind tall trees, and recessed in valleys.

Planners of large-capacity public assembly facilities have begun to sort out some answers to these conflicts:

- Amphitheaters are best located away from residential areas to screen nearby homes from their noise levels.
- Convention centers that accommodate large trade shows are best located outside the CBD, as in Chicago, or at the edge of it, as in Atlanta and Dallas.
- Convention centers in destinations with a magnitude and diversity of amenities to attract professional associations should be sited in the center of those distinctive amenities and attractions, as they are in San Francisco, Boston, San Antonio, and Cincinnati.
- Arenas and ballparks are successful in center-city locations when the available supply of nearby parking is sufficient to reduce the amount of land required and thereby to offset the higher cost of land.

The large numbers of events in these venues (90 to 290 annually) attract large numbers of resident and nonresident attendees (2 to 3 million per year) who may also be induced to shop in nearby retail stores, eat in restaurants, celebrate their victory or mourn their loss in a lively bistro, or, if a team has a large regional following, spend the night. Public assembly facilities can provide a major magnet for a community's urban tourism strategy. In measuring the strength of this magnet, venue location will be as important as the drawing power of the events.

- As to parking, stadiums and large arenas typically require one parking space for every two to four attendees. If mass transit is not available or not used by fans, parking lots or structures must be provided to accommodate as many as 7,000 cars for a 23,000-seat arena and 20,000 or more cars for a 70,000-seat stadium.

Examples of surface parking developed for spectator sport venues may be seen at Nassau Veterans Memorial Coliseum (Uniondale, New York), Giants Stadium/ Byrne Meadowlands Arena (East Rutherford, New Jersey), the Truman Sports Complex (Kansas City, Missouri), and Dodger Stadium (Los Angeles). Parking structures are not cost-effective for ten to 12 NFL events per year. Additionally, 50,000 to 70,000 fans attending a Sunday-afternoon football game are not likely to generate a sufficient volume of retail and restaurant sales to encourage these establishments to open for business if they are normally closed.

Despite these guidelines, local circumstances can create a condition in which developing a venue to host NFL games in the CBD is more cost-effective than locating in exurbia, or "the boonies." Examples of successful center-city venues are provided by multipurpose (football/baseball) and NFL-only stadiums set on the edge or border of the CBD, as in New Orleans, Minneapolis, Cincinnati, Cleveland, Indianapolis, Atlanta, Charlotte, St. Louis, Seattle, and Toronto.

Another concept for the edge of the CBD has been planned in Baltimore. A new NFL stadium has been designed to be erected next to baseball's Oriole Park at Camden Yards. Financing has been approved and has, wisely, been made contingent on securing a franchise. This side-by-side concept was pioneered in exurbia by Kansas City; however, Baltimore will have the first MLB/NFL, center-city, side-by-side venues in recent history.

PARKING AND OTHER PHYSICAL REQUIREMENTS

For an arena or stadium, most of the parking should be placed next to or near the structure, within convenient walking distance. If this parking requirement is not fully satisfied by existing parking facilities, the required site area must be expanded. Parking needs and building footprints will be defined by the market demand analysis, by the parking consultant, and by the building's architect. The amount and location of parking required will be affected by the availability of public transit service to the site, transit ridership and preferences within the local community, and the average size of a travel group for various events.

For example, Madison Square Garden relies on public transit almost exclusively, while Nassau Veterans Memorial Coliseum and Byrne Meadowlands Arena rely almost entirely on cars. For an automobile-dependent community, an arena site without existing and available parking nearby may require 50 to 60 acres for surface parking (at three persons per car), compared with only four acres for the building's footprint. A stadium site remote from existing parking facilities, in an area not serviced by public transit, may require 200 or more acres for surface parking.

Parking structures serving sports facilities located in or adjacent to central cities, like the stadiums in St. Louis and Cincinnati and the new ballpark in Baltimore, can provide additional parking for other CBD visitors or downtown workers during nonevent periods. This extra parking generates added income on nongame days, thereby offsetting some of the parking structure's debt-service costs and enhancing the volume of sales for CBD restaurants and retailers on game days. Parking facilities developed to serve downtown sports venues will also provide added spaces to serve downtown weekday shoppers, business visitors, and employees, thereby enhancing CBD real estate values.

Site area requirements to accommodate the building footprint for a convention center may vary because certain elements of the building program may be stacked. A modern, functional exhibit hall should be contained in one contiguous, rectangular floor area on grade. For this reason, the convention-center footprint can be no less than the total area of the exhibition halls plus circulation, service areas, and lobby/registration and loading areas. For reasons that will be discussed in Chapter 5, design requirements for exhibit-hall floor load limits, truck access, minimum column spacing, and interior circulation will increase costs on sites of limited area that require stacking of elements.

A dramatic example of stacking and the resultant increased development costs is seen in the Washington State Convention and Trade Center in Seattle. Its location in the center of the downtown was chosen to boost its marketability and to bring the greatest economic benefit to the community. Because no large site was available, the sponsor created a site on air rights over the interstate highway that bisects the central core.

Conversely, community leaders in Orlando, Florida, selected a site with ample land for current and future expansion needs at minimum cost. Although the site minimized development costs and provided plenty of room for auto and truck access and circulation, it required a maximum number of parking spaces and may generate less delegate spending and economic/fiscal benefit to the community than would a convention center near to specialty and high-fashion retail shops.

ACCESS

A site near the center of the city's resident population, or its centroid, will minimize travel time for market-area residents and can overcome any negative perceptions they may have about their personal security in attending events. Such a site will maximize the attendance potential for an arena or a stadium.

Consideration should be given to the fact that all attendees will arrive and depart in the same time periods before and after an event. For this reason, multiple traffic lanes serving the venue's parking areas or structures are essential to disperse traffic efficiently and to avoid a wait of an hour or longer to exit the site. A downtown site with multiple points of entry through the local street grid system is usually more efficient than a location at a single freeway interchange.

The 23,400-seat Rupp Arena in downtown Lexington, Kentucky, can collect and disperse autos much faster than the 19,800-seat Freedom Hall Arena on the Watterson Expressway in Louisville. For many years, access to the Watterson was restricted to four lanes. While the center-city Rupp Arena was remote from limited-access highways, its attendees parked (self-dispersed) within a three- to five-block radius of the center. Traffic engineers and parking consultants unfamiliar with this phenomenon may conclude that a site is infeasible or may recommend unneeded or even counterproductive multilevel parking structures.

Maximum parking facilities are needed for a convention center holding a consumer show, like a boat or car show, that draws most of its attendees from local residents on weekends. Compared with arena events such as rock concerts, public shows such as boat or garden shows have arrival and departure patterns that are more evenly distributed over the entire day.

PROXIMITY TO SUPPORT FACILITIES

Successful convention centers attracting professional association meetings must be located within walking distance (three to five blocks) of hotels, restaurants, retail stores, local entertainment, and other attractions. Attendees expect these facilities to be near the center, and their proximity is essential to capturing the amount of money that delegates are estimated to spend in these support facilities. Consequently, such a location is required to obtain the anticipated economic and fiscal impact of the center. In fact, delegate spending is usually the very reason why most centers are built.

The difference between being close to a unique mix of these establishments and being remote from one is reflected in actual surveys of delegates' retail spending. This spending ranges from less than $50 in destinations where specialty shops are remote from the center or are mundane, to over $200 per attendee in other destinations where centers are located near shops that offer unusual and attractive merchandise, as on Newberry Street in Boston or Union Square in San Francisco.

While a sports facility's location near support amenities will generate the greatest economic impact from out-of-town attendees, such a location is not essential to the marketability of a stadium or arena. In contrast, for convention facilities, surveys of meeting planners and association executives usually claim that the lack of unique shopping outlets or a wide variety of nearby restaurants was a main reason for not selecting a center or destination.

New jobs, new commercial development, and increased tax revenues are the benefits or returns that a community receives from its investment in a convention center. Therefore, site selection should be guided by a search for locations that provide visitors with the greatest opportunities to spend their money *and* that provide retailers and hoteliers the greatest proximity to a variety of major customer generators: class A office space, hotels, affluent residents, and visitors to other attractions.

Cities must endeavor to retain occupied class A office space, retail shops, and restaurants in the CBD. Cities that are indifferent to edge-city class A office building development, center-city crime, high downtown parking costs, and high downtown property taxes and that fail to encourage residential areas attractive to affluent households will not obtain the retail shops, hotels, or restaurants they expect to develop in their CBDs by building and subsidizing public assembly centers.

In short, a truly successful convention center must satisfy the facility needs of the user and must maximize opportunities to capture delegate spending at commercial facilities nearby. By their very nature, these commercial uses require a customer base far greater than can be generated by a sports, convention, or entertainment center alone.

MEASURING SITE PERFORMANCE

Some location criteria are more important than others. Some site selection criteria are variable, while others are fixed. The required site area or site holding capacity may be expressed as a range (minimum versus maximum) for a convention center, depending on opportunities for stacking, need for future expansion, and other factors. The minimum site area required for an arena or stadium is inflexible; it is fixed. Creative design cannot reduce the size of a football field.

Criteria such as visibility, economic impact, tax benefits generated, and site cost are variable. Because public sector sponsors are often compelled for political reasons to promote new investment or revitalization by proposing sites that are otherwise inappropriate, a consultant is often retained to evaluate objectively the advantages and disadvantages of each site. Because the various evaluation criteria are of unequal significance, each is assigned a different weight to reflect its relative degree of importance to achieving the objectives of the sponsor. These criteria are often weighted in terms of the proportionate impact that each criterion would have on the center's development cost, and negative cost impacts may be offset

Figure 4-1

ARENA SITE EVALUATION MATRIX (illustrative example)

This table is an example of an evaluation matrix that can be developed for a specific center. The relative importance of the various criteria may differ according to the community. In this particular case, Site C, having the highest total score, was the preferred site.

Evaluation Criteria	Numerical Rating/Weighted Rating				
	Site A Rating/Score	Site B Rating/Score	Site C Rating/Score	Site D Rating/Score	Site E Rating/Score
Physical Characteristics:					
Land Cost[1]	5 / 10	5 / 10	5 / 10	3 / 6	1 / 2
Access	5 / 5	3 / 3	3 / 3	1 / 1	5 / 5
Parking[1]	3 / 6	3 / 6	5 / 10	3 / 6	1 / 2
Land Acquisition[1]	5 / 10	5 / 10	5 / 10	3 / 6	1 / 2
Subtotal	/ 31	/ 29	/ 33	/ 19	/ 11
Market Characteristics:					
Local Market Penetration	3 / 3	3 / 3	3 / 3	1 / 1	5 / 5
Regional Market Penetration[1]	3 / 6	3 / 6	3 / 6	3 / 6	5 / 10
Proximity to Support Services	1 / 1	1 / 1	3 / 3	3 / 3	3 / 3
Acceptability to Anchor Tenant[1]	1 / 2	5 / 10	5 / 10	1 / 2	1 / 2
Image/Visibility	3 / 3	5 / 5	3 / 3	1 / 1	5 / 5
Subtotal	/ 15	/ 25	/ 25	/ 13	/ 25
Financial Feasibility:					
Total Cost	1 / 1	3 / 3	5 / 5	1 / 1	3 / 3
State-Appropriated Funds[1]	3 / 6	5 / 10	5 / 10	1 / 2	1 / 2
Impact on Existing Facility[1]	1 / 2	3 / 6	5 / 10	1 / 2	1 / 2
Economic Benefits[1]	1 / 2	1 / 2	3 / 6	5 / 10	3 / 6
Spin-Off Development	1 / 1	1 / 1	1 / 1	5 / 5	5 / 5
Subtotal	/ 12	/ 22	/ 32	/ 20	/ 18
Total Score	/ 58	/ 76	/ 90	/ 52	/ 54

Key:

Rating	Qualitative Factors	Cost Factors
5	Best	Lowest
3	Adequate	Medium
1	Worst	Highest

[1]Weighted criterion. The weighted criteria were judged twice as important as other criteria in determining the feasibility of site locations. Therefore, the score for each weighted criterion is double the rating. The weighted score is placed to the right of the slash (/). The higher the total score, the more desirable the site.
Source: Price Waterhouse LLP.

(outweighed) by the beneficial effect that the location would have on the center's marketability. Figures 4-1 and 4-2 illustrate site evaluation analyses for an arena and a convention center.

Because site selection criteria are not all fixed and are of unequal importance, designing a site screening process and criteria-weighting methodology is necessary. The first screen would eliminate sites that do not meet the fixed primary criteria (e.g., site size or configuration). The next screen, or second cut, may separate out the sites that do not meet the primary fixed requirements, or the highest-priority "go/no go" criteria (e.g., minimum number of available parking spaces or convention-class hotel rooms within a five-block radius). The third and

Figure 4-2

QUALITATIVE EVALUATION OF CONVENTION-CENTER SITES (illustrative example)

Site Analysis Factors	Factor Importance	Locations					
		Site A	Site B	Site C	Site D	Site E	Site F
Key Screening Criteria:							
Site Size and Expandability	Critical	100+ acres	70–140 acres	15+ acres	70+ acres	65+ acres	50+acres
Adjacent Roads (lanes)	Important	0	2	4	3	2	2
Cost of Land	Important	Average	[1]	High	In Inventory	In Inventory	Not Determined
Capture of Tax Benefits	Critical	Unacceptable	Excellent	Excellent	Excellent	Excellent	Unacceptable
Possible Developer Relationship	Critical	Average	Good	Excellent	Good	Average	Average
Interest by Landholder	Critical	Not Determined	Average	Excellent	Excellent	Moderate	Low
Site Rank[2]		Eliminated	3	2	1	4	Eliminated
Marketability Criteria:							
Destination Appeal	Critical	Poor	Poor	Excellent	Average	Poor	Poor
Proximity to Headquarters Hotel(s)	Critical		Poor	NA[3]	Excellent[4]	Poor	
Proximity to Other Support Hotels	Important		Average	Good	Good	Average	
Proximity to Other Support Meeting Facilities	Important		Excellent	Good	Excellent	Poor	
Proximity to the Airport	Important		Good	Good	Excellent	Good	
Proximity to Support Services	Critical		Average	Excellent	Good	Poor	
Access to Regional Highways	Important		Good	Good	Good	Good	
Site Rank[2]		Eliminated	3	1	2	4	Eliminated
Development Criteria:							
Potential for Joint Operation	Important		Excellent	Good	Good	Good	
Impact on Surrounding Land Uses	Critical		Average	Excellent	Average	Poor	
Economic Impact for Redevelopment	Critical		Poor	Excellent	Good	Poor	
Stimulus for Additional Hotel Development	Important		Average	Excellent	Average	Poor	
Site Rank[2]		Eliminated	3	1	2	4	Eliminated
Overall Site Ranking[2]		Eliminated	3	1	2	4	Eliminated

NA means Not Applicable.
[1]The existing site is owned; if the adjacent parcel is purchased, land costs will be high.
[2]Sites are ranked from 1 to 4, with 1 being the highest ranking.
[3]No hotel is present now; a guarantee for this hotel before development of the convention center is a requirement for this site.
[4]Hotels proposed as project component.
Source: Price Waterhouse LLP.

fourth screens, each a successively finer mesh, will not allow sites to pass through that are less desirable as measured by variable criteria of secondary or tertiary importance (e.g., acquisition cost, ease of site assembly, or clearance of obsolete structures).

The next section of this chapter will explain the reasons why, if possible: (1) identification or nomination of candidate sites should be solicited by invitation in a public announcement published in local newspapers, (2) more than one acceptable site should be identified, and (3) neither the identity nor the relative attractiveness or ranking of the acceptable sites should be disclosed until after the option to purchase has been obtained and a backup site has been optioned or its availability otherwise secured.

ACQUISITION ISSUES

The cost of the site is always an issue, one whose importance is not diminished by the fact that the building must serve the needs of the community for many years. Nearly all development budgets are limited, and site costs will have to be minimized through creative approaches to soliciting developers' proposals, through the creation and marketing of air rights, and through careful evaluation of on-site and off-site land development and infrastructure costs.

In recent years, many communities have asked landowners and developers to submit proposals to sell or grant land for a convention center. When landowners recognize the benefit to their residual holdings, the community can often secure land at a more reasonable cost by avoiding the delays and inflationary effects of relying on site acquisition by eminent domain or condemnation.

To the extent that building sponsors can keep their site selection options open by not announcing the preferred or highest-ranked sites, they can often avoid the ruinous speculation and budget-busting escalation in price that may accompany the announcement of the preferred site or sites. Unfortunately, some governments require that the determination of site preference be made public, thereby guaranteeing speculation and unreasonable claims for higher site acquisition prices.

UNUSUAL SITE ACQUISITION AND VENUE DEVELOPMENT STRATEGIES

The development profiles found among the case studies in this book give many examples of innovative strategies

Development of the Philadelphia Convention Center included the reuse of the Reading Terminal as a magnificent assembly space. The terminal also serves as the connector between the center and a Marriott hotel.

that have proven successful in obtaining sites that would otherwise have been much costlier or even unattainable.

CREATING VALUE BY REZONING

The city of Sacramento induced developers to finance and to operate the ARCO Arena by agreeing to rezone surrounding land, which the development group controlled, for urban development when it would otherwise have been restricted to agricultural use. The city, in effect, sold development rights on the property in exchange for the building and operating of a 17,500-seat venue by some of the landowners.

Similarly, the city of Anaheim granted valuable development rights to the owners of a major league franchise as an inducement for them to lease Anaheim Stadium for their home games. For different reasons, neither the owners of the land around the ARCO Arena nor the Anaheim team owners were able to build their intended developments. What proved a successful strategy for the two local governments has yet to yield the would-be developers the opportunity to realize the values from the rights they were granted.

CREATING VALUE THROUGH SYNERGY AND ENTREPRENEURSHIP

The government of the city-state of Hong Kong offered the developer proposing to build a convention center the right to own and develop commercial buildings on a site it owned in the Wanchai district. This parcel was larger than other available sites on the waterfront and was near the center of the prime commercial district, Victoria, which contains some of the world's most valuable commercial properties. The result, as described in detail in the case study, was the 4.4 million-square-foot complex that includes the Hong Kong Convention and Exhibition Centre (HKCEC), an office tower, a residential apartment tower, and two first-class hotels offering a total of more than 1,400 rooms to accommodate commercial visitors to the city as well as attendees to center events. A diverse calendar of events is presented, composed of trade shows, merchandise marts/exhibitions, and annual conventions or conferences of international professional associations.

In marked contrast to the current status of city and developer success in Anaheim or Sacramento, HKCEC was a win-win situation in that it accomplished the economic objectives of both the private developer and the government. This success is shown in the developer group's participation in an expansion of HKCEC (under construction in 1995) and the participation by some of the group's members in a second development consortium that was later awarded almost identical rights to build the Singapore Convention Center and adjacent commercial buildings.

LEVERAGING THE AWARD OF PROFESSIONAL CONTRACTS TO CREATE A MARKETABLE SITE

The Lexington Center Corporation (LCC) of Lexington, Kentucky, offered the right to design and construct the 24,000-seat Rupp Arena, Lexington Convention Center, and retail mall to a prequalified development consortium that guaranteed to build a 400-room hotel on the site that LCC had selected, which was not close to any existing convention-class hotel rooms. The developer agreed to build and operate the hotel, which was highly successful and was later sold at a substantial profit.

The Lexington Center's consortium was a joint venture between the development subsidiaries of a major construction company and a nationally prominent architectural firm, both of which enjoyed excellent and well-deserved reputations for building and designing major public assembly facilities. The venture earned several million dollars in fees for the construction management,

architectural, and engineering services provided by the joint-venture partners' parent companies.

CREATING VALUE FOR LAND ADJACENT TO A CENTER

Many times, sites have been donated free of charge by the owners of large landholdings in order to obtain the anticipated benefits of the center's impact on the surrounding acreage retained by the donor of the site. In return, the center owner has avoided the acquisition costs of a site conveniently located to suit the needs of its users. Sometimes, as we have seen, this strategy results in a win-win outcome for the center owner and land donor.

Often, however, the land donor discovers that the center will not enhance surrounding land values by an amount greater than the value of the site donated, or even near its market value. Or the center owner discovers that the remote location of the site (1) erodes attendance at events, (2) does not offer the required nearby support amenities, or (3) requires costs for infrastructure, roads, or parking greater than would have been needed to develop the center at another, better located site. Lastly, needless to say, the selection of a site in a floodplain, blighted neighborhood, or public park is not necessarily a cost-effective strategy.

Although many public assembly centers have been successful catalysts for other economic development, most centers developed for that motive have not achieved the expected results. All too often, this arrangement is a lose-lose situation for the developer and the community sponsor. Attendance or occupancy suffers as a result of an undesirable location, and the taxpayer winds up paying more for the center and receiving neither the benefits of a popular venue nor the added tax revenues of the intended development impact.

MAXIMIZING VALUE BY BUILDING ON THE BEST SITE

Ironically, many public assembly facilities would have been more successful at other, more marketable locations. Happily, however, many projects do enjoy extraordinary success, obtain more than their fair share of the market, and maximize operating revenues because they enjoy the benefits of the right site. Examples of facilities richly endowed by their locations are seen in the case studies for Boston's John B. Hynes Veterans' Memorial Convention Center, Baltimore's Oriole Park at Camden Yards, Atlanta's Georgia World Congress Center, and Le Palais des Congrès in Paris.

Chapter 5

DESIGN

The architect's role in the predesign planning process is critical to the success of the project. Studies of site requirements or building footprints will identify alternative configurations for the structure and evaluate their impacts on site circulation, building interior circulation, and preliminary ("order-of-magnitude") development costs. Selecting an architect with a proven track record in designing public assembly facilities can bring valuable experience to the process. Currently, only five or six architectural firms are recognized nationally for specializing in designing arenas, stadiums, convention centers, and amphitheaters.

Efficient design solutions have evolved for each building type. By deviating from these designs, the owner may incur extra development costs and get a less marketable facility. Radical departures from proven design performance criteria should be thoroughly reviewed with experienced tenants and successful center managers. The owner should think seriously before abandoning a boomerang-shaped seating configuration for baseball or an oval design for football. Arena and stadium seating should allow sightlines to be as direct and short as possible to the edge of the court or field of play. A single, main concourse in a 10,000-seat arena will minimize staffing costs, maximize concession sales, and evenly divide access to the upper and lower tiers of seating.

This does not mean that all facilities have to look alike or have the same programs. Nor is it correct to conclude that only architectural specialists can design successful centers or spectator sports venues. Important advances in design solutions have been developed by architects with little or no prior experience with this type of building

(e.g., the Georgia World Congress Center in Atlanta and the Astrodome in Houston).

CONVENTION CENTERS

A successful convention center provides convenient public access to lobby/registration areas near separate banks of meeting rooms and proportionate shares of exhibit space. In an exhibit hall, ceiling heights of 30 feet or more will provide for displays on two- to three-acre floor plates, without attendees' experiencing claustrophobic reactions. This height will also allow two-story booths, effective directional and graphic signage, and ample overhead for trucks. Ideally, attendees can enter the exhibit hall from one side, and freight move-in/move-out can be accommodated from loading docks and ramps on the opposite side. When subdivided into 50,000- or 100,000-square-foot halls with a length-to-width ratio of 2 to 1 or less, the exhibit area will provide an efficient layout of booths.

The total building area is typically two-and-a-half to three times greater than the total of exhibition space and meeting-room space. The ratio of meeting/ballroom space to exhibition space may fall between 1 to 1 and 1 to 4, depending on whether the dominant user groups are professional associations or trade associations. Examples of relationships among public areas, total gross building space, building footprints, and site areas are shown in Figure 5-1.

Meeting rooms should be configured so that public access is separate from service access. Incandescent,

This exhibit area at the Nice Acropolis Convention Centre illustrates the flexibility needed to accommodate exhibitors within an efficient booth/ aisle module.

fluorescent, and other types of illumination with variable intensity levels should be available to correct the color distortion caused by single-source artificial light. Ceiling heights in meeting rooms will vary to accommodate the requirements of various types of audiovisual presentations (for instance, larger rooms usually have higher ceilings). These and numerous other design criteria must be satisfied to ensure that the building properly serves its users and minimizes construction and operating costs.

To enhance a convention center's functionality, various potential user groups—trade show producers, convention meeting planners, and exhibition (decorator) service managers—should provide input during the design process and should critique various design options. Representatives of these groups are interested in evaluating the design and in helping the building designer and owner select interior finishes and performance specifications, such as lighting levels and acoustical characteristics. They are anxious to help because their future events in the building will be more successful if the spaces are logically arranged and appropriately sized.

SPECTATOR SPORTS AND ENTERTAINMENT VENUES

Various types of sports and entertainment events have widely divergent building requirements, although the primary design requirements of their fans and audiences

---

Figure 5-1

EVALUATION AND COMPARISON OF THREE BUILDING PROGRAMS

	Center A	Center B	Center C
Exhibition Space	124,000 SF	95,000 SF	60,200 SF
	(400′ × 310′ × 35′ ht.)	(406′ × 234′ × 32′ ht.)	(222′ × 278′ × 40′ ht.)
Ballroom	12,900 SF	7,900 SF	none
	(140′ × 92′ × 24′ ht.)	(75′ × 105′ × 14′ ht.)	–
Banquet Seating	1,200 persons	790 persons	none
Meeting	39,800 SF	33,440 SF	15,900 SF
Smallest	12′ × 15′ × 9′ ht. = 180 SF	18′ × 25′ × 10′ ht. = 450 SF	20′ × 27′ × 9′ ht. = 540 SF
Largest	30′ × 60′ × 14′ ht. = 1,800 SF	30′ × 64′ × 18′ ht. = 1,920 SF	34′ × 44′ × 12′ ht. = 1,496 SF
Combined Largest	45′ × 133′ × 14′ ht. = 5,985 SF	64′ × 150′ × 18′ ht. = 9,600 SF	44′ × 97′ × 12′ ht. = 4,268 SF
Special Rooms	10,500 SF	6,475 SF	900 SF
Center Offices	7,050 SF	3,574 SF	3,500 SF
Dressing Rooms, etc.	7,175 SF	NA	3,000 SF
Full-Service Kitchen	12,750 SF	13,000 SF	none
Service Kitchen	4,150 SF	400 SF	2,400 SF
Receiving	6,300 SF	29,400 SF	3,750 SF
Storage	15,050 SF	40,650 SF	19,500 SF
Mechanical and Service	23,100 SF	NA	15,050 SF
Public Toilets	13,600 SF	10,820 SF	3,000 SF
Circulation	74,750 SF	51,250 SF	39,900 SF
Miscellaneous	17,150 SF	18,491 SF	9,400 SF
Total Gross Building Area	368,275 SF	310,400 SF	176,500 SF
Footprint	252,000 SF	159,000 SF	173,300 SF
Site Area	430′ × 835′ = 359,050 SF or 8.24 acres	410′ × 415′ = 170,150 SF or 3.91 acres	420′ × 444′ = 186,480 SF or 4.28 acres

---

NA means Not Applicable.

are quite similar. The successful reconciliation of these common needs of spectators with the special requirements for accommodating dissimilar events is more difficult for a multipurpose venue than for one that is intended to serve the needs of one primary use (for example, a tennis stadium or velodrome). The dimensions and shape of the playing surface and the preferred angle of view for a basketball court differ significantly from those for an ice hockey rink, causing some multipurpose arenas to be regarded as better for basketball (America West Arena, Phoenix) or ideal for ice hockey (Maple Leaf Gardens, Toronto). The compromises required for a multipurpose baseball/football (or even football/track) venue are much greater and have proven to be far less acceptable than the required trade-offs for combined NBA/NHL arenas. Rather than trying to accommodate rectangles of different widths and lengths—200 feet by 85 feet (for NHL) versus 110 feet by 70 feet (for NBA)—the baseball/football facility must configure seating for two different geometric shapes—an approximate square (460 feet) versus a rectangle (360 feet by 140 feet). Even more important, two vastly different audience sizes (45,000 versus 70,000) must be accommodated.

Spectator guidelines are, at least from the standpoint of performance specifications, substantially the same for all types of spectator sports. For example:

- Maximize the number of seats in the preferred viewing locations: behind home plate or along the power alleys for baseball, nearer the 50-yard line for football, and center court for basketball.

- Offer a variety of premium seating products (box suites, skyboxes, club seats) in preferred viewing areas to optimize the penetration of major market segments (corporations, individuals with high personal income, upper-middle-income households, and so on).

- Provide optimum ratios of linear feet of concession-counter space, and points of sale per thousand attendees, to optimize net revenue from food and beverage sales.

- Dedicate locations—scoreboards, time clocks, video boards, and the like—with prominent visibility by fans of various types of advertising displays.

These are the types of design criteria that are essential to maximizing revenues from attendees. Numerous other design requirements, dictated by building codes (e.g., plumbing, fire), are particularly onerous for designers of mass spectator venues. Lastly, many other qualitative and aesthetic characteristics can enhance fans' experiences in a facility (e.g., the nostalgic turn-of-the-century architectural styles recreated in Oriole Park at Camden Yards in Baltimore) or can raise community residents' appreciation for a venue design that has become a major commu-

The Pittsburgh Civic Arena has a movable stainless steel roof that takes only 150 seconds to open or close. Completed in 1961, unlike many much younger facilities that have been declared obsolete, it has been modified three times—in 1972, 1989, and 1993—to expand seating capacity and to add new features like super boxes and minisuites to meet changing user expectations.

nity icon (e.g., Yankee Stadium). This holds true even for venues not financed by taxpayers.

ARCHITECT NEEDED AT THE CONCEPT/FEASIBILITY STAGE

Project sponsors should understand the total building footprint and future expansion needs to establish the optimum site area and configuration. At the concept stage, the architect, with the aid of a construction manager or contractor, can advise the client on budgetary requirements by translating function-space requirements (number of spectator seats or square feet of exhibition/meeting-room space) into the total building-space footprint, site area, and configuration required.

This building-space requirement is the basis for determining the estimated, or order-of-magnitude, construction cost: actual unit costs for recently developed, comparable facilities are adjusted for time (inflation) and for location (geographical differences in construction costs). Finally, the architect can develop preliminary sketches to help project sponsors and community leaders visualize how the proposed building may look on the site and how it will relate to nearby activities and structures.

These preliminary design services are as important to the initial planning process as financial and market analyses. A reliable business plan contains both physical and financial plans. The planning process should be in-

This fabric roof, reminiscent of sails, covers a large outdoor terrace at the San Diego Convention Center and is highly functional, given the city's Mediterranean climate. The roof makes for a striking skyline along the waterfront.

teractive among the owner/operator, prospective tenants, the market/financial adviser, the builder, and the designer. At best, it is also in harmony with the master plan for the entire surrounding area.

SELECTING THE ARCHITECT

What previous clients say about an architect, as about any professional adviser, and the success of that architect's projects and assignments will carry more weight than what an architect may claim about his or her qualifications. And the experience or past success of the individual project designer who is given primary responsibility for the design of the project is more important than the past experience of that designer's firm.

Whether the architect's design experience is relevant to the proposed project depends on the specific types and sizes of structures the designer has completed that are successfully serving their users' and owners' needs. Multipurpose civic centers differ considerably in function and layout from NBA or NHL arenas. For these reasons, candidate architects should be asked to provide the names

and locations of all projects built for which they were the designers of record. For each project, they should provide information on:

- The building program, estimated (budgeted) cost, and actual construction cost.
- The current facility manager.
- The project designer.
- The construction manager or general contractor.

Candidate architects should also provide statements describing their understanding and opinions on: the client's and potential users' roles in the design process, other types of consultants required in this process, the merits of the fast-track approach versus the conventional design approach, guaranteed maximum construction costs, factors influencing construction costs, methods of minimizing change orders and the cost impact of changes, the role of the architect in relation to the builder, milestone events and key points in the design process, and other issues that candidates believe are pertinent to the success of the project.

This information will enable the client to select the designer with the best and most relevant abilities and track record. Direct dialogue between the project sponsor/owner and the candidate project designer reveals more about the designer and his or her firm than do elaborate presentations by the architectural firm's marketing directors and principals. Multimedia audiovisual presentations and elaborate brochures, though entertaining, rarely if ever convey information about the experience and the level of enthusiasm, creativity, and relevant expertise that the candidate can bring to the project.

Design competitions are not an effective method of selecting an architect for a public assembly facility unless the contestants have been prequalified. If the owner insists on a design competition, the prequalified contestants should be paid for their work at standard fees. Unlike some trophy office buildings and theatrical retail centers, major event centers will succeed because of the functionality and efficiency of their interiors, rather than the excitement of their exteriors. The configuration of the building must evolve through the collaborative input of the owner, operator (or manager consultant), designer, urban planner, and users. Aesthetic qualities of the structure—interior and exterior finishes, landscaping, setbacks, plazas, entry features, and roofline features—require extraordinary efforts to help these bulky behemoths fit within the context of an existing urban setting. Innovative architectural features can relieve the building of some of its bulkiness, but this much-needed relief should not reduce the center's efficiency for its owner and users.

Unfortunately, labor-saving lifecycle cost features require more money upfront. Larger capital budgets can provide mechanical systems (automated telescopic seating, computer-controlled HVAC and lighting systems, low-maintenance interior finishes) that will minimize future operating budgets. Mid-1990s construction costs for convention centers have ranged from $150 to $300 per square foot. For many centers, a cost differential of this magnitude may only be apparent to an experienced professional designer or builder. In most cases, the cost differential will only be revealed after a look behind the public spaces, inspecting mechanical systems and back-of-the-house facilities.

Because many project sponsors believe that a local architect, who must live with a project after it opens, will be more attentive or conscientious, they are often disposed to retain a local architectural firm, even though this firm has no previous experience with public assembly facilities. Others believe that they must hire an internationally acclaimed or celebrity architect, again without regard to the architect's lack of experience with similar types of public assembly facilities. The consequences of both choices are high risks. Sponsors should not hire inexperienced designers unless they (the sponsors) are willing to wait

while the designers learn, to pay them to learn, and to hope that they can learn. Ideally, the owner will encourage an association of the most qualified design firm with a celebrity architect or a financially stable local architect who possesses full knowledge of local codes and entitlement procedures and is respected in the local business community.

When the project sponsor elects to shorten a multibid process by using the fast-track method, or to lock in a guaranteed-not-to-exceed price by negotiating the construction cost before working drawings are prepared, it is necessary to assemble a development team that, at a minimum, includes an experienced architect, engineer, building operator, and general contractor as principals. If the proposed center is to be part of a mixed-use project and if the developer/owner of the planned private uses retains the same design/build team, that team will endeavor to assure that the two operations are symbiotic, or mutually reinforcing and supportive. For example, the owner/operator of adjacent private uses such as retail or hotel can optimize the linkages to the assembly venue, and the owner of the public assembly facility may obtain greater assurance that the private uses' completion schedule will be properly sequenced with that of the assembly venue.

A combination of public and private uses is often required to enhance the marketability of the project, as, for example, hotel rooms are needed near a convention center. Sometimes, this combination is needed to assure the project's financial feasibility, as when the lease revenues of retail or other commercial space are pledged to and included in the operating revenues of the public assembly facility. In these situations, it may be in the owner's interest to solicit design/build/invest proposals to evaluate the qualifications and guarantees of all essential participants in the project: architect, builder, investor, and developer. Obviously, the formulation, solicitation, evaluation, and selection of a balanced and fully qualified team will call for a complex and unorthodox strategy. However, such a process is a proven way to reduce the risk of failure to attract the private support facilities essential to the success of a venue, to secure a guaranteed cost, and to ensure that construction of the private uses is synchronized with the scheduled completion of the assembly facility.

THE DESIGN PROCESS

As discussed earlier, it is essential to involve the designer at the concept formulation stage to evaluate program requirements, costs, and site area needs. Whether the owner elects the conventional design process or the fast-track process, the major milestones in the completion of the architect's work are the same. The project sponsor must understand these stages in the design evolution process because each stage usually is referred to in the design contract. Moreover, an understanding of these stages will reveal at which points in the process a further refinement of development cost estimates can be obtained. Nonarchitects often use terms describing design completion stages inaccurately: "We only want preliminary or rough schematics" or "I haven't selected a site, but I need a rendering."

CONCEPTUAL

The initial sketches and drawings generally illustrate the scale of the development and the spatial relationships that will exist among building components. Primary functional spaces and areas should be defined, and their locations shown at this basic level of design. Only cost estimates expressed in a wide range will be possible; more frequently than not, these estimates must be based on unit costs for recently built, comparable types of development. These are not drawings and diagrams. Drawings should not be considered illustrative of a specific building until after (1) a site has been identified or selected and (2) a preliminary budget has been approved by the owner.

SCHEMATIC

Schematic drawings provide multiple perspectives: plan views, elevations, building sections, outline specifications, performance specifications, and other information. These drawings are needed to distinguish the scale and relationship among project components in sufficient detail to define and describe functional areas and to enable the estimate of a probable construction cost based on area, volume, and/or unit costs.

DESIGN/DEVELOPMENT

At this level of design, drawings and documents should describe the size and character of the entire project—including architectural, structural, mechanical, and electrical systems—and the intended materials or other essentials particular to the concept or type of project. The availability of materials and equipment; the scheduling; and the energy conservation, user safety, and maintenance requirements should be defined. Outline specifications must be detailed to establish firmly the probable construction costs or, if required, to enable a contractor to provide a guaranteed maximum price (GMP). Also, at this stage these drawings and documents will determine exactly what the building will look like, what its interior finishes will be, and how it will function, based on actual or performance specifications.

Osceola County Stadium in Kissimmee, Florida, is the spring training facility for the Houston Astros major league baseball team and home to the Astros' minor league team, the Osceola Astros. The complex contains a 5,200-seat exhibition stadium, four full-sized practice fields, and a 21,000-square-foot clubhouse equipped with a catering kitchen.

FINAL CONSTRUCTION DOCUMENTS

The construction documents form the basis for bidding and should be reviewed at one or more stages, at least when they are 50 to 60 percent completed, for consistency with design/development plans and specifications. Final drawings should be consistent with previous documents and must be detailed enough to describe fully the work to be done; the materials, workmanship, finishes, and equipment required for the architectural, structural, mechanical, and electrical systems; and the necessary bidding information. The building defined in construction documents and specifications will conform to applicable local codes and will explain possible changes or options in scheduling or construction methods and in all other special requirements that will affect the cost of the work.

These documents should be organized into bid packages to solicit prices for the work, or into a lump-sum bid package, and should state the owner's requirements for completion of the work within a certain time frame.

PARTICIPANTS IN THE DESIGN PROCESS

The designer will often require the expertise of a dozen or more technical disciplines outside those of his or her permanent staff, in addition to the many technical subspecialties employed within a major architectural firm. These outside specialists in the design process include food service/equipment advisers, landscape architects, facility operations managers, user group(s) representatives, acoustical consultants, turf management specialists, and the like. The owner should help select these participants to ensure that all facility features and functions are analyzed

and designed by the most qualified specialists. The spectator sports/entertainment and the meetings/exhibition industries are constantly changing. The development team for a new building should exploit the lessons learned by its predecessors, be sensitive to the changing needs of users, and try to build a state-of-the-art facility with the most cost-effective equipment, high-quality interior finishes, and advanced technology.

The owner can reduce the risk of a single professional discipline's dominating the decision-making process by encouraging a balance of views among development designers, general contractor, and technical advisers. The building will be better designed to serve all of its intended purposes if the owner's attorney, building manager, major tenant, architect, builder, financial adviser, and others are permitted equal input in the planning and design process, with the owner serving as the CEO and final arbiter.

In evaluating building programs and plans for similar venues in other locations, it is essential to remember that each venue was developed to address the unique market opportunities and resources in its community, the specific needs of its users, and the budget adopted by its sponsors or owners. Any attempt to compute rules of thumb (such as the average number of box suites or the ratio of meeting space to exhibition space) is fraught with hazards and should be avoided. Therefore, each public assembly facility's building program should differ from those of its predecessors, just as locations and user-group characteristics differ.

Chapter 6

BUILDING THE CENTER: ALTERNATIVES AND TRADE-OFFS

Builders and owners have devised various methods and alternative construction procedures to enable the owner to accomplish one or more of these primary goals:

- Minimize the cost of the intended project.
- Obtain a fixed, or maximum, cost before financing has been completed.
- Minimize the time required to obtain the fixed or maximum cost.

Unfortunately, selecting a construction method that assures or maximizes the owner's ability to achieve one goal will compromise or reduce the extent to which any other goal is achieved. Hence, no single construction method or builder/owner arrangement enables the owner to accomplish all three goals in equal measure. These alternative construction methods and their trade-offs are described in this chapter.

There is normally a fixed or maximum amount of funding available to pay for all development costs: construction, land, financing, equipment, and so on. This limit may be established or fixed by the owner, to assure an acceptable return on investment; by the lender, to minimize the risk of default or deficiency; or by the financing market, according to the amount of funds annually pledged or dedicated for payment of debt service. There-

fore, for a variety of reasons, the owner is often obligated to obtain project funding before construction can begin.

In most projects, this long-term financing is obtained through the sale of bonds. The owner usually sells all the bonds that the pledged revenue (e.g., a hotel tax or retail sales tax) will support. For this reason, if the prices bid for the project exceed the bond proceeds available, the scope of the project will have to be reduced unless additional funding is found. Often, it is not feasible both to reduce the scope of the project and to retain the number of seats required by the primary tenant or to retain other essential features that the intended customers demand and that are needed to achieve the required level of marketability for the venue.

Unfortunately, the terminology that has evolved to describe these various methods and arrangements can be confusing or misleading because it is not precise and because many terms are synonymous. Quite often, the advantages or disadvantages claimed for one method versus other alternatives are misleading or even untrue. The owner is cautioned to beware of the construction firm that claims that its recommended method is "standard practice in the industry" or "the preferred method." Given all the possible combinations and permutations of methods and arrangements in use today, it is difficult to identify two major projects employing the same method and procedures, or, as some would have it, the same construction delivery option. Figure 6-1 illustrates the methods employed for recently constructed major facilities.

As a baseline or point of reference, it may be helpful to begin with the conventional lump-sum or single-bid method. This method will then serve as the reference point, a prominent and historic landmark. Thus, this chapter can begin its journey of exploration of the various

During construction of the Van Andel Arena in Grand Rapids, Michigan, schedules had to be maintained in all kinds of weather.

Courtesy Huber, Hunt & Nichols

Figure 6-1

BUILDER/OWNER AGREEMENTS SELECTED FOR CONSTRUCTING CENTERS IN THE 1990s

Facility Type/ Location	Name	Single Bid or Lump-Sum Bid GC[1]	Multiple Bids or Construction Management[3] CM+FT[2]	CM+FT+GMP[4]	Design/ Build FT+GMP
Arena					
Buffalo	Crossroads Arena			X	
Chicago	United Center	X			
Cleveland	Gund Arena		X		
Boston	Fleet Center			X	
Phoenix	America West Arena		X		
Portland	Rose Garden		X		
San Jose	San Jose Arena	X			
St. Louis	Kiel Center			X	
Tampa	Ice Palace			X	
Stadium					
Arlington (TX)	The Ballpark in Arlington		X		
Atlanta	Olympic/Braves Stadium		X		
Baltimore	Oriole Park at Camden Yards		X		
Charlotte	Carolinas Stadium		X		
Cleveland	Jacobs Field		X		
Denver	Coors Field			X	
St. Petersburg	ThunderDome	X			
Convention Center					
Baltimore	Baltimore Convention Center		X		
Charlotte	Charlotte Convention Center		X		
Chicago	McCormick Place				X
Denver	Colorado Convention Center			X	
Los Angeles	Los Angeles Convention Center	X			
New Orleans	Ernest N. Morial Convention Center	X			
Orlando	Orange County Convention Center			X	
Philadelphia	Pennsylvania Convention Center	X			

[1]GC = general contractor.
[2]FT = fast track.
[3]There have been no "pure" CM projects identified in recent years.
[4]GMP = guaranteed maximum price.
Source: Price Waterhouse LLP.

other methods and alternative arrangements. Alternatives have evolved to enable owners to achieve the desired balance among the three primary goals: to minimize cost, time, and risk (the risk that project costs will exceed the funds available). Graphic diagrams used to illustrate two of these options are reproduced here with the permission of the Barton Malow Company.

The author wishes to acknowledge the valuable insights and significant contributions provided by Jerry Kerr, executive vice president, Huber, Hunt & Nichols, Inc. (construction); Janet Marie Smith, vice president for sports facilities, Turner Broadcasting System, Inc.; Ron Labinski, senior vice president, Hellmuth, Obata & Kassabaum, Inc., Sports Facilities Group (architects); Tom Ventulett, chairman of the board, Thompson, Ventulett, Stainback & Associates, Inc. (architects); and Dan Graveline, chief executive officer, Georgia World Congress Center and Georgia Dome.

SINGLE OR LUMP-SUM BID BY GENERAL CONTRACTOR

To use this approach, the owner must have the building completely designed, with all working drawings, specifications, and bid documents completed, before single or lump-sum bids can be invited. The final plans, specifications, and other bid documents are then made available for review by interested general contractors (GCs) and their potential subcontractors and material suppliers. An announcement is placed in the local business newspaper and in publications of the trade press, such as the *Dodge Report,* stating that the bid documents, bid procedures, plans, and specifications are available for review and also stating the date and time by which contractors must submit bids.

The owner's architect usually establishes the bid procedures in addition to preparing the bid documents, plans, and specifications. In fact, after the contract has been awarded, the architect normally will be the one who inspects the work of the general contractor to ensure that the project has been built according to the architect's (now the owner's) plans and specifications; who supervises various quality control procedures; and who monitors the progress of the work.

The contract is usually awarded to the builder who submits the lowest bid and is qualified to do the work. In this arrangement, the architect serves as the owner's representative, encouraging the general contractor to remain on schedule, interpreting any ambiguous aspects of the plans and specifications, and generally overseeing the progress of the work on behalf of the owner.

Occasionally, an owner will elect to solicit bids only from construction firms that are prequalified. However,

The ThunderDome, St. Petersburg, Florida, is the first tension-ring, cable-supported, domed baseball stadium built in the United States and one of the largest of its type in the world.

George Cott, Chroma, Inc.

Sources: Barton Malow Company; Price Waterhouse LLP.

Figure 6-2

ELAPSED TIME: LUMP-SUM BIDDING

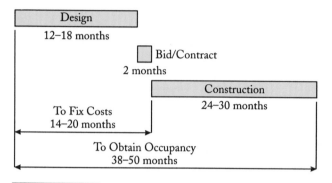

owners or sponsors of projects costing $100 million+, together with their lenders, will in any case require the construction company to provide a performance bond insuring the owner against the loss of monies paid to the successful contractor if the project is not built as specified. Thus, the construction companies are in effect prequalified by the bonding company. In other words, the bonding company must be completely assured that the construction firm is qualified to do the work, in terms of its financial strength, past experience, management expertise, and other factors. If not, the construction company will be unable to obtain the bond required to bid on the project.

TIME REQUIREMENT TO DETERMINE COSTS

Let us say that the single- or lump-sum bid method has been chosen. In an illustrative case, the following realistic needs have been determined:

- The architect requires 12 to 18 months to complete the design and construction bid documents.
- The owner requires two months to bid the work, evaluate bids, and enter into and negotiate a contract with the selected construction firm.
- And the contractor needs a 24- to 30-month construction time.

In this case, then, the total time elapsed from the date when the architect is authorized to begin work until the date when the owner can know the total cost will be 14 to 20 months. The time required from the beginning of design to the point at which the owner can obtain occupancy will be 38 to 50 months (see Figure 6-2). Again, since individual projects may require more or less time, the time frames described in these illustrations are intended to show the relative time differences (shorter or longer) among the different methods, not to show absolute time requirements.

As stated at the beginning of this chapter, all other methods or options that will be compared here with this lump-sum method have evolved to offer one or two major advantages that, by comparison with the single-bid method, may (1) enable the owner to obtain (or sometimes to *think* it has obtained) lower bids for construction costs, or (2) shorten the period of time needed to fix final costs. For comparative purposes, the time requirements for the lump-sum bid process are shown in Figure 6-2.

How project cost is determined

Because each construction firm bidding on the project endeavors to obtain the needed subcontractors and materials by employing the most economical, reliable, and acceptable resources, it is unlikely that all prime or general contractors will select the same subcontractors and material suppliers. Hence, the typical winning bid may not be as low as the sum of the lowest bids for each subcontract and for each type of construction material. This point is illustrated in Figure 6-3.

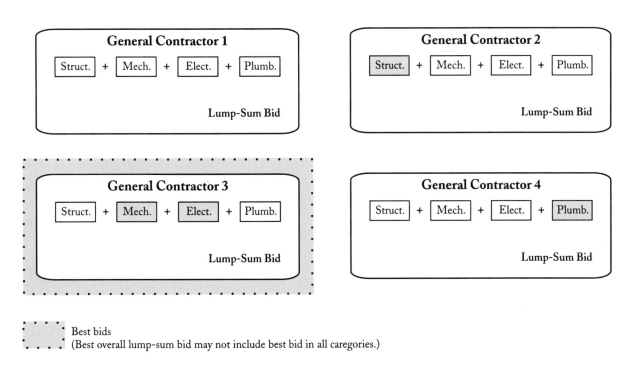

Figure 6-3

Lump-sum bidding: general contracting approach

Best bids
(Best overall lump-sum bid may not include best bid in all caregories.)

Bid Tabulation: General Contractors

	GC1	GC2	GC3	GC4
Structural	$ 560,000	$ 500,000	$ 560,000	$ 575,000
Mechanical	700,000	690,000	600,000	710,000
Electrical	425,000	450,000	400,000	425,000
Plumbing	275,000	250,000	275,000	210,000
	$1,960,000	$1,890,000	$1,835,000	$1,920,000

With GC lump-sum bidding, the owner is not assured of the lowest cost. Any one general contractor's list of subcontractor prices may not contain all of the low subcontractor bids available in the marketplace.

Sources: Barton Malow Company; Price Waterhouse LLP.

Progress photos for Chicago's McCormick Place expansion: from top to bottom, September 1994, June 1995, and September 1995.

For the owner who wants to obtain a lower project cost than may be perceived to be obtainable through the lump-sum bid process, an alternative procedure has been devised: the multibid, or construction manager, method.

CONSTRUCTION MANAGER METHOD

By retaining the professional services of a general contractor for a negotiated fee, the owner sacrifices or trades off the possibility of obtaining another, equally competent contractor whose services may have been retained for a lower fee, as part of a lump-sum bid. The exchange is made to obtain the greater chance for savings perceived to be had when retaining the general contractor to bid each "package" or category of work. The trade-off involves sacrificing the shorter time period available in the lump-sum process. In the construction manager (CM) process, without a fast-track feature, the time required for the owner to determine or to lock in final project costs is longer than with the lump-sum method.

TIME REQUIREMENT TO DETERMINE COST

The elapsed time to determine final project costs will be lengthened by the added time required for bidding and awarding multiple-bid packages, while the total design period plus construction period may remain the same as in the lump-sum bid approach, as shown in Figure 6-4.

While the total time required to design and construct the project is the same as in the example of the lump-sum bid method, the time required to lock in final, albeit lower, costs in this example will be six to eight months longer than with the lump-sum method.

HOW PROJECT COST IS DETERMINED

As stated earlier, the anticipated cost saving seen as obtainable through the CM method should be sufficiently greater than any economies gained through the lump-sum process. And, of course, the extended period needed to determine costs must be acceptable. Otherwise, the perceived savings will not offset the premium the owner will be paying for a construction manager fee. That is, the expected savings must exceed the payment or fee of the construction manager.

The owner is also risking an increase in costs if higher bids are received because they are tendered during a period of high inflation rates. A higher cost caused by inflation may totally offset any savings over the lump-sum method or may even exceed the cost obtained in the single-bid method. In other words, this process does not necessarily result in the lowest total costs if it is employed during a period when prices are escalating faster than expected. Nevertheless, the motive is to achieve the perceived additional savings, as shown in Figure 6-5.

Figure 6-4

ELAPSED TIME: CONSTRUCTION MANAGER

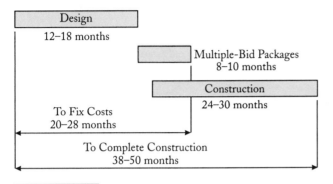

Sources: Barton Malow Company; Price Waterhouse LLP.

Compared with the same work packages bid in the lump-sum process, the CM method as shown in this example results in a 7 percent, or $125,000, savings before deducting the amount of the CM fee (not shown).

Not surprisingly, the delay in determining or fixing the final project costs and the risks attendant on being exposed to price increases over the longer period of time required for bidding have caused owners and builders to devise yet another method. The goal has been to modify the "pure" CM-multibid method by reducing the length of time between the start of the design process and the date on which the final or maximum cost can be determined. Two such modifications or methods that have evolved are not mutually exclusive. They are commonly referred to as the fast-track method and the fast-track method with guaranteed maximum price.

Figure 6-5

BID PACKAGING: CONSTRUCTION MANAGEMENT APPROACH

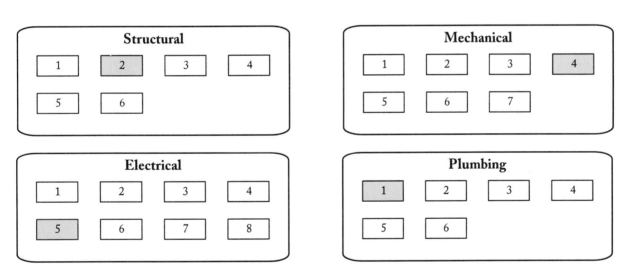

Bid packaging can include best bid in all categories and possibly more bidders in each category.

Bid Tabulation by Package

	#1	#2	#3	#4	#5	#6	#7	#8	Low Bid
Structural	$540,000	$500,000	$561,000	$569,000	$565,000	$575,000			$500,000
Mechanical	715,000	695,000	700,000	600,000	710,000	690,000	$605,000		600,000
Electrical	450,000	445,000	425,000	410,000	400,000	429,000	460,000	$475,000	400,000
Plumbing	210,000	220,000	275,000	255,000	260,000	250,000			210,000

In this example, CM combined total = $1,710,000 before payment of CM fee, which typically ranges from 5 to 7 percent.

Sources: Barton Malow Company; Price Waterhouse LLP.

FAST-TRACK APPROACH

The fast-track method involves overlapping the final stages of the design process and the first phases of construction by bidding some portions of the job, such as foundations and structural work, before the final design for all portions of the work has been completed. In this way, some or all of the delay in the multiple-package bidding process (compared with lump-sum) may be eliminated simply by starting the bidding process earlier.

The disadvantage or trade-off of this method, as compared with the lump-sum bid process, is that the owner accepts the risks that the project cost may exceed budget estimates and that, by the time the owner discovers this fact, much of the work may be in progress or completed. By comparison, again, with the baseline lump-sum method: if the lump-sum bid is unacceptable, the owner may reject it, do a redesign, or modify the scope of the project, then rebid. A sophisticated owner/designer/builder team often will build in a "hedge" against this risk by developing alternative (acceptable though less desirable) material specifications and/or mechanical systems. Or the project team may even build in space reductions to the multiple-bid documents. Each bidder is asked also to quote a price for these "deducts," or alternative design or material specifications that may have been selected at the option of the owner for a lower cost. This technique gives the owner a contingency plan for keeping the project within budget by identifying and building into the bid process opportunities to reduce costs.

By telescoping or overlapping the design/bid/construct activities, it is possible to shorten the total time needed to design and construct the project by as much as two to eight months, as illustrated in this example. Also, the owner can establish total cost in approximately the same time as with the lump-sum bid, i.e., within 14 to 20 months (see Figure 6-6).

FAST-TRACK METHOD WITH GUARANTEED MAXIMUM PRICE

Under a fast-track agreement with guaranteed maximum price (GMP), the owner agrees to a maximum price that has been negotiated with the builder. The owner may place responsibility for the completion of the work, at a not-to-exceed cost, on the builder or both on the builder and on the architect in a joint venture. The architect and builder are now motivated to minimize project costs by preventing the costs bid by subcontractors from exceed-

Figure 6-6

ELAPSED TIME: DESIGN/BUILD METHOD

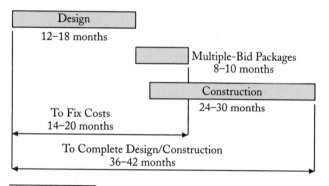

Sources: Barton Malow Company; Price Waterhouse LLP.

ing the costs they have guaranteed. For this reason, the building owner should retain an owner's representative, usually a second, fully qualified, and bondable general contractor or construction company. The owner's representative should be as bondable and as experienced in and capable of constructing the specific type of building ordered as is the designated builder. The owner's rep may advise the owner:

- Which prospective design/build team is most qualified to do the work.
- When the design/development documents are sufficiently detailed and complete.
- When a reasonable price has been negotiated.
- What fees are reasonable for the builders and architects.
- Whether the initial estimates of labor and material costs are realistic.
- When the owner should make payments for the work to the architect, builder, or joint venture.

For example, during contract negotiations with the design/build team, the owner's rep can recommend whether payments made to the design/build team should be based on the percentage of work completed or, alternatively, should be disbursed when material has been delivered to the site, when equipment has been installed and tested, or when the results of quality tests and progress inspection reports have been received.

Advocates of the fast-track method with GMP believe that it encourages "value engineering" to occur through the interaction of the builder, architects, subcontractors, material suppliers, engineers, primary tenants, and owner. It is argued that value engineering can significantly mitigate, if not eliminate, additional costs arising from change orders. For example, if the owner requests changes in the plans to substitute or add a more efficient mechanical system or upgraded interior finishes, the owner's rep may be able to identify a less critical specification elsewhere in the design that could be changed. The owner's rep may then negotiate with the design/build team (1) to make the change early in the process so that the additional cost will be minimized, and/or (2) to reduce the cost of some other part of the work. The latter aim can be achieved by changing—substituting—its scope or specifications in an amount to offset or even to eliminate the effect of the increase in total project costs otherwise caused by the requested change order.

If the owner selects the fast-track method without requiring a GMP, or if the architect is not a guarantor of the maximum price, the architect may serve as the owner's rep as in the conventional method because the architect would then have no conflict between the owner's interests and the prices bid for the work.

When owners want to obtain a guarantee of price or maximum (not-to-exceed) project costs even earlier than is possible through either the multibid/CM or lump-sum/general contractor processes, the GMP is negotiated before the work has been bid. The participant in the process most qualified to provide the GMP, i.e., to assume this risk, is the construction firm or general contractor. The owner negotiates with the builder to obtain a GMP for the work as defined in a design/development pack-

age. As described in Chapter 5, the design/development level of completion is a full stage away (30 percent) from the completion of construction or bid documents. By entering into a contract with the builder at this stage (70 percent of completion), the owner in effect pays the construction firm a substantial "reserve," in addition to the CM fees to which the firm is entitled for providing construction management services, to assume the risk that the costs will exceed the GMP.

Of course, the construction firm is certain to commit to a GMP that exceeds a reasonable estimate of actual bid costs, so as to provide a cushion or a reserve fund in the event that costs exceed estimates. In mutual recognition of the need for this "added" cost, the owner and builder will often negotiate a sharing of the difference, or a split of the savings, between the GMP and the actual costs obtained through the bidding process. The determination of these savings, if any, occurs after all of the work has been completed.

Like the fast-track method without a GMP, this procedure requires that construction drawings and bid packages for various portions of the work be completed in predetermined stages, let out for bid, contracts awarded, and construction initiated while other portions of the work are still being designed and before preparation of their construction drawings has even begun. This requirement reduces the overall construction time by enabling

Flinders Park in Melbourne, Australia, designed and built to provide a world-class tennis facility in which to host the Australian Open tennis championship, has two 350-ton, movable roof sections that enable tennis to be played in the open air on Center Court.

construction to begin sooner and may also (1) reduce interest costs during construction, (2) reduce the risk of project cost increases caused by unexpected cost escalation, and (3) accelerate the opening of the center and the start of cash flow from operations.

The owner's rep should verify the completeness of the design and specifications at the design/development stage, before acceptance of a fixed price or GMP and before authorization for construction to proceed. The owner is thereby assured that the design/development documentation is sufficiently complete to verify the level of building quality expected and to define these expectations before the production of construction drawings. To pursue a fast-track design without an owner's rep is not recommended. Most objections to this method originate from owners who did not retain the services of a qualified owner's rep.

Some public agencies may be precluded from employing the fast-track system with a GMP because of local or state bidding requirements that prohibit the company that is providing the GMP from bidding on the work. This denies the builder the protection of submitting its own bid against bids from other firms that could, in the aggregate, exceed the GMP.

Many architects and builders are skeptical of the fast-track method because disputes can arise out of the ambiguities of incomplete or insufficiently defined design/development documents, or out of the natural evolution of construction details between the design/development stage and the completion of construction documents. These problems can be attributed to the fact that design/development documents define the building design and its level of quality but not how it will be constructed. Furthermore, there have been many cases of owner's reps who, like attorneys, have exploited or abused their role by criticizing the builder over trivial or irrelevant issues to "justify" their fees or to advance their own relationship with the owner.

FAST-TRACK METHOD WITH DESIGN/ BUILD OR TURNKEY OPTION

The so-called turnkey, or design/construct, method involves a lump-sum cost that is negotiated with a builder. The architect is often retained directly by the builder. Because this method is rarely used on large, complex, and one-of-a-kind projects, it is not considered one of the primary options for convention centers, stadiums, or arenas.

The word "turnkey" is normally used to describe a package deal in which the financing of the project is ar-

ranged by the builder and is included in a complete "turnkey package" to finance, design, and construct. Frequently, however, the terms "design/build" and "turnkey" are used interchangeably.

RISKS AND RISK MANAGEMENT

The risks of project delays, budgeted cost overruns, a builder's financial instability, and/or structural failure are increased by the complexity of the project and are inversely related to the experience, reputation, and past performance of the builder and designer. In other words, high risks and multiple risks are to be expected in projects that take 18 to 30 months to build, require heavy loads to be carried on long structural spans, or must be constructed on a tight site with limited storage and restricted access. Options for reducing risk include the GMP, performance bonds, completion bonds, and other forms of contingency "safety nets." Owners must always accept the risks associated with strikes, weather, interest-rate changes, material defects, and subsurface conditions that are unforeseeable or otherwise beyond the control of the general contractor. Even if protection from "acts of God" were available, the cost to obtain "fail-safe" insurance or indemnification would be prohibitive.

For example, if a structural failure occurs during construction, that event usually brings construction to a halt. Traditionally, the owner, builder, subcontractors, designer, material suppliers, and engineers all sue each other and their various insurance carriers. The owner and the owner's project are abandoned to await an unpredictable verdict at some undetermined time in the future. Attorneys specializing in this type of litigation appear to have a greater incentive to delay and obfuscate the judicial process than to expedite an award to resume construction.

Owners and consultants planning the Ocean Center project in Daytona Beach reduced these risks by requiring all participants to use the same, predesignated performance bond and insurance carrier. The owner would thus have been able to obtain relief in a timely manner to complete the project if the cause of a catastrophic event had been attributed to any of the participants/supplies in the construction process. Fortunately, none occurred. However, with this procedure, if a delay had been attributable to a participant, it would not have been necessary to delay the project further to await a determination of which one was at fault before the insurer could grant relief to the owner and thereby enable construction to continue.

The agreement with the insurer also required the owner to establish and maintain a rigorous project completion schedule, cost controls, and quality inspection pro-

Figure 6-7

SUMMARY OF PRIMARY CONSTRUCTION OPTIONS

	Was Total Cost Known before Construction Began?	Was Lowest Cost Obtained?	Has Time to Determine Cost Been Reduced?[1]
Lump-Sum Bid	Yes	Lowest	17 = Moderate
Multiple Bids	No	Lowest	24 = Maximum
Multiple Bids + Fast Track	No	Lowest	17 = Less
Multiple Bids + Fast Track + GMP	Yes	Highest	12 = Least
Design/Build	Yes	Highest	12 = Least

[1]Midpoint of construction process, in months, based on example or illustration in this chapter. Actual elapsed time may be longer or shorter.

cedures and provided for an aggressive role for the owner's rep, who was also required to monitor and report progress to the bonding company and insurance underwriter. For a determined and innovative owner, risk management techniques can be designed and implemented to mitigate, if not avoid, the losses suffered by other project sponsors when the unexpected occurs.

QUICK SUMMARY OF THE FOUR PRIMARY OPTIONS

No single method offers the owner (1) the lowest cost, (2) the shortest time to lock in or limit the maximum cost, and (3) minimal exposure to costs exceeding the budget once the work has commenced. Each of the methods discussed in this chapter offers the owner the chance to achieve more of one advantage and thereby to obtain less of one or both of the other two advantages. These trade-offs or gains/losses are summarized in Figure 6-7.

REAL-WORLD PRACTICES

The basic concepts of several construction arrangements have been described in this chapter to illustrate the reason why each evolved or the motive for which it was developed, as well as to contrast or compare them all with each other. In actual day-to-day practice, though, procedures are rarely as pure as they have been described here.

LUMP-SUM BID

Normally, the general contractor bids less than the sum of the "quotes" or bids received from each subcontractor and material supplier in the expectation that, once the bid has been won, a more favorable price can be negotiated. Therefore, this method does not necessarily result in a higher cost than the multibid method.

CONSTRUCTION MANAGER AND MULTIPLE BIDS

Some builders believe that this method was developed to avoid the big surprise that can occur when the owner has relied on an architect to estimate project cost, rather than on obtaining the services of a builder/construction manager during the design process.

The owner is cautioned against entering into a CM contract that requires the owner to pay a fee based on a multiple (e.g., 1.5 times) of the CM's staff salaries. This kind of arrangement can result in the construction management firm's overstaffing the job to increase fees or to amortize more of its fixed overhead.

FAST-TRACK APPROACH

Some builders and architects complain of problems or extra costs arising from a fast-track process. In these situations, costs and litigation may result from the ambiguities of a partially complete design/development process, as noted earlier. Also, certain materials, such as fabricated steel, may not be specified as early as they would have been in the lump-sum bid method. Early specification is necessary to obtain as low a price from a single order as would be obtained through purchases made in two or three orders in the multibid method. These realities should be taken into consideration when evaluating the advantages and disadvantages of each option.

Chapter 7

MANAGEMENT

More than any other factors, high-quality management and marketing affect a center's occupancy and financial operating performance. Professional and aggressive marketing can influence the supply of events for a building, and professional management will provide well-organized services to the tenant or event producer, giving the attendee an enjoyable and productive experience.

Strange as it may seem, a center manager may function as the CEO for decades, and the building may celebrate many anniversaries before the center owner defines the building's operating objectives, sets booking priorities, or adopts standards or benchmarks for measuring its success. Indeed, the owner may never do these things.

Similarly, a staffing policy may never be articulated. Nonetheless, the mix of temporary, permanent, and contractual personnel—the extent to which specific event services are provided by in-house staff or contracted out—will definitely influence operating costs and service quality.

For many arena events, the facility's net income from food and beverage sales is greater than its net income from rent. For convention centers, this income stream may constitute more than 25 percent of all operating income. Most building owners, however, may be unable to exploit fully this important profit center because elected officials prevent the center from providing services that "compete" with local private businesses.

The quality of management for arenas and stadiums will determine the:

- Ability of the facility to attract and retain professional team tenants.
- Profitability or net income goals of the facility owner.

- Staffing and payroll requirements.
- Building condition and service levels (quality of the attendee experience).

As mentioned earlier, marketing is also crucial to a building's success. To this end, a center's mission or purpose must be defined before criteria can be established to measure its success. A facility must continually be sold to potential users; an arena event contract normally has a term of only one night, while a convention event may extend over as many as seven to ten days. Marketing a convention center is a team effort that may involve staff from the convention-hotel marketing and sales department, the locality's CVB (convention and visitors' bureau), the center sales staff, the food service/catering sales representatives, and local residents who are leaders in the national organizations of which they are members.

From this introduction, it should be evident that the form, size, and structure of management must be defined before the operating budget can be prepared.

ORGANIZATION AND MANAGEMENT STRUCTURE

The purpose of the building, the relationship between the building owner and its management team, and the type of management are factors often considered in determining the organization or management structure.

Pine Knob Music Theatre, Clarkston, Michigan, had a tarnished reputation because of the venue's shortcomings in traffic flow, concessions, and restrooms when it was purchased in 1990 by Palace Sports & Entertainment. With $14 million invested in remodeling and improvement of concessions and restrooms, along with other actions by management, Pine Knob attendance has increased each season.

The financial success of a facility depends on many issues related to organization. Some of those that lie within the control of owners or management include:

- Rental policy and rate schedule.
- Event scheduling, date protection, and booking policy.
- Concession and event/building service contracts.
- On-site parking supply and fees.
- Tenant lease terms.
- Staffing and training issues.
- Maintenance standards and expenditures.
- Energy use and conservation measures.

Some of these factors are controllable on a day-to-day basis, while others are normally enforced by fixed operating procedures or policies. Effective management must be able to make day-to-day operating decisions and to evaluate the results of alternative operating policies.

The basic daily responsibilities of management should include:

- Providing the building conditions, equipment, and event services needed by the tenant for successful events.
- Providing a clean, comfortable environment for attendees, event sponsors, and event service providers.
- Ensuring that food, beverages, and event merchandise are effectively marketed.
- Providing personal and building security year-round and during events.
- Providing for cleanup after events, as well as routine maintenance.
- Maintaining and operating on-site parking facilities.
- Marketing of the facility, as well as advertising for other events as requested by the tenant.
- Motivating and supplying trained staff to deliver friendly, efficient, effective, and high-quality service.

Broader responsibilities of policy and financial control attributable to management and/or ownership include:

- Establishing priorities for scheduling events and for protecting, reserving, and guaranteeing dates.
- Negotiating lease terms, establishing rental rates, and developing profit-optimizing variable pricing policies (yield management).
- Negotiating vendor and service contracts.
- Identifying, prioritizing, and budgeting for capital improvements.
- Promoting the facility for major special events.
- Identifying methods of financing and funding sources for operating deficits, capital improvements, and debt-service requirements.
- Preparing the reports necessary to monitor cash flow and to forecast cash needs.

Owners of arenas, stadiums, and convention centers must decide whether the primary purpose of their facilities is to maximize their economic impact on the local economy, to serve civic event needs, or to achieve target levels of profitability. Currently, many stadium leases with professional teams do not generate sufficient rent to pay all building operating costs (even team event costs), let alone provide operating revenues to pay debt service. The building owner agrees to a "noneconomic" rent to ensure that the team remains in the city and does not relocate to another community or state.

Similarly, arenas in major cities occasionally agree to host major concerts for no rent after concluding that they could earn sufficient revenue from concession and merchandise sales and parking fees to offset the loss of rental income for a date when the building would otherwise have been unoccupied. Conventions and trade shows rarely pay enough rent to cover operating costs. Seldom does a convention center reach an operating surplus. Perhaps, this happens only in centers in major markets in the most attractive destinations, with the best management, citywide marketing efforts, and an unconstrained ability to control food, beverage, and event service delivery.

To maximize operating revenues and to promote resident support for the center, a convention center encourages building occupancy by major consumer shows and other events that attract resident attendees and that pay higher rents than large conventions and trade shows normally will pay. Such operating policies enhance the bottom line of the financial statement but result in lower occupancy for local hotels and a minimal economic impact upon the restaurant and retail sectors. Blocking dates for these resident-oriented events more than 12 or 18 months in advance conflicts with the marketing of dates for conventions or trade shows. For this reason, every building should have a mission statement, and the owner and management must understand the consequences of its booking policy in terms of achieving the desired event mix.

TYPES OF MANAGEMENT

Stadiums and arenas may be operated by their owners, by their primary or anchor tenants, by not-for-profit entities with varying degrees of independence from the owner, or by private management companies. Current trends at major league sports venues provide for operation by their teams on a year-round basis. With few exceptions, convention centers are operated by public (owner) or quasi-public management. In contrast, 20 of 23 major amphitheaters built since 1980, in the top 35 markets, are managed by private companies. The characteristics of each form of management will be discussed in the following sections.

BY THE VENUE OWNER

The management organization may be public or private. A private venue owner/manager is almost always the owner of the professional sports team that anchors the building. For example, Madison Square Garden is owned by the same company that owns the NBA Knicks and NHL Rangers; Great Western Forum in Inglewood (Los Angeles) is owned by the NBA Lakers' owner; and Dodger Stadium is also owned by the team owner.

When a building is owned by local or state government and operated as a department or division of that government, operating efficiency is often constrained or reduced by bureaucratic regulations and procedures. Purchasing procedures; contract approval processes, often requiring the okay of the legislative body; personnel hiring and firing rules; and other government operating practices (which may also include cronyism and patronage) will

The Louisiana Superdome, managed by Spectacor Management Group, was the first public facility to be operated by an independent management company.

hamper the financial and operating performance of the building and may lower employee morale.

Consequently, independent authorities, not-for-profit operations, and private management companies have been used by government-owned buildings to overcome the disadvantages of government management.

BY A NOT-FOR-PROFIT CORPORATION OR AUTHORITY

This kind of entity generally consists of a commission or board of directors whose members are appointed by the government legislative body to act as agents of the local government. The commission or board, however, is usually exempt from some or all of that government's operating regulations and procedures. The directors or commissioners are—it is hoped—successful, intelligent, and civic-minded businesspersons. If they are to manage a convention center, some board members should represent the hospitality industry: hotels, restaurants, airlines, and other interests.

The role of the commission, corporation, or authority is to establish policy, including operating goals, annual budget review, booking priorities, financial needs, and funding plan. The roles of the manager and his or her staff are to implement the policies of the board and to run the day-to-day business of the center. Management should not set policy, and the board should not manage day-to-day operations.

The major disadvantage of this form of management is that the leadership qualities or professional qualifications of board members normally deteriorate over time, as a center loses its glamor and as political favors are paid off by appointments to the board of individuals with lesser vision, knowledge, and leadership ability. The board of directors of the Georgia World Congress Center has been an exception to this norm. For more than 20 years, its board has been composed of the highest-quality civic and business leaders. This may be the result of the center's perennial financial achievements, major expansions, and the aggressive and effective efforts of its CEO to advocate and promote the center's economic importance to the state's executive and legislative leaders, who are responsible for appointing new directors to the board.

BY A PRIVATE MANAGEMENT COMPANY

The profit motive generates incentives to increase revenues and reduce costs. Today, two large center management companies operate more than 50 major public assembly facilities for a management fee or lease. Also, three or four smaller companies operate another 20 or

Figure 7-1

MAJOR FACILITIES WITH PRIVATE MANAGEMENT CONTRACTS (1977-1997)

Year Opened	Convention Center	Arena	Stadium	Amphitheater
1977	–	–	1	–
1979	–	1	–	–
1981	1	1	–	1
1982	1	–	–	–
1983	–	2	1	1
1984	1	1	–	2
1985	1	1	–	–
1986	1	1	–	2
1987	4	5	2	1
1988	5	6	3	3
1989	5	6	3	2
1990	2	4	–	3
1991	–	1	1	3
1992	2	3	–	–
1993	1	3	–	1
1994	1	3	1	1
1995–1997	5[1]	5[1]	–	3
Total	30	43	12	23

[1]Contracts have been awarded, and, except for 1995 projects, buildings are under construction and scheduled to open in 1996–1997.

30 smaller centers. Nearly all contracts contain some form of incentive or performance-related compensation. Since 1972, an increasing number of governments have contracted with private management companies to operate government-owned facilities. The largest publicly owned centers operated by management firms are those that are listed in Figure 7-1.

Some government-owned facilities are unable to give up control by elected officials of hiring practices, as patronage is the officials' means of repaying political debts. These facilities are subject to influence over their event mix and may relinquish control of those aspects of operation that may affect public safety or moral codes, for which the elected leaders may be held accountable. Private management companies, however, may be unfettered by the negative aspects of political obligation and unrestricted in negotiating labor agreements more effectively, obtaining more profitable event contracts, selling more advertising, and increasing the number of commercial events. These goals can be achieved through the companies' established relationships with concert promoters, superstar agents, national association executives, major trade-show producers, and the like. However, if elected officials are determined to exercise their power and influence by interfering with center operations, a community will not be spared this disadvantage through a private management agreement. The pros and cons of alternative forms of management are shown in Figure 7-2.

Although multibuilding management companies have existed since the late 1970s, it was not until the early 1990s that they were able to achieve the critical mass of contracts that they each needed (20+ buildings). At the same time, they have learned to avoid a suicidally competitive environment (e.g., six firms each spending $100,000 in pursuit of a $50,000 management fee). This evolution of survival instincts and prospect selection has provided the economies of scale and professional staff development opportunities that were originally perceived to be uniquely obtainable through this form of management:

■ Specialized professional services that are only economically feasible if several centers share in them. Examples are the services of labor contract attorneys and event marketing specialists.

■ Availability of professional training seminars and procedure manuals for center staff. Workshops and documents cover such fields as accounting and financial reporting, marketing, human resources/personnel, and others.

■ A professional career path on which center staff can advance within a national or international network of centers.

■ Full-service or a la carte contracts. Major management firms are now prepared to respond to any combination of owner needs, from a single function such as building security, event promotion, or food concessions/catering to complete building management or leasing.

The first two decades of this evolution of multibuilding management companies have also tested the effectiveness of a wide variety of incentive and performance compensation arrangements.

Management company executives recognize that outside management is not appropriate for every venue owner. There will always be conditions mandating that a center will be better managed by a major league team, department or agency of state or local government, university, hotel, CVB, not-for-profit corporation, or authority. Centers in Europe, Asia, and other international locations also use all of these forms of management.

Figure 7-2

Advantages and Disadvantages of Alternative Management Structures

	Public Management	Authority or Nonprofit Corporation	Private Management
Advantages	Owner control	Government representation	Greatest operating autonomy
	Financial support	Special-purpose role	Efficiency incentives
	Coordination/sharing of staff/support functions	Increased operating autonomy	Sensitivity to tenants
		Independent revenues	More independence in negotiations with unions
	Bulk-price purchasing	Less constrained by purchasing and civil service requirements	Greater staffing resources
			More objective criteria for accountability
			Less financial risk for government
Disadvantages	Purchasing procedures	Subjection to political influence	Least government control
	Civil service constraints	Lack of incentives	Profit motive versus impact motive
	Contract approval requirements	Bureaucratic inertia	Cost to smaller operations
	Changing political policies	Eroding quality of board membership	
	Lack of incentives		
	Less responsibility to tenants		
	Limited flexibility		
	Lack of dedicated source of funding		

Service Contracts

Some management responsibilities are provided by outside vendors or contractors. Buildings often contract with private vendors or service companies for security, event cleanup, mechanical equipment servicing, and food services. This unbundling may provide greater expertise at lower costs, but it may also prove a difficult arrangement to manage and can obscure accountability for overall performance.

Regardless of the mix of in-house management versus outside contracting, and whatever the type of management, event-related labor is normally contracted for each event: services such as set-up/tear-down, cleanup, ushering, taking tickets, and event security are provided by temporary or part-time personnel. Unless the build-ing achieves extraordinary occupancy (200 days or more for an arena and 250 to 300 days for a convention center), hiring full-time staff for event-related services may not be cost-effective.

Food and Beverage Operations

Food and beverage concessions normally provide a net income to a spectator facility of 35 to 55 percent of gross sales. The range of the profit margin depends on building attendance and annual occupancy, type of events, the food service company's capital investment in equipment, and the seating capacity of the building.

"Catering" refers to services provided for sit-down meal functions, as at banquets or at the cafeteria or buffet-style restaurants that are usually found in convention centers or stadium clubs. These services generally are provided at a lower margin of profit to the building owner but are essential for hosting an event or necessary as an amenity for attendees with box/club seats or for season ticket holders. Careful planning of the food outlets' size, configuration, and location and optimizing of their number are essential. Likewise, the size, location, and layout of the kitchen, holding areas, and stadium club are crucial to the success of these operations.

EVALUATING MANAGEMENT SERVICE QUALITY

When the Ritz Carlton hotels' management company was awarded the Malcolm Baldrige National Quality Award in 1992, many service companies were awakened to the importance of quality of service: how the service was delivered, and the degree of customer satisfaction.

For those service companies that had not already been converted to the value of TQM (total quality management), Tom Peters's anecdotal case studies and financial success stories of Scandinavian Airlines, Federal Express, and Nordstroms department stores provided well-documented evidence of the increased market share and profitability and the enhanced employee morale that could be obtained if the quality of a service could differentiate an enterprise, in much the same way as one expects a company with a superior product to succeed.

Convention centers and spectator facilities are not immune to the growing interest in quality of service. Unfortunately, magazine publishers and trade associations have exploited this interest by promoting their own "awards shows" based on opinion polls, which at best are more akin to popularity contests and at worst are totally unrelated to centers' actual performance and therefore unfair to centers on both ends of the spectrum. Award shows hurt both centers that deserve recognition for their extra efforts and those that want to know how they can do a better job. Unfortunately, these awards are not based on the criteria by which event producers, promoters, and attendees determine quality of service. Consequently, they fail to recognize those centers providing the highest-quality services based on criteria defined by their customers.

Most simple opinion polls are biased insofar as the majority of the responses tend to select centers from among those with the highest attendance figures and the most events. Thus, smaller centers in smaller markets with fewer events will be underrepresented, excluded, or undercounted. A second problem is that most of these polls, relying on ballots by mail, fail to include protection against ballot-box stuffing. And finally, they use criteria that the award's promoter identifies, usually through his or her common sense or "conventional wisdom," rather than using those service characteristics that, in actuality, are most important to the attendee or show producer.

THE PRICE WATERHOUSE SURVEY

Price Waterhouse was retained in 1993 and 1994 by a large number of convention centers to measure how their customers rated the quality of their services. The company agreed to accept this assignment on the condition that participants would not disclose the results of the study, i.e., their final scores. The purpose of this proviso was to encourage participation by centers that may have lacked the resources or self-image to expect a high score.

The survey and analysis were designed to be valid for all participants. The objective was to enable them to discover their strengths as well as their weaknesses, without fear that a low ranking would cause repercussions from their owners or would put them at a competitive disadvantage that their competitors could use against them. (As a slogan, "We're #1" should be left to fans of sports teams.)

IDENTIFYING SERVICE QUALITY CRITERIA

For each center participating in the survey, 35 convention, trade-show, and consumer-show managers were selected based on their proportionate share or mix of occupancy from the *1992 Price Waterhouse Convention Center Annual Report*. If 20 percent of the center's 1992 occupancy consisted of consumer shows, then seven consumer-show producers were polled. Respondents were asked (1) to identify the centers they had used for their past three major or annual events; (2) to indicate which center provided the highest level of service; and (3) to give specific examples or reasons why one center's service was considered superior to the others'.

Responses were grouped by type or category of service and by the five reasons mentioned most frequently by all major types of users identified. It was discovered that the definitions or most frequently mentioned examples of quality of service were the same among the various types of users: the same criteria were most important to producers of conventions, trade shows, and consumer shows. These five most important criteria from the 1993 study are shown in Figure 7-3.

Measuring Quality Levels versus Comparative Rankings

Each participant center was asked to provide the list of all events for the most recent calendar year. For each center, a mix of ten to 12 "ambulatory" (rotating) conventions and trade shows was selected that was proportionate to the mix of events in each of the buildings. A total of ten or more user surveys was completed for each center. Approximately 200 additional groups were contacted, but their responses were not used for one or both of two reasons: either the person interviewed did not attend the event in any of the past three years, or one or more of the past three facilities used were in markets of smaller size, that is, of fewer than 20,000 hotel rooms.

Figure 7-3

Five Criteria for Quality of Service

Criteria	**Examples**
1. Staff Hospitality	■ Staff was friendly, cheerful. ■ Had polite, can-do attitude. ■ Made our staff and delegates feel welcome. ■ They were happy for us to be there. ■ Staff went out of their way to be helpful.
2. Staff Experience/Knowledge	■ Technically skilled. ■ Knew their jobs. ■ Well trained. ■ Made our show/meeting run smoothly.
3. Pre-Event Service	■ Responded promptly to requests. ■ Returned telephone calls the same day. ■ Event coordinator was easily accessible. ■ Initiated suggestions for room set-ups, meal functions, room blocks. ■ Work order was detailed and in writing. ■ Handled plans in a businesslike way. ■ Well organized. ■ Same event coordinator in charge before the event was also in charge during the event. ■ We were notified at regular intervals about how the event was progressing in comparison with our plan.
4. Attentiveness during Event	■ Event coordinator was always easily accessible. ■ Staff delivered on promises. ■ Staff accommodated special requests quickly and easily. ■ Staff anticipated problems early. ■ We found no surprises when we got there. ■ If something did not work, it was promptly repaired or replaced. ■ All room set-ups and equipment were provided as agreed. ■ All services were well organized.
5. Food and Beverage Service	■ Food and beverage orders were delivered as ordered to the right location at the right time. ■ Quality of food was excellent. ■ Appearance/presentation of meals was good. ■ Variety of food and meal choices was extensive. ■ Banquet service was restaurant-quality. ■ Offered a wide range of selections in a broad price range. ■ Prices fair. ■ Service cheerful and friendly.

Most associations' conventions and most trade shows are held annually. It was decided not to ask user groups about their experiences more than three years previously because (1) these impressions might be difficult to recall, (2) many buildings' service levels have changed in four or five years, and (3) many of the event managers did not attend the events or had not been employed by the group over a period exceeding three years.

A number or score for each center was calculated as an expression or approximation of customer satisfaction, based on the comparative ranking of the center (first, second, or third) for each of the five criteria by ten or more users. Consequently, each center's score was not a reflection of how its service compared with that of all other participating buildings but only how it compared with that of the two other centers used by the event. In many instances, the criteria and services that users were asked to rank were not provided by center employees, for example, food and beverage services. It was also apparent that, for some events, the user's response was influenced by a single event or experience, good or bad, that reflected the conduct, experience, skill, and/or friendliness of a subcontractor's staff and not necessarily those of employees of the center. Examples were security, cleaning, or electrical service subcontractors.

The overall score or ranking for each center was an average of its rankings (first being the best, second in the middle, and third last) by each user surveyed. This measure of customer satisfaction for all centers ranged from 1.2 to 2.9 for each criterion. All centers participating in the survey were comparable in size, having approximately 200,000 or more square feet of exhibit space, and were located in major commercial or visitor destinations, that is, in MSAs with 20,000 or more hotel rooms.

At the San Diego Convention Center, an information kiosk directs visitors, while an adjacent gift shop and a business center provide services frequently needed but not often found in convention centers.

DRAWING CONCLUSIONS FROM THE QUALITY-OF-SERVICE SURVEY AND ANALYSIS

In addition to the service-level criteria that the study revealed, participating centers obtained other valuable lessons from the study:

- Responses obtained in exit interviews with users are not consistent with the opinions they disclose in confidential telephone interviews. Therefore, exit interviews may not be regarded as reliable measures of true satisfaction.

- Users often focus on, or measure, service levels and quality by criteria that did not exist ten years ago, such as concierge or telephone rental service.

- Quality of service sometimes depends on the price that the center can charge or the level of subsidy that the

center receives. Unfortunately, some centers are not authorized to hire additional staff to offer prompt responses to user needs, or cannot offer higher wages to attract or retain more conscientious workers. Similarly, some users are unwilling to pay extra fees for in-house event services if these services are not included in the rental charge.

- Some criteria that were most important in 1993 may not be in the top ten for 1998. Of course, retaining a friendly, cheerful staff always seems to be a winning strategy.

- Many destination-related characteristics can sour a user's perception of a center, no matter how well the center's staff members have been trained. In nearly every survey of users that Price Waterhouse staff have conducted over the past 20 years, when event managers have been asked their opinions of the centers, invariably two or three event managers will base their

In San Antonio, the marketing for the Henry B. Gonzalez Convention Center is done by the San Antonio Convention and Visitors Bureau, a city department. The city's world-renowned Riverwalk, which connects the convention center to hotels, shopping, and restaurants, is a major reason why groups are attracted to this city.

evaluations on some condition or event unrelated to the center's operation:

- "They have the best restaurants."
- "Taxi drivers are rude."
- "The weather is always great."
- "Lines at the hotel registration desk are two hours long."
- "Our members love the golf courses there."
- "Air fares to that city are too high."

■ As revealed in the 1993 study, one of the five most important measures of a user's experience was the quality of the center's food. In nearly all centers, food service contracts are not awarded by the center's management; indeed, many center managers have no influence over which concessionaire is selected. Clearly, users do not differentiate between services provided by center employees and those afforded by subcontractor employees (e.g., food and beverage, security, electrical, and janitorial services).

■ Many times, the user will not be able to identify why one center is regarded as providing better service than another without first being asked to name the center that, by comparison, gave the better service and then being asked to give specific reasons or examples for

that preference. Often, the examples or reasons that form the basis for opinions differ from the answers users may give if asked the question "How do you define quality of service?" In other words, user perceptions about service may often differ from the reasons stated in responses.

For example, users' responses when questioned about service quality in the abstract (unrelated to their actual experiences in centers) may reflect criteria expressed in a popular management book or article the users have read recently, motivational speakers they have heard, or even a TQM program being conducted in the center. Hence, the survey asked them to rank centers by level of quality before asking them to name their reasons or to give examples of why they ranked one center ahead of another.

■ Centers that were ranked highest were those with the most rigorous—the most long-term—staff training programs, not those three or four centers that were conducting TQM programs at the time when the survey was conducted.

■ Unlike products, services cannot be tried out or test-driven before they are purchased. Selling services on the basis of quality (versus price) relies more on word-of-mouth referrals or on references or past experience than does the selling of products, which can be evaluated before purchase. An equipment failure—if successfully and cheerfully remedied—can result in higher customer satisfaction than a tenancy without failure. It may sound corny, but many successful centers, when given lemons, know how to make terrific lemonade.

Price Waterhouse looks forward to conducting a follow-up survey every five years to determine what changes, if any, have taken place in each center's score and the extent to which service criteria may have changed.

MARKETING

The successful convention center will have its own marketing department, will work closely with a well-funded and professionally staffed convention and visitors' bureau (CVB), and will enjoy an effective relationship with the sales and marketing directors of the major convention-oriented hotels. In most cities, these alliances, though necessary for success, are not always achieved. A hotel is often reluctant to block rooms during its peak season or to share leads for multiple-hotel events unless it is itself the headquarters hotel. The CVB is sometimes a department of city government or of the chamber of commerce, or it is underfunded. Center management is often oriented toward operations or gate shows and may regard event promotion as the show producer's or event manager's responsibility.

Typically, the CVB prepares three- to five-year marketing plans and budgets and solicits events that book 18+ months in advance. The building staff will market events with less than 18 months' advance notice and fill-in-type events, such as local functions and shows, receptions, banquets, and merchandise mart–type shows. The CVB will market large, multihotel conventions and trade shows that tend to book three to six years into the future.

In the most successful destinations, all of these actors work as a team to promote the city and its center at major meeting-planner and trade-show conventions, such as those of the American Society of Association Executives (ASAE) and the International Association of Exposition Managers (IAEM). Responsibility is shared for staffing the city's exhibit; staffing the hospitality suite; obtaining resources for printed brochures; soliciting in-kind contributions to cover airline tickets, restaurant meals, receptions at the convention center and major hotels, hotel rooms, and so on; for familiarization ("fam") trips; and pursuing leads and prospects.

For arenas and stadiums, marketing is primarily the responsibility of the building's staff, event promoters, athletic team management, and other event sponsors. The venue negotiates discounted rates at which event promoters can obtain television, radio, and newspaper advertising. Though promotion costs are borne by the event producers, the experienced building manager can help guide promoters to the most effective media outlets for particular types of presentations and help lead them to discounts and trade-outs.

The building's marketing plan should set forth the various sales activities and marketing programs to be undertaken (e.g., group sales), assign responsibilities for each task, establish criteria for measuring the effectiveness or success of each task, and provide a detailed budget and time frame for the completion of each activity. A financial strategy will describe the sources of funding for the plan. The success of an arena or stadium marketing plan can be measured within a relatively short time. By contrast, because conventions and trade shows are booked years ahead, a convention center's ultimate success and the long-term effect of its marketing effort are not realized until many years after the effort has been made.

Chapter 8

FINANCIAL OPERATIONS: BUILDING REVENUES AND EXPENSES

The income statement for a public assembly facility reveals, in most cases, whether the facility generates an operating surplus or a deficit. Many professional sports venues and nearly all convention centers require operating subsidies. In North America, only two or three convention centers in major markets consistently generate enough operating income to pay operating expenses, and approximately the same number of recently built venues for major league sports pay all operating expenses and most debt service from their operating revenues.

A careful analysis of the project's financial operations—of its income statement—will also reveal the underlying objective or motives of the primary tenant or tenants (usually the team or, in a convention center, the trade show or convention manager) and of the building owner (usually the local or state government).

Because the motives of landlords and tenants have changed over the past 20 to 30 years, the financial operating characteristics of the building also will reflect the age of the building. Many physical features of centers built between 1985 and 1995 were not provided in buildings designed and constructed in the 1960s or 1970s. For example, only a few arenas and stadiums built 20 years

ago offered enclosed luxury box suites, an extensive variety of food service, and large seating capacities: 20,000+ and 70,000+ for arenas and stadiums, respectively. Similarly, most convention centers developed in the '60s and '70s did not include ballrooms or banquet halls, contiguous exhibit space exceeding 150,000 square feet, or a wide variety of food service options. Only since the second half of the 1980s have major league teams received revenues from the sale of naming rights or shares of parking or concession revenues in publicly owned stadiums.

Public assembly facility operations, like other hospitality enterprises such as hotels and theme parks, are management-intensive. But a center's dependence on operating or debt-service subsidies is usually determined by the terms of the leases with primary tenants, rather than by its occupancy or by the performance or operating efficiency of its management team. Primary tenant lease terms that specify the distribution of event revenues and responsibility for event-related expenses are normally negotiated by the building owner, not by management. The presence or absence of high-quality service levels and cost-effective management can enhance the quality of events or reduce a center's occupancy. But management expertise and service levels are rarely able to influence the center's need for subsidy. Management is unable to determine whether the bottom line will be written in black ink or red when lease terms and operating policies and procedures are set by others. This chapter seeks to explore these issues in greater detail.

To summarize, the size of the operating surplus or loss will be influenced partly by a center's level of use and by the physical characteristics of the building. In nearly all cases, the ultimate need for operating subsidies will be primarily determined by the operating objectives of the

Restaurants like the Front Row and specialty retailing like that at The Ballpark at Arlington, Texas, provide previously unrecognized revenue opportunities for sports facilities.

Figure 8-1

ILLUSTRATIVE OPERATING REVENUES AND EXPENSES IN 1995 (millions)

	Sports and Entertainment Venue		Convention Center	
Period of Construction	1965–1975	1985–1995	1965–1975	1985–1995
Occupancy/Use	One Pro Team	One Pro Team	Typical	Typical
Operating Revenues				
Rentals	$2.0	$ 4.0	$1.0	$1.0
Food Service	1.0	3.0	0.2	1.0
Parking	1.0	1.0	0.1	0.4
Premium Seats		10.5		
Naming Rights		0.5		
Event Services			0.1	0.6
Advertising and Promotion	0.5	0.5		
Other	0.5	1.0	0.1	0.5
Total	$5.0	$20.5	$1.5	$3.5
Operating Expenses				
Salaries, Wages, Benefits	$2.0	$ 4.5	$0.9	$1.6
Utilities	0.5	1.2	0.6	0.6
Insurance	0.2	0.3	0.2	0.3
Marketing and Sales	0.2	0.2	0.2	0.5
Maintenance, Repairs, and Supplies	0.1	0.8	0.3	0.3
Depreciation and Replacement	0.5	0.5	0.2	0.2
Nonreimbursed Event Costs	1.0	2.0	0.1	0.5
Total	$4.5	$ 9.5	$2.5	$4.0
Net Operating Income	$0.5	$11.0	$(1.0)	$(0.5)

building owner and primary tenant or tenants, as reflected in the major "deal points" of the lease agreement. The primary sources of operating revenues and major types of expenses are illustrated in Figure 8-1. As shown, the differences in levels and sources of operating income for centers that resulted from deals negotiated between 1985 and 1995, as compared with buildings constructed in 1965 through 1975, are dramatic.

OPERATING REVENUES

RENTALS

ARENAS AND STADIUMS

In older sports venues, the rental revenue received by the facility from an event presented by the tenant or lessor was usually a single fixed rate, for example, at 10 percent of gross ticket revenues. Rent paid by family shows was normally less than rent paid by concert promoters. Over the past two decades, however, a wider array of rent deals has been developed that typically reduces the rent paid by and the financial risks to concert promoters and team owners alike.

More venues have been built that serve overlapping market areas. And while the supply of stadiums and arenas has increased, the supply of performers seeking arena venues has declined because there are fewer touring acts, making shorter tours. Also, professional sports leagues have opted to limit the number of new franchises, compared with the number of willing buyers, so as to enhance the quality of the sport and (coincidentally) the prices charged for expansion teams. Team owners have benefited from the imbalance between the supply of teams and the increasing number of communities (and now states) competing for their occupancy. This heightened demand has enabled team owners to secure single-purpose venues (e.g., baseball-only versus baseball/football venues) and to obtain more of the cash flow from operations, as facility owners have increased the share going to the teams as an inducement for their residence.

During this same period, outdoor amphitheaters accommodating 10,000 to 30,000 attendees have been built in 25 of the top 35 markets. The impact on the number of arena concert events caused by the combined effects of these changes in the supply and demand for arena dates has resulted in: lower rents paid to venue owners; more special-purpose venues for major league sports (fewer two-team facilities); and major shares of the cash flow and profit centers, which had previously been retained by the building, now allocated to professional teams and touring acts. Buildings and concert promoters are forced to survive on lower margins and to absorb some or all of the financial risks of poorly attended games or concerts. Previously, a greater share of these losses was absorbed in part or totally by team owners, promoters, or acts.

Between 1988 and 1995, more than 80 percent of NBA and NHL teams moved to a new arena, had one under construction, or obtained a commitment from a government entity that had promised to develop a new arena for them. Team relocations and additions of new teams resulting from expansions of all major leagues have likewise resulted in a wave of new stadium construction. Motives that may previously have been attributed to a team owner's "greed" must now be recognized and acknowledged as essential to attain financial parity with competing franchises.

Faced with escalating player salary demands and unstable broadcast revenues, team owners in disparate markets are compelled to seek parity with their competitors' increased financial strength, which has most often been obtained from new revenue sources that are only possible in a new building:

- Premium seating, such as box suites and club seats.
- Event parking that is controlled by the center.
- Other arena (non–major league team) event revenues.
- Naming rights and other sponsorship opportunities.
- Increased food and beverage services, outlets, and sales.
- Payments when attendance declines below a specified level.
- In a single-purpose venue, rights to all revenues that were previously shared with a second team in a dual- or multipurpose center.

New agreements occasionally provide rental rates that appear comparable to previous agreements. These agreements, however, usually also contain new provisions that entitle the team owner to additional income from new revenue sources or event-related services provided without charge that had previously been an extra expense to the tenant under the terms of the older lease for the venue. Examples are day-of-event costs, use of practice facilities, and use of office space.

As shown in the illustration of an operating statement for a sports venue (Figure 8-2), revenues made available in newer buildings can provide a team with a $5 million to $15 million increase in annual cash flow. The amount depends on the extent to which debt service on the new center is funded from the building's net operating revenues or subsidized by a pledge of revenue from other sources. An analysis of arena leases negotiated between 1985 and 1995 reveals revenues pledged to

Figure 8-2

ILLUSTRATIVE OPERATING AND INCOME STATEMENTS FOR NEW NBA/NHL ARENA (millions)

Operating Revenues	
Net Rental	$ 6.0
Suite Leasing, Net of Tickets	11.0
Premiums for Club Seats	3.0
Net Concessions	4.0
Net Merchandise	0.3
Net Food and Beverage	0.7
Net Parking	2.3
Advertising and Naming	2.7
Gross Operating Revenues	$30.0
Operating Expenses	
Salaries, Wages, and Benefits	$ 4.5
Utilities	1.7
Insurance	0.5
Maintenance, Materials, and Supplies	0.9
Nonreimbursed Event Costs	2.4
Gross Operating Expenses	$10.0
Net Operating Revenues	$20.0[1]

[1]New arenas typically provide $5 million to $15 million more in net operating income than pre-1980 venues. Older facilities normally do not offer suites, club seats, or naming rights. Added revenues are also realized for additional seats (10 to 20 percent), more profitable concession facilities, parking, and so on.

pay debt service from non-center-related sources ranging from 10 to 80 percent, with most leases being in the 20 to 40 percent range.

Rental formulas reflect the increased complexity of team and building financing. Many agreements provide for some minimum rent level, plus added rent calculated at varying percentages of the revenue generated by alternative attendance levels. These formulas vary according to tenant and landlord appetites to trade off financial risks, e.g., to obtain break-even income at low attendance and to forgo some of the upside or extraordinary gains from an unusually successful season. Similar agreements are structured with concert promoters who are required to guarantee large fees to superstars who may take 95 percent of the box office receipts. The promoter works in the expectation of a sellout performance to obtain the potential 5 percent fee, and the building owner accepts a "free rent" deal in exchange for higher revenues generated by the superstar from food concessions, parking, event service fees, and a percentage of merchandise sales (posters, recordings, T-shirts). For some major acts, merchandise sales per attendee exceed the average ticket price.

CONVENTION CENTERS

Only rarely do the rate schedules for two convention centers enable direct comparison. Rental paid by a convention or trade show will be determined by:

- The number of days that an event requires to move in, convene the delegates, present the event, and move out.
- The amount of exhibit space and meeting-room or ballroom space the event requires.
- The amount of exhibit space it rents to exhibitors.
- Specific dates (e.g., holiday periods) or season of the year, and number of hotel rooms occupied.
- How far in advance of the event date the agreement is signed or the deposit is paid.
- Which furnishings, equipment, or services are included in the rental.
- The number, type, and cost of food service functions, cocktail receptions, and the like.

An effective rental rate per occupied square foot of exhibit space or per attendee can be calculated on the same basis on which a hotel calculates its ADR (average daily rate) earned per occupied room. Figure 8-3 compares the averages and the ranges of effective rents charged by all primary centers in various-sized markets in 1989 and 1994. These rates do not reflect complimentary services or equipment; nor do they reflect rebates that may

Offering the highest-quality convention services, such as room set-up crews and catering, is critical to a convention center's reputation when marketing the center.

have been paid to the center by hotels occupied by event attendees, to reduce the standard rental rates as an inducement for the association to select the center and the destination.

Convention centers do not enjoy a spectator venue's ability to increase rent to offset monetary inflation by linking rent to a percentage of box office gross revenues. In fact, convention-center effective rents have declined in constant dollars as a result of tenant resistance to increases in rental charges. Centers in the most attractive markets and destinations have succeeded in protecting their operating margins (ratios of operating revenues to expenses) by:

- Increasing parking rates, if they have parking facilities.
- Marketing exclusive or nonexclusive event services like electricity, booth security, and telephones.
- Offering a wider variety and a higher quality of food and beverage services.
- Competing more aggressively for local banquets, receptions, and assemblies.
- Charging extra fees for services or equipment that were previously provided as part of the rental fee.

A diverse range of rental agreements and terms is found in major centers today, much wider than that available 30 years ago: from "four walls, broom-clean" to fully decorated halls and meeting rooms, including microphone and speaker's podium. In the early 1990s, one center in Australia offered the use of its fully furnished, equipped center for a fixed price per attendee that included, in addition to the use of the center, lodging, meals, local transportation, and round-trip air fare from North America.

Figure 8-3

EFFECTIVE RENTAL RATES IN 1989 AND 1994

Market Size[1]	1989				1994			
	Conventions/ Trade Shows		Consumer Shows		Conventions/ Trade Shows		Consumer Shows	
	Average	Range	Average	Range	Average	Range	Average	Range
Gateway City								
East	$.03	$.02–.04	$.03	$.01–.04	$.04	$.02–.10	$.05	$.00–.10
Central	.02	.00–.04	.03	.01–.10	.04	.02–.05	.04	.03–.05
West	.04	.02–.05	.04	.02–.07	.04	.01–.08	.04	.03–.06
All	.03	.00–.05	.03	.01–.10	.04	.01–.10	.04	.00–.10
National City								
East	$.04	$.01–.07	$.06	$.02–.14	$.08	$.01–.14	$.12	$.04–.20
Central	.02	.01–.05	.02	.01–.04	.02	.01–.03	.04	.01–.05
West	.02	.01–.04	.04	.03–.04	NA	NA	.04	NA
All	.03	.01–.07	.04	.01–.14	.04	.01–.14	.06	.01–.20
Regional City								
East	$.03	$.02–.04	$.03	$.01–.05	NA	NA	NA	NA
Central	.03	.01–.06	.04	.01–.10	$.05	$.03–.07	$.06	$.03–.11
West	.03	.01–.06	.05	.02–.08	.04	.02–.06	.05	.04–.05
All	.03	.01–.06	.04	.01–.10	.05	.02–.10	.06	.03–.12

NA means Not Available.

[1]Size of market refers to the number of hotel rooms in the metropolitan area, as reported by Smith Travel Service. Gateway markets are ones with more than 20,000 rooms; national, with 10,000 to 20,000 rooms; and regional, with fewer than 10,000 rooms.

FOOD SERVICES

SPORTS AND ENTERTAINMENT VENUES

It may seem axiomatic that per capita sales of food and beverages at the same event in different venues will vary according to the accessibility of food services to the customer. Each serving station available for attendees to purchase food items or drinks is referred to as a "point of sale." Older arenas and stadiums typically offered concessions from a limited number of permanent stands or counters built into the concourses behind the seating areas. Congestion and long lines caused by the limited width of the concourse and number of stands made purchases a lengthy process and discouraged sales. Also, fans were reluctant to leave the game and risk missing a key play.

Newer venues offer double or triple the number of points of sale in wide, colorful, and well-lighted concourses. Video monitors are mounted near concession stands to enable fans to watch the game while standing in line. A wider variety and higher quality of food items are offered to attendees, who will typically spend more for well-prepared, cheerfully served, and attractively displayed alternatives to hot dogs and soda thrust at them by grumpy attendants. Per capita sales per attendee in new venues have increased 25 to 30 percent over those reported by older facilities.

The percentage of gross sales that a concessionaire is willing to pay a building owner will increase with higher annual attendance, larger number of events, and increased efficiency of the vending, preparation, and storage facilities. The share paid to the building will decrease in response to the level of investment in equipment or upfront cash payment that the concessionaire is required to make and with the level of uncertainty about future events and attendance levels expected, e.g., by a new team in a new market. Consequently, agreements can range from 20 to 50 percent of gross food and beverage sales paid to the center.

CONVENTION CENTERS

Until the mid-1980s, many major centers did not have a banquet hall or preparation kitchen. It was assumed or even required that any major receptions or food functions would be held in a hotel ballroom. Convention-center lobbies, prefunction areas, and corridors were not designed to accommodate food service or vending stands. Often, eating and drinking in carpeted areas was discouraged. Exhibit halls offered built-in spaces in perimeter walls to vend stadium-type concessions. The trade-show manager could usually opt to close off these wall openings to accommodate more booths and to place food stands or locate buffet lines at alternative locations within the exhibit area—strategically sited to influence visitor flow—or in the hallways outside the exhibit area. Because the show producer did not share in food sale revenues, however, offering valuable space for these services was regarded as a necessary inconvenience to prevent attendees from leaving the exhibit.

Modern convention centers in attractive destinations and large markets may earn as much as 50 percent of their net operating revenues from their share of food and beverage sales. Products are offered from pushcarts; portable stands; sidewalk cafes; themed food courts; "branded" food outlets; formal, white-tablecloth banquets offering five-course, restaurant-quality meals; banquets featuring tableside "Escoffier" service; and cafeterias. Over the past two decades, many convention centers have made the transition from K rations to haute cuisine. Figure 8-4 shows food and beverage sales per capita for conventions with and without trade shows and for consumer shows, revealing the range of service levels that existed in 1994. It is still challenging, not only to decorate an exhibit hall to look like a ballroom but also to serve tasty meals that

are prepared off site and that arrive fully assembled in the back of a truck.

PARKING

Higher land costs in a downtown are usually offset by the higher income from increased use of parking facilities and by the reduced number of on-site spaces required for parking, in comparison with remoter settings. Although land costs may be less in an exurban setting, a 70,000-seat football stadium could require 250 acres for surface parking that might only be occupied from 12 to 15 days per year. By contrast, the parking decks in downtown Atlanta, serving the Omni Arena and Georgia Dome, or in Cincinnati, at Riverfront Stadium and the Coliseum, are filled every weekday with downtown employee parking and available on weekends and evenings for game attendees. It is not essential to acquire 250 acres for parking if the venue only needs to add 2,000 to 5,000 spaces for VIP parking or to supplement existing spaces, or if a large share of attendees arrives by subway. Estimates of parking revenue must therefore be adjusted for the percentage of attendees using public transit.

On a peak day, crowds of several thousand people may be attracted to a large trade show at a major convention center. Thus, parking requirements may be calculated on the same basis as for spectator-event venues. Unlike ballgames and concerts, however, major trade shows are held on weekdays, and attendee arrival and departure patterns are spread over the entire day. These trade-show events may attract 30 to 40 percent of their attendees from among residents of surrounding metropolitan areas who commute by private automobile. Without park-and-ride rail transit, a center should be prepared to offer 5,000 or more unoccupied parking spaces for attendees or risk losing events to competing centers or markets that can provide such facilities.

Parking rates will be determined by the importance of an event and by local customs. Some fans are elated to find a parking space near Madison Square Garden, even though the four-hour charge is $20. Conversely, potential visitors to a boat show in a suburban market may refuse to attend the event if asked to pay even a nominal parking fee. Compared with poor food service facilities, inadequate parking facilities can have a more adverse effect on the level of gross revenues. If attendees perceive parking to be expensive or unavailable or expect long delays in leaving a multilevel garage after an event, attendance will be reduced. The marketability of a building, as measured by event attendance, will be directly influenced by inadequate parking, ingress and egress delays, and unsafe parking facilities.

Figure 8-4

FOOD AND BEVERAGE EXPENDITURES PER CAPITA IN 1994

Market Size[1]	Conventions with Trade Shows	Conventions without Trade Shows	Consumer Shows
Gateway	$4.03–$24.03	$0.00–$59.64	$0.24–$4.13
National	0.59–18.64	0.24–8.01	0.26–3.85
Regional	0.15–13.78	0.30–5.96	0.16–1.34

[1]Size of market refers to the number of hotel rooms in the metropolitan area, as reported by Smith Travel Service. Gateway markets are ones with more than 20,000 rooms; national, with 10,000 to 20,000 rooms; and regional, with fewer than 10,000 rooms.

Convenient transit access reduces parking demand and makes a public assembly facility more accessible both to visitors and to the community it was built to serve.

Center-city venues must make extra provisions to overcome any public perception of personal safety or security problems, even when the potential risk of assault or auto break-ins is statistically less than at suburban shopping malls, which are often unjustifiably perceived as more secure.

PREMIUM SEATING

From the days of the first-century Roman Colosseum, where Nero enjoyed a reserved ringside seat, to more recent offerings of box seats such as the restored ones at Washington, D.C.'s Ford's Theatre, spectator-event centers have had a long history of accommodating VIPs in preferred seating areas. During the last quarter of the 20th century, stadium and arena owners have discovered that this concept is not only an additional luxury but also a major profit center capable of financing an entire facility.

By marketing to upper-income segments of a team's fan base, franchise owners have demonstrated the revenue-generating potential of premium seating at preferred viewing locations, in the form of luxury box suites and club seating areas. The financing of Texas Stadium in the 1970s and, to a greater extent, Joe Robbie Stadium in the 1980s are perfect examples of stadium owners' benefiting from this strategy. Companies that rank among the largest employers in their communities have proved to be prime candidates for luxury box suites, while upper-income business professionals have been the major target market for club seats.

Great Western Forum in Inglewood, California, has found that the extraordinary demand for premium seating in preferred "Senate Seat" locations at Lakers and Kings games and at concerts has enabled the arena to earn several thousand dollars from each of the 3,500 Senate Seats.

Spectator venues for major league sports typically generate a premium of $500 to over $1,000 per seat per season, in addition to the higher prices for tickets, for the right to reserve a private box suite or a club seat in a preferred location with extra leg room and access to a members-only club concourse, preferred parking, and upscale food service. The Forum in Inglewood has demonstrated its ability to exact a premium for the right to occupy seats in a preferred viewing area without the private concourse amenities or larger seats typically associated with premium seats on a club level. In 1995, premium seats attained their highest level of stratification to date at the United Center in Chicago, which has six concourses: three serving the public and three accessible to holders of box suites and club seats only.

Long-term revenue potential from premium seating is determined primarily by:
- The number of larger corporate employers in a market.
- The number of high-income households in the market.
- The number of locally competing, major league venues with premium seats or suites.
- The relative popularity of the team.

Premium seat sales have also been influenced by civic boosterism, as in Albany, New York, or by special events like the Rose Bowl. However, these are temporary or unstable conditions on which to rely after the first lease term has expired.

Revenue streams from premium seats are produced at major soccer stadiums throughout Europe, major college football stadiums, amphitheaters, and choice venues for minor league baseball. One university in the southeastern United States has had great success in leasing long-term parking spaces near its football stadium for "premium tailgating" privileges.

PERMANENT SEAT LICENSES

New NFL venues in Charlotte and St. Louis have succeeded in obtaining $140 million and $50 million, respectively, from the sale of permanent seat licenses (PSLs). Indeed, Charlotte's NFL stadium actually offers the only truly permanent seat license in professional sports. The America's Center in St. Louis sells what it calls a "personal" seat license, though because of the length of its term, it is tantamount to a permanent seat license. In this case, fans bought a license for 30 years, which corresponded to the stadium's bond financing term. Because the life of the stadium may not exceed this term, however, this arrangement could be considered equivalent to permanent licensing.

In August 1995, Oakland, California, attempted to sell ten-year seat licenses with a five-year renewal option. This effort was not completely successful because many observers believe that the Oakland seat license is not marketable as an appreciable asset, given its limited term, and thus may not be seen as having the same value as a lifetime license.

As of January 1996, no arenas in the NBA or NHL had sold PSLs. The closest thing to a PSL sold at a professional arena was found at the Charlotte Coliseum. In this case, charter seat rights were granted to purchasers of charter season tickets. A fan paid a deposit of $300 to $500 for season tickets before Charlotte gained an NBA franchise. This deposit was applied to the season ticket purchase, and the fan was guaranteed the right to buy season tickets for that specific seat location for a lifetime. Approximately 15,000 deposits were collected on a total of 23,000 seats. Once the city had been awarded the NBA franchise, however, the ultimate cost of the seat right became $0 because the money was applied to the purchase price of the season ticket. Thus, this is not a true PSL. On the other hand, the original purchaser's right to buy those season tickets (or those charters) was and is transferable and is now selling for $2,500 to $25,000.

NAMING RIGHTS

The value of this revenue source is determined by factors similar to those affecting premium seat values: the presence of a major corporate headquarters and the prestige of the team or venue. Values are further enhanced to the extent that the sponsor's name and corporate logo are repeated in key locations to increase the potential for TV broadcast viewership for a given event.

Premium seating and special suites like this one at Joe Robbie Stadium represent a major revenue source.

EVENT SERVICES

Revenues from event services such as concessions, catering, audiovisual aids, security, cleaning, and telephones are most important to convention centers. As mentioned earlier, this is one of the limited means by which centers have been able to increase operating income and offset real dollar declines in rental revenues. The local political climate, however, often prevents centers from competing with local businesses offering these services.

ADVERTISING AND PROMOTIONS

As of this writing, revenues from advertising and promotions apply almost exclusively to spectator venues. Consumer product suppliers have recognized opportunities to increase the impact of their marketing efforts. By combining advertising (display panels, dasher boards, scoreboards) with pouring rights (for beverage distributors), special-event sponsorships, broadcast advertising, new product introductions, and program advertisements, spectator facilities have learned to offer custom packages that may involve flexible payment-rate schedules, use of luxury boxes, and other forms of "trade-outs."

OPERATING EXPENSES

Management opportunities to influence operating expenses are extremely limited. Methods of controlling payroll costs are largely restricted by the level of use and by local labor conditions. Venues with 100 events or fewer per year may maintain a small staff of permanent, full-time employees. Conversely, venues with 250 events per year can obtain the financial advantages of retaining key-event service (day-of-event) employees on a full-time basis and recapturing their expense by charging event producers less than they might otherwise have to pay for less skilled and less reliable temporary employees. Similar decisions can be made regarding entering into contracts for such functions as event security and janitorial service, versus providing these services with an in-house staff.

Lastly, if a team is managing a center, the venue owner will obtain savings by using the team's marketing staff or accounting department to service the center's needs, then paying the team for its pro rata share of this expense, instead of duplicating staff, department heads, office space, and so on. Thanks to the many combinations and permutations of these different means of staffing a center, it is rare to find two public assembly facilities with similar staffing plans, payroll costs, contract services expenses, or numbers of employees. Comparing income statements from different venues is usually not appropriate.

INSURANCE

This cost typically consists of property and liability insurance premiums. The cost for each type of coverage is based on the value of the building, the type or types of events hosted, and the number of attendees. Insurance companies specializing in coverage of public assembly facilities are reliable sources for estimates of these costs.

UTILITIES

Energy costs are based on local area electric or other energy costs, facility usage, building efficiency, the size of the building, and the number of degree days. Supplying enough electricity to heat an arena filled with 20,000+ spectators, each radiating 98.6 degrees Fahrenheit, may not be necessary, even when the temperature outside the facility is below freezing. With the same outside temperature, though, a half-filled facility will require considerable energy to heat and maintain attendee comfort.

Computer-based energy conservation systems have proven cost-effective investments if costs are amortized over the life of the equipment. These systems adjust the lighting for full occupancy, partial occupancy, cleaning crews, or TV broadcast requirements and turn the lights off when rooms are not occupied. Similarly, these systems regulate the use of heat, air conditioning, ventilation with outside air, and recirculation of internal air to minimize energy costs given any combination of outside temperature/humidity, building occupancy, and other events or activities taking place in the building.

MARKETING AND SALES

These expenses, like depreciation and replacement reserve, are often not included in a center's operating statement. An arena or stadium usually relies on its primary tenant or tenants or on event producers to market or promote each event, while a convention center often relies totally on a sales staff and budget provided by the local convention and visitors' bureau. These arrangements are inadequate for centers seeking to maximize their event-related income. Most successful centers provide their own in-house sales staff, even though their departmental cost and budget may be included in generic line items such as salaries, travel, or supplies.

Public assembly facilities that enjoy high occupancy rates recognize the value of promoting themselves as entertainment centers. They encourage market-area residents to consider their facilities' locations and event schedules when seeking entertainment, just as these citizens might routinely scan the current offerings at a local multi-screen cinema or performing arts center. With the increasing competition among the growing number of spectator sports and entertainment venues, sales and marketing staffs often must secure a sought-after touring act by promoting their venues as "the place to be" and offering event promoters a range of cost-effective programs with which to advertise their events. Discounted advertising rates, trade-outs, and promotions with local deejays or other celebrities are examples of established strategies from which an event producer may benefit, and many promoters have come to expect them.

It is not unusual to find a convention center that is marketed by a team of professionals from four or five separate organizations: building sales staff, the local CVB, hotel sales staff, food service contractors, and event producers. Each organization benefits from a well-attended event. Convention centers have fewer dark days when a professional marketing staff aggressively solicits events for dates within the 12- to 18-month advance booking period during which additional major trade shows or conventions are unlikely to schedule.

Typically, the CVB is primarily responsible for securing events that attract out-of-town attendees requiring multiple hotels, such as professional and trade association events. The center sales staff focuses on corporate meetings, consumer shows, social and civic events, merchandise sales and shows, and a wide range of other activities requiring the use of meeting rooms, ballrooms, exhibit space, and related services. These users' requirements are too large to be accommodated in local hotels or restaurants, and demand may arise when local facilities are fully booked, e.g., during the holidays.

MAJOR REPAIR AND REPLACEMENT RESERVE

Annual allocations for major repairs and replacements are usually not budgeted and set aside in a reserve fund to cover future renovations or replacement of major equipment and furnishings. This item is a real expense, as discussed in Chapter 10. As such, it is just as important to a center's success as expenditures for insurance or maintenance and should be recognized and budgeted. Likewise, in calculating the net value of a center (its value after depreciation), an appraisal of the center should consider the remaining useful life of chairs, carpets, mechanical systems, and other furniture, fixtures, and equipment, in much the same way as it would consider the cost of deferred maintenance as a reduction in the building's current value.

Financial planning for public assembly facilities does not always provide adequate funding or reserves for replacement of capital equipment and for the periodic renovations or updating required to retain a center's marketability. This oversight can result in costly unanticipated shutdowns of operations, violations of lease agreements with anchor tenants, negative public relations, and erosion of market share. Public assembly facilities serve big-business users and routinely host events that attract massive crowds. When 50,000 teenagers have jammed into a stadium for a concert, or when 20,000 enthusiastic fans have paid $50 per ticket for an arena seat to view a highly publicized, closed-circuit TV boxing match, the lighting or sound systems should not fail. When parents bring their children to an arena for an ice show or circus, the interior finishes and fixtures should be clean and in attractive condition.

A trade-show promoter or convention organizer may have hundreds of thousands of dollars committed to a successful exhibition; the building should not detract from the guest's experience and appreciation of the major investments in exhibits. Private entrepreneurs do not want to wait for a town council's budget to be resolved before they are assured of a successful event. The building should have adequate reserves dedicated to pay for unforeseen breakdowns, as well as for periodic modernization. Most major capital expenses are predictable, and reserves for replacements can be budgeted. With proper business planning, promises can be kept and the public's confidence in the facility sustained.

NONREIMBURSED EVENT COSTS

Accurate cost accounting is essential to effective management decisions. Many center managers maintain a separate bank account into which they deposit funds paid by event producers for reimbursement of day-of-event costs, such as ushers, security, ticket takers, and post-event cleanup. Funds from this account are disbursed to pay the temporary workers and service contractors who make up the day-of-event staffing and labor pool.

The decision not to commingle operating revenues—which are dedicated to paying annually budgeted, fixed operating costs—with revenues received to pay day-of-event expenses is a means of preventing the misapplication of revenues dedicated to pay event costs. Although many centers offer fixed-price or package deals that include rent, event staffing, and so forth, it is still important for management to measure the fixed versus the variable event-related costs. The cost of event labor for which the building is not reimbursed by the tenant should be deducted from the rental income for the events involved. In this way, one can measure these events' cost-effectiveness or profitability in comparison with other events in the center and with similar events in comparable centers.

OPERATING SUBSIDY REQUIREMENT

A variety of taxes may be used to finance public facility operations. Most important to a center's financial stability is the pledge of a dedicated source of income, such as ticket fees or taxes on a stable revenue stream like hotel room rentals. If the facility's net operating cost becomes a line item in the local government's annual budget, the facility is doomed to compete for funds each year with other municipal, county, or state government departments providing more vital community services like public housing, police, and fire protection. Furthermore, annual fund allocations will be heavily influenced by the all-too-frequent budgetary setbacks suffered by governments: declines in certain tax revenues, labor contract increases, across-the-board cuts, and the like. A facility that needs funding to pay net operating expenses would be well advised to delay development until a dedicated revenue stream or tax can be obtained.

Chapter 9

ECONOMIC IMPACTS: FISCAL BENEFITS VERSUS DEBT AND NET OPERATING COSTS

Identifying and measuring the specific economic consequences of a proposed development will enable project planners to determine the proper building size, to identify funding sources, and to gauge the possibilities or the necessity for additional hotel or commercial retail development. Many types of economic or development impacts are common to sports/entertainment venues and to convention centers alike, while others are unique to each of the two types of enterprise.

IMPACTS UNIQUE TO ARENAS AND STADIUMS

The theory of economic impact analysis is based on the premise that a facility hosts events that produce or export entertainment services and that import new dollars, spent by visitors, into the economy. This it does to the extent that it attracts attendees who would not otherwise spend dollars in the local economy. The new income is produced not only by nonresident spending but also by expenditures of local residents who, without the local center, would attend the same or similar events in venues outside the locality.

Given this premise, new income must be traced to where it is spent and then respent by successive recipients within and outside the local economy, producing what is called the multiplier effect. Through this methodology, one can measure the total benefit to the local economy deriving from new income, sales, jobs created, and taxes generated from the first round of (direct) spending and all subsequent (indirect or induced) spending rounds.

The first step in the analysis is to define the specific boundaries of the economic area within which the impact is to be measured. The local economy, or "economic universe," can be a neighborhood, a city, a county, an MSA (metropolitan statistical area), or a state. The economic universe must be defined to determine its exported services, imported revenue, and nonresident attendees. For example, nearly one-half of an NFL team's revenue comes from TV broadcasts; all of this income is new or incremental to the local economy. Therefore, it is important to determine how much the franchise spends on locally purchased supplies, equipment, rent, and other needs; how much is spent on team salaries and what percentage of the team resides within the locality; and what percentage of the team's budget is paid to nonresident businesses and individuals.

Remember that the economic impact will be reduced by the amount spent by local residents attending the event who would probably spend those dollars elsewhere in the local economy if the venue at which the event was held did not exist. It must also be determined how many of these total fan dollars are spent on concessions, merchandise, parking, and tickets. How much of the total ticket expenditures at a concert will the touring

The long-term economic impact of a facility like the Los Angeles Coliseum, which has been home to two Olympic games, is impossible to quantify.

Rupp Arena in Lexington has kept people at home rather than in Cincinnati or Louisville for concerts, games, or family shows.

act or cast and the promoter take out of the community? Certainly, for instance, the "leakage" for payments made to performers at an arena in Los Angeles will differ from that for an arena in Wichita, if the performers in both cases live in Los Angeles.

Expenditures by local residents must also be calculated when residents otherwise would have spent their dollars in a facility in another locale, or economic universe. For example, before the Rupp Arena was built in Lexington, Kentucky, local citizens traveled to Louisville or Cincinnati to attend concerts or to take their children to family shows. Similarly, because most NFL Jet and Giant season ticket holders reside in New York State, their expenditures would mean an increased (if not new) economic gain to New York State if the franchise or franchises could be lured back from New Jersey to facilities in New York.

To summarize, income is generated by fans, by tenants/events, and by the facility itself as money is spent within the local economy. To determine the economic impact, it is necessary to identify those center-dependent expenditures within the local economy that would not have occurred if the arena or stadium did not exist. To argue that spending by local residents will create jobs or income, it must be shown that their expenditures would otherwise have been made outside the local economy.

IMPACTS THAT DISTINGUISH CONVENTION CENTERS

Most events in large convention centers in major metropolitan areas attract the majority of their attendees from out of town. Figure 9-1 shows a breakdown of spending by convention delegates in 1993.

Large trade shows and conventions attract not only attendees and delegates but also exhibitors, association staff, and exhibition service contractors who stay in hotels and patronize local restaurants and retail shops. Spending per delegate by associations, exhibitors, and service contractors substantially increases the economic benefits of a convention or trade show, as shown in Figure 9-2. Return on investment (ROI) is measured in terms of new tax revenues created by convention delegates and trade-show attendee spending, in addition to the center's operating surplus or loss. ROI is reduced by the center's development cost, as amortized over its economic life.

While stadiums and arenas are built to entertain local residents, the primary motive for the development of convention centers is to attract nonresidents whose spending will infuse new money into the economy and create new jobs, increased sales, and more tax revenues. National conventions and trade shows draw more out-of-town and overnight attendees than do regional, state, or district events. Major cities and popular tourist destinations with an abundance of large, convention-class hotels and excellent air service capture more events with a

Figure 9-1

CONVENTION DELEGATE EXPENDITURES AT ALL TYPES OF CONVENTIONS IN 1993

Type of Expenditure	Total Expenditures[1]	Daily Expenditures
Hotel Rooms	$294.16	$ 84.53
Hotel Restaurants	77.25	22.20
Other Restaurants	78.53	22.57
Hospitality Suites	21.11	6.07
Entertainment	10.97	3.15
Recreation	5.00	1.44
Sporting Events	2.49	0.72
Sightseeing	9.63	2.77
Retail Stores	82.69	23.76
Local Transportation	12.31	3.54
Auto Rentals	16.66	4.79
Gasoline	9.19	2.64
Other	18.21	5.21
Total per Delegate	$638.20	$183.39

[1]Assumes 3.48 days per delegate.

Source: *1993 Convention Income Survey*, published by the International Association of Convention and Visitor Bureaus.

Figure 9-2

ASSOCIATION EXPENDITURES AT ALL TYPES OF CONVENTIONS IN 1993

Type of Expenditure	Average Expenditures[1]	Daily Expenditures
Exhibition-Space Fee	$14,937.95	$ 2,999.59
Additional Room Rentals	2,268.06	455.43
Food and Beverages	36,186.34	7,266.33
Staff Living Expenses	4,099.47	823.19
Equipment Rentals	7,429.62	1,491.89
Services Hired	5,719.72	1,148.54
Other	9,814.48	1,970.78
Total per Event	$80,455.64	$16,155.75
Average Spending per Delegate	$ 56.81	

[1]Assumes 4.98 days per convention.

Source: *1993 Convention Income Survey*, published by the International Association of Convention and Visitor Bureaus.

Figure 9-3

AVERAGE SPENDING PER DELEGATE IN 1993: INTERNATIONAL, NATIONAL, AND REGIONAL VERSUS STATE AND LOCAL CONVENTIONS

Type of Expenditure	International, National, and Regional[1]	State and Local[2]
Hotel Rooms	$382.26	$142.34
Hotel Restaurants	96.50	44.88
Other Restaurants	101.50	38.48
Hospitality Suites	31.12	5.19
Entertainment	15.17	4.15
Recreation	6.55	2.65
Sporting Events	3.49	0.94
Sightseeing	13.85	2.55
Retail Stores	96.82	59.76
Local Transportation	17.92	2.73
Auto Rentals	23.90	3.85
Gasoline	9.34	8.93
Other	20.40	14.61
Average Total per Delegate	$818.82	$331.06

[1]Assumes 4.10 days per delegate.
[2]Assumes 2.42 days per delegate.
Source: *1993 Convention Income Survey*, published by the International Association of Convention and Visitor Bureaus.

national membership or attendee base than do destinations with fewer hotel rooms and limited air service. These major destinations attract events with a longer length of stay and consequently higher delegate expenditures. Figure 9-3 illustrates the difference in spending by delegates at international, national, and regional events, as compared with state and local events.

Smaller convention centers and community centers typically host more events for local attendees than do larger centers in more popular destinations for tourists or business visitors. A convention center in a metropolitan area containing 5,000 hotel rooms may attract a small national convention, a few regional and state events, and several consumer shows. Consumer shows—like stadium or arena events—attract primarily local residents. Figure 9-4 shows the substantial range of economic impacts generated by centers in "gateway" cities (those with more than 20,000 hotel rooms), "national" cities (10,000 to 20,000 hotel rooms), and "regional" cities (fewer than 10,000 hotel rooms). This wide range of impacts results from the disproportionately larger share of national convention and trade-show delegates attending events in centers located in destinations with large inventories of hotel rooms.

DIRECT SPENDING AND THE MULTIPLIER EFFECT

Local business establishments receiving expenditures from event attendees at public assembly facilities respend this income for their various operating costs, such as payrolls, supplies, and services. If all businesses and other recipients of attendee spending reside in the local economy and respend their income locally, the local economy will capture 100 percent of the first and second spending rounds. Obviously, in each successive round of spending, some dollars will be paid (leaked out) to nonlocal sources. These leakages will diminish the size of each spending round, ultimately reducing it to zero.

The ability of a local economy to capture a high percentage of successive spending rounds will depend on its size and diversity. Studies of these phenomena are made possible by the use of econometric studies and input/output models that are designed to mimic local transactions. These studies are used to estimate the magnitude of the income and employment multipliers for each sector of the local or state economy, as broken down by SIC (standard industrial classification) business code. For example, the multiplier for one dollar

Figure 9-4

Total nonresident attendee spending in 1994, by market size[1]

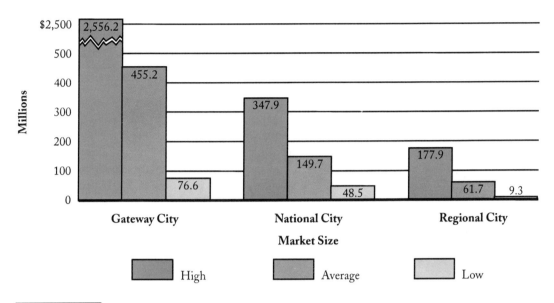

[1]Size of market refers to the number of hotel rooms in the metropolitan area, as reported by Smith Travel Service. Gateway markets are ones with more than 20,000 rooms; national, with 10,000 to 20,000 rooms; and regional, with fewer than 10,000 rooms.
Source: Price Waterhouse *Annual Convention Industry Report* (1995).

spent at a hotel may be less than that for one dollar spent at a local bakery.

Larger, more diverse economies have higher multipliers than do smaller communities because they are more likely to retain a larger portion of each successive round of spending. If the multiplier for an entire local economy is a weighted average of all of the separate multipliers for each sector of the economy, a city like Chicago may have a multiplier of two, which means that the total impact, or sum, of all expenditures through successive rounds is two times the initial expenditure.

It is proper to quantify each type of expenditure, e.g., hotel, taxi, or restaurant; enter it into the computerized input/output model; and calculate for the local economy. The econometric model is created from data obtained from an analysis of all businesses, broken down by type and size, in the local economy; the result is a measure of the value of the goods and services that each individual business imports and exports and of their relationships to each other. Through this process, the multiplier is calculated. Its use will produce a reliable and credible estimate of the local business activity resulting from visitor spending.

Results of economic impacts

It is not uncommon for a major new facility to cause new businesses to open, existing enterprises to expand, or new buildings to be built to house businesses such as an exposition services company, a catering firm, a security service, a new hotel, or a new restaurant. Many mixed-use developments (MXDs) contain a public assembly facility as a major component, if not as the centerpiece. Examples include Prudential Center in Boston, Lexington Center in Kentucky, Le Palais des Congres de Paris, Madison Square Garden, Suntec City in Singapore, Atlanta's Omni-CNN Center, and many others.

Careful analysis must be conducted to determine the share of event-generated expenditures that may realistically be captured by nearby businesses. The number and types of events, average attendance, and the capacities of nearby competitive businesses are all important factors. Many new hotels, restaurants, and the like have failed because they depended too much on capturing an unrealistic share of spending by a facility's attendees. Nevertheless, many new and existing businesses will benefit

An international boat show like this one at Earls Court in London attracts attendees from around the world who stay to eat, shop, and tour as a part of their visit.

from public assembly facilities; the number of new jobs, sales, and taxes they generate may be estimated through an economic impact analysis.

A public assembly facility can be an important component of a downtown revitalization or redevelopment plan. The role of the downtown as an entertainment center with specialty shops and restaurants has emerged in many cities to replace the regional retailing that abandoned most central cores in the 1960s and '70s. Entertainment elements and hotels make an attractive environment for Class A office space, which in turn reinforces and augments support for hotels, shops, and restaurants. The typically large supply of off-street parking facilities in a downtown both supports and is supported by a public assembly facility. This synergism has become very important to many successful downtowns, such as Cincinnati, Atlanta, Portland, Stockholm, Makuhari (near Tokyo), and many others.

ADDITIONAL COSTS

Occasionally, a community becomes concerned about the costs for the additional municipal services like police protection, water lines, and sewer capacity that a new facility will require. Traditionally, additional costs for off-site improvements (for water, sewer, roads, and so forth) required by a new center are included in the funding requirements and financing for the facility, that is,

they are included as part of the development cost. Costs for day-of-event traffic control and security services are usually reimbursed by the event producers or paid by the center as part of other day-of-event costs, such as expenses for ushers and ticket takers. The facility pays for solid waste disposal and monthly water and sewer services as would any other private development, and these costs are included in the annual operating budget.

Exceptions to this practice occur where the city or county public works crews maintain landscaping, remove snow, and perform other services, but such "free" services are uncommon today. All too frequently, a center is charged for a share of local government administrative costs, and the amount of the charge far exceeds the cost to the center if it had been able to obtain the administrative services it needed from alternative sources.

IMPLICATIONS FOR A FINANCING PLAN

One of the more useful applications of fiscal (new tax-revenue) impact analysis is in identifying funding sources and in structuring a center's financing plan. Ideally, those parties that receive the tangible benefits of the facility should pay pro rata shares of the annual net operating and debt-service costs.

If a convention facility generates substantial hotel room occupancy and retail sales, and if there is a strong enough supplementary market demand for these uses, for example, from downtown office visitors and employ-

The development of the Blossom Music Center increases the salaries of the members of the Cleveland Symphony Orchestra by adding a summer season; provides entertainment to a broad audience with its diverse schedule of classical, rock, and pop programs; and helps fund the symphony from its profits.

ees, then a new hotel or specialty retail development may be feasible. The economic impact analysis should facilitate planning for capital financing by answering questions such as: How many new hotel rooms, or how much additional retail and restaurant space, will be occupied? How much tax revenue will be generated from new retail sales, hotel room rentals, new building property taxes, and ticket taxes? Which government entities receive these taxes?

The cost-to-benefit ratio is particularly useful when it is known who pays the costs and who receives the benefits. If new taxes cannot be captured by the entity bearing the cost burden, a cost-to-benefit ratio of 1 to 10 is no help!

Sometimes, the existing tax structure does not permit the center developer to obtain the benefits in a tangible, or negotiable, form. But it is sometimes possible to amend or reconfigure the tax structure to enable the entity that is generating the additional spending to capture the new taxes. Frequently, a new facility will require legislation by the state or local government to provide a new tax—or an increase in an existing tax—on retail sales, hotel room rentals, restaurant meals, admissions to events, and nearby benefiting property. Likewise, if new private commercial development is warranted, land next to the new facility can be reserved for sale or lease to a private developer. In these ways, the impact analysis can quantify how much new business is being created, which development planning initiatives are needed to activate the new development, and, as specifically as possible, who benefits from these gains.

Recent fiscal impact analyses of convention centers have shown that state governments are receiving the largest share of tax-revenue increases generated by new convention centers. For example, studies of new tax revenues for city-sponsored convention-center development in Missouri, Massachusetts, and Illinois have revealed that state-level entities are receiving shares of total new taxes generated of 62 percent, 79 percent, and 70 percent, respectively. As a result of the findings of these types of studies as to beneficiaries, many states, including Georgia, Washington, Massachusetts, Illinois, New York, and Maryland, have decided to fund entirely or to assist in the annual financial support of new facilities. Whether the state assumes these obligations directly or remands a state tax-revenue increase to the sponsoring city or county through subventions, the community should know the extent to which its state treasury is benefiting

The Georgia World Congress Center, with 2.5 million square feet of space, was financed by the state of Georgia. Its existence was a key element in Atlanta's successful bid to host the 1996 Olympics.

and should work through its local legislative delegation to secure all or part of the new revenue.

While a public-assembly event in a specific city may be the primary motive for an attendee to plan a visit, other cities and regions within the state—particularly popular tourist-destination states like Massachusetts and Florida—may also reap benefits from attendee leisure travel before or after the event. For this reason, an analysis of the economic benefits induced by public assembly facilities should include the extra impact of added leisure-travel spending by convention delegates for pre- and post-event touring.

CONCLUSION

Public assembly facilities are promoted, built, and run for a wide variety of motives. These centers benefit various public and private groups in different ways. In each case, the combination of motivations, methods, and results is unique to local circumstances. Because the development process for this kind of facility cannot be standardized, the varied case studies in this book are intended to illustrate how sponsors of successful centers have designed financing plans given their own specific circumstances, resources, and goals. It is hoped that readers will learn from these accomplishments.

Chapter 10

FINANCING AND FUNDING

The cost to secure the intended benefit of a publicly financed convention, sports, or entertainment facility usually includes much more than the annual mortgage payment or debt-service (principal and interest) payments on the bonds. Furthermore, the amount of bonds sold may be two times greater than the construction cost. If the "sticker shock" following the opening of construction bids does not dampen support for a center, then the size of the bond issue often will have the same effect.

For many centers whose sponsors have bitten the bullet but still only provide funding for development costs, the center fails to function or to deliver the expected benefits because essential features, equipment, or reserves were cut from the budget. These unfunded costs often include parking facilities, food service equipment, essential pre-opening marketing costs, and funding of required reserves for the inevitable emergencies: major capital repairs, equipment needed but unanticipated in the budget, and other unforeseen requirements.

The financing plan should address:

- Development costs and net operating expenses.
- Sources of funds, and future revenue estimates for each source.
- Alternative methods of financing or funding annual fixed costs and operating subsidy.

Each of these topics will be discussed separately to help avoid what for many people is the confusion or mystique associated with the discussion of finance. The last section of this chapter will present various examples of funding plans for different types of facilities.

FUNDING NEEDS

The needs analysis must begin with a listing of all costs for the planning, development, operation, renewing or replacement, marketing, and support facilities for the center. The funding needs or budget analysis should not end unless and until all costs have been identified, including so-called indirect costs. The most effective means of ensuring the completeness or all-inclusiveness of this task is to make a careful inspection or evaluation of the total development, financing, and operating costs of similar centers. Evaluation will require in-depth analysis and interviews with key persons involved in the development, marketing, and operation of other centers: owners, operators, anchor tenants/teams/user groups, concessionaires, sales and marketing staff/CVB, local government finance director, financial advisers/bond underwriters, service contractors, and others.

PREDEVELOPMENT EXPENSES

Funding for planning and predevelopment expenses is usually harder to find than money for project construction because intangibles are valued more in hindsight or in their absence than they are during the predevelopment planning process. But this kind of funding should be recognized as an essential, integral part of the project itself. Unlike an office building, hotel, highway, fire station, or water treatment plant, a convention center's or sports facility's building program is one of a kind, and the center's location and site requirements should be determined by careful analysis of the needs of its unique mix of users. These needs often will vary with the other characteristics of the community in which an event or show will be held. A center built in the wrong location, with an inappropriate building program, or lacking funds to manage or market itself adequately will not fulfill its promises.

Therefore, if a center sponsor cannot fund predevelopment and predesign planning expenses of $1 million, it should seriously reconsider its intention to develop a $100 million center. More important, the sponsor should question the reliability of underfunded analysis of development costs and estimates of operating costs. Predevelopment planning costs must cover:

- Establishing and funding the operation and expense of a task force or committee to investigate the market support or user need for the facility.

- Identifying prospective user groups, building and site requirements, location characteristics, development and operating costs, and funding sources.
- Conducting studies of design options, site planning, and physical feasibility: building footprint and total size requirements, estimated construction costs, site load-bearing characteristics, vehicular circulation and parking studies, food service/acoustic/other technical needs analyses, and environmental impact studies.
- Obtaining predevelopment professional services for site survey, load testing, appraisal, legal counsel, and so on.
- Securing the right or option to purchase a site.

It is often essential to recruit the most respected and experienced civic project sponsors and business leaders to guide the predevelopment planning process. The credibility of their findings will depend on their track records for firsthand, hands-on management of other major, successful, one-of-a-kind projects. These community leaders ought to tour centers in other communities and to meet with their operators and tenants. It is especially helpful for them to meet their counterparts who, like themselves, were responsible for predevelopment planning. These planning expenses will usually be the most productive and will produce the highest values of all costs in the planning process.

Because a large percentage of centers in other communities clearly have not been properly planned, it is necessary to obtain upfront the public's confidence in the individuals leading the center's needs analysis and planning process. Thus, project planners should anticipate the need to overcome the initial skepticism of the press or elected officials, who may fear another boondoggle or a white-elephant public works project. Spending the first project dollars to ask the community's best minds to evaluate what others have done, that is, to conduct a reality check on other centers, and to determine the probability of success for a similar type of center in their own hometown will usually lay a strong foundation for a sound business plan. Or, just as important, it may result in an objective decision to abandon further plans for a center.

DEVELOPMENT COSTS

Besides predevelopment planning costs, development costs typically include expenses for bond issuance, land acquisition, off-site improvements, construction, and architecture and engineering fees. As stated at the start of this chapter, it is not unusual for total development costs to come to more than twice the cost of construction, as shown in Figure 10-1.

Hazards of underestimating center costs include the surprise or shock to project sponsors from several other doubling effects. First, the construction cost for the center will not be $75 per square foot, as it is for warehouse space, but $150 per square foot, as for hotel meeting rooms and banquet halls. Second, the gross building area required to accommodate 400,000 net square feet of exhibit, meeting, and ballroom space will be 800,000 square feet. Furthermore, the total development cost for the building in this example will not be $120 million (800,000 square feet x $150) but actually $200 million ($120 million in construction costs + site + soft costs + FF&E [furniture, fixtures, and equipment] + infrastructure + parking garage + off-site improvements + financing cost + interest capitalized during construction +++++). Business leaders experienced in funding total development costs for retail uses, offices, and hotels will not be dismayed at these doubling effects.

OPERATING EXPENSES

Operating expenses are usually greater than operating revenues for most public assembly facilities. Increasing competition for visitor spending and major league sports franchises has necessitated that the anticipated new tax dollars generated by a center be used to pay for net operating costs, i.e., those that remain after deducting operating revenues. New tax revenues must also be forfeited

Figure 10-1

COMPARISON OF CONSTRUCTION COSTS WITH TOTAL DEVELOPMENT COSTS

Construction	$100,000,000
Architect and Engineer Fees (soft costs)	11,000,000
Furniture, Fixtures, and Equipment	9,000,000
Site Acquisition (including appraisal)	15,000,000
Site Improvements, Demolition, etc.	6,000,000
Business Relocation Expense	12,000,000
Off-Site Improvements, Access Roads, etc.	18,000,000
Parking Garage	24,000,000
Bond Issuance (legal, printing, etc.)	2,000,000
Capitalized Interest Funding Cost	1,000,000
Underwriting Fees/Discount	2,000,000
Bond Sale Proceeds	200,000,000
Predevelopment Planning	1,000,000
Support Facilities	5,000,000
Total Development Costs	$206,000,000

United Center in Chicago is a joint venture between the owner of the Bulls and the owner of the Blackhawks and was privately funded with loans from the First Bank of Chicago of $140 million and $35 million in equity.

to pay annual debt service or the amortization of capital costs. Should government subsidy be justified, and if so, to what extent? The determination of how much subsidy may be reasonable is the subject of Chapter 9.

The importance of funding the full costs of a professional management staff and other operating expenses is at least as great as that of funding the costs for a state-of-the-art building. There are as many examples of successful centers with Class A operations in Class B buildings as there are in the reverse situation, if not more. Over time, the former combination is more profitable than the latter. Operating costs are discussed in Chapter 8.

REPLACEMENT

Replacement cost may be equated with true depreciation costs and should be considered an annual expense in addition to operating expense. This is the estimated annualized cost for major repairs, replacement, renovation, and improvements.

Many stadiums built in the 1970s with 30-year financing and still in good physical condition are being replaced in the 1990s, after only two decades' use, because they have been determined to be functionally and economically obsolete. As much as ten more years of debt payments remain to be funded on some buildings that have been razed. Therefore, economic life may be defined as the period during which a building is both

physically and financially functional, i.e., in competitive condition. The period of time it takes to wear out a carpet, chairs, or an air conditioning unit is obviously much shorter than the economic life of the building. It is essential to provide for these periodic capital improvements, equipment replacements, and major repairs, as well as for complete interior renovations. Most hotel owners and many centers provide for an annual allowance or payment of X percent of the original costs or Y percent of the operating budget to fund or build a reserve for these expenses.

Failure to provide for these expenses annually will result in future funding problems when these needs arise, and deferring repair or replacement will cause a loss of business. Unlike a pothole in the street, deferred maintenance in a public assembly facility will reduce future operating revenues because the facility's users, unlike a community's residents, do have venues in alternative destinations from which to choose.

MARKETING

Marketing costs for a convention or spectator-event center are proportionate to the vulnerability of its market share to the predatory habits of its competitors. The more centers a facility competes against for attendees or tenants, the greater its annual sales and marketing costs will be. Moscone Center in San Francisco and United Center in Chicago do not have to market themselves as aggressively as do convention centers or spectator venues in less popular destinations or in markets with two or more competing centers. Unfortunately, marketing budgets for civic centers, CVBs, and convention-center sales departments are normally funded from the same sources, which supply funding for the annual debt service incurred for financing construction costs.

Consequently, the funding of marketing costs for a public assembly facility must be considered while identifying funding sources for development and operating costs. Failure to identify and plan funding for marketing often means that the building's management and the local convention and visitors' bureau, its marketing group, will end up competing for the same hotel tax revenues.

SUPPORT FACILITIES

Support facilities have historically included parking garages and, more recently, hotels, festive retail, and entertainment centers. Communities that have funded all or most hotel development costs to enhance the marketability of their convention centers include Memphis, Minneapolis, Visalia (California), Providence, and many others. Many more cities are currently planning to do likewise, as are Miami, Tampa, Houston, and Chicago.

As Ludwig von Mises has observed, however, "Government intervention always breeds economic dislocations that necessitate more government intervention." This view may be related to the doctrine of the slippery slope, namely, that once you start slipping (subsidizing), you cannot stop. It often leads to counting the benefit of one visitor's spending several times over in order to justify the subsidies required for the center, its operation, its marketing, its hotel, its nearby attractions, and so forth.

Evaluating the justification for subsidizing support facilities can be based solely on fiscal impact considerations and often is. Or these facilities can become the focus of editorials espousing political and pseudo-economic philosophy. An objective analysis of site location requirements, parking, hotels, and other uses will usually reveal the need for support facilities before the center is built, rather than after.

AN OVERVIEW OF SOURCES OF FUNDING

Martin Millspaugh has observed that a project sponsor will often request its financial adviser to design an innovative funding plan, saying, "Don't be bound by what has been done by others," and "Don't give us a conven-

tional, plain-vanilla financing plan." Then, after the plan has been presented, the same sponsor will demand of the consultant: "Don't forget to name three examples in which the proposed financing method has proven successful in other cities, for similar projects."

In this context, readers are not advised to let their imaginations be their guides. The funding sources that have typically been identified and pledged to support center costs will ideally be those that meet the following criteria:

- The source is not pledged to fund the local government general fund, so that its use to fund a new center will not be expected to cause a tax increase.
- It is not specifically or exclusively dedicated to another purpose. That is, it is available, not previously committed.
- It is paid largely or completely by nonresidents.
- It equals the amount of increase in revenue produced by a tax that will generate more revenue because of the economic activity generated by the center, e.g., because of attendee spending. Sources that are most commonly pledged to fund center operations, marketing, and debt service are shown in Figure 10-2.
- The increase in an existing tax rate or levy of a new tax will not put the community at a competitive disadvantage.

SPECTATOR SPORTS AND ENTERTAINMENT CENTERS

Arena, stadium, and amphitheater development costs have historically been supported through state and local government bond financing. In recent years, though, more innovative financing techniques have been used to minimize the burden on taxpayers for debt repayment. Gone is the exemption from federal taxes of the interest received on municipal bonds that have been issued to finance facilities with a single, dominant private tenant or franchise. To fill the gap, widely varied financing techniques have been developed. For example, Giants Stadium and Byrne Meadowlands Arena in East Rutherford, New Jersey, were financed with parimutuel tax revenues from an on-site race track. This financing was in effect a diversion of tax revenue that otherwise would have flowed to the state of New Jersey's general fund, as similar revenue does in most other states.

The Cowboys' Texas Stadium in Irving, Texas, and the Dolphins' Joe Robbie Stadium in Miami were financed primarily through revenues from the sale and rental of box suites and premium seats. This method of financing depends heavily on a team's local popularity; in the case of Joe Robbie Stadium, it also rested on the willingness of the owner to enhance the security of the

Figure 10-2

FUNDING SOURCES

Source	Where Used
Casino taxes	Las Vegas
Center operating revenue	Chicago
Certificate of participation/lease-leaseback	St. Louis
Commercial building lease revenue	Santa Clara, Lexington
Development rights on adjacent land	Anaheim, Miami
Facility-specific admissions tax	Minneapolis
Increase in excise tax/sales tax for specified period	San Antonio
Increased hotel tax rate	Atlanta, St. Petersburg
Land appreciation through favorable rezoning	Sacramento
Municipal development of parking facilities	Milwaukee
Parimutuel tax revenue	New Jersey
Private contributions	Indianapolis, Chapel Hill, Milwaukee
Rights to concession franchise in other venues	Anaheim
State general obligation and revenue bonds/appropriations	(Several)
State incremental revenue/benefit subvention	St. Louis, Maryland
Sports lottery	Maryland, Oregon, Wisconsin
Tax increment financing	Salt Lake City
Use of land for venue at no or below-market cost	Miami

construction loan by a pledge of the team. The stated benefits of an arena or stadium frequently include the value of the facility as a recreational amenity for the citizens of a community, the new taxes and spending generated by out-of-town attendees, and the enhancement of the community's image or name recognition. Considering the wide range of types of benefits and mixes of bene-

ficiaries, perceived or real, it is not surprising—indeed, it is more common—to find a combination of financing methods and a variety of different funding sources used to underwrite the various subsidy requirements of a single center.

SIX STADIUMS

GEORGIA DOME

Business, civic, and government leaders began discussing the advantages of constructing a new stadium in Atlanta in the early 1980s. The existing Braves/Falcons stadium was less than 20 years old at that time. The development process, however, took more than eight years to complete. In 1985, the state, city, and county governments, along with local business leaders, formed a committee and contributed funds to study a myriad of options for a new stadium. The committee concluded that a domed stadium would generate more public support in Atlanta than would a second open-air stadium.

Georgia Dome construction was funded by state revenue bonds, which were to be repaid by sales of box suites and club seats, as well as by a portion of city and county hotel tax. This hotel tax was already in place when

To obtain the totally private funding required for Joe Robbie Stadium, the franchise owner had to put the franchise up as security for the completion of construction.

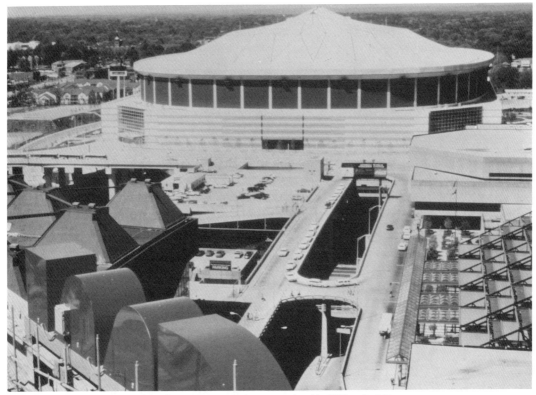

The financing and development of the Georgia Dome, which was completed in 1992, took eight years.

the Georgia Dome was developed, and there was no increase in the tax rate. Total cost of the facility was approximately $214 million, which included $14 million for site acquisition and $200 million for construction. The stadium has a maximum seating capacity of 80,000 and offers 102,000 square feet of exhibit space, which is used nine to 12 times a year to support events at the adjacent Georgia World Congress Center.

Because the Georgia Dome has shown a small surplus in each year, operations have not been subsidized. Replacement costs for the facility are funded through a reserve similar to that of the Georgia World Congress Center. Marketing costs are paid from the operating revenues of both the Georgia Dome and the Georgia World Congress Center, through the joint marketing department of the Congress Center Authority. Parking, which was developed at the time of the construction of the dome, was financed by the original bond issue.

ORIOLE PARK AT CAMDEN YARDS

Construction of Oriole Park at Camden Yards in Baltimore began in July 1989 and was completed in April 1992. The Maryland Stadium Authority, an independent agency of the state government, oversaw the facility's

planning and construction. The ballpark has a maximum seating capacity of 48,262, including 3,757 club seats and 72 private suites, and affords 5,200 parking spaces on site.

Costs for the development of Oriole Park totaled $237 million, including $100 million for site acquisition,

The Warehouse at Camden Yards, which extends the entire length of the right-field sideline, was rehabilitated for use as an office element in the new Orioles ballpark, providing another income stream for the overall funding package.

$106 million for construction, and $31 million in other costs. These costs were financed entirely by the state. Although the city provided about $46 million in infrastructure improvements, mainly highway and road construction and renovation, these improvements were already included in the city's ten-year plan. The ballpark's development did accelerate the completion schedule. The city also contributes $1 million per year toward payment of the state's general obligation bonds. Both the $46 million and the annual $1 million payment are financed through the city's general fund.

The state's portion has been funded by a general obligation bond issue financed by a cash "sports" lottery operated statewide, using $1 scratch-off tickets. This lottery is a special, additional series dedicated to the Mary-

land Stadium Authority solely for the development of Camden Yards baseball and football stadium. Predevelopment costs were funded by the stadium authority and a special commission appointed by the mayor.

Operating costs are covered by Oriole rent. There is no operating deficit at Camden Yards. Though the stadium lost 25 games in 1994 because of the baseball strike, these lost games were split between two fiscal years. Thus, the facility was able to generate enough revenue for both fiscal years to cover operating costs. Replacement costs are covered by a state fund deriving from Orioles revenues, as is the capital improvement fund, part of the stadium authority's operating revenues. This fund requires a minimum payment of $200,000 per year and a maximum payment stipulated by the lease with the Orioles of $800,000 per year. Marketing costs are paid by the Orioles.

COMISKEY PARK

Chicago's Comiskey Park began construction in May 1989 and opened in April 1991. Owned by the Illinois Sports Facilities Authority and operated by the Chicago White Sox, the stadium has a maximum seating capacity of 44,321, which includes the seating accommodated in 90 private suites and 1,800 club seats. There are 7,500 on-site parking spaces.

Total project costs for Comiskey Park approximated $187 million: $135 million for building construction and stadium FF&E costs, $30 million for site acquisition, $8 million for architect fees, and $14 million for contingencies, underwriting, and other miscellaneous costs. The facility, which was primarily funded by bonds issued by the Illinois Sports Facilities Authority, finances its costs with revenue from a 2 percent hotel/motel tax levied in the city of Chicago and from rental payments made by the White Sox. The team pays rent to the Illinois Sports Facilities Authority on a per attendee basis for full paid attendance above 1.2 million and also pays the authority a portion of its broadcast revenues.

The team, which receives an annual $2 million operating subsidy from the authority, operates Comiskey Park and is responsible for paying all stadium operating expenses.

INDIANA CONVENTION CENTER AND RCA DOME

The Indiana Convention Center opened in Indianapolis in 1972 with 124,000 square feet of exhibit space. The second phase of the project, begun in 1982, included the construction of the RCA Dome.

Marion County, Indiana, issued $15.5 million in general obligation bonds in 1969 for the purpose of con-

New Comiskey Park is owned by the Illinois Sports Facilities Authority and was funded with revenue bonds, backed by a 2 percent hotel/motel tax.

HOK Sports

The RCA Dome in Indianapolis was funded by a public/private construction financing campaign.

structing the original Indiana Convention Center. Funds to cover the cost of the second phase, which totaled $95 million, including $78 million for the RCA Dome, were raised by a successful public/private construction financing campaign. The Lilly Endowment and the Krannert Charitable Trust gave $30 million in gifts and grants, while the sale of county excise tax revenue bonds raised an additional $48 million. A 5 percent hotel tax and 1 percent food and beverage tax are collected within Marion County to pay debt service on these bonds, with the remaining revenue from the taxes going to the complex's capital improvement and operating fund.

In 1991, Marion County revenue bonds were sold to finance a $43 million Phase III expansion and renovation that took place in 1993. This financing retired the old debt and combined it with Phase III needs to take advantage of lower interest rates at the time. The center and RCA Dome receive no property taxes; nor will property taxes be used to pay off the revenue bonds. Rather, these revenue bonds are financed through excise taxes in the form of county hotel/motel taxes, food and beverage taxes, a professional sports admissions tax on dome events, and a tax on cigarettes.

The revenue generated per year from the hotel/motel tax within Marion County is approximately $9.5 million, while the food and beverage tax generates some $10.6 million per year within the county. The county admissions tax and cigarette tax produce roughly $650,000 and $350,000 per year, respectively. In 1994, the total collection for these four taxes approximated $21 million.

The capital improvement fund, which is financed by the hotel/motel tax, restaurant tax, admissions tax, and cigarette tax, is used to cover operating costs and replacement costs, as well as marketing for the complex. The replacement fund budget must be no lower than $5 million per year and has historically ranged from $5 million to $7.5 million. Though center staff markets the convention center in conjunction with the Indianapolis Convention and Visitors' Association, the capital improvement board is responsible for RCA Dome marketing and maintenance.

ALAMODOME

San Antonio's Alamodome was completed in 1993. The 65,000-seat stadium is located adjacent to downtown San Antonio and is connected via walkways under Interstate 37 to the convention center and HemisFair Park. The stadium floor offers 160,000 square feet of exhibition space and is occasionally used for consumer and trade shows.

Total cost of the Alamodome was $186.3 million, which was funded by a state-legislated half-cent sales tax within San Antonio and surrounding cities. This tax was permitted for a five-year period and generated enough funds to retire all debt for construction of the dome.

Operating costs of the Alamodome are funded by the facility's revenues. It requires no subsidy. Marketing costs of the facility are covered by the CVB, while replacement costs are funded based on projections of revenues. The Alamodome also has an emergency fund for capital improvements.

CERVANTES CONVENTION CENTER AND TRANSWORLD DOME

When the original Cervantes Convention Center in St. Louis was completed in 1977, it provided approximately 240,000 square feet of prime exhibit space. In 1993, Phase II construction was completed, increasing exhibit space by 100,000 square feet. A domed stadium, the TransWorld Dome, adjacent to Cervantes Convention Center, was completed in 1995 and contains 70,000 fixed seats and an additional 162,000 square feet of exhibit space on the stadium floor.

Figure 10-3

STADIUM DEVELOPMENT COSTS AND FINANCING SOURCES (millions)

Stadium	Cost	General Obligation Bonds	Revenue Bonds	Private Contributions	Other Sources
Georgia Dome	$214	–	$214	–	–
Oriole Park at Camden Yards	287	$283	–	–	$ 4
Comiskey Park	187	–	178	$ 9	–
RCA Dome	95	15.5	48	30	0.5
Alamodome	186	–	–	–	186[1]
TransWorld Dome	265	265	–	–	–

[1]Sales tax revenues that had accumulated within the locality before dome completion.

Total cost of Phase I construction (the convention center only) was about $30 million. Repayment of the bonds sold to fund this phase was made from a pledged increase in the city's restaurant tax rate and a $2 surcharge on occupied hotel rooms.

Phase II construction (the expansion of the convention center) cost approximately $130 million, which was paid from the proceeds of bonds backed by annual appropriations from the general revenue fund of the city of St. Louis.

Budgeted to cost $265 million, the dome receives funding from a series of tax-exempt bonds issued by the St. Louis Regional Convention and Sports Complex Authority. City, county, and state appropriations will repay the bond issues, with the state of Missouri furnishing 50 percent of the financing and the city and the county sharing equally in the repayment of the remaining 50 percent. To finance its share, the county is increasing its hotel room occupancy tax.

Under its agreement with the sports complex authority, the St. Louis Convention and Visitors' Commission is responsible for marketing the dome and convention center, as well as for operating the center. Before the stadium was completed in 1995, the operating subsidy was paid from the city's general fund. But as of October 1995, the net operating costs of the Cervantes Convention Center and the TransWorld Dome are paid by the St. Louis Regional Convention and Sports Complex Authority. Future replacement costs are estimated at approximately $4 million per year and are financed by appropriations from the city, county, and state.

Figure 10-3 summarizes the revenue sources used to cover stadium construction and development costs at the six facilities described in this section.

A CHECKLIST OF INDIVIDUAL FINANCING SOURCES AND METHODS

NAMING RIGHTS

A large amount of upfront capital can be raised through either the sale or the lease of a facility name to a private corporation. Venues that have used this financing vehicle include:

- BankOne ballpark in Phoenix, with a payment of $66 million over 30 years.
- America West Arena in Phoenix, with $26 million over 30 years from America West Airlines.
- Fleet Center in Boston, with $30 million over 15 years from Fleet Bank.
- Hardee's Walnut Creek Amphitheatre in Raleigh, North Carolina, with a Hardee's payment of $1.2 million.

With a number of larger corporations evaluating new forms of advertising, this type of financing is often a viable option.

SALES OF ADVERTISING RIGHTS

Advertising rights within a stadium or arena are sold or leased to derive an annual source of revenue. Interior advertising usually consists of scoreboard messages during an event and billboards placed throughout the facility.

Recently, buildings have been trading the capital costs, installation, and operating expenses of new computer-controlled scoreboards for all or part of the advertising generated by this equipment. For example, a stadium contracts with a scoreboard manufacturer to install such a system, and in return the manufacturer receives a major share of the advertising rights. The manufacturer then pays the stadium a fixed or percentage rent annually, based on the revenue the ads generate.

SEAT PREFERENCE BONDS

Seat preference bonds are sold to individuals or corporations, allowing them the right to purchase season tickets in prime viewing locations within an arena or stadium. This revenue source is a viable alternative when the stadium project is popular and supported by the general public. Texas Stadium successfully sold $19 million in seat preference bonds to finance most of its original construction costs. A refinement of this concept, the permanent seat license or PSL, was developed and promoted by Max Muhlman to raise $150 million to cover 62 percent of the cost of constructing Carolina Stadium in Charlotte.

JOINT DEVELOPMENT REVENUES

Real estate development adjacent to a sports facility site might well include hotel and office components. Ground lease revenue from hotel and office developers can produce an annual stream of funds that supplements other income available for debt service. Obviously, this potential relies on the marketability and availability of adjacent land for a major commercial building.

GENERAL OBLIGATION BONDS

When general obligation bonds are used to finance stadium and arena facilities, annual debt-service payments are made from the community's general fund. Because the facility may be operated by a department of the local government, any excess revenue coming from operations can be paid into the general fund. This revenue may be sufficient to retire the debt, or it may be pledged to an enterprise fund and dedicated to pay for future capital improvements or to cover operating deficits. Regardless of the level of net operating income or deficit, the governmental unit is obligated to pay debt service from any and all available sources.

REVENUE BONDS

Revenue bonds are secured by defined or specific tax revenue sources. The most obvious source of revenue is the annual proceeds from facility operations after expenses have been deducted. This source is sometimes referred to as a "straight" revenue bond. Most revenue

bonds, however, are supplemented or backed by additional dedicated revenue sources like a hotel room tax, an admission tax, a food and beverage tax, or a general sales tax. Without one or more of these additional revenue sources, most arenas or stadiums could not generate enough income from operations to make a revenue bond a viable financing option.

Special-purpose tax levies represent a means by which capital costs may be linked with recurring benefits, and the levies are typically aimed at those sectors of the local economy that directly benefit from the public assembly facility. But because this source of funding is a specified revenue stream, it is not backed by the full faith and credit of a governmental entity, as is a general obligation bond, and the interest rate is usually higher than the cost of general obligation borrowing.

TAX INCREMENT BONDS

Tax increment or tax allocation bonds are secured by a pledge of the net increases in property taxes resulting from the added taxable buildings within a defined redevelopment district. The success of this type of financing depends on the establishment of a strong redevelopment district that is successful in attracting new commercial development projects. Most major metropolitan areas have access to state legislation that enables the use of this financing technique.

INTERGOVERNMENTAL AGREEMENTS

These are joint agreements between two units of local government, for example, a city and a county, in which each unit agrees to fund a portion of the proposed facility.

One source of development funding is the naming of the facility. Hardee's paid $1.2 million to the Hardee's Walnut Creek Amphitheater in Raleigh.

Special venues like the Pettit National Ice Center, the only Olympic training facility for speed skating in the United States, need unique benefactors. Jane and Lloyd Pettit have donated more than $6 million to the development of the $13.3 million-dollar facility and have established an annual endowment fund for operations.

Spreading the cost of the facility among two or more government entities lessens the financial burden of building the facility. This method is also fair because a new public assembly facility, particularly an arena, benefits more people than just the citizens of the community in which it is located. For example, the Mid-South Coliseum in Memphis was financed by a joint city-and-county agreement in which the city supplied 60 percent of the funds and the county provided the remaining 40 percent.

COLLEGE OR UNIVERSITY FUNDING

Educational institutions or systems have provided funding assistance for the construction of arena facilities. These facilities have not always been located on university property or owned by the university. Naturally, the facilities meet many of the needs of the university by providing a home for varsity sports programs, as well as space for educational programs. Student activities fees are the primary source of revenue for most university facilities.

PRIVATE DONATIONS

Private donations represent another potential form of funding. In many cases, an individual benefactor or a foundation provides these funds. The Dean E. Smith Center at the University of North Carolina, Chapel Hill, was funded solely through private donations, primarily from alumni. Bradley Center, home of the Milwaukee Bucks, was funded almost entirely by a grant from Jane Pettit in memory of A.E. Bradley, her father.

ILLUSTRATIVE FINANCING PLANS FOR FOUR ARENAS/RELATED FACILITIES

An examination of how arena sponsors have devised their own, sometimes unique financing plans can provide some insight into creative yet realistic solutions of the funding issue. Funding experiences at the following centers are here examined: the Charlotte Coliseum in Charlotte, North Carolina; the Dean E. Smith Center at the University of North Carolina; Lexington Center in Lexington, Kentucky; and the Leon County Civic Center in Tallahassee, Florida.

CHARLOTTE COLISEUM

The Charlotte Coliseum provides permanent seating for 22,000 people and with portable seating will hold 23,800 spectators for basketball. The city's share of construction costs of $47 million were financed entirely by general obligation bonds issued by the city of Charlotte. This bond issue, which passed a public referendum in November 1984, included an additional $16 million for various road improvements.

The annual debt service for these bonds is paid from the city's general fund. In addition to traditional general fund sources, such as ad valorem taxes, approximately $2 million per year from a hotel room tax is earmarked for the retirement of the debt. This represents the city's share of the 3 percent room tax designated for use on visitor-related facilities.

DEAN E. SMITH CENTER

The Dean E. Smith Center arena, with a total seating capacity of 22,000, opened in 1986 on the campus of the University of North Carolina at Chapel Hill. Funding for the $33.8 million facility came exclusively from private donations made to the university's Education Foundation, which raises money for athletic scholarships.

LEXINGTON CENTER

Lexington Center contains a 24,000-seat arena, a 62,000-square-foot exhibit area, eight meeting rooms, and a 1,100-seat theater known as the Opera House. In addition, 100,000 square feet of specialty retail and a 370-room hotel are among the privately developed components of this mixed-use and mixed-ownership development.

The following sources contributed funds in these approximate amounts to offset the annual operating expenses and debt-service requirements of Lexington Center:

Operating revenues of public assembly facilities (rents, concessions, parking, and other)	$2,000,000
Hotel lease rental (1979–1980)	500,000
Retail lease rental	300,000
Display advertising	100,000
Income from investment of bond reserve funds	400,000
Contribution from county hotel taxes	500,000
Additional income from parking facility	200,000
Funds from city/county payroll tax generated by Lexington Center operations	100,000
Annual value to city of debt owed to federal government by city's urban renewal agency (debt was cancelled as a result of Lexington Center development)	300,000
Net added cost to city/county government	500,000
Total: Covers annual debt service at $2,600,000, plus operation expense at $2,300,000 per year (1988)	$4,900,000

Lexington Center's total 1974 project cost of $49.2 million, including the Opera House and excluding the hotel, was funded from the following sources:

Earnings on bond funds invested during construction	$6,100,000
Contribution from city/county hotel tax revenues during construction	1,000,000
Contribution from city/county general fund during construction	1,100,000
Grant from state of Kentucky	4,000,000
Bond sale proceeds	37,000,000
Total	$49,200,000

This financing plan illustrates a successful effort to link operating and capital cost funding from ten different sources (city, county, state, hotel, retail, college team, arena operations, parking, hotel tax, and reserve fund earnings) to the various groups served by the center and by the tax increases it generates.

LEON COUNTY CIVIC CENTER

Tallahassee, the state capital of Florida, opened its new civic center complex in 1981. The facility contains an arena with 13,500 seats, 40,000 square feet of exhibit space, a full-preparation kitchen, and six meeting rooms seating from 65 to 1,200 people. Total project costs of $33.4 million (in 1978) were met from the following sources:

Florida State University/Florida A&M University	$12,200,000
Leon County	6,000,000
City of Tallahassee	6,000,000
Economic Development Administration (federal grant)	3,200,000
State of Florida	6,000,000
Total	$33,400,000

The center's annual net operating deficit each year is funded from the city, county, Florida State University, and Florida A&M University, thereby allocating costs to the various sectors of the community that benefit from the facility.

A CLOSER LOOK AT THE FINANCING OF CONVENTION CENTERS

Convention centers often are financed from hotel tax revenues. Like stadiums and arenas, they also receive substantial financing from general obligation bonds. And in rare instances, as at Lexington Center, a financing plan can be structured with a pledge of multiple revenue streams. The difficulty in structuring a complex plan like that of Lexington Center is amplified by the need to execute numerous public/private agreements simultaneously. Failure to obtain timely support from any one of the participants would have caused a complete reconfiguration of the project. Lexington succeeded only because of the dedicated, long-term support of the community's civic and business leadership. Most communities would be well advised not to attempt to secure such complex financing.

Some communities have explored the feasibility of financing their convention centers with revenues pledged from nearby hotel properties. These financing plans have identified various funding sources from special assessment districts to room reservation fees. While such methods are logical and make sense in theory, to date no financing plan has relied on them. The strategy of the special assessment district would be to tax the visitor-supported commercial property or revenues of the hotels closest to the convention center, on the presumption that they would derive the greatest direct benefit from the center's operation. Room reservation fees would be based on the Atlantic City CVB funding concept: hotels would pay a certain fee for rooms occupied by visitors attending events at the convention center, assuming that these visitors can be identified. As of this writing, neither of these techniques has been used to finance the development of a convention center. More traditional methods of financing convention centers are illustrated in Figure 10-4.

Ideally, those who benefit financially from the development would pay, in proportion to their benefit, to finance the center. In practice, the fiscal structure in most locations means that far more tax revenues generated by convention centers go to state government than to local government. Delegate spending in major cities generates taxes from hotels, retail sales, restaurant food and beverage sales, and wage/income taxes, among other sources. Recent studies have revealed that state-government benefits from the tax-revenue increases generated by convention centers are four to five times greater than local government tax benefits.

Not surprisingly, compelling arguments have been made for state governments to share the responsibility for developing convention centers. Furthermore, studies of the travel patterns of convention delegates and trade-show attendees in certain areas reveal extensive leisure visits to other parts of the state before and after a meeting. This is especially true in tourist destinations like California, Oregon, Washington, Colorado, and Florida. In other words, a convention center generates substantial pre- and post-event tourism, which benefits the state and localities, further justifying the state's participation in financing the center. Indeed, states recently have become much more involved in convention-center financing. Notable examples include Massachusetts, Georgia, New York, Washington, Oregon, Colorado, Missouri, Louisiana, Illinois, Pennsylvania, Rhode Island, Indiana, and Maryland.

The story of the Baltimore Convention Center illustrates how a state worked with a city to finance a new center in the mid-1970s. The state of Maryland financed the facility according to an agreement with Baltimore that set specific goals and quotas for the city to meet regarding tax revenues to the state from convention-center delegate spending.

ILLUSTRATIVE FINANCING PLAN FOR A CONVENTION CENTER

The original Baltimore Convention Center, which was constructed in 1979, provided 195,000 square feet of exhibit space. It is now undergoing a two-phased expansion: the first stage of expansion will increase exhibit space by 105,000 square feet and will cost $151 million, and the second stage, estimated to cost approximately $9 mil-

lion, will consist of renovations to older parts of the building and will not begin until the new section is complete. It is expected that both stages will be complete in 1997.

Total cost of the original Baltimore Convention Center was $51 million. The state of Maryland authorized $35 million to aid in planning, design, and construction of the original center, while the city provided the balance. The state's authorization required an agreement between the city and state in which the city pledged to fulfill its obligations to this debt if it was unsuccessful in attracting an agreed-upon number of nonresident attendees annually.

A convention-center committee was formed and devised a formula to determine whether spending by out-of-state meeting attendees at convention-center events for a given year generated enough hotel/motel tax revenue for the state so that it could meet the debt service. To compute state hotel/motel tax revenue generated by convention-center activity, the committee used data collected from motels and hotels within a 20-mile radius of the center. To obtain the amount of state hotel/motel tax revenue collected per delegate-day, the city and the state agreed upon a formula that reflects the distinctions between the spending habits of in-state delegates and those of out-of-state delegates. The convention-center committee is responsible for the data collection and computation of state hotel/motel tax revenues, as well as for monitoring state tax policy and implementing any needed changes in the formula. Any deficiency in state tax revenue from a particular year that is greater than the cumulative surpluses from previous years will be paid by the city.

Funding for the current $151 million expansion is being provided both by the state of Maryland (66 percent, or $101 million) and by the city of Baltimore (33 percent, or $50 million). The city's portion was made available by a revenue bond issue financed through an existing 7 percent local hotel tax. There is currently a pledge to increase the hotel tax to cover the city's portion of the debt service. The state's portion was funded by general obligation bonds financed by a combination of a state sales tax ($46 million) and the general revenue fund of the state ($55 million). The city does not receive any of the income from the 5 percent statewide sales tax.

Predevelopment costs for the most recent expansion were made available by the city, the state, and the private sector, at 25 percent, 50 percent, and 25 percent, respectively. Approximately $1.7 million was budgeted for predevelopment planning, including design and site plans. At least in part, the monies loaned to fund this budget were repaid by the proceeds of the general obligation bond issue for the center.

Figure 10-4

Illustrative Financing Methods for Convention Centers (millions)

City	Total Cost	Sources
Baltimore Convention Center		
Phase I	$51.0	$35.2—State appropriations
		$15.8—City appropriations
Phase II	151.0	$100.4—State general obligation bonds financed by state sales tax and general revenue fund
		$50.6—City revenue bonds financed by city hotel tax
Dallas Convention Center		
Phase I	$8.9	General obligation bonds financed by property taxes
Phase II	32.0	Revenue bonds financed by hotel/motel and alcoholic beverage taxes
Phase III	33.0	Revenue bonds financed by hotel/motel and alcoholic beverage taxes
Phase IV	90.9	Revenue bonds and certificates of obligation financed by increased hotel/motel and alcoholic beverage taxes
Georgia World Congress Center		
Phase I	$35.2	State general obligation bonds
Phase II	93.0	State general obligation bonds
Phase III	98.0	State general obligation bonds
Los Angeles Convention Center		
Phase I	$35.0	30-year bonds, certificates of participation
Phase II	487.0	Revenue bonds financed by hotel/motel tax and Community Redevelopment Agency funds

Center operating deficits are funded by the city using a portion of its hotel tax, while replacement costs are included in a fund jointly provided half by the city and half by the state. The Maryland Stadium Authority assumes some maintenance of the facility, and marketing costs are funded by the city through its CVB and center staff. According to the Baltimore CVB, however, the bureau has not received any funding for the marketing of the center in the last year. At present, the CVB is soliciting the state, city, and private businesses to fund a proposed $235,000 annual marketing budget for the center for the next three years. Negotiations are currently taking place on this issue. The bureau, which spent about $100,000 on marketing the expansion of the center last year, obtained this money from other areas of its own budget, as there was no funding from the city.

PART II
U.S. CASE STUDIES

CHASTAIN PARK

ATLANTA, GEORGIA

Originally envisioned as a showplace for recreation, Chastain Park has served metropolitan Atlanta residents for more than 50 years. So, too, has its amphitheater.

DEVELOPMENT STRATEGY

In the 1940s, a group of Fulton County commissioners led by Troy G. Chastain decided to develop a recreational showpiece to attract residential development to the area. An amphitheater, stables, 18-hole golf course, tennis center, pool, and picnic grounds were all constructed as part of the original development of Chastain Park on county-owned land. Many of these facilities were built by the Works Projects Administration (WPA) and by labor from a temporary prison farm nearby.

The city of Atlanta annexed Chastain Park as part of its 1952 Plan of Improvement. In September 1946, the Fulton County Commission had named the park in honor of Chastain, having developed it as Chastain had intended. The only major additions to the original design have been the ballfields, built in 1952, and the gymnasium, erected in 1972.

DESIGN AND SITE ISSUES

Chastain Park occupies the site of a Creek Indian village on the floodplain of Nancy Creek in northern Fulton County. Over the years, this floodplain has been filled with land to a depth of more than ten feet, and it is believed that the remains of the Indian village exist below this fill. Development of the 268-acre park began in 1940, when riding stables were built to house horses for shows and for the nearby polo fields. New stables were built in 1945. Later, the stables were converted into a restaurant and the polo fields into ball fields, which were considered more useful to the general public.

An 18-hole golf course designed by Walter Hagan was added in 1943. In 1948, the National Public Links Golf Tournament was held at Chastain Park—the first time it was ever held in the South. Before the tournament, a main clubhouse was built, and the original one became the women's clubhouse. In 1986, to lessen the city's maintenance responsibility, the golf course was leased to American Golf, a private organization that maintains the links.

Chastain, determined that the park would be a model recreational facility, built a tennis center with nine courts that was said to rival Jekyll Island (a resort area located off the coast of southern Georgia). A new tennis-center pro shop has been completed to replace the former one, which was destroyed by fire in 1979. The courts themselves have been remodeled over the years.

The original Olympic-size swimming pool was designed with competition in mind. Indeed, swimming teams came from as far away as Havana to compete at the Chastain Park pool. A bathhouse that was built in addition to the pool has since undergone many renovations.

An amphitheater was also a part of Chastain's original plan. The site chosen was a natural bowl formation, and the venue was designed to resemble another facility

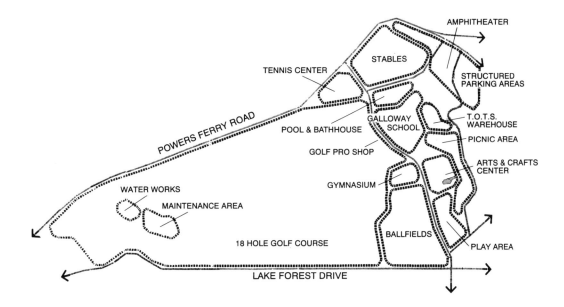

Map labels:
AMPHITHEATER
STABLES
TENNIS CENTER
STRUCTURED PARKING AREAS
POWERS FERRY ROAD
GALLOWAY SCHOOL
T.O.T.S. WAREHOUSE
POOL & BATHHOUSE
PICNIC AREA
GOLF PRO SHOP
ARTS & CRAFTS CENTER
GYMNASIUM
WATER WORKS
MAINTENANCE AREA
18 HOLE GOLF COURSE
BALLFIELDS
PLAY AREA
LAKE FOREST DRIVE

in Richmond, Virginia. The 6,000-seat amphitheater opened in June of 1944.

The only major recent addition to the park, a gymnasium, was completed in 1972. This facility includes a weight room, gymnasium/basketball court, locker rooms, and one handball/racquetball court. The Northside Youth Organization partially funded the gymnasium's development.

MARKET ORIENTATION

The park, which is situated in an affluent residential neighborhood in northeastern Atlanta, attracts visitors from a 50-mile radius to enjoy the facilities. Access to Chastain Park is easily gained from Interstate 75.

The Chastain Park amphitheater is leased to the Atlanta Symphony and to Southern Promotions, a company that promotes popular music concerts. The summer season draws people from all over metropolitan Atlanta with middle-of-the-road and nostalgia performers such as John Denver, Patti LaBelle, Stevie Nicks, and Neil Sedaka.

FINANCING

The park's most recent renovations, which cost about $500,000, were funded by the city of Atlanta.

LESSONS LEARNED

- Because of development around the park, traffic management is a problem. When the park was originally developed, most residents did not own automobiles.
- Nearby residents have expressed their concern about noise from concerts, and the city requires that all concerts end by 11:00 p.m. As a voluntary measure, the parks department monitors every concert to ensure that the sound level is less than 85 decibels.

PROJECT DATA

CHASTAIN PARK
ATLANTA, GA

Owner: City of Atlanta
Developer: Fulton County/City of Atlanta
Architects: Walter Hagan (design of golf course)
Planning Began: 1940

PROJECT INFORMATION
Site Area: 268 acres
Total Parking: 1,100
Amphitheater Seating: 6,000

BLOSSOM MUSIC CENTER

CUYAHOGA FALLS, OHIO (CLEVELAND AREA)

Roger Mastroianni

Blossom Music Center, summer home of the Cleveland Symphony Orchestra, is one of the more respected cultural and entertainment facilities in North America. Honoring the Dudley S. Blossom family, longtime supporters of the Cleveland Orchestra, the facility is owned and operated by the Musical Arts Association as a nonprofit organization. Located on the edge of an unspoiled national recreation area, Blossom attracts users with its picturesque setting, diverse schedule, accessibility, and fine musical entertainment.

Blossom was opened in 1968, in commemoration of the Cleveland Orchestra's 50th-anniversary season. The center has an exclusive agreement with an outside agency to promote all contemporary/popular music concerts. The income generated by its rock concerts helps to maintain and improve the facility, as well as to meet a portion of the costs of symphonic programs.

DEVELOPMENT STRATEGY

Blossom Music Center was conceived in 1966, when the board of trustees of the Musical Arts Association recognized the need for a summer home for the Cleveland Symphony Orchestra. The trustees realized that not only would a facility like Blossom boost salaries of the orchestra's musicians, but also it would give music lovers outside Cleveland's downtown the chance to hear music performed by an internationally recognized orchestra.

Accordingly, the board asked Pietro Belluschi to serve as architectural adviser for the project and engaged the firm of Schafer, Flynn & van Dijk to design the complex. Christopher Jaffe was invited to complete the preliminary acoustical design work for Blossom's pavilion, while Heinrich Keilholz, the German acoustical engineer responsible for the acoustical renovation of Severance Hall in Cleveland, was employed to design Blossom's acoustical shell. Ground was broken on July 2, 1967, and, after a fast-track design/construction period, Blossom Music Center's inaugural concert took place on July 19, 1968, as part of the Cleveland Orchestra's 50th-anniversary celebration season.

DESIGN AND SITE ISSUES

The Blossom complex is anchored by Blossom Pavilion, which has won awards such as the 1969 Architectural Award for Excellence from the American Institute of Architects. Consisting of two buildings, the pavilion's main structure stands at the base of a natural bowl formation and seats 5,281 people under its roof. A four-acre, grassy seating area slopes up from the pavilion and holds a maximum of 13,500 additional persons, each with an unobstructed view of the pavilion's 3,500-square-foot stage. Lawn seating is illuminated by three 85-foot light towers, each supporting 16 to 22 lighting instruments.

The Blossom stage has its own air conditioning system, which expels hot air through ventilators on the top of the rear wall while drawing cooler air from the sides. A mechanical dehumidifying system complements this natural air flow and maintains a continuous current of air around the performers at a constant temperature and humidity.

Beneath the stage are two levels of rooms that provide support services for performers and technicians. The first level contains dressing rooms, practice rooms, storage space, and a recording studio for taping the orchestra's concerts. A subbasement beneath the dressing-room level contains the air dehumidifying system, an emergency power generator, and major electrical junction boxes.

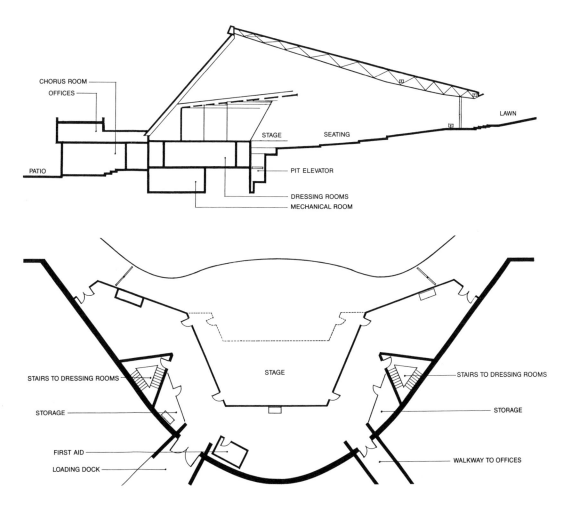

The 10,000-watt sound reinforcement system projects sound through three groups of speakers: one, at the edge of the pavilion roof overlooking the lawn; a second, at the lip of the acoustical shell; and a third, along the apron of the stage. This last group is composed of portable speakers. No amplification is needed within the pavilion during orchestra concerts, although some is required for special events. The additional speakers serving the pavilion's lawn seating project sound that reaches the listeners at the same instant as the sound is made on stage.

An ancillary building standing to the rear of the main pavilion is connected to it by a covered walkway at stage level. It houses a chorus room, an open terrace, private dressing rooms, the orchestra's library management offices, and studios for guest soloists and permanent and visiting conductors.

Other facilities and services include:

■ Eells Art Gallery, which presents major works of well-known artists on the evenings of orchestra performances. Situated just inside Blossom's main gate, the gallery often features chamber music performed by students from the Blossom Festival School.

■ The Frank E. Joseph Garden, planted in 1970 to honor the chairman of the board of the Musical Arts Association, who spearheaded the drive to develop Blossom. The garden contains assorted trees and flowering shrubs.

■ The Bandwagon Gift Shop, which is open on most performance evenings and offers distinctive gift items. It is operated by the Junior Committee of the Cleveland Orchestra, with proceeds benefiting the orchestra.

■ The Green Room, located at stage right, which provides a setting in which musicians and other performers await stage calls and greet friends and patrons following concerts.

■ The Blossom Restaurant, which houses three facilities: a refreshment stand; a main dining hall offering a complete menu before each concert and a select menu afterward; and the Blossom Club, a private dining room restricted to members and their guests.

■ Other buildings on the site include a box office and an administrative office, which are located outside the main gate, and a first-aid room and security office, which are just inside. All buildings on the grounds feature wood siding treated with a natural preservative, in keeping with the center's natural, wooded surroundings.

Blossom Music Center occupies an 800-acre site between Akron and Cleveland in Ohio's Northampton Township. With approximately 100 acres currently developed, the site lies within the boundaries of several park and recreational areas that extend north of Akron along the banks of the upper Cuyahoga River. The music center's activities are enhanced by the ambience of this natural setting, which has been protected through the use of underground utility lines, wooded buffer zones, and only minimal landfill and excavation. All of these techniques have helped to retain the site's original topography.

The site was chosen by the Musical Art Association's site committee in 1966 for its picturesque qualities and its accessibility. A few miles south of Exit 12 on the Ohio Turnpike (I-80), which serves northeast Ohio and links Youngstown with Toledo, the site also lies two miles west of Ohio Route 8 and enjoys ready access from Interstates 271 and 77. Local event traffic is handled primarily via an existing road that was graded, widened, and resurfaced in 1970 to ease traffic flow in and out of the center. The tree-lined, divided main entrance drive connects with a circular road surrounding the various parking lots, while a secondary access road empties onto an outside road from the entrance drive.

Several paved parking lots, buffered from each other and from the main grounds by wooded areas, accommodate more than 2,500 automobiles and 25 buses. Space for an additional 5,000 cars is available in unpaved overflow lots, and a parking lot for concert subscribers adjoins the main gate. Pedestrian traffic is separated from that of cars via a pedestrian bridge leading from the parking areas to the main gate. Jeep trains are operated at many concert performances to transport patrons to and from the pavilion and parking areas.

FINANCING

Blossom Music Center was developed at a cost of just over $10 million. Development funds were raised entirely from private sources as part of the Cleveland Orchestra's 50th-anniversary capital drive. Capital improvements are financed by private donations and fund-raising activities, which also cover any operating deficits that Blossom might incur.

MARKET ORIENTATION

Blossom's concert series, held from June through mid-September, hosts some 60 performances each season, including 30 performances by the Cleveland Orchestra and 30 special attractions, among which are rock, pop, and country music concerts.

Because of the center's reputation, no extraordinary marketing effort has been necessary. In most cases, promoters contact Blossom to host their events. Nonsymphony events are advertised and marketed by the individual promoters.

LESSONS LEARNED

- Blossom's fast-track design/construction method resulted in hundreds of thousands of dollars in additional post-opening costs for repairs and improvements as a result of incomplete design/development documents.
- The accelerated building schedule also required around-the-clock work shifts during the last two months of construction to meet the opening-day deadline. It is estimated that the facility could have been built for 20 percent less, had the opening date not been targeted to commemorate the symphony's 50th anniversary.

PROJECT DATA

BLOSSOM MUSIC CENTER
CUYAHOGA FALLS, OH

Owner: Musical Arts Association
Architect: Schafer, Flynn & van Dijk, with Pietro Belluschi as architectural adviser
Primary Users: Cleveland Symphony, other classical music concerts, pop/rock concerts
Year Planning Began: 1966
Year Construction Began: 1967
Year Construction Completed: 1968

PROJECT INFORMATION
Site Area: 800 acres
Total Seating Capacity: 18,781
    Fixed Seating: 5,281
    Lawn Seating: 13,500
Total Parking Spaces: 7,525
    Surface Spaces (paved): 2,525 (including subscribers' lot)
    Overflow Spaces (unpaved): 5,000

ECONOMIC INFORMATION
Total Project Cost: $10,000,000
Funding Sources: Private donations (total amount)

CONCORD PAVILION

CONCORD, CALIFORNIA

Winner of the American Institute of Architects' highest award, Concord Pavilion is a beautiful outdoor entertainment facility. The pavilion is a premier open-air showplace for summer entertainment, situated in a natural crater among the foothills of Mount Diablo with a panoramic view that extends to the Carquinez Straits, where the Sacramento River empties into San Francisco Bay.

DEVELOPMENT STRATEGY

The idea for the pavilion developed in 1969, when Carl Jefferson, a local civic and business leader, convinced the city of Concord to host a week-long music festival. By the early 1970s, the annual Concord Jazz Festival had earned a national reputation. As Concord and Contra Costa County grew, so did the interest in a center for culture and entertainment. With community support, the city opened Concord Pavilion on May 16, 1975.

DESIGN AND SITE ISSUES

Concord Pavilion is located on 122 acres that lie some 28 miles northeast of downtown San Francisco. The pavilion is open on three sides and, before 1996, featured an adaptable circular stage under a one-acre canopy. Also until 1996, seating capacity was 8,750, of which 3,500 were reserved seats and 5,250 were lawn seats. On-site parking then offered 3,700 spaces.

In 1992, renovations to the pavilion stage were made whereby the space above the stage was enlarged by 36 percent. Also, a high-definition video screen system was added at that time for the use of audience members on the lawn and in the side seats.

The pavilion received a $16 million renovation in 1995/1996, with a grand reopening in the spring of 1996. The renovation increases seating capacity to 12,730, with 7,500 reserved seats, 5,000 lawn seats, and 230 seats in luxury boxes. Parking also increased, by 1,700 spaces. Renovation also included: (1) the addition of 40,000 square feet of new plazas for improved concession sales and product signage; (2) the creation of state-of-the-art staging and production facilities to include a greatly enlarged, adaptable proscenium stage to meet the needs of today's major touring attractions; and (3) the installation of luxury boxes with food and beverage service and with

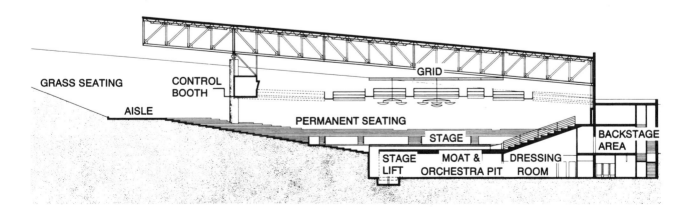

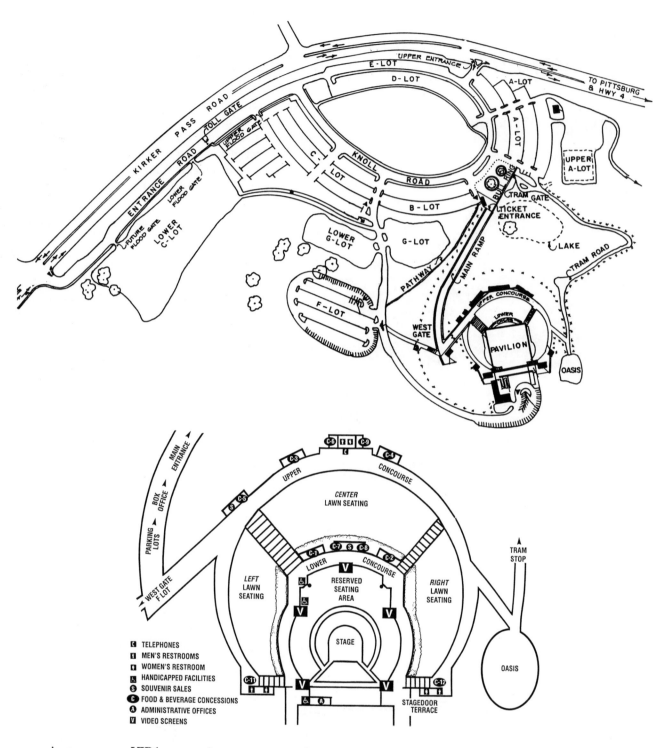

TELEPHONES
MEN'S RESTROOMS
WOMEN'S RESTROOM
HANDICAPPED FACILITIES
SOUVENIR SALES
FOOD & BEVERAGE CONCESSIONS
ADMINISTRATIVE OFFICES
VIDEO SCREENS

convenient access to a VIP lounge, private restrooms, and VIP parking. Among the principal design participants for the new pavilion are internationally renowned architect Frank O. Gehry and six-time Tony Award–winning theater design consultant Jules Fisher.

Concord Pavilion is served by the Bay Area Rapid Transit rail line, which connects to the county's public transit service.

FINANCING

For the original construction in 1974, a revenue bond of $4.25 million was issued, along with a $2 million federal public works grant. In 1995, financing for the renovation was provided through the sale of revenue bonds.

Concord Pavilion is a nonprofit agency of the city of Concord; operations are supported through event revenues, fund-raising activities, and sponsorships. The pavilion receives no public or government subsidy to finance its operating expenses.

MARKET ORIENTATION

After the 1996 expansion, annual attendance is expected to exceed 420,000 at more than 70 events, bringing an

PROJECT DATA

CONCORD PAVILION
CONCORD, CA

Owner: City of Concord
Architects: Frank O. Gehry & Associates
Year Completed: 1975
Renovation to Be Completed: 1996

PROJECT INFORMATION
Site Area: 122 acres
1995 Total Seating Capacity: 8,750
    Fixed: 3,500
    Lawn: 5,250
1996 Total Seating Capacity: 12,730
    Fixed: 7,500
    Lawn: 5,000
    Premium Box Seats: 230
Total Parking:
    1995: 3,700
    1996: 5,400

ECONOMIC INFORMATION
Original Costs:
    Construction (1975 dollars): $4,750,000
    Total Project (1975 dollars): $6,250,000
    Total Project (1994 dollars):[1] $16,938,000
Original Financing: $6,250,000
    City of Concord Revenue Bond: $4,250,000
    Federal Public Works Grant: $2,000,000
1995–1996 Renovation Costs:
    Construction: $13,600,000
    Total Project: $16,400,000
1995–1996 Financing:
    City of Concord Revenue Bond: $16,400,000

Note:
[1]Calculated based on the consumer price index.

expected revenue of $11 million. Thanks to the area's mild climate, Concord Pavilion's season is exceptionally long, usually running from April through October. As a publicly operated, not-for-profit facility, the pavilion has built a national reputation within the performing arts industry for combining commercial success with public service. Through what is considered a model community service program, one out of every four people admitted to events at the pavilion attends free of charge.

The pavilion offers a wide range of entertainment, cultural, and community events, including the JVC and Concord Jazz Festivals, world-renowned symphony orchestras, rock and popular concerts, children's programs, local school events, Olympic-style wrestling, and boxing tournaments.

LESSONS LEARNED

Commercial success, achieved by attracting and successfully marketing popular touring performers, provides income from tickets and ancillary events and lures corporate sponsorship dollars. All of these resources are necessary for survival. This success and the support of the facility's nonprofit citizens' group are essential components in the development of a community and cultural performing arts program that fulfills the public mandate to enrich the lives of the entire community, without public subsidy.

RED ROCKS AMPHITHEATRE

MORRISON, COLORADO (DENVER AREA)

Red Rocks Amphitheatre is set in the midst of Red Rocks Park in the Rocky Mountain foothills near Morrison, Colorado, 15 miles west of Denver. The unparalleled beauty of the amphitheater and park, with its twin 300-foot sandstone rocks (Creation Rock and Ship Rock), along with its near-perfect acoustics, has attracted a variety of musical performers since its development in the early 1940s. The natural geological formation, originally known as the Garden of Angels, is not duplicated anywhere else in the world.

DEVELOPMENT STRATEGY

Red Rocks began as a vision of John Brisben Walker, who purchased the park in 1906. His first project was the construction of a funicular railroad to the top of Mount Morrison to provide easier access to the theater. Walker scheduled concerts on a temporary stage in Red Rocks Park between 1906 and 1910, but plans for the development of a full-scale outdoor theater dwindled after World War I due to personal financial problems. Proposals presented to the city of Morrison and the state of Colorado met with little interest from public officials.

Walker offered Red Rocks Park to the city of Denver for $100,000 in 1923. A committee appointed by then-Mayor Ben Stapleton proposed that the city purchase the park, but it was not until 1928 that the city finally bought Red Rocks and its valuable water rights from Walker for $54,133.

The Great Depression delayed development of the theater and of a scenic road through the park, but at the same time it stimulated a great public works project, providing work for the unemployed. Construction of the theater and of the Alameda Highway leading to the park was made possible through federally financed labor in the Civilian Conservation Corps (CCC).

In 1935, Mayor Stapleton appointed George Cranmer as manager of parks and improvements. Cranmer played a key role in the recruitment of the CCC, allowing theater development to proceed through the Depression. The amphitheater was completed in 1941 and dedicated on June 15 of that year. A total of 12 years had been necessary to complete the project, from planning to dedication (1928–1941).

DESIGN AND SITE ISSUES

The design of Red Rocks Amphitheatre began when Cranmer engaged Burnham Hoyt, a Denver architect, to develop the basic plans. Cranmer proposed that the National Park Service, which had jurisdiction over the CCC camps, supply the labor and pay the cost of the concrete, steel, cement, and stone. Burnham and Cranmer would provide engineering plans and supervise construction. The Park Service agreed, and construction began in 1936.

One problem presented by the unique setting of Red Rocks Park was a hillside covered with boulders, which would have to be removed before the floor of the theater could be leveled and seats installed. Cranmer feared that if construction did not move quickly, the environmentalists of the day might try to halt the project before it ever got started. He ordered the boulders removed at once. Holes were drilled in the bases of all the rock formations and dynamite inserted. The CCC foreman notified Cranmer of the date when the boulders were to be destroyed so that Cranmer could leave town and be unavailable for comment. Once the boulders had been blown up, progress was underway. Cranmer successfully avoided the mayor and the press until they were satisfied that the removal of the boulders had revealed a beautiful natural theater.

Key to the success of the original design was an echo of the natural landscape through the use of indigenous building materials and the wide spacing of benches. The seating provides ample leg room, with a full three feet of space between rows. Patron circulation within the amphitheater is facilitated by stairways, which are hidden from the main seating area by tree-filled planter boxes. Stairways within the seating area were laid at inconsistent angles and widths, encouraging patrons to move toward perimeter aisles when exiting. This system reduces repeated and annoying obstruction of the seated audience.

Much of the original design remains today, despite various upgrades and restorations throughout the years. Red Rocks is a 640-acre park, with the amphitheater itself covering 50 acres. Initially, the theater's capacity was 10,000, but it currently seats 9,200 in 69 tiered rows. The stage, only ten feet from the first row of seats, is a permanent concrete pad 60 feet wide and 70 feet in depth. It is covered by a structured steel roof with adjacent steel speaker towers. At the theater's opening, no loudspeakers were necessary because of the superb natural acoustics.

Parking at Red Rocks accommodates 3,500 vehicles in six lots, with several supplemental spaces available. The city and county of Denver operate and manage parking services through a service contractor.

FINANCING

Funding for the development of Red Rocks came from federal, state, and local governments. The operations and marketing functions are financed through operating, rent, and parking revenues. Due to its management structure, however, the amphitheater is not permitted to apply all profits back to the facility. Instead, financing is funneled through the Denver Division of Theaters and Arenas, which manages several other area facilities as well.

The number of events and the revenue generated at Red Rocks in recent years have fluctuated. In 1988, Fiddler's Green Amphitheater, an 18,000-seat facility, opened in south Denver, causing revenues at Red Rocks to drop significantly. But since that time, the number of shows has steadily increased to rival pre-1988 concert seasons, thanks to a strong concert market.

There are several potential opportunities to increase facility revenue. The first and most obvious way would be to boost the number of shows. Second, a greater seating capacity would allow for a higher profit margin at each concert. Adding concerts depends on a number of factors, including effective marketing, promoter interest, and area competition. If seating were to be expanded, an increase in parking space would be required, which would also generate additional revenue. Another option for revenue enhancement would be to raise the parking fee.

MARKETING ORIENTATION

Although Red Rocks opened in 1941, there was little use of the amphitheater during the war years. Two interesting "firsts" occurred in 1947, however. This, the first year in which the now-annual Easter Service was held, was also the first year when a series of concerts was offered. The success of this series encouraged the mayor to approve plans for the organization of a nonprofit corporation to present concerts and other entertainment at Red Rocks.

Throughout the next 15 years, the amphitheater hosted a variety of events, most of them classical music performances such as those of the Denver Symphony Orchestra and the Mormon Tabernacle Choir. Beginning in 1962, however, there was a drastic change in the type of programming staged at Red Rocks, with the introduction of rock-and-roll concerts. Among the acts presented were performers such as the Beatles, the Beach Boys, and the Mamas and Papas. The accent on rock music has carried over into the 1990s, with contemporary acts such as ZZ Top, Indigo Girls, and Big Head Todd & the Monsters.

Theater management is provided by the city and county of Denver's theaters and arenas division. There is difficulty in generating monies for upkeep and upgrades because Red Rocks's profit margin in any given year is not earmarked for reinvestment or improvements to the amphitheater.

RED ROCKS AMPHITHEATRE
MORRISON, CO

Owner: City and County of Denver
Operator: City and County of Denver Theaters and
   Arenas Division
Builder: Civilian Conservation Corps
Architect: Burnham Hoyt, Denver
Primary Users: Concerts
Year Planning Began: 1928
Year Construction Began: 1936
Year Construction Completed: 1941

PROJECT INFORMATION
Site Area: 50 acres
Seating Capacity: 9,200
Parking Spaces: 3,500
Stage Size: 4,200 square feet

ECONOMIC INFORMATION
1994 Renovations: $750,000
   General Repair: $520,000
   Modifications to Comply with the Americans with
      Disabilities Act: $20,000
   First Aid/Security Building: $156,000
   Miscellaneous: $54,000

LESSONS LEARNED

- The movement to develop Red Rocks Amphitheatre benefited from federally financed labor made available during the Great Depression. By capitalizing on the surplus of labor, the developers gained support for the construction of the facility from the city of Denver and the state of Colorado.
- Red Rocks's seating capacity has become a problem in recent years. Performers wishing to appear before larger audiences can play one show at a competing facility, such as Fiddler's Green, for less cost than playing multiple nights at Red Rocks. This reduces the profit margin per show at Red Rocks, along with the number of acts willing to play the facility. At present, the Colorado Historical Society prefers to preserve the theater's aesthetics, thereby delaying any seating expansion for the time being.
- At present, Red Rocks does not carry a license to serve alcoholic beverages. Introducing these concessions would boost the revenue generated by the facility.
- Despite its small size, Red Rocks Amphitheatre sustains some of the highest expenses for event presentation, due to its remote location and physical characteristics. The construction of a new loading dock and truck ramp would alleviate some of these expenses.
- Fortunately, despite some inconveniences, Red Rocks remains a desired venue for artists to play because of its unique environment and breathtaking beauty.

PINE KNOB MUSIC THEATRE

CLARKSTON, MICHIGAN (DETROIT AREA)

Pine Knob Music Theatre has a reputation as the top open-air venue in the state of Michigan, if not the nation. It has been nominated as the best outdoor concert venue by *Pollstar* and *Performance* magazines every year since 1991.

DEVELOPMENT STRATEGY

When it first opened in 1972, Pine Knob Music Theatre was the largest outdoor arena in the United States, and it soon became a popular summertime attraction for area rock-and-roll fans.

But as the industry changed over the years, so did concertgoers. More sophisticated audiences began to notice the pavilion's physical shortcomings and general indifference to customer service. Consequently, attendance dropped, and Pine Knob filed for Chapter 11 bankruptcy protection in 1980.

In early 1984, the Nederlander Organization, which had been managing the property, purchased the amphitheater and began making improvements that started to increase attendance. In 1990, Nederlander sold Pine Knob to Palace Sports & Entertainment, which had planned to build an amphitheater, the Palace Gardens, on its Palace Arena property. The Palace Gardens project was abandoned, however, because of environmental problems.

DESIGN AND SITE ISSUES

The original Pine Knob complex included the amphitheater, a golf course, and a ski resort, which are all now under separate ownership. The Pine Knob Music Theatre, a pavilion standing at the base of a natural bowl, offers covered seating for 7,350 and lawn seating for 8,000. Behind the stage are seven dressing rooms, administrative offices, four loading docks, and a catering room. Patrons have access to concessions in 13 locations and to merchandise at three locations. The Courtyard restaurant, which is a private VIP area for Royalty Seat (season ticket) holders, serves a full dinner menu with seating for 400. The Plaza reception lounge is available for pre- and post-event gatherings and private parties of up to 250 people.

The venue is reached from Interstate 75, at the Sashabaw Road interchange, and provides on-site parking for 5,000 cars.

Extensive renovations completed since Palace Sports & Entertainment purchased the facility have included: doubling the number of restrooms; tripling concession-service points of sale; repaving and improving parking; installing additional video screens for lawn patrons; enhancing the landscaping; and padding the pavilion seats. Nine-foot-by-12-foot electrosonic video walls located on both sides of the stage enhance concert viewing, while the pavilion design allows sound to carry easily to the rear of the house.

FINANCING

In 1980, Pine Knob's owners filed for Chapter 11 bankruptcy, reporting more than $15.5 million in debts. In 1984, Nederlander Organization, in conjunction with Northern Equities Corporation, purchased the amphitheater and the ski complex for $14.1 million. Nederlander later assumed sole ownership of the amphitheater and sold it to Palace Sports & Entertainment in 1990. Since then, Palace Sports & Entertainment has invested more than $14 million in remodeling.

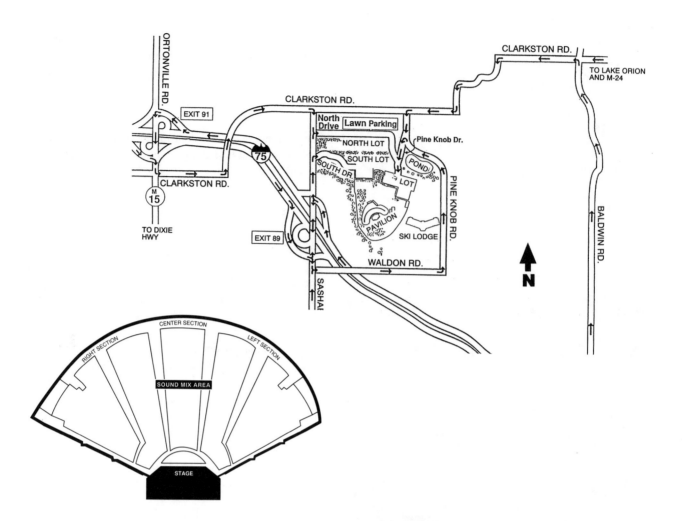

MARKET ORIENTATION

The Pine Knob concert season operates from May to September, with approximately 80 events per year drawing attendees from within a 75-mile radius. Events include rock, pop, alternative music, jazz, classical, adult contemporary, and country music concerts, along with family and variety shows.

LESSONS LEARNED

Palace Sports & Entertainment bought Pine Knob because it was already built and because people knew where it was. But Pine Knob had a tarnished reputation because of the venue's shortcomings in traffic flow, concessions, and restrooms. Since the 1990/1991 renovations and with improved management, Pine Knob attendance has increased each season. Further renovations are planned, including additional restrooms and video screens for lawn patrons.

PROJECT DATA

PINE KNOB MUSIC THEATRE
CLARKSTON, MI

Owner: Palace Sports & Entertainment
Architects: Rossetti Associates, Birmingham, Michigan
   (renovations)
Primary Users: Musical concerts, family shows
Year Construction Completed: 1972
Renovations: 1990, 1991

PROJECT INFORMATION
Site Area: 84 acres
Total Seating Capacity: 15,253
   Fixed Seating: 7,253
   Lawn Seating: 8,000
Total Parking: 5,000

ECONOMIC INFORMATION
Renovations: $14,000,000

HOLLYWOOD BOWL

HOLLYWOOD, CALIFORNIA

The Hollywood Bowl first emerged as an entertainment venue in the 1920s; within ten years, it had established itself as a Los Angeles institution, which it remains to this day. The facility has found success as a dramatic site for symphony, opera, and ballet performances, as well as jazz and pop concerts, and has been emulated in both form and spirit across the United States.

DEVELOPMENT STRATEGY

Hollywood Bowl and the Hollywood myth evolved in the same era. In 1919, a group of arts-minded citizens founded the Theater Arts Alliance and promptly announced their intention to build a "community park and art center" at which they could stage outdoor performances similar to the theatrical events of ancient Greece. At the time, Hollywood did not have a public park or any public space in which to present live entertainment. The

alliance purchased 59 acres at Bolton Canyon, a location selected because of its superb acoustical properties. The site lay just outside the Los Angeles city limits and afforded a natural amphitheater formation.

"The Park" was applauded by theatergoers, music lovers, nature buffs, politicians, real estate developers, and others as a welcome addition to the community. There was an acknowledged need for a public park because of the overwhelming success of several existing outdoor events, among them the Easter sunrise service, which attracted thousands of guests.

Christine Wetherill Stevenson, heiress to the Pittsburgh Paint Company fortune and organizer and president of the Theater Arts Alliance, contributed almost half of the site acquisition cost of $47,550. When alliance members discovered that Stevenson wanted to use the facility to promote the theosophical tenets of universal brotherhood, however, the alliance changed the name of its organization to the Community Park and Art Association. Artie Mason Carter assumed responsibility for the Park and championed its role in community activism and arts education. She passionately promoted the Park, thereafter referred to as "the Bowl."

Tickets were priced at twenty-five cents, and although thousands of tickets were sold, revenues were never enough to retire the debt on the property. By 1924, the value of the Bowl site had reached $1.5 million (more than 30 times its 1919 selling price), and arrangements were made to deed the facility to Los Angeles County to avoid the escalating taxes. The county would contribute money for the operating budget and capital improvements and would lease the Bowl back to the Community Park and Art Association for 99 years. The organization reorganized as the Hollywood Bowl Association and named Artie Carter as president. When she resigned in 1926, she left a legacy of affordable seats for Bowl patrons.

In 1934, Allan Balch, a previous Hollywood Bowl president, became president of the Symphony Association, creating a link between the Bowl and the Los Angeles Philharmonic Orchestra, which had been closely associated since the 1921 Easter sunrise service. Hollywood Bowl remains the summer home of the Philharmonic.

DESIGN AND SITE ISSUES

The two primary requirements for an outdoor production arena were an amphitheater for the audience and a performance space for musicians and actors. The early structure had expressed two fundamental ideas: (1) nature (columned trellises set against decorated walls), and (2) ancient history (Greek urns placed on either side of the stage, linking the Bowl's design to ancient Greece).

In 1925, Los Angeles County designated funding for permanent improvements to the Bowl. The facility had been a dirt amphitheater with movable wooden benches and stage. Allied Architects was contracted to draw up plans for a $300,000 project, and construction began in March 1926. The hillside was graded and hollowed to increase seating from 15,000 to almost 18,000. Four hundred new boxes were built, for a total of 550 boxes, and concrete partitions divided the sections of seats and boxes. An orchestra pit and stage were erected atop a concrete bunker. The new amphitheater opened in June 1926, just in time for the summer concert season. In July of that year, a new structure for musical performances was built, made up of a wood-frame shell with five walls in curved sections rising to meet the proscenium arch. Unfortunately, these improvements altered the Hollywood Bowl's acoustics: the concrete shell projected sound to the center seating area, where it reverberated unpleasantly.

In 1929, a semicircular shell of cement and asbestos was constructed by Allied Architects at a cost of $33,000. But the acoustic problem was not solved, and in the 1950s the Bowl underwent further remodeling. A reflecting pool was installed in 1953, and sound towers were added a year later, along with a fountain that sprayed in rainbow hues. To increase the season ticket base, new boxes were eventually added, and the custom of picnicking at the Bowl began. In 1980, Frank Gehry designed the award-winning fiberglass spheres that hang from the shell to reflect and distribute sound.

Additional renovations have included a new parking deck behind the stage (1981); restored cedarwood benches (1983); an electronic entrance marquee (1984); and new access ramps (1991). A multiphase renovation is currently in progress, entailing upgrades of infrastructure, addition of code-compliant restroom facilities, other adaptions to ADA requirements, and general improvements.

FINANCING

The Hollywood Bowl site was purchased in 1919 by the Theater Arts Alliance for $47,550. In 1924, the Community Park and Art Association (the former Alliance) deeded the completed facility to Los Angeles County, which assumed financial responsibility.

MARKET ORIENTATION

Hollywood Bowl's season extends from June until mid-October and attracts about 800,000 attendees. The Los Angeles Philharmonic Orchestra and the Hollywood

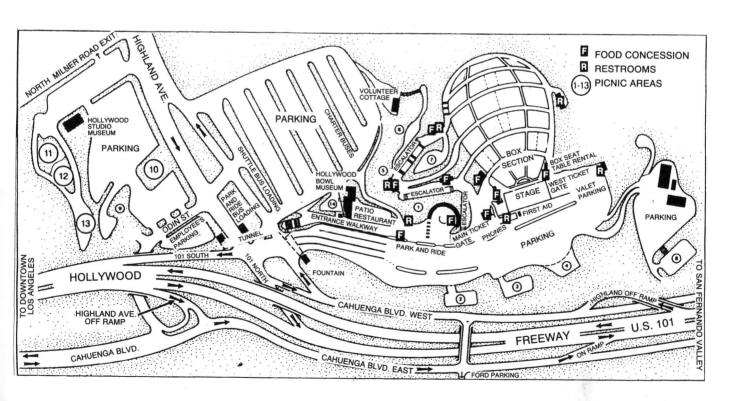

Bowl Orchestra are the primary tenants, although anywhere from 12 to 20 additional events are presented annually. Acts have included: Harry Connick, Jr., Bonnie Raitt, and Garth Brooks.

LESSONS LEARNED

As one of the nation's oldest amphitheaters, Hollywood Bowl has remained successful over time by continually making adjustments to keep pace with audience demand. In this way, the facility has been able to retain a diverse audience by presenting a range of performances from symphony concerts to country music shows. Hollywood Bowl remains one of the most popular and well-known outdoor concert venues in the country.

PROJECT DATA

HOLLYWOOD BOWL
HOLLYWOOD, CA

Owner: Los Angeles County Department of Parks and Recreation
Developer: Theater Arts Alliance
Architects: Allied Architects
Year Planning Began: 1919
Year First Renovation Completed: 1926

PROJECT INFORMATION
Site Area: 59 acres
Total Seats: 17,965
Total Parking: 3,120

ECONOMIC INFORMATION
Site Acquisition Cost: $47,550
Total Project Cost (1919 dollars): $47,550
Total Project Cost (1994 dollars):[1] $412,661
First Renovation Costs (1926 dollars): $300,000
Second Renovation Costs (1929 dollars): $33,000

Note:
[1]Calculated based on the consumer price index.

BLOCKBUSTER DESERT SKY PAVILION

PHOENIX, ARIZONA

When veteran Broadway producer Zev Buffman and the Blockbuster Entertainment Corporation formed a joint venture to build a chain of 20,000-seat amphitheaters throughout the United States, the Blockbuster Desert Sky Pavilion was among the first to open. Its opening, on November 9, 1990, featured a sold-out "Storm Front Tour" concert by Billy Joel. Buffman believes that amphitheaters should provide an affordable entertainment option. He says that taking the family to the symphony could be a major undertaking, but when the show costs only $8 and you can attend while reclining on a grassy slope under the stars, the occasion is more accessible and appealing.

DEVELOPMENT STRATEGY

Blockbuster Desert Sky Pavilion is a multipurpose facility designed to host concerts, Broadway shows, operas, ballet performances, and sporting events like boxing. It was envisioned as the nation's first open-air amphitheater to operate year-round.

The city of Phoenix built and owns the pavilion, which occupies a 65-acre site. To develop an amphitheater in Phoenix was the idea of Zev Buffman, who observed that Phoenix was the largest market in 1987 without a state-of-the-art amphitheater. In addition, Phoenix's large winter population of tourists would mean additional attendees for pavilion events.

DESIGN AND SITE ISSUES

Blockbuster Desert Sky Pavilion stands near Interstate 10 and Interstate 17, within 30 minutes of most locations in the Phoenix Valley.

The amphitheater features a full Broadway stage and an orchestra pit with room for 100 musicians. Separate, 8,300-square-foot back-of-house and administrative offices are located behind the stage.

The pavilion has a seating capacity of 20,000, including approximately 9,000 covered, reserved seats and 11,000 "festival-style" seats on the concert green, the grassy knoll extending behind the covered, fixed seating. The reserved seating also comprises corporate box seats. There are 96 food and beverage serving stations, or points of sale, distributed throughout the amphitheater.

Desert Sky Pavilion was designed with enhanced acoustic quality. Stage and roofing materials used in construction were selected for their ability to promote sound quality by reducing and/or enhancing reverberation, depending on the needs of the event. A signal-delayed speaker system was also incorporated into the pavilion design, allowing for amplification of the stage performance without distortion of sound quality before sound reaches the audience on the concert green.

The effect of concert sounds on neighboring communities was also a major consideration in the pavilion's design and layout. To minimize this effect, a roof was built over the fixed seating. Noise-absorbing material was placed in the roof, behind the main speakers, and in the stage and back stage areas. An earth berm rising 34 feet above the level of the stage floor and an eight-foot-high wall surrounding the berm perimeter increase

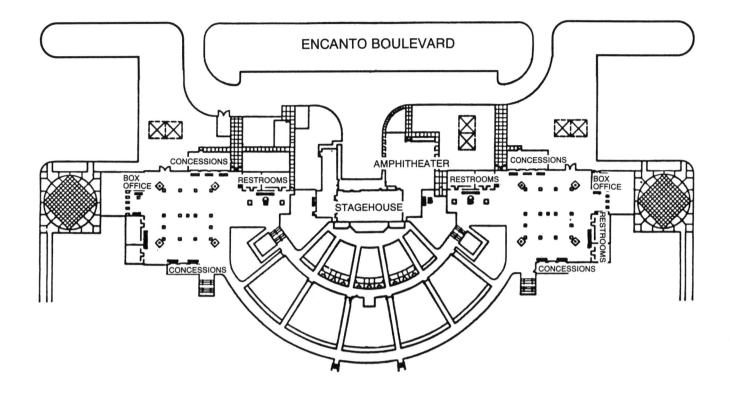

ENCANTO BOULEVARD

CONCESSIONS   AMPHITHEATER   CONCESSIONS

BOX
OFFICE   RESTROOMS   RESTROOMS   BOX
OFFICE

STAGEHOUSE   RESTROOMS

CONCESSIONS   CONCESSIONS

the effective height of the shielding to 42 feet above the stage floor.

The city of Phoenix is responsible for maintaining the 42-acre parking lot, which affords 5,800 parking spaces. There are two VIP parking lots, where valet parking is offered. Additional overflow parking for 1,000 cars is available within a short walking distance.

FINANCING

To construct the pavilion, the city of Phoenix issued $12 million in bonds authorized for a large pool of public improvement projects. The city bought the land and built the amphitheater and the infrastructure to support it at a total cost of $19.8 million, including $5.8 million for land acquisition, $2 million for infrastructure, and $12 million for construction.

Amphitheater Entertainment Corporation (AEC), a Buffman-Blockbuster joint venture, signed a 60-year agreement with the city to lease and manage the venue. As part of the lease agreement, AEC agreed to make bond principal and interest payments each year to the city of Phoenix. These payments have been structured to minimize the corporation's payment obligations in the early years.

MARKET ORIENTATION

Blockbuster Desert Sky Pavilion hosts about 40 performances per year, including occasional Broadway musicals, dance performances, comedies, classical music, and jazz, but primarily consisting of contemporary and country music shows. Among other productions, the pavilion has staged the *Nutcracker* ballet. The amphitheater also hosts local functions such as school music competitions, Cinco De Mayo celebrations, Easter sunrise services, and community events.

LESSONS LEARNED

- Surprisingly, some concert activity has taken place during the summer months. Many observers thought that performers would avoid the high summer temperatures of Phoenix, but 12 concerts were held in the first summer.
- Blockbuster Desert Sky Pavilion opened in 1990, a year-and-a-half before the NBA Suns' new America West Arena. Initially, there was aggressive competition for performers between the two facilities. Now, it seems that performers who prefer outdoor shows perform at Desert Sky, while acts preferring indoor

PROJECT DATA

BLOCKBUSTER DESERT SKY PAVILION
PHOENIX, AZ

Owner: City of Phoenix
Developer: Whizzed Amphitheater Corporation
Architects: Helmuth, Obata & Kassabaum (HOK),
    Kansas City, Missouri
Year Planning Began: 1989
Year Completed: 1990

PROJECT INFORMATION

Site Area: 65 acres
Total Seating Capacity: 20,000
    Fixed: 9,000
    Lawn: 11,000
Total Parking: 5,800 on site

ECONOMIC INFORMATION

Site Acquisition Cost: $5,800,000
Infrastructure Cost: $2,000,000
Construction Costs (1990 dollars): $12,000,000
Total Project Cost (1990 dollars): $19,800,000
Total Project Cost (1994 dollars):[1] $22,100,000

Note:
[1]Calculated based on the consumer price index.

shows appear at America West Arena or Veteran's Coliseum.

- It was believed that the large local Hispanic market could be tapped readily by booking major Hispanic performers and advertising on Spanish-language television and radio stations. In reality, this has been a slow process and must evolve over time. Recently, the Hispanic market seems to be responding more favorably to ethnic performances held at the pavilion.

- The investment in the high-cost, sophisticated staging equipment necessary for Broadway shows, such as fly lofts, was not profitable. It seems that amphitheaters may not be able to provide the theatrical ambience required for Broadway shows.

HARDEE'S WALNUT CREEK AMPHITHEATRE

RALEIGH, NORTH CAROLINA

Hardee's Walnut Creek Amphitheatre is a performing arts center specifically designed for concerts. Situated on 77 acres of beautifully wooded parkland in southeast Raleigh, the amphitheater has ranked among the top ten most successful amphitheaters in the country each year since its opening in 1991. The facility is part of Raleigh's nationally honored city parks system.

DEVELOPMENT STRATEGY

Development of the amphitheater began in the late 1980s, when the city of Raleigh launched a concerted effort to expand its parks and recreational facilities. The site was originally considered for a professional baseball facility. When Raleigh was unable to secure a franchise, however, city leaders began researching other possibilities.

Roger Krupa, director of the Raleigh Civic Center, suggested to the city that amphitheaters were the new wave in entertainment presentation. City officials approached PACE, a concert promotion company based

in Houston, with a proposal for an amphitheater in Raleigh. As Raleigh officials were impressed by other PACE facilities, they signed an agreement for a $13.7 million amphitheater, with PACE furnishing some $2.2 million and the city $9 million toward the facility and $2.5 million toward other improvements.

DESIGN AND SITE ISSUES

"The Creek," as it is affectionately known, has a seating capacity of 20,000: 7,000 fixed seats in the open-air pavilion and 13,000 in lawn seating. Four-, six-, and eight-seat VIP boxes, which can be leased seasonally, are elevated for superior viewing and feature table service with gourmet menus and VIP parking. "Starseats" in the venue's Gold Circle section are also available seasonally and include the same parking privileges. At the Caribbean Club, a private club for corporate sponsors, box seat holders, media, and special guests, the patio setting incorporates an indoor bar, buffet, and closed-circuit television.

To provide performers with privacy and accessibility, the amphitheater has six large dressing rooms within a few feet of the main stage. State-of-the-art sound, natural outdoor acoustics, and strategically positioned, big-screen video monitors on the lawn and in the pavilion deliver exceptional sight and sound to all seating areas.

Ample seating is available for the physically challenged, and assistive listening devices may be had on request. The Creek is a barrier-free facility. The loading dock accommodates nine semi-trailers and eight crew buses. For attendees, parking for 6,500 cars is provided in five adjacent lots.

FINANCING

The city of Raleigh furnished $11.5 million, which it raised through the sale of certificates of participation. The Walnut Creek Financial Assistance Corporation was set up as a nonprofit entity to issue the debt, to enter into a lease with PACE, to receive payments from that firm, and eventually to retire the debt.

The management/rental agreement requires PACE to pay monthly installments to the city in the amount of 7 percent of gross revenues during the lease term. Gross revenues include total revenues from the use and operation of the amphitheater and parking facilities but do not include payments received from concessionaires in upfront/capital contributions. Additionally, the first $2 million of revenue generated during each of the first two years of operation and the first $1 million received during the third year were excluded from gross revenues.

The initial lease term extends for 20 years, with an option to renew for an additional 20. PACE is obligated to pay the city $1 million on the last day of the initial lease agreement, plus a renewal fee of $1.5 million at the commencement of the renewed lease.

Wilson Rogers, general manager of the facility, acknowledges that at a project cost of $13.7 million, The Creek was an expensive proposition for the city. Compared with other types of facilities, however, the amphitheater has been a bargain. With its 20,000-seat capacity, the Creek's cost breaks down to approximately $700 per seat. In contrast, an indoor arena averages $3,000 per seat for construction alone; at that rate, this venue could have cost the city upwards of $60 million. But Rogers believes that Raleigh found a way to provide the highest-quality entertainment at a fraction of the cost.

MARKET ORIENTATION

The Creek was designed primarily for concerts, with the season beginning in late April and continuing through October. Between 35 and 45 performances representing every musical style—rock, pop, country, jazz, rhythm and blues, oldies, and more—are presented each season. Acts and events hosted at The Creek have included Michael Bolton, Lollapalooza, and Festival New Orleans. In 1994, Jimmy Buffett sold out three shows, and Reba McEntire, the Eagles, Aerosmith, and Alan Jackson also performed before sellout crowds.

In its first season, the amphitheater drew some 275,000 people to southeast Raleigh. The Creek finished among the top five highest-grossing amphitheaters in the country in 1993, when attendance totaled more than 450,000, with 45 shows and seven sellouts. As of July 1994, the facility had risen to the number-two spot.

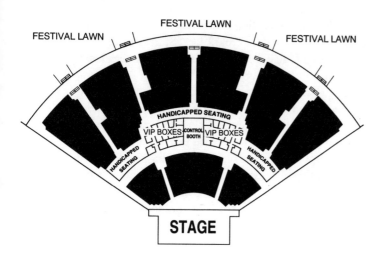

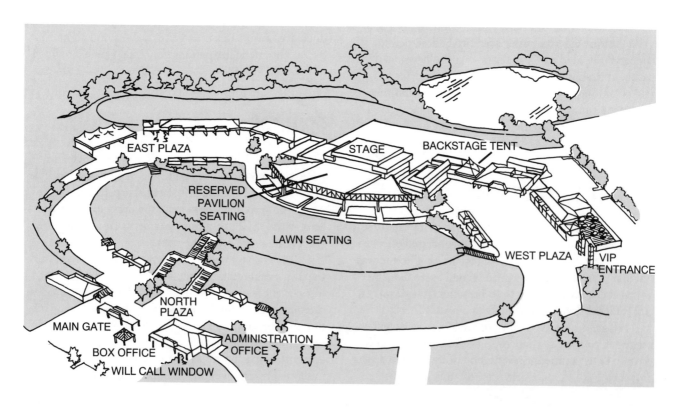

PROJECT DATA

HARDEE'S WALNUT CREEK AMPHITHEATRE RALEIGH, NC

Owner: City of Raleigh
Operator: Pavilion Partners (Sony, PACE, and Blockbuster), in association with Cellar Door of the Carolinas
Architect: Abe Sustaita & Associates
Primary Users: Concerts, festivals, special events
Year Planning Began: 1987
Year Construction Began: 1991
Year Construction Completed: 1991

PROJECT INFORMATION

Site Area: 77 acres
Seating Capacity: 20,000
    Fixed: 7,000
    Lawn: 13,000
Total Parking Spaces: 6,500 on site

ECONOMIC INFORMATION

Total Project Cost (1991 dollars): $13,700,000
Total Project Cost (1994 dollars):[1] $14,500,000
Funding Sources:
    PACE: $2,200,000
    City of Raleigh:[2] $9,000,000
    City of Raleigh:[3] $2,500,000

Notes:
[1] Calculated based on the consumer price index.
[2] For the facility.
[3] For additional improvements.

The amphitheater also hosts company picnics, meetings, fundraisers, and many kinds of public and private special events.

LESSONS LEARNED

Some residents who live near Hardee's Walnut Creek have complained about increased traffic and noise in their once-quiet neighborhood. The city and PACE have worked diligently to address these concerns, making adjustments in the amphitheater's speaker system, paving access roads, redirecting street lights, and posting traffic attendants to discourage parking in residential areas. The city has also built a privacy fence near adjoining property, and leaders have met with residents to discuss additional long-term solutions.

GLEN HELEN BLOCKBUSTER PAVILION

SAN BERNARDINO, CALIFORNIA

The Glen Helen Blockbuster Pavilion is the third amphitheater to be developed by the joint venture between veteran Broadway producer Zev Buffman and Blockbuster Entertainment Corporation, the first two being Desert Sky Pavilion in Phoenix and Blockbuster Pavilion in Charlotte.

DEVELOPMENT STRATEGY

Before 1993, San Bernardino and Riverside counties (the "Inland Empire") constituted one of the largest entertainment markets in the nation without a modern venue for spectator entertainment with a seating capacity of at least 10,000. The Glen Helen Blockbuster Pavilion, which stands in Glen Helen Regional Park, was conceived and built to capture this large and rapidly growing market.

The 1,250-acre park developed an existing bowl that had previously been used for occasional concerts, was owned by the San Bernardino County Parks Department. The Glen Helen Blockbuster Pavilion, which opened in July 1993, hosts concerts and other entertainment events.

DESIGN AND SITE ISSUES

The pavilion was initially developed as a traditional open-air amphitheater with a total of 16,800 seats: 10,451 fixed seats and 6,349 lawn seats on a grassy slope behind the permanent seats. As infrastructure improvements were added, the area for lawn seating was expanded to bring its total capacity to 35,000 seats. And during the pavilion's third season, which began in May 1995, the venue was able to accommodate stadium-size events accommodating 65,000 (approximately 10,000 fixed seats and 55,000 lawn seating).

The original development included infrastructure improvements supplied by the county, so that access to the park can now be gained from Interstates 15 and 215. A new interchange on Interstate 15, completed in May 1995, provides direct access to the park and parking lot, which furnishes nearly 25,000 spaces. Food and beverage concessions are available in a food court on the grounds.

FINANCING

The county financed the development from three sources: funds provided by the Buffman/ Blockbuster joint venture, funds designated for park improvements, and proceeds from the sale of bonds.

Total project cost was $18 million, with the county financing $14 million (taxable and tax-exempt) and Buffman/Blockbuster $4 million. The county also financed the new freeway interchange at a cost of $5.7 million. Buffman/Blockbuster has leased the land from the county for 25 years plus options and pays the county an average annual rent (debt service) of approximately $1 million, plus a percentage of ticket and concession sales when levels of these proceeds exceed original projections.

MARKET ORIENTATION

The 65,000 person capacity enables the pavilion to target stadium-size concerts. The venue also hopes to present occasional symphonies, Broadway shows, and ballets.

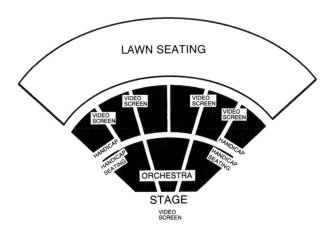

LAWN SEATING

VIDEO SCREEN
VIDEO SCREEN
VIDEO SCREEN
VIDEO SCREEN

HANDICAP SEATING
HANDICAP SEATING
HANDICAP SEATING
HANDICAP SEATING

ORCHESTRA

STAGE

VIDEO SCREEN

LESSONS LEARNED

■ The Inland Empire is a rapidly growing market, but there was concern that residents from Los Angeles and Orange counties would not drive to San Bernardino for a concert. Surprisingly, 31 percent of the pavilion's attendees come from more than 45 miles away in Los Angeles or in Orange County. Some 16 percent come from 30 to 45 miles away in the more distant parts of the Inland Empire, which stretches to the Nevada and Arizona borders. Only 33 percent come from the 20-mile radius local market, with 13 percent traveling between 20 and 30 miles and 20 percent between one and 20 miles. The remaining 20 percent of concertgoers are tourists or visitors from outside the four-county area. This extraordinarily large market area may result from traffic patterns that make it is easier to travel to the Inland Empire than to Los Angeles and Orange counties.

PROJECT DATA

GLEN HELEN BLOCKBUSTER PAVILION
SAN BERNARDINO, CA

Owner: San Bernardino County
Developer: Buffman/Blockbuster
Architects: Wolff, Lang, & Christopher, San Bernardino
Year Planning Began: 1992
Year Construction Completed: 1993

PROJECT INFORMATION
Site Area: 1,250 acres
    Amphitheater: 56 acres
    Parking: 220 acres
Seating Capacity: 65,000
    Fixed: 10,000
    Lawn: 55,000
Parking Spaces: 25,000

ECONOMIC INFORMATION
Total Project Cost (1992 dollars): $18,000,000 (all phases)
Total Project Cost (1994 dollars):[1] $18,705,631
Financing:
    Buffman/Blockbuster: $4,000,000
    San Bernardino County: $14,000,000

Note:
[1]Calculated based on the consumer price index.

■ Occasionally, fierce competition arises between the area's two major competitors: Irvine Meadows in Orange County and Glen Helen Blockbuster Pavilion. As a rule, performers generally prefer to schedule performances in Los Angeles, with additional southern California appearances at either Irvine Meadows or Glen Helen.

KNICKERBOCKER ARENA

ALBANY, NEW YORK

Knickerbocker Arena is a 17,500-seat multipurpose facility that has been hailed as the "crowning touch in the revitalization of downtown Albany." The facility serves the community as a sports and entertainment center as well as a venue for family shows.

DEVELOPMENT STRATEGY

The arena was conceived by county executive James Coyne. He was also responsible for the development of Heritage Park, a minor-league baseball stadium and hockey rink, home of the U.S. Olympic hockey team. After the facility had been designed by Crozier Associates, Architects, construction began in 1986 and continued until completion in January 1990.

DESIGN AND SITE ISSUES

Situated in downtown Albany, Knickerbocker Arena stands in the heart of the Capital District Region. A pedestrian skywalk connects the complex to the Nelson

A. Rockefeller Empire State Plaza, home of the New York State government. The arena complex contains 20,000 square feet of retail space and 51,000 square feet of exhibition space, using the arena floor, concourse, and exhibit hall. With its 17,500-seat capacity, the arena is the third largest multipurpose arena in New York State and also the largest facility in the United States with an Olympic-size hockey rink.

The "Knick" Showcase is an intimate, 6,000-seat auditorium created within the arena by a curtain panel system that allows flexible seating configurations. Each of the curtain panels can be lifted to add more seats if sales exceed 6,000.

There are 25 luxury suites, each seating 16 and available through one of three lease packages. Gold Suite benefits include 16 free tickets to all arena events and four complimentary parking passes for the adjoining garage. This package is leased for three years at $40,000 per year. Silver Suite benefits allow the suite user the flexibility of viewing only certain events. Tickets are purchased as desired, and the suiteholder enjoys the right to reserve all 16 tickets for each event. The Silver Suite package is leased for three years at $25,000 per year. And Sportsman Club benefits feature the same assigned seat for each sporting event in a corporate suite for one year. This seating arrangement can be purchased in blocks at $1,250 per seat, or individually at $1,500 per seat, which includes a parking pass.

A 1,000-space parking garage is located behind the facility. There are 10,000 supplemental spaces within an eight-block radius of the arena. Knickerbocker offers a portable basketball floor, four locker rooms, seven dressing rooms, and one officials' locker room.

FINANCING

Knickerbocker Arena was developed at a total cost of $69.4 million, with the construction cost totaling $65 million. The facility was funded by various sources, though most of the financing came from Albany County general obligation bonds totaling $51.4 million. Additionally, the Urban Development Corporation (UDC) funded $6.5 million through New York State bonds, while the UDC Project Development contributed another $5 million. The remaining $6.5 million was funded by Albany County's general fund. To assist in financing the facility, a 1 percent hotel/motel bed tax was levied countywide.

Arena operations and marketing expenses are covered by ticket sales, parking income, and concession revenues.

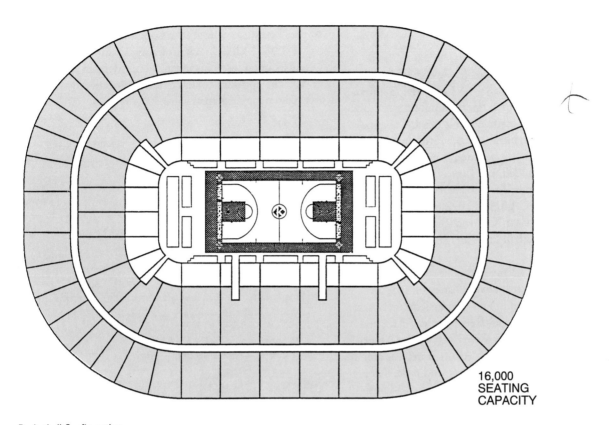

16,000
SEATING
CAPACITY

Basketball Configuration

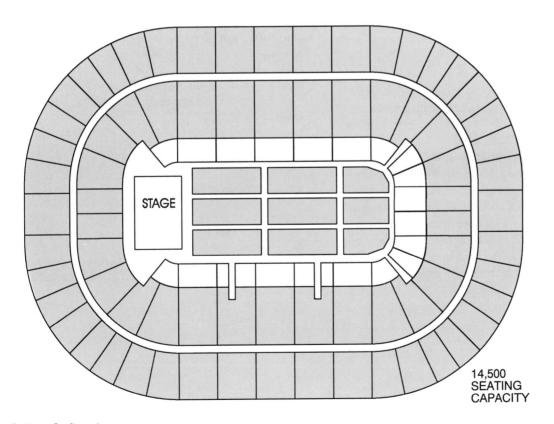

14,500
SEATING
CAPACITY

Endstage Configuration

135

Market Orientation

Albany County owns Knickerbocker Arena, while Spectacor Management Group (SMG) of Philadelphia manages the facility. SMG, which operates public assembly facilities under long-term contracts or leases and assumes full responsibility for financial and operating management, is also responsible for booking events held in the arena. Events have included the Metro Atlantic Athletic Conference (MAAC) men's and women's basketball tournament and, for the NCAA, the 1992 men's ice hockey Final Four, the 1994 East Regionals, and the 1995 Division 1 men's basketball first- and second-round championships.

Other events and family shows hosted by the arena include Sesame Street Live, Disney on Ice, the Pepsi Tennis Classic, World Wrestling Federation bouts, and the Albany International Beer Festival. Knickerbocker is home to the Albany River Rats of the American Hockey League, as well as the Albany Firebirds arena football team. Concerts, motor sports, and rodeos are also staged in the arena. SMG has established a working relationship with Team USA, the U.S. Olympic hockey team, which uses the facility for games and international tournaments.

Lessons Learned

- Arena seating was recently made more flexible with the installation of a curtain system, which creates a showcase setting, providing an intimate environment for crowds of up to 6,000.
- Throughout the preconstruction and construction stages, the management group joined in weekly construction meetings and worked with the local architect to improve seating and row alignments, creating better sightlines. This high level of communication between management and the development team led to a smooth opening of the facility and enabled it to host 60 performances in its first 59 days of operation.

- Knickerbocker was able to solicit and win the bid for the 1992 NCAA hockey championship before the facility's opening. This award demonstrated at an early date the confidence that event promoters displayed in the arena and its management.

Project Data
Knickerbocker Arena
Albany, NY

Owner: County of Albany
Operator: Spectacor Management Group, Philadelphia
Builder: Beltrove, General Contractor, Albany
Architects: Crozier Associates, Architects, Albany
Primary Users: Albany River Rats (hockey), Albany Firebirds (arena football)
Year Planning Began: 1981
Year Construction Began: 1986
Year Construction Completed: 1990

Project Information
Maximum Seating Capacity: 17,500
Exhibition Space: 51,000 square feet
Retail Space: 20,000 square feet
Total Parking Spaces: 1,000 on site[1]

Economic Information
Site Acquisition Cost: $4,000,000
Construction Cost: $65,400,000
Total Project Cost (1990 dollars): $69,400,000
Total Project Cost (1994 dollars):[2] $77,500,000
Funding Sources:
   Urban Development Corporation: $6,500,000
   Urban Development Corporation Project Development: $5,000,000
   County General Obligation Bonds:[3] $51,400,000
   County General Fund:[3] $6,500,000

Notes:
[1]Ten thousand supplemental spaces lie within an eight-block radius.
[2]Calculated based on consumer price index.
[3]Funded by a 1 percent, countywide hotel/motel bed tax.

ARROWHEAD POND OF ANAHEIM

ANAHEIM, CALIFORNIA

Arrowhead Pond of Anaheim is a multipurpose arena designed to be a landmark building for Orange County and the city of Anaheim. The arena was built to provide a venue for high-quality entertainment and, ideally, to attract a professional hockey or basketball franchise. The Pond now stands as home to the National Hockey League's Mighty Ducks of Anaheim.

DEVELOPMENT STRATEGY

In 1988, the Anaheim City Council and the city manager began the effort to build an arena by selecting a site near Anaheim Stadium that they believed was superior because of its visibility and freeway access. In June 1990, the city council passed agreements that finalized land acquisition and relocation and that settled management and concession issues allowing Ogden Entertainment Corporation, a private facility management firm, to enter into a public/private partnership with the city. Later

that year, the sports division of Hellmuth, Obata and Kassabaum (HOK), Inc., completed the building design; groundbreaking took place in November of that same year.

In December 1992, the National Hockey League granted two conditional expansion franchises, one to Orange County and one to Miami. One of the conditions stipulated that the franchise must have secured a lease with a suitable venue. In February 1993, a three-way agreement was signed between Ogden, the city of Anaheim, and Disney that cleared the way for Disney's expansion hockey franchise to begin playing in the 1993–1994 season.

Arrowhead Pond opened on June 17, 1993, with a Barry Manilow concert.

DESIGN AND SITE ISSUES

The Pond is located near five major freeways that provide direct access from throughout southern California. Seven lots supply parking for 4,500 cars, with an additional 17,000 spaces at nearby Anaheim Stadium.

The arena seats 19,400 for boxing, 18,200 for basketball, and 17,200 for hockey. Seating is arranged on three levels: terrace, club, and plaza. The facility uses a portable riser system, which allows seats to be placed at the correct angle for any event. Seat risers float on a cushion of air that permits ease of movement during event changeovers.

Arrowhead Pond has 84 luxury suites, leasing for $75,000 to $105,000 per year, and 1,724 club seats lo-

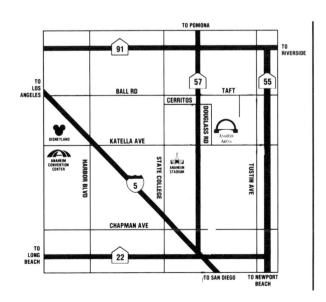

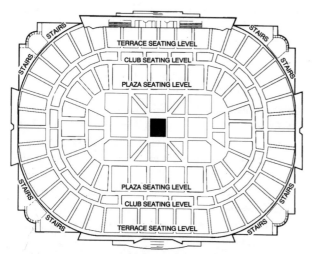

Center Stage/Boxing Configuration—19,400 Seating Capacity

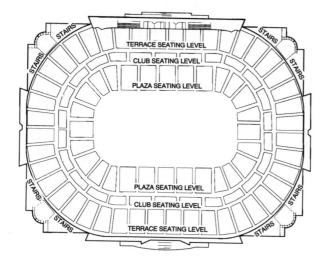

Hockey Configuration—17,200 Seating Capacity

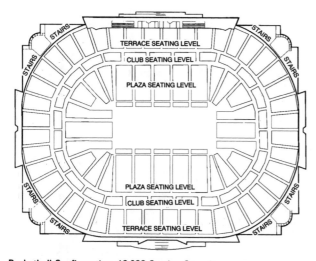

Basketball Configuration—18,200 Seating Capacity

cated on the terrace and club levels. All 84 suites and 1,400 (81 percent) of the club seats are currently (1996) leased. Suites seat ten, 12, or 14 guests depending on their size, with suite amenities including a refrigerator, wet bar, television, and telephones.

There are ten concession stands on the terrace level and four specialty concession areas on the plaza level.

Ten miles of piping are enclosed within the arena's concrete floor. When ice is needed for an event, brine is pumped through the piping to freeze the concrete. A thin sheet of water is pumped onto the floor and is frozen to the concrete. Logos and ice markings are painted on the ice. Finally, when another layer of ice has been added, the ice is about one inch thick.

FINANCING

Initially, the project was funded through a city bond issue of $126.5 million. Later, Ogden Entertainment relieved the city of its debt service and took over management of the facility.

Half of the Pond's revenue comes from corporate and individual leases of luxury suites and club seats. Rent from sports teams and event organizers accounts for an additional 20 percent of revenue.

The city of Anaheim receives a share of the profits only if these exceed Ogden's debt payment. Disney leases the arena and shares in the revenues from suite leases and permanent signage.

MARKET ORIENTATION

The Mighty Ducks and the Los Angeles Clippers (who play ten games per year at the facility) are the major tenants at Arrowhead Pond. The arena also hosts the Splash, a team of the Continental Indoor Soccer League. After Roller Hockey International introduced a professional league for indoor roller hockey, its Anaheim franchise, the Bullfrogs, began playing home games at Arrowhead Pond in July 1993. The circus, rodeos, ice shows, concerts, tennis, college and high-school basketball, motor sports, wrestling, and local functions are among the many other events held at Arrowhead Pond. In 1994, the Pond hosted 182 events, which were attended by 1.8 million people.

In its first year of operation, Arrowhead Pond of Anaheim received four awards from trade publications, including Best New Arena, New Venue of the Year, Venue of Merit, and Arena of Merit. In its first full year,

PROJECT DATA

ARROWHEAD POND OF ANAHEIM
ANAHEIM, CA

Owner: City of Anaheim
Architect: Hellmuth, Obata, & Kassabaum, Inc., Sports
 Facilities Group, Kansas City, Missouri
Primary Users: The Mighty Ducks of Anaheim (hockey),
 Los Angeles Clippers (basketball), Splash (indoor
 soccer), Bullfrogs (roller hockey)
Year Construction Began: 1990
Year Construction Completed: 1993

PROJECT INFORMATION

Total Seating Capacity:
 Hockey: 17,200
 Basketball: 18,200
 Boxing: 19,400
Total Parking Spaces:
 On Site: 4,500
 Nearby: 17,000

ECONOMIC INFORMATION

Total Project Cost (1993 dollars): $126,500,000
 Soft Costs: $56,500,000[1]
 Construction Costs: $70,000,000
Funding Source:
 City Bond Issue: $126,500,000[2]

Notes:
[1]Includes architectural fees, legal fees, and territorial rights payment due to the NHL's LA Kings.
[2]Later relieved by Ogden Entertainment.

it was also listed as the third-highest-grossing venue in North America for concert activity by *Amusement Business* and *Pollstar*. *Performance* magazine voted Arrowhead Pond the Arena of the Year for 1994.

LESSONS LEARNED

The arrangement between Disney, with its marketing expertise, and Ogden, contributing facility management, provided joint responsibility for selling the luxury suites. The venue and the NHL team also have created new opportunities for Disney by linking the NHL, Disney merchandise, and movies. Merchandise featuring the Mighty Ducks' mascot, "Wild Wing," currently (1995) outsells all other NHL logos and accounts for a large share of the league's retail merchandise sales. In addition, Disney's "Mighty Ducks" movies have helped promote the sport.

UNITED CENTER

CHICAGO, ILLINOIS

The United Center is a privately funded, state-of-the-art multiuse arena. Home to the Chicago Blackhawks National Hockey League team and the Chicago Bulls NBA team, the United Center also hosts concerts, sporting events, and family shows.

DEVELOPMENT STRATEGY

The United Center was developed as a joint venture between the owner of the Blackhawks and the owner of the Bulls to replace the antiquated Chicago Stadium, also the property of the Blackhawks' owner. Ironically, Chicago Stadium had been considered state-of-the-art when the National Hockey League was formed and played its inaugural season there in 1929. Planning began for the United Center in 1989, and construction was completed in 1994.

DESIGN AND SITE ISSUES

Sited on 45 acres, one mile west of Chicago's Loop and four blocks north of I-290 at Damen Avenue, the United Center contains nearly 1 million square feet of floor space. The arena has nine team/star dressing rooms, six locker rooms for sports teams, and 46 permanent concession stands offering 194 points of sale. Catering is also available.

"Fandemonium," the United Center's sportswear store, includes the Bulls/Blackhawks Hall of Fame and a 70-seat theater showing highlights of the greatest moments in team history. The arena also has four permanent merchandise stands.

The United Center seats 24,500 for concerts, 20,500 for hockey, 21,500 for basketball, and 25,000 for wrestling/boxing. On-site parking for 5,000 cars is available in secure, well-lit lots. All parking lots are fenced and continually patrolled. Twenty-five entry lanes and cashiers make access swift and exiting easy.

The United Center has 216 unusual private luxury suites, each offering 12 to 16 seats, for a total of 2,600 suite seats. The suites are located on three levels (lower, club, and penthouse), and each is served by its own private elevator and concourse. Lower-level suites rise 19 rows off the floor, club-level suites are 27 rows off the floor, and penthouse-level (skybox) suites offer an outstanding view from above the top rows of seats. The 3,300 club seats are found between the two lower suite levels, and access to them is gained from their own private concourse.

MARKET ORIENTATION

The United Center is home to the Chicago Blackhawks and Chicago Bulls. The arena will host more than 175 events annually, including some 100 Bulls/Blackhawks preseason, regular-season home games, and play-off games. It was designed to accommodate all major touring musical performers, sporting events, and family shows.

FINANCING

The $175 million United Center was privately financed through the First Bank of Chicago. The entire project will be paid for by the Bulls and the Blackhawks.

LESSONS LEARNED

- It was always anticipated that the United Center would have a high profile because it was built in a union town, using union laborers who took pride in their work and are avid home-team fans.
- Because the United Center is a new building, it is going through an adjustment period. For example, the food service staff have had to adapt to the added responsibility of expanded concession services on six levels and to the demands of catering for 216 suites on three levels.

PROJECT DATA

UNITED CENTER
CHICAGO, IL

Owner: United Center Joint Venture
Architects: Hellmuth, Obata & Kassabaum (HOK), Kansas City, Missouri
Year Planning Began: 1989
Year Construction Began: 1992
Year Construction Completed: 1994

PROJECT INFORMATION
Site Area: 45 acres
Total GBA: 960,000 square feet
Seating Capacity:
    Basketball: 21,500
    Hockey: 20,500
    Concerts: 24,500
    Wrestling/Boxing: 25,000
Total Parking: 5,000

ECONOMIC INFORMATION
Total Project Cost (1994 dollars): $175,000,000
Financing:
    First Bank of Chicago:[1] $140,000,000
    Equity: $35,000,000

Note:
[1]Includes 12 agent banks.

- United Center's financial success can be attributed to the successful preleasing of a large number of suites. Not only does this center offer more private seating than any other indoor arena, but also every suite was leased before groundbreaking. Preleasing helped to pay for a major part of the construction costs and to reduce the amount that had to be financed.

OCEAN CENTER

DAYTONA BEACH, FLORIDA

The Ocean Center in Daytona Beach is a 10,000-seat, multipurpose facility that serves the community as a sports and entertainment center, as well as a venue for conventions and meetings. Located one block from the Atlantic oceanfront, the center is in the heart of the Daytona Beach resort area along U.S. Highway A-1-A. The facility adds a new facet to this traditionally tourist-oriented community.

DEVELOPMENT STRATEGY

During the early 1970s, Daytona Beach felt the aftershocks of the energy crunch as tourism began to decline, weakening the local economy and making it heavily dependent upon visitors to Cape Canaveral and the beaches. Also, increasing competition from Orlando, with the advent of Disney World and other prominent tourist attractions, lessened Daytona Beach's desirability as a destination. As a result, the central or core beach areas of Daytona Beach began to decay, as hotel properties,

suffering from high vacancy rates, showed the effects of fewer dollars in property upkeep and maintenance and as poor market conditions forced plans for new hotels to be dropped. The decline of the central beach areas of Daytona Beach was also reflected in the surrounding retail and restaurant establishments dependent upon tourists. A community and government effort was spawned in this environment to pursue diversification of the visitor and convention markets.

In 1974, the Daytona Beach Chamber of Commerce joined with Volusia County in commissioning a study of current market conditions and of a proposal to build a convention/civic center. This three-part study found that a multipurpose facility in the Daytona Beach area would create a demand for a different segment of the hotel market. At the time, however, county officials lacked the resources to finance any land acquisition or project development.

In 1978, voters approved a local-option hotel tax intended as a funding source for the proposed civic center. Accordingly, Volusia County retained a multidisciplinary team of consultants to devise and implement a specific development strategy for the proposed facility, covering:

- Site selection.
- Building program, estimated usage, and financial operating estimates.
- Development budget and financing strategy.
- Development timetables, methods of contracting, and methods of project management.
- Executive recruitment and preopening operating objectives.

Members of the consulting team included economic/market and development consultants, architectural designers and engineers, building managers, financial advisers, and traffic and parking engineers.

The study recommended a specific site in the Daytona Beach vicinity and suggested that the project would serve as a public investment in the redevelopment of the beach district. The criteria used to evaluate potential sites encompassed site acquisition costs, any threat of delays, development costs and financing plans, subordination of the land to hotel mortgage or civic center bonds, any guarantee of hotel development, and traffic issues.

The source of funding identified was the state's newly enacted local-option tourist development tax, which empowers counties to levy a resort tax. The consultants also recommended an innovative design/build approach by which design teams composed of architects, engineers, and contractors would each submit a single proposal with a guaranteed maximum price.

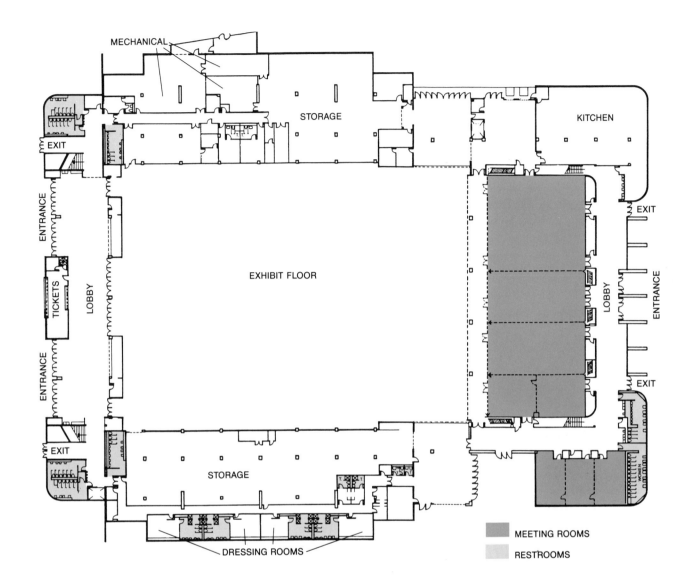

MECHANICAL

STORAGE

KITCHEN

EXIT

ENTRANCE

TICKETS

LOBBY

EXHIBIT FLOOR

EXIT

ENTRANCE

LOBBY

ENTRANCE

EXIT

EXIT

STORAGE

WOMEN

DRESSING ROOMS

MEETING ROOMS

RESTROOMS

Site acquisition controversies and a period of high interest rates in the early 1980s delayed the project. It was not until 1983 that revenue bonds were issued and construction began on the Ocean Center.

DESIGN AND SITE ISSUES

The center's design showcases its versatility and its capability of making quick changeovers from spectator event to exhibition event. For instance, the facility can be set up for a sporting event one night and then converted within eight hours for convention or trade-show activity. Movable walls add to the flexibility to handle multiple or different-sized events. Concert seating can accommodate up to 10,000 people, and because there are only 4,200 perma-

nent seats, the portable seating structures can be stored away to convert the arena into a 46,000-square-foot exhibition hall. If additional room is required, movable partitions allow for 14,000 square feet of adjoining banquet/meeting space to be used as exhibition space, for a total of some 60,000 square feet of continuous space.

Two other features added to the design of the facility during construction were a catering kitchen for attracting meetings and conventions that require food service and the icemaking equipment that would allow the center to be used for ice shows, hockey exhibitions, or public skating. Project construction costs amounted to $24 million for the center, with an additional $3.5 million for adjacent surface parking improvements. Total project development costs including land aquisition were about $42 million.

Volusia County purchased some 18 acres of land for the Ocean Center site in the designated community redevelopment district, a special tax assessment district in Daytona Beach. The land, mostly residential property, was an assemblage of approximately 100 parcels and took almost three years to acquire, as many homeowners sued the county during and after the eminent domain proceedings. There was also controversy over the vacation of the right-of-way of Grandview Street. Many residents complained that this street was a well-traveled north/south connector to Main Street, which runs from the beach district to the mainland. The Daytona Beach City Commission, however, ruled in favor of the county. Total cost for the land assemblage (including land for parking) and for the purchase of rights-of-way came to $8.8 million.

PROJECT DATA

OCEAN CENTER
DAYTONA BEACH, FL

Owner: Volusia County
Developer: Volusia County
Architect: Ellerbe Architects, Minneapolis
Primary Users: College basketball, professional wrestling, Sun Devils (hockey), conventions, trade shows, consumer shows
Year Planning Began: 1974
Year Construction Began: 1983
Year Construction Completed: 1985

PROJECT INFORMATION
Site Area: 18 acres
Total GBA: 225,000 square feet
    Exhibition Space: 46,000 square feet[1]
    Meeting Space: 14,000 square feet
Total Seating Capacity:[2] 10,000

ECONOMIC INFORMATION
Site Acquisition Cost: $8,800,000
Construction Cost: $24,000,000[3]
Total Project Cost: $42,000,000
Funding Sources:
    Local-Option Hotel Tax (1978–1983): $9,000,000
    Revenue Bond Issue (1983): $29,000,000
    Interest on Capital Improvement Fund: $4,000,000

Notes:
[1]Movable partitions can make 60,000 square feet available.
[2]Only 4,200 seats are permanent.
[3]Plus $3.5 million for adjacent surface parking improvements.

FINANCING

Enactment of the local-option tourist development tax by Florida's state legislature in 1977 provided the source of funds and gave the impetus to push the Ocean Center from an idea into a reality. Volusia County, like all Florida counties, was enabled to levy a 2 percent tax on hotel rooms, with use of the monies restricted to funding CVBs, backing the construction and development of convention facilities, and generally promoting tourism. The land purchase was completely financed through tourist development tax revenues, which had started to accrue several years before the land assemblage took place, from 1980 to 1983.

In 1983, Volusia County issued $29 million in revenue bonds to construct the Ocean Center and to develop adjacent parking lots. Other sources of financing included $9 million from tourist tax revenues that had accumulated before construction and another $4 million from interest earned on capital improvement funds during construction.

Despite the tourist development tax, the county still needed an interlocal agreement with the city of Daytona Beach to issue the bonds. Basically, the agreement allows the city to guarantee the bonds with a pledge of state revenue-sharing income and a portion of the franchise fees from utilities. This agreement added $3 million of debt security annually to the Ocean Center bond issue.

MARKET ORIENTATION

The Daytona Beach market is not large enough to compete for most national and regional trade shows and conventions that would use the larger facilities located, for instance, in Orlando or Miami. Daytona Beach, however, has been able to capture significant levels of concert activity, smaller conventions, and state association meetings since the center's opening in September 1985.

The Daytona Beach Marriott, which opened in January 1989, added 400 first-class hotel rooms directly across the street from the Ocean Center. However, tourist-oriented motels in the vicinity of the center have made it difficult to assemble large, convention-quality room blocks convenient to the facility.

In addition, the Ocean Center continues to be a strong venue for family shows, such as the circus and truck and tractor pull competitions. Sporting events include collegiate basketball (Stetson University, Daytona Community College, and Bethune-Cookman College), plus championship wrestling and Daytona Sun Devils (Sunshine State Hockey League) games.

LESSONS LEARNED

Officials associated with Ocean Center's development are pleased with every aspect of the design, building program, and construction process. Some points of experience gained include:

- An innovative, fast-track process allowed for more than 100 change orders to be made during the construction period. Only two months before scheduled groundbreaking, a 40,000-square-foot wing and an ice floor were added, and the building was turned to an east/west orientation without causing delays in the construction process.
- At groundbreaking, only 30 percent of the design was on paper, allowing for owner-initiated changes to be made throughout the entire process with a minimal amount of disruption.
- Volusia County hired the building manager at groundbreaking to further influence the final design of the center. It is difficult to hire a building manager almost

24 months before a facility is ready for occupancy, and Volusia County's ability to do this was a notable accomplishment. The 24-month construction period was comparable to that of a conventional approach to construction; however, the changes Volusia County made could have delayed center construction far beyond two years.

McNichols Sports Arena

DENVER, COLORADO

The McNichols Sports Arena and Entertainment Complex in Denver, Colorado, is a 17,000-seat arena located next to Mile High Stadium off Interstate 25, near downtown Denver. The arena and the entertainment complex, although not built at the same time, are both owned by the City and County of Denver Division of Theaters and Arenas. The Denver Nuggets professional basketball team is the arena's primary tenant.

DEVELOPMENT STRATEGY

In the early 1970s, the state of Colorado and the city of Denver were candidates to host the 1976 Winter Olympic Games. The question of whether to host the Olympics, however, became a political hotbed. The incumbent mayor of Denver, William McNichols, Jr., was a major proponent of the Olympic movement in Denver, but the governor opposed the idea. As the debate heated up, the issue came to a vote in 1972. Two questions were placed on the city ballot: (1) should Denver and Colorado host the 1976 Winter Olympics? and (2) should Denver build a new sports arena?

The citizens of Denver voted to decline hosting the 1976 Winter Olympics but did elect to build a new arena. The vote led to a bond issue to finance the construction and development of McNichols Sports Arena. In 1973, the City and County of Denver Public Works Department hired the Denver architectural firm of Sink, Combs, Dethlefs to design the arena. A general contractor was not hired; rather, the public works department implemented a phased construction with multiple prime contracts.

DESIGN AND SITE ISSUES

McNichols was designed to accommodate a variety of sporting events, such as basketball, hockey, tennis, and boxing, with seating capacities ranging from 16,000 to 20,000. The roof rises 85 feet above the arena floor. The facility features two seating levels, with the upper level overlapping the lower so that the roof area is reduced and upper-level viewing distances shortened. Seating is divided equally between the upper and lower levels.

The elevation of the upper seating section allows spectators on the concourse level to view arena activity as they circulate from the entrance to the seating aisles. The concourse level provides access to all seating and contains the concession stands and restrooms. Construction costs for the 252,000-square-foot arena in 1973 were $11.4 million, of which $9.7 million were hard costs.

The city purchased the 20-acre site for $3 million. Access from all directions is excellent, and a natural change in elevation lends itself to public access on the concourse level and service access at floor level. McNichols was built on the embankment portion of the site, leaving the maximum level square footage for parking. McNichols has a 5,500-space parking lot that it shares with Mile High Stadium. This parking is ample for the arena, although not adequate for stadium events. Fortunately, bookings for both venues are handled by the city, so that conflicts in scheduling that could cause parking problems are avoided.

In 1986, the city reached a lease renewal agreement with the owners of the Denver Nuggets that, in addition to spelling out rental terms, established a renovation program for McNichols Sports Arena. The Nuggets' owners were responsible for the $12.9 million renovation, all of whose stages from design through construction were completed within ten months, and which included:

- A new Arena Club (11,000 square feet, with 400 seats for dining).
- Three themed restaurants (15,000 square feet, with 316 seats for dining).
- Enlarged public concourses.
- Additional restrooms.
- An instant replay scoreboard.
- A stereo sound system.
- Upgraded food and beverage concessions.
- Upgraded luxury box suites (expanded to 18 seats each).
- Ten new box suites.

The Arena Club has a glass facade on the eastern side and gives easy access to and from the concourse. The three themed restaurants were added directly off the concourse to raise additional revenues and to afford spectators a variety of dining choices before, during, and after events. These restaurants are also open during non-event days.

FINANCING

Funding for the original construction and development of McNichols Arena came primarily from two sources:

the city of Denver issued a $10 million general obligation bond to finance construction, while the federal government gave the city $3.9 million in revenue-sharing funds. Federal revenue sharing was a 1970s program that gave cities monies with no constraints on how it must be spent. Another $1.8 million came from a capital improvements fund and the remainder from various other sources. Total cost for arena and parking lot construction and site acquisition was $16.2 million.

Arena renovations were paid for in a rather unusual fashion that was agreed upon in the lease. Improvements were paid for out of the operations of the arena before any split between the team and the city, thus sparing the citizens a vote on a bond issue. The agreement also conferred more responsibility on the Nuggets for marketing the facility and called for a stream of revenue guarantees to the city.

MARKET ORIENTATION

McNichols Sports Arena is home to the NBA Nuggets and IHL Grizzlers. The Nuggets attracted nearly 700,000 fans in the 1993–1994 season. The arena also hosts other

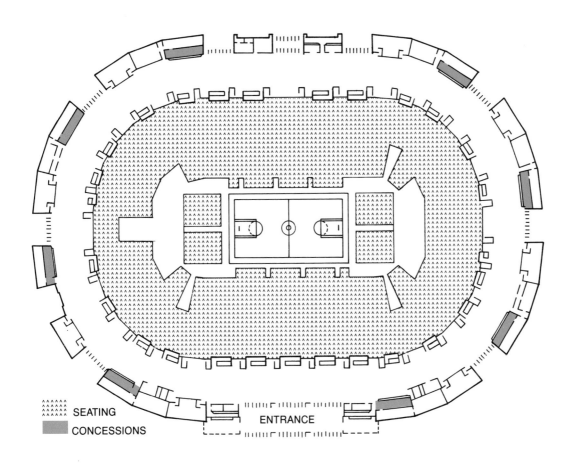

SEATING

CONCESSIONS

ENTRANCE

sporting events, such as boxing and wrestling. Concerts and family shows like circuses, ice shows, and truck and tractor pulls fill the rest of the events calendar.

LESSONS LEARNED

McNichols Arena officials were generally pleased with the original facility's construction and design. While loading and service area space was adequate when the building opened in 1975, over the years, as concerts and touring shows required more space for equipment, the arena was faced with internal traffic congestion during pre- and post-event hours. The main problems occurred backstage, where event production personnel setting up equipment and concessionaire staff receiving deliveries competed for the same space. The 1987 renovation increased food service and storage area. The issue was finally resolved when additional service space was added in 1994 to provide separate areas for loading and service personnel.

PROJECT DATA

MCNICHOLS SPORTS ARENA
DENVER, CO

Owner: City of Denver
Developer: City of Denver Public Works Department
Builders: Multiple (27) prime contractors, working within a phased construction program
Architect: Sink, Combs, Dethlefs of Denver
Manager/Operator: City and County of Denver Division of Theaters and Arenas
Primary Users: Denver Nuggets (basketball), Denver Grizzlers (hockey), concerts, family shows
Year Construction Began: 1973
Year Construction Completed: 1975

PROJECT INFORMATION

Site Area: 20 acres
Total GBA: 252,000 square feet
Total Seating Capacity:
    Basketball: 16,700
    Hockey: 16,215
    Concerts: 18,200
Total Parking Spaces: 5,500

ECONOMIC INFORMATION[1]

Site Acquisition Costs: $3,000,000
Site Development Costs: $1,757,367
Construction Costs: $9,769,249
Consulting Fees:
    Architectural/Engineering: $784,000
    Construction Management: $867,742
    Financing: $21,642
    Reserve for Contingencies: $1,673,384
Total Project Costs: $16,200,000
Funding Sources:
    General Obligation Bond: $10,000,000
    Federal Revenue-Sharing Funds: $3,900,000
    Capital Improvements Fund: $1,800,000
    Other Sources: $500,000

Note:
[1]In 1975 dollars.

THE PALACE OF AUBURN HILLS

AUBURN HILLS, MICHIGAN

The Palace of Auburn Hills is a multipurpose sports and entertainment facility that is home to Detroit's NBA Pistons, the IHL Vipers, and the Neon indoor soccer team. The Palace was designed with special consideration for patron comfort, security, and accessibility, with an emphasis on public-space ambience, seating configuration, sightlines, and acoustic qualities. The facility has received many design and technical awards, among them *Pollstar* magazine's 1992 Arena of the Year, *Performance* magazine's 1988 Best New Venue, and several other Arena of the Year awards.

DEVELOPMENT STRATEGY

The Palace was designed and built on an extremely aggressive fast-track schedule. Facility design began early in 1986, and site work started in June of the same year, barely four-and-a-half months into the design process. Construction also proceeded at a very rapid pace in order to achieve completion in time for the Pistons' 1988–1989 season.

DESIGN AND SITE ISSUES

The Palace is located in Auburn Hills, 25 miles north of downtown Detroit and immediately north of the I-75/M-24 interchange. It is strategically sited in an area that has become a major entertainment center of southeastern Michigan. The Pontiac Silverdome, four miles south, is home to the Detroit Lions NFL team. Also within ten miles of the arena are two outdoor amphitheaters, Pine Knob Music Theatre and Meadow Brook Music Festival.

The 61.3-acre site provides parking for more than 8,400 cars in a parklike setting. A generously proportioned, landscaped plaza that surrounds the building gently slopes from the northwest at the concourse level, to the club/main entry level, to the loading dock on the floor level. Approximately 12 acres of the site are designated as wetlands. Site design considerations included preservation and enhancement of the wetlands, integration of the large stormwater detention basins into the wetlands and the natural topography, and meeting the stringent landscape requirements of the city of Auburn Hills. The ultimate goal of the project was to create an exciting, people-oriented entertainment venue while adhering to good engineering and environmentally responsible principles.

The exterior of the 485,000-square-foot circular structure is covered with brick-faced, precast concrete panels arranged in a decorative diagonal pattern, with concrete and tile medallions for accents. Expansive glass entries and skylights, in addition to a ring of high windows, bring natural light into the arena and provide a spectacular view of the site from the upper balcony level.

The 21,454-seat Palace offers 180 private box suites at three levels. All levels are connected to the members-only, club-level restaurant and bar. At the front of each suite, facing the arena, are ten to 14 seats reserved for suite holders. Ranging from 186 square feet to 450 square feet, all suites have a private entrance, living room, wet bar, and restroom. Each is equipped with furniture, appliances, television, telephone, and decorative accessories. Suite holders are offered ten color schemes and five furniture styles from which to choose. Private suites enjoy preordered food and beverage catering service from the central kitchen.

Fifty-two notable suites are found at rows 16 and 17 above the arena level to afford spectator viewing from mid-level. The most convenient features of these club-level suites are their location near and accessibility to the courtside level. Located only a few rows above the arena floor, they offer an outstanding view of all types of spectator events. In addition, 48 concourse-level suites are

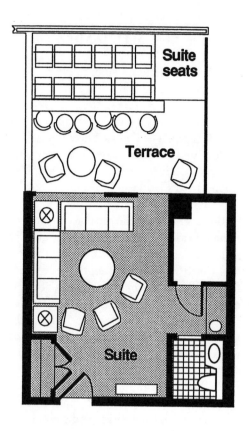

are guaranteed attendance at 100 events, including all Pistons home games. Currently, all suites are leased.

All of the seats in the arena are fully upholstered for comfort, appearance, and superior acoustics. Though a noise reduction coefficient (NRC) of 40 to 45 is common in most arenas, the Palace has an NRC of 35, equivalent to that of a normal office building's ambient noise level. These acoustics enhance musical productions, conventions, and other activities.

Arena patrons are served by ten concession stands and two fast-food facilities at the concourse level. In-stand food vending is also provided.

The Palace also houses the Pistons' administrative offices and team facilities, visiting team locker rooms, dressing rooms, arena management offices, and a rooftop heliport.

FINANCING

The Palace was funded entirely by a private ownership group, Arena Associates, Inc., including the owner of the Pistons, William Davidson. Much of the capital came from presales of private suites.

offered at rows 25 and 26, and 80 suites are to be found on the penthouse level; several of the latter are leased on a timeshare basis to colessors.

Suite leases range from $30,000 to $120,000 per year and run for three-year periods. Included in the cost are tickets, parking passes to a private lot, and membership in the club-level restaurant and bar. Suite holders

MARKETING AND MANAGEMENT

The Pistons' season-ticket package sales exceed 15,000. Many concert events have played to capacity audiences as well. With more than 175 events per year, the Palace attracts more than 2.5 million persons annually.

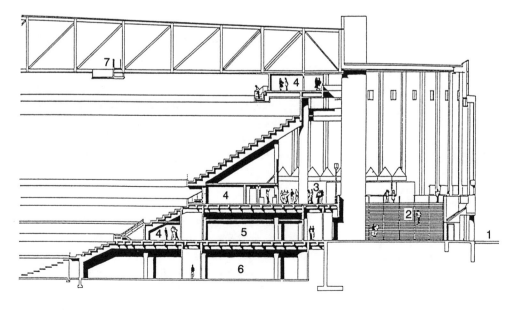

TYPICAL STADIA SECTION

1. ENTRY PLAZA
2. FOYER
3. CONCOURSE
4. PRIVATE SUITE
5. RESTAURANT / CLUB / ADMIN.
6. LOCKER / STORAGE SERVICE
7. TRUSS LEVEL CATWALK

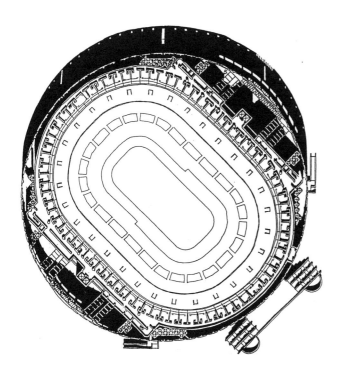

The arena is a state-of-the-art basketball facility yet can accommodate concerts requiring an indoor setting with excellent acoustics. Because it offers an unobstructed view, the Palace is also a good setting for circuses, ice shows, rodeos, and other family events.

The venue is self-managed by Palace Sports & Entertainment, which handles every aspect of arena management except concessions, and which also runs two nearby outdoor amphitheaters, Pine Knob and Meadow Brook.

LESSONS LEARNED

■ Early on, it became apparent that the building lacked both administrative office space and storage space, forcing the use of off-site space for these purposes.
■ Permanent ice capabilities were added in 1992, allowing for more family shows on ice and the addition of

PROJECT DATA

THE PALACE OF AUBURN HILLS
AUBURN HILLS, MI

Owner: Arena Associates, Inc. (William Davidson, majority owner)
Operator: Palace Sports & Entertainment
Builder: R.E. Dailey Construction Company, Detroit
Architect: Rossetti Associates, Birmingham, Michigan
Primary Users: Detroit Pistons (basketball), Detroit Vipers (hockey), Detroit Neon (indoor soccer)
Year Planning Began: 1986
Year Construction Began: 1986
Year Construction Completed: 1988

PROJECT INFORMATION
Site Area: 61.3 acres
Total GBA: 485,000 square feet
Arena Floor: 30,000 square feet
Total Seating Capacity:
    Basketball: 21,454
    Hockey: 20,182
    Concert: 16,762–22,533
Private Suites: 180
Total Parking Spaces: 8,400 on site

ECONOMIC INFORMATION
Total Project Cost (1989 dollars): $62,000,000
Funding Sources: Private

a professional hockey team. This adaptability was possible because the building was originally designed to allow for an ice-arena configuration.
■ The extremely ambitious fast-track construction schedule necessitated the use of a combination of cast-in-place and precast concrete structural elements. Also, economics and construction speed dictated that the interior face of the exterior building panels had to be the interior building finish as well. What evolved was a precast, insulated concrete panel system that was fabricated and erected with virtually no problems.

JACK BRESLIN STUDENT EVENTS CENTER

EAST LANSING, MICHIGAN

The Jack Breslin Student Events Center, which stands on the Michigan State University (MSU) campus, is an all-event facility designed for conventions, trade shows, concerts, and other functions of interest to the university and the East Lansing community.

DEVELOPMENT STRATEGY

The 15,000-seat center was named for Jack Breslin, who served as an administrator (among many other roles) at MSU for almost 50 years. Breslin Center and its multi-purpose arena were completed in 1989, replacing the 49-year-old Jenison Field House.

DESIGN AND SITE ISSUES

The Breslin Center contains three levels: the arena floor, mezzanine, and concourse. The arena floor level is the location of locker rooms, mechanical areas, and press rooms. The mezzanine level features a lobby and four 1,000-square-foot meeting rooms, administration offices, and MSU basketball offices. Also on this level is an auxiliary gymnasium with an additional 8,190 square feet of space.

The concourse, or the main entry level of the building, gives access to upper- and lower-level seating. There are eight luxury suites on the concourse level, accommodating up to 12 people each, and platform seating for 165 handicapped persons.

At the perimeter of the basketball court are 12 rows of telescopic bench seating. Because all seats offer an unobstructed view, even the seats farthest away from the floor (only 127 feet) are considered good ones.

The million-dollar sound and light systems afford excellent acoustics and computerized lighting. Concessions are on the concourse, with catering services available.

FINANCING

The total construction cost of the center, $43 million, was paid from student fees which are paid with tuition costs.

MARKET ORIENTATION

The Breslin Center accommodates men's and women's basketball, as well as commencement ceremonies, concerts, trade shows, conventions, and other special events.

LESSONS LEARNED

- The Breslin Center was designed to accommodate handicapped persons by complying with the new ADA standards and by providing listening devices and interpreters for hearing-impaired patrons.
- Only one box office was incorporated into the design, sufficient for basketball but not for other events (family shows, concerts, exhibitions, and the like) that need ticket windows at the gates.

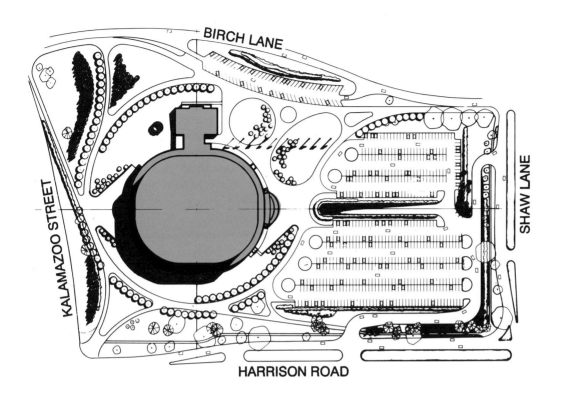

BIRCH LANE

KALAMAZOO STREET

SHAW LANE

HARRISON ROAD

PROJECT DATA

JACK BRESLIN STUDENT EVENTS CENTER
EAST LANSING, MI

Owner: Michigan State University
Architect: Giffels/Hoyem Basso, Michigan; HNTB Sports
  Facilities Group, Kansas City, Missouri
Primary Users: Michigan State University (basketball)
Year Planning Began: 1985
Year Construction Began: 1986
Year Construction Completed: 1989

PROJECT INFORMATION

Site Area: 900,000+ square feet
Total GBA: 254,000 square feet
  Exhibition Space: 17,500 square feet
  Concourse Area: 30,000–45,000 square feet
Seating Capacity: 15,100
Parking Spaces: 550 on site, 3,500 adjacent

ECONOMIC INFORMATION

Total Project Cost (1986 dollars): $43,000,000
Total Project Cost (1994 dollars):[1] $57,202,555

Note:
[1]Calculated based on the consumer price index.

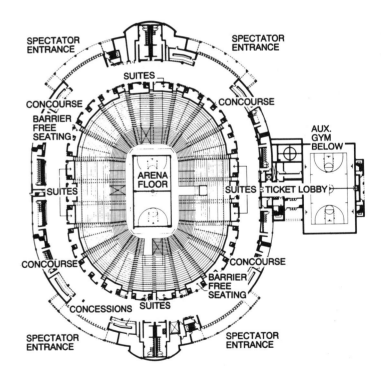

MARKET SQUARE ARENA

INDIANAPOLIS, INDIANA

Sited in downtown Indianapolis, the 17,000-seat Market Square Arena has been the home of the Indiana Pacers since its opening in 1974. The arena has also hosted numerous national and international events, including the NCAA men's basketball tournament and the Pan American Games. In addition to high-profile sporting events, the arena was the venue of Elvis Presley's last concert. "The King" sang his last performance at Market Square on June 26, 1977. In 1994, the IHL Indianapolis Ice made its new home at Market Square Arena.

DEVELOPMENT STRATEGY

Market Square Arena is the product of a partnership between Market Square Associates and the city of Indianapolis and is probably one of the earliest examples of public/private development of public assembly projects.

In 1971, an agreement between Market Square Associates and the city was reached with the support and endorsement of Mayor Richard Lugar. The agreement outlined the commitments of both parties in the construction, development, and financing of the arena, parking garages, and ancillary development. Market Square Associates (MSA) included the F.C. Tucker Company, Mid-Republican Construction Company, and Indiana Professional Sports, Inc. (the Pacers).

Under the agreement, the city purchased and cleared the downtown Market Street site, which in turn was leased to Market Square Associates for $150,000 annually. MSA built two 600-car parking garages, over which the city built the arena, which was to be managed by MSA. The city financed the arena's land acquisition and construction, while MSA financed construction of the parking garages. As part of the agreement, MSA obtained permission to develop an adjacent parcel of land. The development plan for this parcel called for a first phase that included a 12-story office building with an adjoining 846-car parking facility to be completed concurrently with the arena. The second phase was to include an additional 12-story office building.

Development of the arena and adjacent office buildings was part of a strategy to revitalize downtown Indianapolis, particularly the Market Square vicinity. The idea was to bring people to this area during the day for work and at night for entertainment, in the hope that the increased pedestrian traffic would spur the growth of supporting restaurants and retail establishments. Property values would increase, and so would property taxes. Therefore, the cost of development to the general population would be more than paid off by the ancillary development, such as the City Market, a renovated festival retail center.

In 1983, the city sold the arena to the Capital Improvement Board (CIB) of Marion County, which owns the RCA Dome and the Indiana Convention Center. The CIB undertook a $3 million renovation of the arena. The roof was replaced, repairs were made to the concourse, the exterior was repainted, and new restrooms were added. The CIB did all this work as part of an agreement with the Pacers' new owners, Melvin and Herb Simon, who also have the management contract for the arena.

DESIGN AND SITE ISSUES

Market Square Arena was built at a time when federal regulations overseeing worker safety and the environment came into being in the form of OSHA and EPA. Enforcement of these regulations cost the city $400,000. The approximately four-acre downtown site was found to be located over an underground river, which hampered and delayed the project; land acquisition and site clearing cost about $2 million.

The arena has a maximum seating capacity of 18,000 for concerts, 16,000 for Indianapolis Ice hockey, and 16,500 for Indiana Pacers basketball.

FINANCING

In 1971, the city issued a $12 million, 30-year general obligation bond for the purpose of buying the site and building Market Square Arena. Financing for the garages was handled privately by Market Square Associates through the Indiana National Bank. The cost of the garages came to $3.5 million each. As stated in the agreement, MSA leased the land for $150,000 and also leased the arena for $360,000, its payments thus totaling $510,000.

Cost overruns on the project were paid from federal revenue-sharing funds, which were created in 1972 and given to cities with no strings attached. Indianapolis received $12 million from this source in 1973. (Two years later, the U.S. General Accounting Office surveyed the uses of these funds, and Indianapolis was found to be the only city to have used them for sports facility development.)

When ownership of the arena transferred to the CIB, the CIB agreed to pay $510,000 a year.

MARKET ORIENTATION

The arena's primary tenants are the NBA Indiana Pacers and the IHL Indianapolis Ice; sporting events account for roughly half of the arena's annual use. The Pacers attracted 800,000 fans in the 1994–1995 season. Other events held at the arena include concerts, ice shows, and circuses.

LESSONS LEARNED

Market Square Arena demonstrates that development of public assembly facilities by public/private partnerships can work and can benefit both parties.

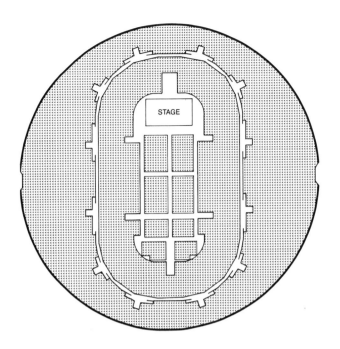

PROJECT DATA

MARKET SQUARE ARENA
INDIANAPOLIS, IN

Owner: Capital Improvement Board (City of Indianapolis/Marion County)
Primary Users: Indiana Pacers (basketball), Indianapolis Ice (hockey)
Year Planning Began: 1971
Year Construction Completed: 1974

PROJECT INFORMATION
Site Area: 4 acres
Seating Capacity:
    Basketball: 16,500
    Hockey: 16,000
    Concerts: 18,000
Parking:
    On Site: 1,275
    Nearby: 10,000

ECONOMIC INFORMATION
Funding Sources:
    General Obligation Bond:[1] $12,000,000
    Federal Revenue-Sharing Funds: $12,000,000
    Market Square Associates: $7,000,000[2]

Notes:
[1] Issued by the city of Indianapolis.
[2] For parking garages.

THOMAS & MACK CENTER

LAS VEGAS, NEVADA

The Thomas & Mack (T&M) Center is located on the campus of the University of Nevada at Las Vegas (UNLV). The center, which is owned and operated by the university, has as its primary tenant the UNLV men's basketball team, the Rebels. However, the 18,000-seat arena not only accommodates UNLV sporting events but is also a popular venue for major concerts and other nonsporting events.

DEVELOPMENT STRATEGY

The primary force behind the drive to fund and build the Thomas & Mack Center came from the Rebels Athletic Foundation and its then-president, William W. Morris. Interest in building an on-campus facility mounted in 1977, when the Rebels' coach, Jerry Tarkanian, led the team to the NCAA men's basketball championships. Tarkanian complained that he could not bring top teams to Las Vegas because the arena that UNLV then used at the Las Vegas Convention Center only held 6,327 spectators, and the university was unable to pay the mini-

mum guarantees required to draw the top competition. Another limitation that this earlier venue imposed on the university's athletic department was low ticket sales resulting from the arena's limited seating capacity.

In 1977, the Rebels Athletic Foundation presented a proposal to the Nevada state legislature outlining a building program for a new continuing education and special-events facility. The proposal called for an 18,000-seat arena to be built on campus and to include a continuing education center to house the offices of the athletic department, thereby freeing office space in the physical education complex. The continuing education facility, a 29,000-square-foot component of the center, would include a 300-seat auditorium, eight classrooms, a kitchen, a conference room, 11 administrative offices, and a lobby and would be situated next to the athletic department offices. Both components would have separate ingress and egress from the arena.

The legislature accepted the proposal and began planning and designing the facility. The state's department of public works, which managed the development and construction of the center, selected the architectural team of Carl Warnicke, Architect, and Cambiero & Cambiero, Architects, to design the Thomas & Mack Center. Mardian Construction of Phoenix was hired as the general contractor.

DESIGN AND SITE ISSUES

The UNLV campus covers about 335 acres, of which the T&M Center occupies 53 acres in the southeastern quadrant of the campus. The site had been chosen during the master planning of the university. There is a main entrance to the facility's parking and another general public entrance to the back parking lots.

During construction, design problems were discovered in the seating structure. The original design followed the Rebels Athletic Foundation's proposal recommendations, with an emphasis on a basketball configuration. There was no allowance for flexibility in seating, however; the concrete seating structures extended almost to courtside. The newly appointed manager, Dennis Finfrock, ordered the concrete structures to be jackhammered at a cost of $445,000. This alteration allowed the T&M Center to adapt its seating configuration to host large family shows and rodeos but forced a postponement on paving the parking lots because the center was on a fixed budget. Paving on the parking lots was finally completed in 1987, almost three-and-a-half years after completion of the structure itself.

FINANCING

The state legislature voted to finance the project with a slot tax rebate in 1978. Originally, the lawmakers wanted to issue bonds that were exempt from the bonded indebtedness provision in the Nevada bylaws: Nevada law prohibits the state from having a total outstanding debt of more than 1 percent of the assessed value of property held in the state. Thus, a friendly lawsuit was filed to determine whether these bonds would come under the bonded indebtedness provision. The courts ruled that they would.

In 1981, the state of Nevada issued $40 million in general obligation bonds for the purpose of building the T&M Center at UNLV, as well as the Lawlor Special Events Center at the University of Nevada at Reno. The state stipulated that the two centers were to be completed at approximately the same time and budgeted at fixed ceilings of $30 million for T&M and $26 million for the Lawlor Events Center. Additional funding for the two projects came from the Special Capital Construction Fund for Higher Education ($12 million) and anticipated interest on the construction fund ($4.5 million).

Monies for the Special Capital Construction Fund for Higher Education and its special fund come from a portion of the proceeds of the state's slot tax, an originally federal tax that amounts to a per-machine assessment on all coin-operated gaming devices. Proceeds from this tax are allocated as follows: $5 million to the Capital Construction Fund for Higher Education; 20 percent of the tax to the special fund; and the balance of the proceeds from the tax to the state distributive fund, to be earmarked for elementary and secondary education. Although the state is generally obligated to the bond issue, the capital fund and the special fund serve as pledged sources for the issue.

The state also mandated that both facilities be revenue-producing, that is, that revenue from operations must cover operating and maintenance expenditures. If either facility should operate at a deficit, the overage would be funded from the general operating funds of the respective university.

MARKET ORIENTATION

Thomas & Mack Center was built primarily to serve the needs of UNLV's athletic department. But if the center wants to operate at a surplus, it is not able to rely on UNLV sports alone. Management has been aggressive in bringing concerts and family shows to the center. At first, the center faced opposition from local hotel groups that did not want competition for entertainment. Because of its size, however, T&M Center can accommodate performers and groups who need larger stages and more seats than the hotels can provide.

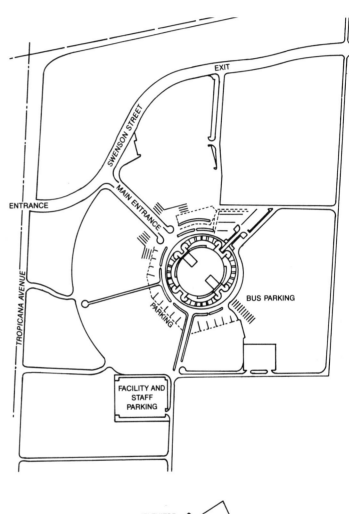

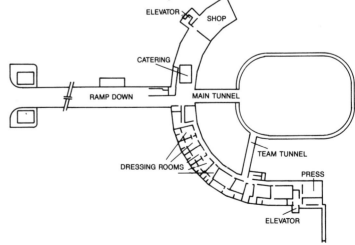

Probably the biggest coup that center management has accomplished is bringing the National Finals Rodeo (NFR) to the T&M Center from Oklahoma City. This ten-day event, held every December, averages nearly 12,000 fans per day. In addition to the NFR, the T&M Center hosts the Helldorado Rodeo in June. Neither of these events could have been held in the center if the cement seating structure had not been moved back.

LESSONS LEARNED

- A facility can be built to serve a primary function such as basketball yet still have the physical versatility to accommodate other events. Removing the concrete seating structure gave T&M Center the ability to accommodate large events like rodeos. This alteration may have made the difference between an operating deficit and a surplus.
- In retrospect, officials involved in the development of the center would have performed a better legal search to determine whether or not the funding issue would

PROJECT DATA

THOMAS & MACK CENTER
LAS VEGAS, NV

Owner: University of Nevada at Las Vegas
Builder: Mardian Construction, Phoenix
Architects: Carl Warnicke, Los Angeles, with Cambiero & Cambiero, Architects, Las Vegas
Primary Users: UNLV (basketball), concerts, family shows
Year Planning Began: 1977
Year Construction Completed: 1983

PROJECT INFORMATION
Site Area: 53 acres
Total Seating Capacity: 18,000
Total Parking Spaces: 5,500

ECONOMIC INFORMATION
Total Project Cost: $30,000,000
Funding Sources:
    General Obligation Bonds (1981): $40,000,000[1]
    Special Capital Construction Fund for Higher Education: $12,000,000[1]
    Accrued Interest: $4,500,000

Note:
[1]These monies funded the construction of the Thomas & Mack Center at UNLV and the Lawlor Special Events Center at the University of Nevada at Reno.

come under the state's bonded indebtedness provision. Delays caused by the friendly suit delayed construction.
- Other delays might have been curtailed had there been some outside review process of the construction management role played by the state's public works department.

LEXINGTON CENTER/ RUPP ARENA

LEXINGTON, KENTUCKY

Lexington Center is noted as one of the first and most successful public/private convention center projects in the nation. Constructed in 1976, Lexington Center consists of a 70,000-square-foot convention center, a 23,000-seat sports arena (Rupp Arena), and 70,000 square feet of net leasable retail space. In 1977, a 366-room Hyatt Regency hotel, integrated into the complex, was opened to complement the center. And in April 1994, a 55,000-square-foot addition to the convention center was completed, adding 30,000 square feet of exhibit space and thereby increasing the total contiguous exhibit space to 62,000 square feet. The $16 million addition was funded by $15 million of general obligation bonds issued by the commonwealth of Kentucky and $1 million from the Lexington Center Corporation reserves.

DEVELOPMENT STRATEGY

Development of Lexington Center was undertaken by the not-for-profit Lexington Center Corporation (LCC). Construction of the complex was financed through a $41 million issue of revenue bonds, a $2.6 million con-

tribution from the state government, and $2 million in private donations, which were used to develop an adjacent 1.1-acre urban park operated and maintained by LCC. Land leases for both the hotel and the retail space supplement the operations of the center.

FINANCING

The developer of the hotel had a variety of financial incentives for participating in the project, including the fee income for developing the entire complex, the leasehold interest in the hotel, and the master lease of the retail complex. The structure of this deal was considered equitable for both parties: the community could not "give away the store" to attract a hotel, as is often the case in such arrangements.

The original agreement required the hotel to pay to LCC 6 percent of all gross receipts, plus 50 percent of all net receipts after debt service. Duration of the lease was 30 years, with six renewal options of ten years each. The mall was operated by the owners of the hotel. The term of the mall lease was also for a period of 30 years, again with six renewal options of ten years each. Rent paid to LCC by the hotel owner was $3.50 per leasable square foot. These two leases supplemented the operations and debt service of the center in the amount of approximately $1 million annually, the hotel lease contributing $650,000 and the mall lease adding $350,000.

In 1990, the then-current holder of the hotel and mall leases fell into arrears on payments of rent and was in imminent danger of bankruptcy. A second not-for-profit corporation, Lexington Hotel Mall Corporation (LHMC), a sister corporation of LCC, was formed for the express purpose of acquiring the leases on the hotel and mall and holding them until the marketplace was conducive to returning those assets to the private sector.

MARKET ORIENTATION

Today, three distinct management entities are present in the complex: Hyatt, operating the hotel; LHMC, operating the mall; and LCC, which operates Rupp Arena and associated convention and trade-show facilities.

The hotel has, as part of the original agreement, exclusive catering rights for the entire complex, though Rupp Arena has an in-house concession operation. Hotel catering staff are responsible for banquet catering at functions in Lexington Center, while LCC staff assist in setting up these events. Catering sales fall under the ground lease contract, so that only 6 percent of gross catering sales are returned to LCC.

Lexington Center staff conduct most event services and event set-ups for the arena, exhibition hall, and Lexington Center's meeting and ballroom space. Compensation for these services is derived from rent plus equipment and labor charges, as in a standalone operation.

A central utilities plant is in place for the entire complex and is controlled by Lexington Center. Lexington Center measures the utility consumption of the hotel and bills the hotel operator accordingly. Similarly, a portion of the parking serving the complex is leased to the hotel operator and used to accommodate hotel guests and retail visitors.

The center is marketed by three entities: (1) the well-established Greater Lexington Convention and Visitors' Bureau; (2) Lexington Center's sales staff, who promote the arena and its convention facilities; and (3) the Hyatt's sales staff, who promote the hotel, its meeting space, and the entire complex.

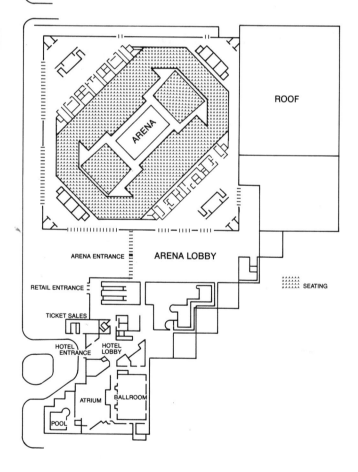

LESSONS LEARNED

Overall, the financial and operating relationship between Lexington Center and the Hyatt has been a good one. Conflict has arisen in the following areas, however:

- *Catering.* Hyatt has tended to operate its catering activities much as it would a hotel banquet room. Sometimes, menu prices have been perceived as high, though the quality of food service has been good. Since the acquisition of the hotel lease by LHMC, earlier concerns over inflexible menu offerings and prices have diminished.
- *Booking.* While it is clear that the hotel sales staff and the LCC sales staff have many common objectives, constant reminders must be given to these parties that their individual booking objectives and priorities come into conflict frequently and that those priorities must sometimes be compromised for the benefit of the total complex.
- *Physical plant.* The hotel and Lexington Center meeting rooms are separated by a large lobby and by the retail mall concourse. This separation has reduced the effective use of the entire hotel/convention-center meeting-room block as one complex. Each meeting-room location is served by hotel or center staff. To date, this has generally not been an issue because service and equipment have been fairly consistent, but this situation has been a source of friction from time to time.

Many positive features exist in the operating relationship for Lexington Center, including:

- *Service levels.* Lexington Center management is committed to providing service consistent with that of the Hyatt Regency. The autonomy gained by the provision of a not-for-profit corporation, and a commitment from management to offer high-quality service at the center, are the keys to this success.
- *Unified goals.* LCC is very aware that the primary purpose behind the development of convention and exhibit space was to generate added occupancy in all of the community's hotels, and LCC booking policies recognize that objective. Similarly, arena booking policies reflect a recognition of the importance of major basketball tournaments and other sporting events as economic generators for the community. Thus, goals for the arena focus on sports, entertainment, and cultural activities.
- *One-stop shopping.* Although the tenant has to negotiate the building contract with Lexington Center and the hotel and catering contract with Hyatt, a strong communication link between the two concerns exists, and a fairly unified face is presented to the facility user.

BRADLEY CENTER

MILWAUKEE, WISCONSIN

The Bradley Center in Milwaukee was a gift to the state of Wisconsin from Jane and Lloyd Pettit in memory of her father, Harry Lynde Bradley, a chairman of the Allen-Bradley Company. The center opened in October 1988 and is the home of five sports tenants: the NBA Milwaukee Bucks, the IHL Milwaukee Admirals, the Marquette University Golden Eagles men's basketball team, the NPSL Milwaukee Wave soccer team, and the AFL Milwaukee Mustangs arena football team. The $84 million structure features glass-enclosed lobbies, three concourses, and movable seats and accommodates both sports and nonsports events such as con-

certs, ice shows, family entertainment, and even motor sports, with minimal changeover time between events.

DEVELOPMENT STRATEGY

The preexisting facility, the Milwaukee Exposition and Convention Center and Arena (MECCA), is a downtown complex that once met Milwaukee's needs for sports and entertainment events, along with conventions and meetings. This venue, known as the MECCA Arena, is separate from the convention hall and served as Milwaukee's primary arena from 1950 to 1988. But the MECCA Arena has some limitations that in the 1970s and 1980s prohibited accommodating top-name entertainers and professional sports teams: the building is small, compared with other venues in similar-sized cities; it has only 9,000 permanent seats; and its capacity for basketball is only 11,052. Another distinct disadvantage is the age of the facility, which has drawn complaints from teams and fans alike, as well as from concert promoters and operators of touring family shows.

In the mid-1980s, the changing market demanded that a larger and more modern facility be implemented because the MECCA Arena could no longer compete with newer and larger venues. The MECCA board, amid rumors of the Milwaukee Bucks' leaving town, commissioned a study to evaluate the feasibility of expanding the current arena or of building a new one, without an increase in general property taxes.

In March 1985, shortly before the study was completed, the Pettits announced their plans to fund the construction of a new arena to be named the Bradley Center. The Pettits' announcement made the public financing issue a more manageable problem. Now public expenditures would be limited to site assembly and infrastructure, and Milwaukee would have its new arena as a private gift.

The Pettits created and funded the Bradley Center Corporation to build and to operate Bradley Center initially, until all construction was complete and its operations stabilized. In June 1993, the Bradley Center Corporation, a 501(c)(3) nonprofit, merged with the Bradley Center Sports and Entertainment Corporation, which was created by Chapter 232 of the Wisconsin statues. The merger completed the transfer of the center to the people of the state of Wisconsin. The Bradley Center Corporation selected Hellmuth, Obata & Kassabaum (HOK) to design the center, with engineering work to be done by Geiger Associates and construction management by Huber Hunt & Nichols, Inc.

DESIGN AND SITE ISSUES

The Bradley Center accommodates 18,600 attendees for basketball, 17,800 for hockey, and 20,000 for concerts, with a total area of 550,000 square feet. Design emphasis was placed on flexibility. For the fans' comfort, the designers increased the space between rows from 18 inches, as in the MECCA Arena, to 32 inches. But the increased seating capacity and extra legroom in the three-level building have not been added at the expense of the sightlines. From the top row to the center of the court, the distance is only 177 feet, with the box suites only 113 feet from center court. There are 68 box suites in the Bradley Center, all located on the second of the three levels. Fans reach the three concourses via 16 escalators and two elevators. In addition, there are 12 concessions stands, four merchandise stands, and 24 public restrooms. The center provides separate team facilities for the Admirals, Bucks, and Golden Eagles.

Originally, the Bradley Center was to adjoin the Milwaukee County Stadium, but a traffic study indicated that transportation and parking problems already existed at that site. The Bradley Center Corporation was then approached by city officials to locate the facility downtown. Eight sites were presented to the board of directors of the Bradley Center Corporation, who chose the same one recommended for a new arena by the MECCA study.

The site encompasses approximately six acres and lies across the street from and just north of the MECCA complex. The city agreed to purchase the land, relocate its tenants, and clear the site, as well as to provide 2,450 parking spaces within a specified boundary. Milwaukee purchased the site in December 1985 for $6.3 million, with the total land costs coming closer to $10 million once the tenants had been relocated, the existing improvements demolished, and utility lines relocated. This land

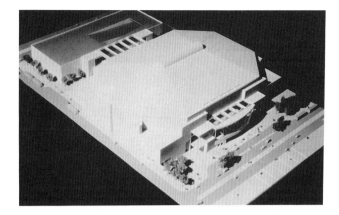

was then deeded to the Bradley Center Corporation. The city later spent $730,000 to improve the appearance of the pedestrian and street environs of the Bradley Center.

FINANCING

Although the city did not finance construction of the building, it invested a large sum for land acquisition and tenant relocation costs. These expenditures were financed primarily through general obligation bonds. The city committed itself to providing 2,450 parking spaces in the form of parking garages, surface parking, or arrangements with existing parking facilities. Accordingly, the city's redevelopment authority built two parking garages: a 905-space garage was built diagonally across from the Bradley Center, and the second garage, with approximately 850 spaces, stands about two-and-a-half blocks from the center. The remainder of the spaces are on existing surface parking lots or in private parking garages that allow public use during event hours.

The approximate total development cost of both garages was $23 million. The city redevelopment authority issued a $25.5 million revenue bond for the construction of both new garages, which the city leases from the authority. The revenue bond issue is backed by the lease payments from the city to the authority: the lease payments are expected to generate enough revenue to meet the debt-service requirements of the bond, but the city is obligated to make the lease payments should operating revenues from the parking garage not meet debt-service requirements.

MARKET ORIENTATION

The five teams that occupy the center support about 135 events, giving the Bradley Center a solid core of sports

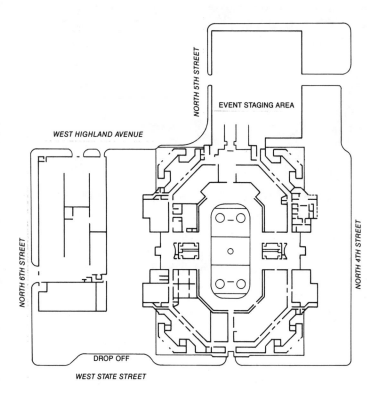

NORTH 5TH STREET

EVENT STAGING AREA

WEST HIGHLAND AVENUE

NORTH 6TH STREET

NORTH 4TH STREET

DROP OFF

WEST STATE STREET

events. The size and seating capacity of the arena have helped it to attract both top acts and traditional family shows. Also, the Bradley Center gives Milwaukee an advantage in attracting national or international sporting events, such as NCAA regional basketball tournaments. After six years of operation, the facility has hosted more than 1,200 events and 11 million patrons.

LESSONS LEARNED

To address the issue of the two potentially competing facilities, the Bradley Center Corporation and the city of Milwaukee signed an agreement giving the Bradley Center the authority to book sporting and entertainment events for both the Bradley Center and the MECCA Arena.

PROJECT DATA
BRADLEY CENTER
MILWAUKEE, WI

Owner: State of Wisconsin
Builder: Huber Hunt & Nichols, Inc., Indianapolis
Architect: Hellmuth, Obata & Kassabaum (HOK), Kansas City, Missouri
Primary Users: Milwaukee Bucks (basketball), Milwaukee Admirals (hockey), Marquette University Golden Eagles (basketball), Milwaukee Wave (soccer), Milwaukee Mustangs (arena football)
Year Planning Began: 1985
Year Construction Began: 1986
Year Construction Completed: 1988

PROJECT INFORMATION
Site Area: 6 acres
Total Seating Capacity:
    Basketball: 18,600
    Hockey: 17,800
    Concerts: 20,000
Total Parking Spaces: 12,000 within a six-block radius

ECONOMIC INFORMATION
Site Acquisition and Improvement Costs: $10,730,000[1]
Construction Costs: $107,000,000[2]
Total Project Cost (1987 dollars): $117,730,000
Total Project Cost (1994 dollars): $136,045,775[3]
Funding Sources:
    Jane and Lloyd Pettit (private): $84,000,000
    Revenue Bond: $25,500,000[4]
    General Obligation Bonds: $12,000,000[4]
Total Financing: $121,500,000

Notes:
[1] Includes $6.3 million for site purchase and approximately $3.7 million for relocations and demolition.
[2] Includes cost of building two parking garages.
[3] Calculated based on the consumer price index.
[4] City financing from revenue and general obligation bonds exceeded its costs due to debt-service reserve.

PITTSBURGH CIVIC ARENA

PITTSBURGH, PENNSYLVANIA

The Pittsburgh Civic Arena has served the metropolitan community of Pittsburgh since 1961. The 18,500-seat, multipurpose facility has housed the Civic Light Opera, the Pittsburgh Penguins hockey club, and the Duquesne University basketball team. Although the Civic Light Opera no longer performs in the Civic Arena, the arena has been the stage for many touring rock and pop groups. The most striking feature of this facility is its retractable stainless steel roof, which allows the arena to appear domelike when closed and to be open-aired when the roof is drawn back. This feature not only makes Pittsburgh's Civic Arena distinctive but also reveals its advantages and disadvantages.

DEVELOPMENT STRATEGY

The reasons for developing the Civic Arena were twofold. First, the arena would be home to the Civic Light Opera, which, at the time, played in the 56,500-seat uncovered Pitt Stadium, and influential civic leaders wanted to preserve the ambience, weather permitting, of concerts "under the stars." Second, the arena would be the initial and most important phase in the redevelopment of the blighted Lower Hill section. The 95-acre Lower Hill area is located immediately east of Pittsburgh's center city and Golden Triangle area.

The arena's 20-acre site was leased from the Urban Redevelopment Authority by the Civic Arena. The terms of the 45-year lease include annual lease payments of $100,000 and an option for a 40-year extension. The lease period has since been amended, with a 50-year extension, to reach the year 2031.

Groundbreaking for the arena took place in 1959, and the facility opened in 1961. Its total cost came to $16.2 million in 1960 dollars, with $9 million attributed to the stainless steel retractable roof. The Civic Arena was designed by the Pittsburgh architectural firm of Mitchell & Ritchey (now Deeter Ritchey Sippel), with Amman & Whitney Engineers of New York City serving as design and mechanical engineers for the roof structure.

DESIGN AND SITE ISSUES

The original structure featured 9,280 upholstered seats on three levels. Seating capacities varied with the type of event. For example, seating for Penguins hockey games was expanded to 10,500; basketball could accommodate 11,900; and center-stage events such as boxing and political rallies, could seat 13,600. However, 2,100 seats have been lost for opera performances, because the stage structure for end-stage events occupies the space normally filled by a section of permanent seats. To prepare for this kind of performance, hydraulic lifts raise the section of seats, revealing the 118-foot by 64-foot stage. In their raised position the seats form a proscenium arch over the stage and allow stage lighting and curtains to be hung.

The original exhibition area, behind the stage on the first level, provided 50,000 square feet for flat floor expositions and trade shows. This exhibition space was not configured to host trade shows since its area curved underneath the upper seating levels along the outer perimeter of the building. Because it was divided by two meeting rooms, gate entrances, and escalators leading to the upper seating levels, the space was not contiguous. When combined with the floor space of the arena, this facility provided almost 90,000 square feet of exhibition space.

The most intriguing feature of the Civic Arena is its retractable roof. The idea of building a multipurpose structure that can adapt itself to weather conditions was considered very impractical by many, but the Civic Arena's architects and engineers were able to realize this concept. The eight-section roof consists of 7,800 separate pieces covering approximately four acres. Two sections are fixed, and six are movable along a curved railroad track lying inside the concrete ring girder.

The roof is supported by a 260-foot cantilever frame that is anchored into the ground across the access road and reinforced by the concrete ring girder; the cantilever arm, flanked by two fixed steel sections, forms a point at the top of the roof from which the movable sections rotate. Each section has an individual motor, synchronized with the others, so that the roof can be retracted from the main control room. The process of fully opening or closing the roof takes approximately two-and-a-half minutes.

The roof is only opened after hockey season because the hanging lights used to illuminate the rink have to be removed for the opening process to occur. The roof can be partially opened, about one-eighth of the way, for an event such as a tractor pull, to vent exhaust fumes. From mid-May to mid-September the Civic Arena may use the roof only five to 10 times, with the most often-used configuration being the "summer amphitheater." This set-up uses a half-house seating configuration with the roof rolled back to reveal the Pittsburgh skyline.

The Civic Arena underwent a series of expansions in the early 1970s to meet the growing demand for sporting and entertainment events. The first expansion, in 1972, created a press box for the media on the upper level of the east rim. In the following year, 1,000 seats were added at the lower level; modifications had to be made to the edge of the ice floor to allow for the addition. Along the west rim, 23 luxury boxes (skyboxes) were built, adding some 300 seats.

Over the years, the facility has been expanded numerous times, increasing seating capacity for hockey to 17,400 and for concerts to 18,500. Also, eight scoreboard monitors have been installed underneath the balconies to accommodate those fans whose views of the main scoreboard are obstructed. During this installation, the design and engineering team of Biggie-Shaflucas, Architects, and Rupley, Bahler, Blake, Engineers (Buffalo), had their task made easier because they could rotate the roof back and use cranes to fit the steel and pour the concrete. At the time, the Pittsburgh Civic Arena was among the 20 largest arenas in the country.

The Civic Arena underwent an extensive renovation that was completed in January 1989. The $12 million renovation, financed by general obligation bonds issued by the authority but with the direct backing of the county and city, included a new marquee, landscaping, paved parking, newly replaced sections of seats, renovated dressing rooms, new concession stands, additional office space (obtained by the conversion of exhibition space), and a renovated restaurant, offices, and restrooms.

In 1993, the Pittsburgh Penguins, as primary tenant, funded $4 million of a $4.5 million expansion to the Civic Arena. The expansion added 1,100 seats on two new balconies and also added some 200 seats in six superboxes (12 to 16 seats per box) and 16 minisuites (eight seats per suite). In addition, the press box was relocated to the opposite side of the arena floor, and 88 club seats were installed in the former press-box location. The city funded the remaining $0.5 million cost of this expansion.

FINANCING

Originally, the $16.2 million Pittsburgh Civic Arena was funded through a combination of public and private sources. The city of Pittsburgh and Allegheny County

formed the Public Auditorium Authority of Pittsburgh and Allegheny County to fund and operate it. The authority issued $15 million in revenue bonds guaranteed by supporting agreements by the city and county, should arena operations not cover the debt service. The city and county appropriated $450,000 each to pay the annual debt service. And the Edgar S. Kaufmann Charitable Trust made a $1 million gift to the project. Other sources of financing included public grants from both the city and county and smaller gift contributions.

In 1975, a $4 million expansion was financed through a similar bond issue that was backed by supporting agreements from the city and county. However, a $0.25 seat charge (ticket tax) was imposed to retire the debt service of this latest issue. Revenue from this surcharge on tickets exceeded the debt service amount, so that the city and county did not need to appropriate additional monies for this debt issue. In 1979, the original $15 million issue, plus the $4 million issue, were refunded in a single issue.

In 1991, the Spectacor Management Group signed an agreement with the auditorium authority to operate and manage the arena. Lease payments to the authority were equal to the amount of debt service on the refunded issue.

MARKET ORIENTATION

Until 1966, when the National Hockey League voted to expand, the Civic Arena's primary tenant was the Civic Light Opera, which performed there until 1970, when Heinz Hall was opened. The event calendar was rounded out with other concerts, sports exhibitions, and family shows such as circuses and ice shows. The exhibition hall also served as Pittsburgh's main convention center, providing space for consumer shows, conventions, and trade shows.

During 1966 and 1967, the Pittsburgh Penguins team of the National Hockey League was formed and became the primary sports tenant, averaging more than 7,400 attendees per game in their first season. The Penguins have played approximately 40 home games, and over the years attendance has gradually increased, with average home game attendance approaching capacity. High attendance figures have been especially notable in the early 1990s, with the Penguins' back-to-back Stanley Cup championships in the 1990–1991 and 1991–1992 seasons.

The Civic Arena has also hosted the home games of Duquesne University's basketball team, which accounted

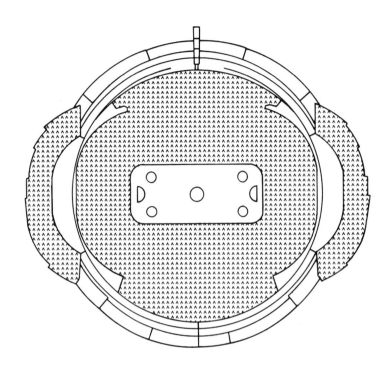

for approximately 15 dates per year. These games were generally held during the week and rarely on Saturdays. The 1987–1988 season marked the last year that Duquesne played in the Civic Arena, as the university's new 6,200-seat facility became ready at the beginning of the next season. The University of Pittsburgh plays most of its home dates at its own campus gym, but uses the Civic Arena to play approximately six dates against Big East Conference and other high-profile opponents to accommodate the expected sellout crowds.

Typical annual utilization for the Civic Arena comes to some 20 to 25 concerts (mainly rock and pop), 12 professional wrestling matches, two circuses/ice shows, and a few consumer shows. Consumer shows and conventions have been minimal since the opening of the David L. Lawrence Convention Center in 1981. The arena draws approximately 2 million people annually from its media market area with a population of more than 2.9 million.

LESSONS LEARNED

No major problems have arisen concerning the building structure or roof structure, but observations regarding other aspects of its operation have been made in retrospect:
■ The arena has outlived its usefulness as an exhibition hall, due to changes in convention center user needs

and to the fact that nowadays, an arena cannot effectively serve as a multi-purpose, spectator and exposition facility.

- One glaring mistake may have been made when the original construction was funded. Although funding for the arena did provide a reserve fund for operations and maintenance, it did not include a capital improvements fund. This omission has forced the authority to ask the city or county for additional funds for capital improvements, major repairs, or replacements. Thus, funding for these projects has become subject to political as well as budgetary considerations.

- As for the Lower Hill redevelopment goal, it is difficult to determine how much impact the arena has had in spurring revitalization of the area. It should be noted that in the mid-1960s, the Hyatt Corporation built a 400-room hotel in the Lower Hill area, and, albeit slowly, redevelopment has occurred. Only one major parcel remains vacant today, and it is used for parking during arena events. In contrast, Pittsburgh's Three Rivers Stadium was built in 1970 with a similar objective of city redevelopment, but its vicinity has not exhibited the same economic development activity as has the Lower Hill area.

- The cost that the admissions tax and ticket surcharge have added to the total price of tickets has placed the venue at a considerable competitive disadvantage since the new Star Lake Amphitheatre was opened in 1990. Concert promoters have all but abandoned their use of the Civic Arena when given the opportunity to book the amphitheater, which is free of local ticket taxes.

PROJECT DATA

PITTSBURGH CIVIC ARENA
PITTSBURGH, PA

Owner: Urban Redevelopment Authority, Pittsburgh
Developers: Public Auditorium Authority/Civic Arena Corporation, Pittsburgh
Architects: Mitchell & Ritchey, Pittsburgh (now Deeter Ritchey Sippel)
Roof Engineers: Amman & Whitney Engineers, New York, New York
Primary Users: Pittsburgh Penguins (NHL)
Year Construction Began: 1959
Year Construction Completed: 1961[1]

PROJECT INFORMATION
Site Area: 20 acres
Total Seating Capacity:[2]
    Originally: 9,280–13,600
    Currently: 17,400–18,500

ECONOMIC INFORMATION
Site Acquisition Cost[3]
Construction Costs/Civic Arena: $7,200,000
Construction Costs/Roof: $9,000,000
Total Project Cost (1960 dollars): $16,200,000
Funding Sources (1961):[4]
    Revenue Bond Issue: $15,000,000
    City and County Appropriations: $900,000
    Edgar S. Kaufmann Charitable Trust: $1,000,000

Notes:
[1]Expansions occurred between 1972 and 1975, from 1988 to 1989, and in 1993.
[2]Varies with event.
[3]Leased.
[4]Also: revenue bonds (1975), $4,000,000; general obligation bonds (1985), $12,000,000; and primary-tenant funding (1993), $4,000,000.

ARCO ARENAS

SACRAMENTO, CALIFORNIA

The ARCO Arena is the first project of a multi-year effort by a group of private businessmen and marks the beginning of their phased development plan. The Sacramento Sports Association (SSA), a California general partnership, was founded in 1978 for the purpose of promoting professional sports in Sacramento and building a privately financed arena and stadium.

The SSA was responsible for bringing the National Basketball Association's Kansas City Kings to Sacramento in 1985 to play in the privately financed ARCO Arena, so named for the corporate sponsorship of Atlantic Richfield. This arena, however, was designed and built to be temporary and was referred to as ARCO 1. The Kings are now housed in a permanent arena, ARCO 2, one-half mile from the North Natomas community and three miles north of downtown Sacramento. The permanent arena is one of two components of a proposed sports complex, the other to be a stadium suitable for baseball or football. The sports complex represents the first phase of a 1,600-acre community master planned by the Capital Gateway Partnership, of which the SSA is a partner.

DEVELOPMENT STRATEGY

In accomplishing its goal, the SSA faced an uphill battle. The political climate in Sacramento since the late 1960s and 1970s had been extremely averse to growth and de-

velopment, particularly in North Natomas. In 1974, the city adopted a land use policy that preserved agricultural land until it was deemed ready for urbanization. In effect, this plan virtually halted development plans in the vicinity. But in spite of the political climate in Sacramento, the SSA was able to start a successful petition drive that brought the sports complex and development issue to the forefront by placing a stadium issue on the 1979 ballot.

Although the SSA's proposal was not voted in (voters did not know that the development would be privately financed), momentum in the community was mounting for resolution of these land use and development issues. A Sports Stadium Task Force was organized to study the issue and to select a suitable site. After months of deliberation, the task force selected two sites, one of which was owned by the SSA. However, the city council again voted to keep North Natomas agricultural for the next five years.

Undaunted by this setback, the SSA purchased the Kansas City Kings for $10.5 million in June 1983. Its intention was to keep the Kings in Kansas City. But poor attendance in Kansas City and growing enthusiasm in Sacramento made the option of relocating the Kings to Sacramento a more viable one, and in April 1985, the NBA Board of Governors approved the relocation of the Kings to Sacramento.

The SSA, as a partner in the Capital Gateway development, submitted a proposal to develop 1,622 acres in North Natomas. The plan included 170 acres for the sports complex, 140 acres for high-density residential uses, 140 acres for commercial projects, 850 acres for industrial development, and the remaining 332 acres for green space, road infrastructure, and interchanges. After a three-year battle, an amended plan was approved in February 1986. This plan outlined the total community development (7,681 acres) of the Capital Gateway project, calling for 200 acres for the sports complex, 2,715 acres of residential, 160 acres of commercial, 2,106 acres of office/industrial/manufacturing, and 2,500 acres dedicated to green space, infrastructure, parks, and public buildings.

The temporary ARCO Arena was built on a 40-acre site just outside the city limits, thus avoiding the "political minefield": in contrast to the city, the county did not have an antigrowth policy. Total development cost for ARCO 1 came to only $12 million and was completely privately financed. ARCO 1 seated 10,333 for basketball, which made it the smallest arena among the NBA franchises. There were only four box suites, of which two were leased: one was the owner's box, while the other was used as an event control room.

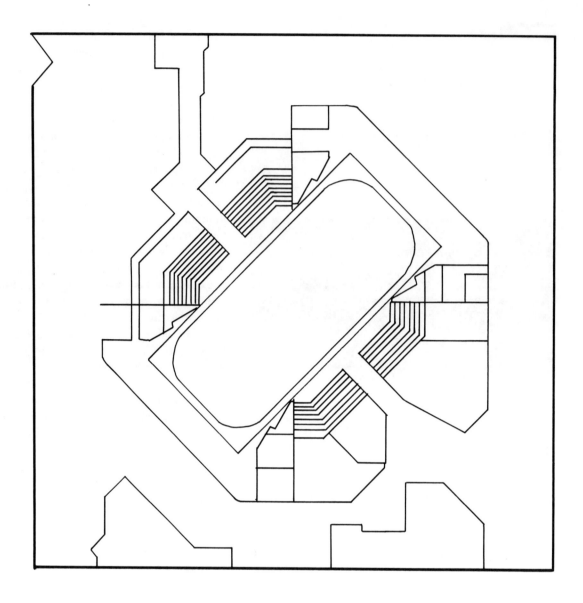

The temporary character of ARCO 1, however, was its most peculiar aspect. The utilization outlook for the arena was only two to three years. At the time that it was being built, there was still uncertainty about final approval for the permanent arena; certainly, if the permanent arena became a dead issue, then this arena might be expanded. The temporariness of ARCO 1 was probably a good indicator of the confidence that the SSA had in its ultimate goal.

ARCO 1 was designed so that it could be converted into a 120,000-square-foot, three-story office building or hospital. The seats and seating structure were wooden. Upon removal of these, the scoreboards, the HVAC system, the food preparation equipment, the concession stands, the locker room and training equipment, and the

tenant finish improvements for the Kings and ARCO Arena offices, ARCO 1 became a three-story shell. These items were to be used in the construction of the permanent ARCO Arena, as the SSA did not want to own two competing facilities.

Owning and operating a temporary arena for two years before constructing a permanent one afforded the SSA's architect, Rann Haight, the benefit of this experience and knowledge to be applied toward designing ARCO 2. The temporary arena was a small one and provided an intimate setting for fans, while the permanent arena was designed primarily for basketball, but with the flexibility to handle other events. The basketball court in the permanent arena has an east/west orientation, and other sporting events (hockey, arena football, indoor soccer, and so on) have a north/south orientation. ARCO 2 expanded the seating to 16,400 for basketball by filling in the corners of ARCO 1's plan and adding six rows of seats. According to Haight, "The net effect is that the farthest seat from the basketball floor is only 30 feet farther away than in ARCO 1." Haight also expanded the locker rooms in ARCO 2 to NBA standards, as well as providing amenities for fan comfort. Among these are 26 box suites, ten permanent concession stands, 310 toilets (compared with 118 in ARCO 1), four merchandise stands, and two cocktail lounges.

ARCO 2 sits on 105 acres, which cost $1.8 million, or about $17,500 per acre. More than 11,000 parking spaces are available on the site.

ARCO 2 marks the beginning of the first phase of the Capital Gateway, which has a total projected build-out cost of $8 billion and a development area greater than 65 million square feet. Total cost of the new 412,000-square-foot arena was $41 million. It was completed in September 1988, approximately 60 days before the opening of the Kings' 1988–1989 season.

The second major component of the sports complex, the proposed 65,000-seat stadium for baseball or football, is designated to be built on the remaining 95 acres, only 60 feet from ARCO 2.

FINANCING

The SSA stressed from the beginning that this project would not be built at taxpayer expense. It would be privately developed, owned, and operated. This strategy not only helped the SSA to gain the city's approval for land use changes, but also it gave the SSA total control over the project because of its ownership of the land, building, and team. In 1992, a controlling interest in the Sacramento Kings and ARCO Arena was purchased by Maguire Thomas Partners, a Los Angeles real estate company. The SSA maintains a nonactive, minority interest in the team and arena.

MARKET ORIENTATION

Maguire Thomas Partners own and operate ARCO Arena, as well as its primary tenant, the Sacramento Kings.

In addition to basketball, ARCO Arena hosts other sporting events; concerts; family shows like ice shows, circuses, and truck pulls; and local events.

PROJECT DATA

ARCO ARENAS
SACRAMENTO, CA

Developer: Sacramento Sports Association
Owner: Maguire Thomas Partners
Builder: JB/L & L Construction, Sacramento
Architect: Rann Haight, Sacramento
Construction Completed: 1988

PROJECT INFORMATION
Site Area: 105 acres
Seating Capacity:
    Basketball: 17,000
    Concerts: 17,500
    Ice Event: 14,000
Total Parking Spaces: 11,000

ECONOMIC INFORMATION
Site Acquisition Cost: $1,800,000
Construction Costs: $37,500,000
Soft Costs: $1,700,000
Total Costs: $41,000,000
Funding Source: Private financing (bank loan convertible to mini-permanent loan)

LESSONS LEARNED

- The SSA went through an invaluable learning process by owning and operating ARCO 1, which was in essence a two-thirds scale model, before building the permanent arena. This experience had a dramatic impact on the design of the new facility:
- Fan proximity to the court, and the primary emphasis on basketball, were high priorities in the design process. So were performer areas such as locker rooms and dressing rooms. Public areas and concessions became larger to accommodate patrons.
- Not only did ARCO 1 have an effect on the design implications of ARCO 2, but also it affected the operations of the new arena.
- The community bears no expense in the construction or operation of this project.
- Private ownership of the facility, coupled with ownership of the team, avoids many of the problems typically encountered by teams that are tenants of municipally owned arenas.

SUN DOME

TAMPA, FLORIDA

The University of South Florida (USF) campus in Tampa is the site of the 11,346-seat Sun Dome. The sprawling 958-acre campus is situated in a rapidly growing northeastern section of Tampa between I-275 and I-75. The 30-year-old university, which is a member of the Metro Conference, today has a total student population of approximately 38,000. Although the Sun Dome is the home court of the USF Bulls basketball team, it was planned to function as a multipurpose facility. Completed in 1981, it is also used for other school functions, athletic and academic, as well as for community and commercial events such as concerts and consumer shows.

DEVELOPMENT STRATEGY

In the mid- and late 1970s, the state of Florida examined the status of the university system's athletic facilities. It found that the three major state universities, with a total student population of 74,000 (24,000 at USF) in 1978, had below-par or virtually nonexistent spectator sports centers. At that time, the University of Florida's basket-ball team played in a 75-year-old gymnasium that held only 4,000 to 5,000 fans. Tully Gym, which also seated 4,000 to 5,000, was home court for the Florida State University basketball team. USF, in probably the worst situation of the three, had a gym that seated fewer than 1,000 fans.

The Sun Belt Conference declared the USF facility unacceptable for conference play, forcing the men's team to play conference games elsewhere, including the Curtis Hixon Convention Center in Tampa, the Bayfront Center in St. Petersburg, and the Lakeland Civic Center in Lakeland. Nonconference games were played in the USF gym. This arrangement made it difficult for students and alumni to attend games. Games played in Lakeland, for instance, were 50 miles away from the campus.

Each of the state universities was asked to submit proposals for student athletic centers to the state's board of regents. Two proposals were put to a student vote at USF, one to build a new theater and one to construct a new arena. The vote resulted in a proposal for the Sun Dome. The state of Florida hired architects Moore, May & Harrington of Gainesville to design a pair of multipurpose facilities that would serve the short- and long-term needs of the University of Florida and USF. To reduce design costs for both universities, the architects were to produce the same facility for each school.

SITE AND DESIGN ISSUES

The architects' design incorporated many features that were considered state-of-the-art at the time, including an air-supported fiberglass roof. The dome's base is contoured as a 120,000-square-foot octagon shaped by eight steel cables. The air-supported roof features four large fans that maintain an interior air pressure adequate to support the 21-ton roof. This system is controlled by a computer that responds instantly to changes in the weather or to electrical outages. In the event that the roof fully deflates, it sags no lower than the concrete ring around the top of the building, which is still higher than the top row of seats.

Not only is an air-supported roof less expensive to build than a concrete and steel-reinforced roof, but it is also energy-efficient, allowing ample sunlight to pervade the arena during the daytime, thus reducing the need for artificial light. The white coating on the roof reflects 70 to 75 percent of the sunlight, and an inner membrane reduces heat transfer to keep air-conditioning costs lower. At night, the internal light flows out through the roof, creating a glow visible from a great distance.

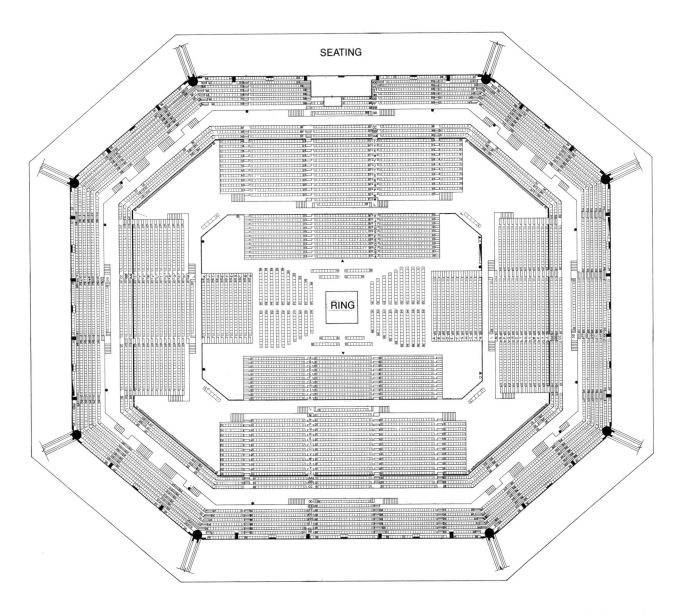

SEATING

RING

The dome has three seating levels, with the main and mezzanine levels retractable to allow for a total maximum floor space of 53,000 square feet (on two levels). This makes the Sun Dome an ideal place for small consumer shows and locally oriented trade-show exhibitions with as many as 120 booths. The Sun Dome has one 2,500-square-foot meeting room that can be used for business meetings, presentations, or school functions. Dome administrative offices, as well as offices for the men's and women's basketball teams, men's baseball and soccer, and the athletic association are located on the Sun Dome's lower level.

Adjacent to the dome are surface parking lots capable of handling 4,000 cars, with two separate entrances to ease traffic flow before and after events. The dome and its parking lots occupy about 80 acres of land. Conven-

ient access to and from a main local thoroughfare and easy access through the university's road infrastructure were primary reasons for this particular site's selection. In addition, the site is on high ground, so that no drainage problems exist.

FINANCING

In Florida's state university system, student tuition is allocated to cover four fees: building, capital improvement trust, health, and matriculation. The capital improvement trust (CIT) fees are local, that is, each university is credited with a certain number of dollars generated from these fees. The school is then allowed to use the fees to construct student activity facilities other than classroom buildings.

Over the years, the CIT funds had accumulated to an enormous sum. Hence, the state had the means either to upgrade or build new student activity centers. All funding for the dome's original construction came from the CIT funds. Although Sun Dome, Inc., is building its own internal capital improvement fund, most funding for renovations or additions will still come from the CIT funds.

The original budget for the dome was $12 million. The O'Connell Center and the Sun Dome were constructed concurrently, but the CIT funds began to run low and the Sun Dome's construction budget was cut to $8 million, causing design features that had been implemented in the O'Connell Center to be stricken from the Sun Dome project. For example, the air-supported roof on the O'Connell Center extends to ground level, whereas the Sun Dome roof covers only the top portion of the building.

Because of this same budgetary problem, other features were omitted, such as a natatorium, meeting rooms, permanent concession areas, indoor access to HVAC and administrative offices, and more efficient airlocks to control the entryways. Cost overruns on the project inflated its final price tag back to the original $12 million, all of which came from pledges of future CIT funds.

During renovation, which began in 1993, the Sun Dome entryways were enclosed and an auxiliary gymnasium added to allow more flexibility in scheduling the facility's main arena. This was accomplished through an allocation of $5 million from CIT funds from the state university system.

MARKET ORIENTATION

The Sun Dome is managed by a not-for-profit corporation, Sun Dome, Inc., thus allowing management to operate the facility unencumbered by state government and university bureaucracy. This organizational approach enables dome management to respond quickly in the competitive Tampa Bay market, a strategy that has paid off financially. Although operated separately from the university (USF pays Sun Dome, Inc., a management fee), close ties exist between the two entities. USF basketball games and commencements account for about 20 event days annually, and USF pays little rent. Admission to USF events is free to students, and scheduling for USF enjoys priority over other events.

In an effort to maintain the viability of Sun Dome, Inc., as a management company for the future, the com-

pany has "annexed" several sports complexes on the USF campus. In the face of the current, uncertain entertainment market and the possibility of even greater competition from newly constructed facilities in the Tampa Bay area, it had become clear that additional sources of revenue would be needed to maintain the company in the down periods. The USF golf course, which hosts 50,000 to 60,000 golfers per year; a 4,000-seat outdoor soccer and track facility; a 2,500-seat baseball facility; and three smaller sports venues have been added to the management agreement with USF. This diverse grouping of facilities provides not only additional revenue streams but also cross-utilization of resources and economies of scale. It remains to be seen whether the long-term existence of Sun Dome, Inc., can rely solely on this relationship.

The Sun Dome, primarily used as a university sports arena and convocation center, is nevertheless the dominant venue serving the Tampa and central Florida con-

PROJECT DATA

SUN DOME
TAMPA, FL

Owner: State of Florida
Developer: State of Florida
Architect: Moore, May & Harrington, Gainesville, Florida
Primary Users: University of South Florida basketball games and school functions, community events, concerts, family shows
Year Planning Began: 1978
Year Construction Completed: 1981

PROJECT INFORMATION
Site Area: 80 acres
Exhibition Space: 53,000 square feet (on two levels)
Total Seating Capacity: 11,346
Total Parking Spaces: 4,000

ECONOMIC INFORMATION
Original Project Cost (1981 dollars): $12,000,000
Renovations (1993 dollars): $5,000,000
Total Project Cost (1994 dollars):[1] $24,000,000
Funding Sources:
   Capital Improvement Trust:[2] $12,000,000
   Capital Improvement Trust:[2] $5,000,000

Notes:
[1] Calculated based on consumer price index.
[2] Derived from 25 percent of student tuition fees.

cert market. With relatively easy access from I-75 and I-275, the facility offers the 2.5 million people in the Tampa Bay area their largest concert facility besides the 74,000-seat Tampa outdoor stadium and the 50,000-seat domed baseball (Devil Rays) stadium in nearby St. Petersburg. In 1994, the Sun Dome staged nearly 50 concerts, with an average attendance of 5,600. It attracts top performing artists such as pop and country stars Elton John, Alan Jackson, and Neil Diamond and has hosted operatic tenor Luciano Pavarotti. In addition to USF basketball, the Sun Dome accommodates other sporting events, among them tennis, gymnastics, boxing, and professional wrestling, which is presented about six times annually. These events draw capacity crowds and produce above-average revenues from merchandise and concessions.

The dome hosts family shows such as *Sesame Street Live* (seven shows a year), the *Muppet Babies,* and the Harlem Globetrotters. However, design limitations, as discussed below, have precluded the dome from presenting ice shows and circuses. The Sun Dome also hosts trade and consumer shows. Aggressive marketing of these types of events has meant the difference between profit and loss—an atypical situation for a university arena.

LESSONS LEARNED

Several design limitations in the Sun Dome prohibit the staging of some kinds of events:

- Probably the most severe design error was the exclusion of a rigging support system for stage lighting and sound, initially preventing dome management from presenting concerts that require overhead stage lighting (and most concerts do!). A rigging support system was added in 1983 at a cost of $370,000, enabling the facility to attract many touring acts that had previously been unable to play this venue.
- A major limitation of the air-supported roof is still unresolved: its inability to accommodate circuses requiring overhead rigging support. This drawback limits the dome to staging only those circuses performed at

floor level or that are physically self-supporting. These circuses tend to be smaller and to book shorter runs.

- Another design limitation that has adversely affected the use of the dome is that the field of view, or sightlines, for the audience was designed for a basketball court. Many other arena sports, including indoor soccer, are designed to use hockey-floor dimensions.

In addition to reducing the available seating to 4,000, however, an indoor soccer configuration would obscure sightlines from the field of play outside the area of the dimensions of the basketball court; fans would literally be on top of the action, unable to see that portion of the ice floor beneath or behind their lines of sight.

- A lack of icemaking equipment at the Sun Dome prevents the facility from offering a cost advantage to touring ice shows and skating exhibitions. It is more costly for these shows to provide portable icemaking equipment than to perform in venues that offer a permanent ice floor. This capability was either not included in the original design or eliminated for budgetary reasons.
- Because of budgetary restrictions during initial construction, the Sun Dome's entry and lobby areas were left incomplete. During the 1993 renovation, three of four exterior main entrances were enclosed. In addition to enhanced customer convenience and comfort, these expanded air locks serve as additional lobbies and provide space for extra restrooms and concessions.

ANAHEIM CONVENTION CENTER

ANAHEIM, CALIFORNIA

Major changes have taken place in the meetings and convention industry since Anaheim Convention Center opened its doors in 1967. Today, the newly remodeled and expanded facility continues to keep pace with those changes and satisfy meeting planners' needs.

DEVELOPMENT STRATEGY

In 1964, a group of Anaheim hotel/motel owners identified the need for a convention center to host meetings, trade shows, and community events. They endeavored to build the center privately but soon realized that the project could not be accomplished without government support. They were successful in convincing the city of Anaheim to undertake the project. In return, the hotel/motel owners agreed to support a local-option hotel room tax to finance construction.

The convention center was a high priority until a major league baseball team agreed to locate in Anaheim if it had a new stadium. This put convention center plans on hold while Anaheim Stadium was built. Convention center construction finally began in 1965 and was completed in 1967.

There were two primary reasons for building the convention center. Anaheim was becoming more and more popular as a tourist destination, largely because of Disneyland. Hotels and motels were being built to accommodate these visitors, and it was anticipated that a convention center in Anaheim would attract out-of-town visitors to meetings and trade shows during Disneyland's off-peak periods. The center would also provide area residents with a venue for community events. It was estimated that revenue from the hotel room tax would enable the convention center to break even financially and therefore not to be an economic burden to the community.

The city council approved a unique joint-powers relationship between the Anaheim Union High School District and the city of Anaheim, with both of these entities guaranteeing the bonds. The joint-powers relationship was based on three requirements: 1) that the high school district received first priority for one date per year; 2) that the center would host five community events (e.g., ice shows, auto shows, home and garden shows) each year; and 3) that conventions and trade shows were required to book one year or more in advance. These requirements proved extremely successful for the center, the city, and the school district.

The majority (95 percent) of center operating expenses are covered by operating revenues. The funding for the remaining 5 percent of expenses is obtained through subsidies from the city. Except for food service and exhibitor telephones, which are contracted out, all services at the center are operated entirely by the city of Anaheim. Operating most services in-house contributes to the convention center's success because it allows the city to set and maintain high quality control standards. Anaheim Convention Center is recognized for its formal staff training programs, developed by its first CEO, Tom Leigler, which are known as The Anaheim Way.

SITE ANALYSIS

The original convention center design included a small exhibition hall, meeting rooms, and a theater. Before construction, the theater was replaced by an 8,700-seat arena that also serves as a multipurpose room. It was named an "arenatorium" and received awards for its design concept.

The 56-acre convention center site lies directly across the street from Disneyland, on Katella Avenue.

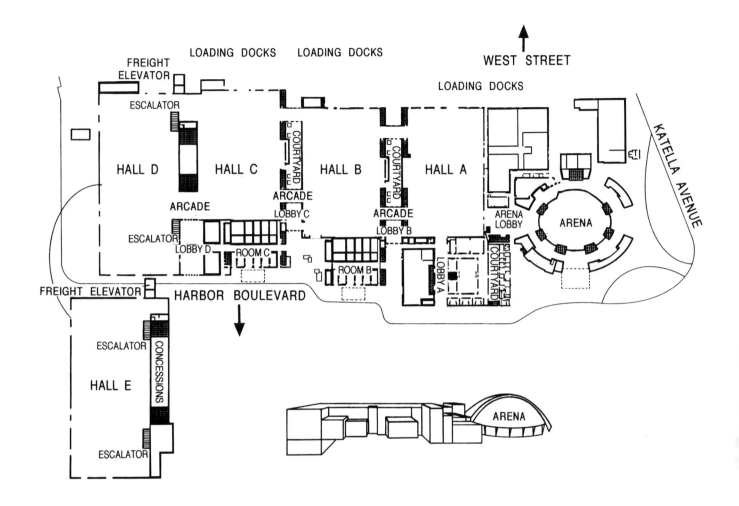

It is surrounded by 18,000 hotel rooms. The center has a total of 985,000 square feet of space, consisting of five exhibition halls, an arena, and three rooms that can be used either for exhibit areas, for receptions, or for meeting space. Six additional, divisible rooms are available for meetings. There are 4,150 on-site parking spaces.

The center has undergone four expansions ("betterments"), which were essential to keep pace with area, convention, and trade-show industry growth.

The fifth betterment, scheduled to begin in 1997, will bring Anaheim Convention Center well over the 1-million square-foot mark. Because the center has booking commitments into the year 2010, construction will be completed in phases over a period of approximately five years. The proposed renovation will include new meeting rooms, a large common lobby, and more exhibition space. The existing Center Drive will be converted into a pedestrian mall, and the arena will be replaced by a new exhibition hall. Existing meeting rooms and two of the multipurpose rooms will be converted into a common lobby, with meeting-room space above.

FINANCING

Anaheim Convention Center was built in 1967 and financed by a $15 million bond issue. A 3 percent hotel room tax was later levied to retire the bonds. Expansions and renovations have been financed with additional bond issues. In 1974, Hall B and Room B were added at a cost of $8 million. In 1982, Hall C and Room C were built, and additional land was acquired for a total of $36 million. In 1990, Hall D, additional parking, and a modernization were completed at a cost of $64 million. And in 1993, parking space was converted into exhibition space for $11 million.

MARKET ORIENTATION

Anaheim Convention Center has been and continues to be successful in booking national trade shows and conventions. It operates at near-capacity levels throughout most of the year. The center's success can be attributed to the southern California location; the large population base; abundant hotel room supply; two headquarters hotels on site offering 2,600 rooms, meeting rooms, and ballrooms; excellent air and road access; and the city's appeal as a tourist destination. The center's plan to replace the arena with more exhibition space will enhance its marketability for conventions and trade shows.

LESSONS LEARNED

- Because of the rapid growth of the southern California population and economy and an abundant supply of proximate hotel rooms, the convention center has enjoyed high occupancy levels since it opened. The management structure of the center, which is almost entirely operated by the city, has proven extremely efficient because it enables the city to maintain a level of high-quality service.
- Because adequate land was not acquired before the early 1980s, obtaining land for future expansions has been expensive and difficult. A master plan could have avoided this problem.
- Some of the areas used for truck marshaling were lost through expansion. A temporary area is currently being used, but a permanent area has yet to be designated.
- The absence of a master plan has resulted in design flaws, such as exhibition halls without common lobbies and great walking distances between meeting rooms and parking lots. New construction should remedy these flaws.

PROJECT DATA

ANAHEIM CONVENTION CENTER
ANAHEIM, CA

Owner: Community Center Authority (CCA), Anaheim
Architect: Adrian-Wilson; Howard, Needles, Tammen & Bergendoff (HNTB), Los Angeles; Leason-Pomeroy Associates, Costa Mesa.
Primary Users: Conventions and trade shows
Year Construction Began: 1965
Year Construction Completed: 1967
Expansions/Renovations: 1974, 1982, 1990, 1993

PROJECT INFORMATION
Site Area: 56 acres
Total GBA: 985,000 square feet
    Exhibition Space: 626,000 square feet
    Meeting Space: 70,638 square feet
Arena Seating Capacity: 8,700
Total Parking Spaces: 4,150

ECONOMIC INFORMATION
Original Project Cost (1967 dollars): $15,000,000
Original Project Cost (1994 dollars):[1] $65,479,042
Renovations:
    Hall B and Room B Expansion (1974 dollars): $8,000,000
    Hall C, Room C, Land Acquisition (1982 dollars): $36,000,000
    Hall D, Additional Parking, Modernization (1990 dollars): $64,000,000
    Additional Exhibition Space (1993 dollars): $11,000,000

FINANCING
Original Bond Issue: $15,000,000[2]

Notes:
[1] Calculated based on the consumer price index.
[2] Not including additional bond issues and bond refinancing for renovations and expansions.

GEORGIA WORLD CONGRESS CENTER

ATLANTA, GEORGIA

In 1992, upon the opening of the Georgia World Congress Center's second expansion, the center became the premier facility of its kind in the southeastern United States. The generally European title of "congress center" is appropriate because the facility's goal is to attract international delegates. The expanded Georgia World Congress Center (GWCC), adjacent to downtown Atlanta, spans six city blocks, with more than 42 acres of floor space—a total of 2.5 million square feet. It offers 950,000 square feet of exhibit space, 76 meeting rooms, and a 33,000-square-foot ballroom.

DEVELOPMENT STRATEGY

Atlanta's evolution into a convention and trade-show destination has been an ongoing process of development for more than 20 years. In 1970, the formation of an ad hoc committee to study the feasibility of developing a convention and trade-show facility in Atlanta began the development process. In 1971, the Georgia State General Assembly authorized development of the conven-

tion center and followed this up in 1973 by dedicating $35 million in general obligation bonds for construction of the GWCC. The development of the first 350,000 square feet of exhibit space, Phase I, began in 1974, and was completed in 1976.

Because of excess demand for the GWCC, the state resumed the development process in 1979, commissioning a feasibility study for Phase II, an expansion of the center. The study, which indicated that an expansion was warranted and would be used, also stressed that delay would mean added construction costs and lost convention business. As a result of the study's research findings, the state authorized $10 million in general obligation bonds to secure additional land and retain architects. Another $83 million was authorized in 1981 in the form of general obligation bonds to construct the second phase, which would double the size of the existing facility. Construction took place from 1981 to 1984.

Again because of excess demand for the facility, another market analysis study was commissioned and planning began in 1988 for Phase III, a second expansion. Increased exhibit space was proposed to enable the center to meet the growth demands of a number of its existing show producers, as well as to offer opportunities for new markets. The awarding of the 1996 Olympics to Atlanta added an incentive for the proposed expansion, as the GWCC would be used as the media center for the games and the venue for table tennis, fencing, judo, weight lifting, handball, and wrestling events. Thus, the Georgia legislature approved the development of Phase III in 1988. Acquisition of property and architectural design were completed in the following year; site preparation began in 1989 and was finished in April 1991, whereupon construction contracts were awarded for Phase III, which was completed in 1992.

DESIGN AND SITE ISSUES

The original site consisted of 13 acres adjacent to downtown Atlanta, near the Omni Arena and its office, retail, and hotel complex. Five of the original acres were acquired for $2.2 million, with the remainder donated by then–Omni owner Tom Cousins. Site acquisition costs for the first expansion were $7 million.

From the beginning, the demand for the facility exceeded its available days and capacity. Therefore, the architectural firm that had designed the original center was selected to study the expanded center's intended size, its relationship with its components, and its pedestrian and vehicular access, providing conceptual drawings with

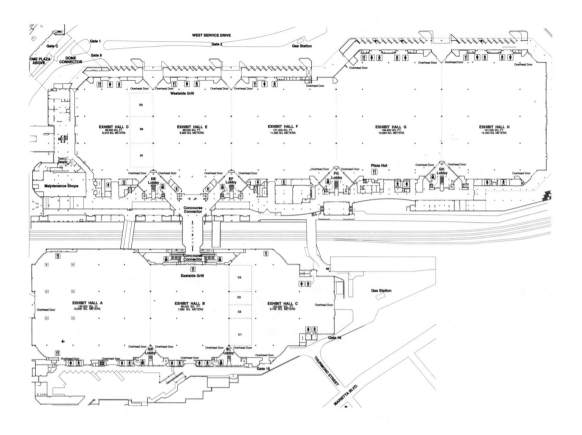

cost estimates for the expanded GWCC. At the same time, a study commissioned by the state's office of planning and budget analyzed the potential economic impact of the center as it then stood and compared it with that of the proposed expanded GWCC.

The architects' Phase II expansion designs included an additional 300,000 square feet of exhibition space, all on one level; 100,000 square feet of new meeting space; a 33,000-square-foot, finely finished ballroom; and 24 new loading docks, as well as crate storage areas. The expansion plans integrated the new facilities with the existing one via a 35,000-square-foot entrance lobby.

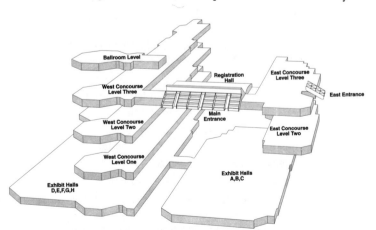

Construction would be phased so as not to interrupt events already scheduled at the GWCC. Groundbreaking for this expansion was held on September 17, 1981. Hotel development kept pace, with the addition of 10,000 new rooms to Atlanta's hotel room supply.

Phase III, the latest GWCC expansion, added another 310,000 square feet of exhibition space in 1992, making the total square footage of the building more than 2.5 million. This phase broadened the range of services offered by the center, which is now the second largest convention center in the nation. Taking into account the adjacent Georgia Dome, the two venues constitute one of the largest convention, sports, and entertainment complexes in the world.

More than 17,000 parking spaces are available within eight blocks of the facility. Two parking decks offering a total of 1,260 spaces and two surface lots with a total of 2,600 spaces are located next to the complex. In addition, there is a staging area for 200 buses or trucks.

The GWCC Authority has approved construction of a parking deck and plaza on International Boulevard alongside the center. The combined deck and plaza, which will improve pedestrian access and traffic flow at the complex and add 1,000 parking spaces, is scheduled for completion before the 1996 Olympic Games.

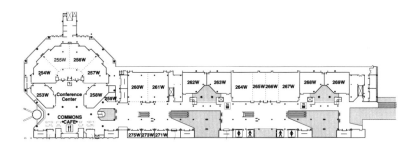

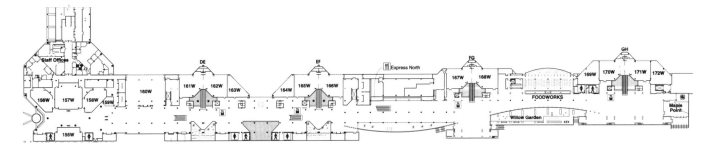

Georgia World Congress Center is accessible via Hartsfield International Airport in Atlanta and two commuter airports nearby. Also, the MARTA transit system services the center with the adjacent Omni-GWCC-Dome rail station, linking the congress center/dome complex to all of metropolitan Atlanta.

FINANCING

Financing for Phase II, GWCC's first expansion, was not accomplished without leaping several fiscal and political hurdles. The need for the estimated $89.5 million expansion came at a time when the Georgia state legislature was faced with particularly tight budget restraints. Bond financing was under strict scrutiny, given the unstable financial market of the late 1970s, and the project size was the largest ever considered by the state, except in highway development. Several times, the project came dangerously close to being shelved because of extraordinarily high interest rates on bonds; project bonds were sold in phases in the hope of securing lower interest rates during the life of the project. Also, politically the project had to overcome regional opposition among some state legislators, who wanted state funds allocated to local projects. The final cost of financing the project came to over $103 million.

The proposal of Phase III also came during a difficult budget year for the Georgia General Assembly. The state recognized the need for expansion, however, and gave its support for funding by authorizing general obli-

gation bonds totaling $18 million for land acquisition and architectural design, $5 million for demolition and site development, and $75 million for construction of the third phase.

MARKET ORIENTATION

The Georgia World Congress Center has been the number-one destination for trade shows in the southeastern United States since its expansion in 1984. In recent years, the facility has ranked among the nation's highest in occupied square footage for large conventions and trade shows. GWCC's success as a convention/trade-show destination is attributable in large part to the support that the center has received from the state's

PROJECT DATA

GEORGIA WORLD CONGRESS CENTER
ATLANTA, GA

Owner: State of Georgia
Builders:
  Phase I: Ira Hardin Construction, Atlanta
  Phase II: Dugan Meyers Construction, Atlanta
  Phase III: Hardin Construction Group, Inc., Atlanta
Architect (all phases): Thompson, Ventulett, Stainback & Associates (TVS), Atlanta

	Phase I	Phase II	Phase III	All
Year Planning Began:	1971	1979	1988	
Year Construction Began:	1974	1981	1991	
Year Construction Completed:	1976	1984	1992	

PROJECT INFORMATION

	Phase I	Phase II	Phase III	All
Site Area (acres):	13	15	14	42
Total GBA (square feet):	750,000	+1,100,000	+650,000	2,500,000
Exhibit Space	350,000	+300,000	+300,000	950,000
Meeting Space	115,500	+100,000	+14,500	230,000
Total Parking Spaces:[1] 17,000				

ECONOMIC INFORMATION

	Phase I	Phase II	Phase III
Site Acquisition Cost:	$2,200,000	$7,000,000	$18,000,000
Construction Costs:	$27,000,000	$86,000,000	$75,000,000
Total Soft Costs:	$6,000,000	$10,000,000	$5,000,000
Total Project Cost:	$35,200,000	$103,000,000	$98,000,000
Funding Sources:			
State General Obligation Bonds	$35,000,000	$93,000,000[2]	$98,000,000[3]

Notes:
[1] Available within eight blocks of the center.
[2] Including $10 million in 1979 to secure the land and retain architects, and $83 million in 1981 for Phase II construction.
[3] Including $18 million in 1988 to secure land and retain architects, $5 million in 1989 for site preparation, and $75 million in 1991 for Phase III construction.

---

general assembly; Georgia was one of the first states to approve state funding for facilities intended to attract international and national meetings to its cities. As of 1995, these states include Washington, Oregon, Colorado, Louisiana, Maryland, Pennsylvania, New Jersey, New York, Massachusetts, Illinois, Missouri, Kentucky, and Indiana, in addition to Georgia.

The state of Georgia and the city of Atlanta take a team approach to bringing convention and trade-show business to Georgia. As part of the team concept, promotion of other Georgia cities as convention and trade-show destinations is done on the GWCC premises, for the state is interested in attracting meetings to Georgia and sharing the economic benefits among several of its cities. GWCC was the first U.S. convention center to set up an international program, including seminars for associations; toward this end, it affords simultaneous translation and equipment services.

GWCC is owned by the state of Georgia and managed by the 11-member GWCC Authority, whose members are appointed by the governor of Georgia and serve on a voluntary basis. The responsibilities of the executive director of the authority include overall planning, organization, staffing, and operation of both the GWCC and the Georgia Dome. The executive director, who was named in 1976 when the center was under construction, has guided the facility through its official opening and overseen the completion of the first two expansions, which have tripled the size of the facility.

A self-supporting venue, GWCC has not required an operational subsidy since 1982.

LESSONS LEARNED

Among the insights gained on this project have been the following:

- The Georgia State Assembly, through its financial support, has basically created its own destination in Atlanta by constructing the largest trade-show facility of its kind in the southeastern United States. Economic benefits accruing from the state's action have already returned its initial investment in sales taxes and hotel/motel taxes, through the sales of goods and services to national and international attendees at conventions and trade shows. Given the continued demand for space and the competition in this marketplace, management is contemplating an expansion after the 1996 Olympic Games that would increase overall space by another 400,000 to 500,000 square feet.

- From the opening of the first phase, GWCC management has been able to learn about the changing characteristics of the meetings and exhibition industry and to determine how the facility, either through architectural or mechanical design, could interact with various functions. More specifically, center management saw a need to supply an adequate ratio of meeting rooms to exhibition space to maximize the potential use of the center. Thus, groups that are more meetings-intensive can use the facility even while an exhibition or trade show is being held.

- Another design characteristic concerns restrooms. Many groups are either predominantly male-oriented or female-oriented. Rather than overbuild restrooms, the center designed them to be "unisex" facilities to allow for greater flexibility from event to event.

- Fine acoustic quality is an important feature for exhibition halls, so that different groups can be accommodated at the same time with minimal noise conflict.

- To accommodate the movement of attendees and to ease pedestrian traffic flow, at least three reversible escalators were installed.

- Storage rooms for in-house services are separated by service function, such as janitorial or maintenance, to keep better track of inventory.

- Separate entrances and service corridors are incorporated into the design to allow caterers access to meeting rooms and ballrooms without encumbering public spaces.

- GWCC mechanical features include extra electrical service to meeting rooms and hallways to accommodate overflow exhibitions. Also, air conditioning units service zones of the building as needed and are able to operate on different fuel sources to minimize energy costs. GWCC has incorporated these features into its expanded space.

- The professional quality and leadership of its board of directors has distinguished the GWCC authority from nearly all other authorities or not-for-profit corporations created for this purpose. The calibre of appointees and their level of interest have not deteriorated over the 20 years since GWCC's creation.

THE JOHN B. HYNES VETERANS' MEMORIAL CONVENTION CENTER

BOSTON, MASSACHUSETTS

The expanded and renovated Boston Hynes Auditorium, now called The John B. Hynes Veterans' Memorial Convention Center, opened in January 1988. The $234 million project has significantly increased the state's share of national and regional convention business. The decision to reconstruct the Hynes Auditorium was made in the late 1970s, under Mayor White's administration, and the city filed legislation in 1979 to request state funding for the convention center project. The state enacted legislation in 1980 enabling the city to receive funds for the Hynes project. The renovation and expansion completely redeveloped the aging Hynes Auditorium, which in the past, even in its poor condition, achieved high levels of demand.

The center is located in the Back Bay area of Boston, next to Copley Square. It is interconnected with the Sheraton hotel in Prudential Center and with the new Westin and Marriott hotels. The combination of the hotels and center with Boston's other cultural assets in the immediate area has resulted in one of the most convenient and attractive walking environments in the country.

The new Hynes facility offers exhibition space totaling 193,000 square feet and 41 meeting rooms. It also includes a 25,000-square-foot ballroom and 143,000 square feet of lobby and prefunction space, of which 30,000 square feet is available for registration purposes.

DEVELOPMENT STRATEGY

The reconstruction/expansion of the Boston Hynes Auditorium into a convention center was the response of business and community leaders to the need for more convention/exhibition space in Boston. The city conducted studies to determine the needs of meeting planners with regard to conventions. The results of the study indicated that without an expansion in the size of the convention center, Boston would lose its competitive edge in the convention market to other large facilities across the United States. The study recommended that the most effective and practical way for the city to retain and expand its convention business was to reconstruct the new convention center on the existing Hynes Auditorium site, primarily because there were so many adjacent hotel rooms.

In 1982, state legislation was enacted to create the Massachusetts Convention Center Authority (MCCA). The authority was created to own and manage the new Boston Hynes Convention Center. This newly formed state agency worked closely with the Boston Redevelopment Agency (BRA) in undertaking this redevelopment project. The law required that the Boston Hynes Auditorium expansion take place on land owned by the city of Boston and the Prudential Insurance Company.

The construction development process encountered a number of obstacles. First, the project became one of the most complicated eminent domain actions in Massachusetts history because the center's site occupies air rights over the Massachusetts Turnpike. The site was partially an air rights site over a rail bed, as well as over the Massachusetts Turnpike, and the balance of the site belonged to Prudential Insurance. Thus, MCCA, itself a newly established entity, had to deal with three landowners in a complicated negotiation. Finally, a tremendous amount of development and redevelopment was occurring adjacent to and around the site, and transportation issues and site linkages created numerous problems that had to be solved.

Other problems included relocating utilities, finding new premises for displaced tenants, moving complicated equipment such as computer and air conditioning installations, building overpasses over the rails and the turnpike, eradicating hard-to-remove asbestos, and awarding the hundreds of contracts required to conform with state laws.

The original plans for the expansion and renovation of the Boston Hynes Auditorium called for phased construction to allow continuous operation of the facility throughout the construction period. However, after much deliberation and with the support of the local hotel industry, MCCA recommended a complete closing of the facility for three years during construction. This alternative was chosen to ease the construction process and to avoid the delays often encountered by phased construction projects. The closing of the old Hynes made strict adherence to project schedules critical.

DESIGN AND SITE ISSUES

The original John B. Hynes Auditorium was built in classic WPA style and was similar to many of the civic and cultural centers built during the 1930s, and even through the late 1940s (as veterans' or war memorial auditoriums). By the 1970s, the Hynes was handicapped by many undersized and poorly serviced meeting rooms, numerous pillars in the exhibition hall, poor access and egress, and inadequate registration areas.

About the only vestige of the original facility remaining is its location. The balance of the facility was completely redeveloped. The result is a remarkable and workable meeting complex. The market analysis conducted for the study concluded that although Boston could attract larger exhibitions, preservation of the location was a prime consideration. Therefore, only 193,000 square feet of exhibition area could be provided, and that area had to be on two levels. Further, the market study concluded that perhaps an appropriate twofold approach for Boston, with its special qualities as a city, would be to offer the capacity for one large event requiring 193,000 square feet of exhibition space, or two moderately sized events on different levels, each with a complement of breakout meeting space. The building's original configuration lent itself well to this approach, and the following design evolved:

- A lower-level subbasement, including the entrance lobby, administration, the tunnel for the Massachusetts Turnpike, and the truck and service area.
- A plaza level, including two exhibition halls with a total of 82,000 square feet of exhibition space, 14 meet-

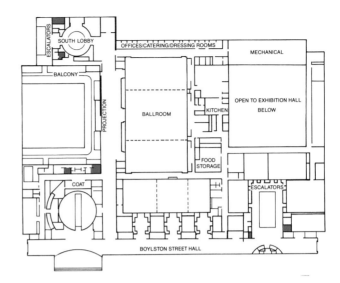

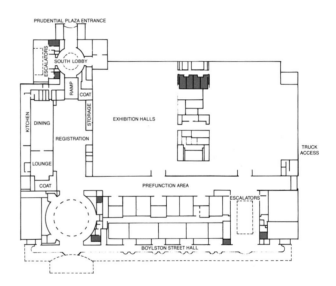

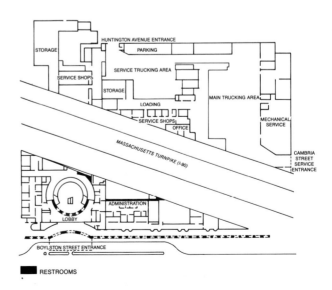

■ RESTROOMS

ing rooms offering 20,209 square feet of space, registration and prefunction areas, and two entrances.

- A second level, offering two exhibition halls and a multipurpose room totaling 111,000 square feet, and 12 meeting rooms with 20,385 square feet.
- A third level, offering a 24,426-square-foot ballroom and 15 meeting rooms containing a total of 29,272 square feet.

The entire convention center can be used by one event, or each level can be used independently, as each has its own separate access. Because Boston has such a good transportation system and because the site and surrounding hotels can be reached by the subway system (the "T"), no parking was provided on the site. The convention center is operated in conjunction with a public parking garage at the nearby Boston Common. The Boston Common garage, located on several blocks, was renovated in 1995, providing 1,450 parking spaces.

The convention center occupies a 5.5-acre site, the major portion of which was created on air rights. Four of these acres are owned by the city, while 1.5 acres were owned by the Prudential Center. The center has a premier location, three miles from Logan International Airport and only two blocks from an entrance to the Massachusetts Turnpike. Near the center are more than 7,000 convention-quality hotel rooms, 5,000 of which stand within three blocks of the Hynes. Interconnecting skywalks link most of the major hotels with the convention center.

PROJECT DATA

JOHN B. HYNES VETERANS' MEMORIAL CONVENTION CENTER
BOSTON, MA

Owner: Massachusetts Convention Center Authority (MCCA), Boston
Developer: MCCA/Boston Redevelopment Authority (BRA), Boston
Architects: Howard, Needles, Tammen & Bergendorf (HNTB); Kallman, McKinnell & Wood; and Perez & Associates, all of Boston
Year Planning Began: 1979
Year Construction Completed: 1988

PROJECT INFORMATION
Site Area: 5.5 acres
Total GBA: 548,700 square feet
    Exhibition Space: 193,000 square feet
    Meeting Space: 70,000 square feet
    Ballroom Space: 24,426 square feet

ECONOMIC INFORMATION
Site Acquisition Cost (includes utilities, relocation, insurance, and other costs): $66,100,000
Construction Costs: $168,100,000
Total Project Cost (1988 dollars): $234,200,000
Total Project Cost (1994 dollars):[1] $288,642,100
Funding Sources:
    State-Backed General Obligation Bonds (1984):[2]
        $100,000,000
    State-Backed General Obligation Bonds (1985):
        $100,000,000
    State Appropriations and Interest Earnings: $34,200,000
Total Funding: $234,200,000

Notes:
[1]Calculated based on the consumer price index.
[2]Implicitly derived from state-levied tax on hotel room occupancy.

FINANCING

The cost of the expansion and renovation of the facility was $234.2 million. This comprised construction costs of $168.1 million, plus $66.1 million for the costs of acquiring space from Prudential, utilities relocation, insurance, and other soft costs associated with major construction projects. The state legislature authorized state-backed bonds in two increments: $100 million in 1984 and another $100 million in 1985.

As noted earlier, the state legislature created the Massachusetts Convention Center Authority (MCCA) to acquire and operate the Boston Hynes Convention Center. A primary source of revenue to pay debt service on the bonds came (implicitly) from the hotel-room occupancy tax that the state levied. In 1983, the MCCA purchased all land, buildings, and fixtures at the convention center from the city of Boston, as well as the city's rights to the parking garage under the Commons or Public Garden.

MARKET ORIENTATION

The target markets for the convention center are moderately sized national trade shows and conventions of professional associations. Boston, because of its location and its distinctive metropolitan environment, has traditionally hosted a large number of national and regional meetings. Because there are two other trade show facilities in the Boston area, the Hynes wanted to position itself to serve events requiring high-quality meeting space and to provide nearby hotel rooms for nonresident attendees.

The MCCA and the Boston Convention and Visitors' Bureau have mounted a very aggressive sales and marketing campaign for the expanded convention center. A number of new incentives have been employed to encourage meeting planners to bring their meetings to the new center.

LESSONS LEARNED

Boston has been a highly competitive meeting destination, and the opening of the expanded John B. Hynes Convention Center has strengthened Boston's market share of large convention business. This accomplishment was the result of several tactics, including:

- Boston has succeeded with its historic Back Bay location and, despite many obstacles, has elected to expand its older convention facility on the premise that the location within the center of the city is what makes the Boston destination attractive to conventions.

  The key obstacle to developing on this site was that, although Boston is a major city, it would have to enter the market with a middle-sized building in an industry that perceives that "bigger is better and biggest is best." Although the site presented numerous complicated construction problems, the decision to retain the center at its present location has resulted in high attendance levels and occupancy rates.

- City, state, and hotel industry representatives unanimously agreed to close down the Hynes during construction rather than risk delays that might postpone the completion of the expanded center. Intense debate marked this decision because many events held dates at the center, and several major hotels had just been built near the center, expecting that a major

share of their occupancy would come from events at the Hynes. Because the center project involved a complete redevelopment, however, the only course was to "bite the bullet" and close. All the hotels and other exhibition facilities worked hard to accommodate existing bookings, and even with the strength of Boston's lodging demand the hotels coped well with these problems. Virtually no goodwill was lost, and the decision to close was vindicated.

- The state took the initiative to support Boston's effort to expand its exhibition facilities by creating an authority to develop and operate the convention center and by issuing the general obligation bonds.

- As Seattle did for its new convention center, Boston chose the most marketable location and saw strengthening the center city as a key reason for its site selection. Boston's strategy of penetrating the middle-tier market and focusing on simultaneous events has been a well-conceived one and has served the city well.

187

SAINT LUCIE COUNTY CIVIC CENTER

FORT PIERCE, FLORIDA

Saint Lucie County Civic Center is centrally located on Florida's eastern coast, midway between West Palm Beach and Cape Kennedy. Tourism is fast becoming a major industry for the county because of its beaches, public recreational facilities, and good location. The civic center is one of five major recreational facilities in Saint Lucie County, along with Lawnwood Recreation Complex, The Savannas (freshwater fishing), Indian River Memorial Park Amphitheater, and the South Beach Boardwalk. In response to a need for a multi-purpose facility in which to hold a variety of events, construction began on the civic center in April 1976 and was completed in the following year. The venue is the only one of its kind in the Saint Lucie/Martin/Indian River tricounty area.

DEVELOPMENT STRATEGY

Saint Lucie County Civic Center functions as an arena, exhibit hall, banquet hall, theater, and convention cen-

ter. It has hosted a wide variety of events, including the International Citrus Expo, Amara Temple Shrine Circus, home shows, boat and RV shows, the Lipizzan Stallions, the Treasure Coast Opera Society, and concerts featuring such performers as Foreigner, Ronnie Milsap, and Confederate Railroad. Because of increased trade-show use, however, the number of concerts held at the civic center has declined.

The civic center was built to meet the demand within the county and environs for concerts and trade shows. Before center construction, a fairgrounds and a jai alai *fronton* were the primary public assembly venues in the area, and the county commission encouraged the development of a civic center as a more appropriate, purpose-built venue for concerts and trade shows.

DESIGN AND SITE ISSUES

The civic center occupies a ten-acre site, offers 24,000 square feet of unobstructed floor space, and has a maximum seating capacity of 5,000. Center amenities include banquet and catering capabilities and star and cast dressing rooms. A ceiling-to-floor curtain divides the arena or exhibit area into northern and southern portions: with its theater floor plan, the south hall seats 2,100 persons, while the north hall can be configured to provide banquet accommodations for up to 800 diners. There are 500 on-site parking spaces.

FINANCING

Saint Lucie County Civic Center was financed by county-issued bonds secured by the local hotel tax. In Florida,

Billy Howard

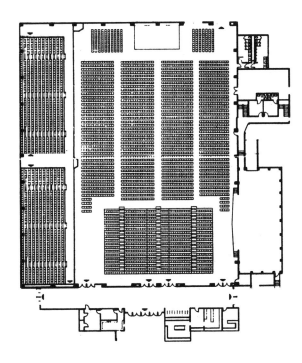

PROJECT DATA

SAINT LUCIE CIVIC CENTER
FORT PIERCE, FL

Owner: Saint Lucie County
Architect: Reigler Associates
Year Construction Began: 1976
Year Construction Completed: 1977

PROJECT INFORMATION

Site Area: 10 acres
Total GBA: 32,000 square feet
Exhibition Space: 24,000 square feet
Total Parking Spaces: 500

ECONOMIC INFORMATION

Total Project Cost (1977 dollars): $6,750,000
Total Project Cost (1994 dollars):[1] $16,240,000
Funding Source: Bonds

Note:
[1]Calculated based on the consumer price index.

every county is authorized to levy a hotel tax of up to 3 percent that must be approved by local referendum, or local "option." These taxes can be pledged to repay bonds whose proceeds may be used for any facility that can be shown to increase tourism.

MARKETING AND MANAGEMENT

The facility is marketed by the center itself and through advertising sponsored by the convention and visitors' bureau. Local and repeat business accounts for considerable center use.

LESSONS LEARNED

- Because there was not enough supervision by the county during building construction, deficiencies in the building, such as poor roofing, are notable.
- In an attempt to cut costs, the county delayed hiring a center manager until after construction had been completed. If hired earlier, a manager could have overseen construction and perhaps prevented some of the center's layout deficiencies.
- The building was constructed with more than $10,000 worth of equipment and fixtures that are rarely used. Speakers that were built into the acoustical ceiling are impractical and have never been used.

INDIANA CONVENTION CENTER AND RCA DOME

INDIANAPOLIS, INDIANA

Though the Indiana Convention Center opened in 1972, groundbreaking for the adjacent, 60,000-seat RCA Dome (formerly the Hoosier Dome) did not occur until 1982. Located in downtown Indianapolis, the Indiana Convention Center/RCA Dome complex hosts a large number of conventions and trade shows each year, including many state association meetings, while the RCA Dome is home to the Indianapolis Colts National Football League franchise. Indianapolis has capitalized on its image as a sports-oriented city noted for car racing, basketball, and football in order to create a sports-themed environment for visiting convention groups.

DEVELOPMENT STRATEGY

In addition to the Dome, the original convention center was expanded in 1991 to increase the exhibition, assembly, and banquet capacity of the center.

During the 1970s, Indianapolis business and community leaders set out to convince NFL officials that the city would be an ideal place for an expansion team. But a primary obstacle in securing a franchise was that the city had no stadium. And if a stadium were to be built, who was going to pay for it, and how would it be financed?

At the same time, Indianapolis was finding it difficult to meet the increasing demand to accommodate more conventions; the center had to expand if the city was going to remain competitive as a national, state, and regional convention and meeting destination. In 1980, the idea of building a facility that could serve both convention and sports purposes was conceived. Skepticism abounded with regard to the financial hurdles, but support for the combined-use project gained momentum toward the end of 1980.

Convention-center expansion and the addition of the RCA Dome, at a total cost of $94.7 million, were financed through local tax initiatives, aided by $30 million from foundation grants and endorsements. The local community was supportive, voting in favor of building the dome on its first referendum.

DESIGN AND SITE ISSUES

The Indiana Convention Center/RCA Dome occupies a site in the heart of downtown Indianapolis. The city owned the 7.25-acre site adjacent to the convention center on which the dome was developed, and because of extensive public support for the project, few political obstacles were encountered once development was underway. The site selected and the proposed design also found widespread acceptance.

The complex was designed with two purposes in mind: to provide a high-caliber sports facility to attract a professional football franchise, and to offer premier exhibition and banquet space to convention and trade-show groups. The lighted, air-supported, and translucent roof of the RCA Dome has become a landmark in the Indianapolis cityscape. The facility's concrete exterior with metal trim was chosen to blend the existing convention center's architecture with that of the futuristic dome, which offers 60,500 permanent seats.

In 1992, the dome underwent several improvements, including the addition of two new video screens, a club-level renovation, and improvements in concourse ventilation and accessibility for disabled persons. Further expansion and renovation in 1993 increased the convention center's meeting space by 22,050 square feet and added the 36,000-square-foot Sagamore Ballroom, two skywalks to adjacent hotels, a new lobby and registration area, and additional prefunction space. The complex now houses a total of 301,500 square feet of column-free exhibit space, including the stadium floor and 127,595 square feet of meeting space in 52 meeting rooms, including three ballrooms. In 1994, the balance of the space was refurbished.

The convention center/dome project has been a major catalyst for development and redevelopment within the downtown, complementing other local projects. After the announcement of the second phase, comprising the expansion of the convention center and the addition of the RCA Dome, several new developments augmented the revitalization of the area around the complex:

- A 578-room Westin hotel.
- A 1,000-car parking garage with a $6 million public park on its top floor.
- The Pan American Plaza, which houses two skating rinks and a 12-story office complex, home to many national sports governing bodies.
- The transformation of Union Station into a dining, entertainment, and shopping complex.

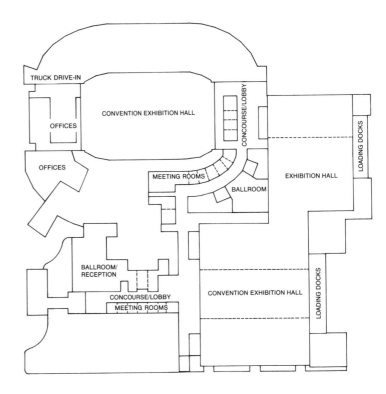

FINANCING

Marion County, Indiana, issued $15.5 million in general obligation bonds on August 13, 1969, to help finance construction of the original Indiana Convention Center. When the second phase of the project—expansion of the convention center and construction of the RCA Dome—became a reality in 1982, funds were raised by a successful public/private construction financing campaign. Thirty million dollars in private grants was received from the Lilly Endowment and the Krannert Charitable Trust, and the sale of excise tax revenue bonds raised an additional $47,250,000. A 5 percent hotel tax and a 1 percent food and beverage tax are collected by the state partially to pay debt service on these bonds. The remain-

der of this revenue goes to the convention center's capital improvements and operating fund, as well as to marketing, which is handled by the Indianapolis Convention and Visitor's Association in conjunction with the complex's marketing department.

In May 1991, revenue bonds were sold to finance the third phase, the expansion and renovation that took place in 1993. The complex consolidated old debt to take advantage of lower interest rates at that time. The facility does not receive any property taxes; nor will they be used to pay off the revenue bonds. Rather, the complex receives only excise taxes on hotels/motels, food and beverage sales, cigarettes, and professional sports admissions at the dome.

MARKET ORIENTATION

With expansion of the convention center and addition of the dome, Indianapolis has achieved the status of a premier convention destination. Historically dominated by state meeting activity, the city is now poised to compete with other nationally attractive cities in the region, such as St. Louis, Columbus, Cincinnati, and Milwaukee. Indianapolis hosts many national events while maintaining its market competitiveness in the state and regional markets. Further, the city's strategy of promoting its sports image in concert with its convention promotional

exhibit halls, the number of conventions and trade shows held at the facility has increased substantially. This trend is expected to continue in the future. The complex also has an advantage in terms of revenue generation because of the many sporting and entertainment events that take place in the RCA Dome.

In 1994, the CIB of Marion County announced an agreement in principle to rename the Hoosier Dome the RCA Dome. According to officials, the name change is the first step in the CIB's program to expand private sector involvement and minimize taxpayer support. For RCA, sponsorship of the dome links their name with championship performances in sports and entertainment.

LESSONS LEARNED

The Indiana Convention Center/RCA Dome has enjoyed much success in its early years of operation. Among the consequences of its development have been the following:

- The dome has become home to the Colts NFL franchise.
- The city is continuing to attract a large share of the state's convention business, largely because of its central location.
- The success of the project has been due in large part to the strong guidance and determination of business and community leaders, who sought and gained the support of the Indianapolis public.
- In both development strategy and design, the project's creators were resourceful and imaginative. The development of the RCA Dome as an expansion to the convention center was a relatively new approach for a city/county government to entertain. As to design, the project was one of the first air-supported stadium roof structures ever built.
- The city of Indianapolis has seen a higher-than-average level of downtown redevelopment since the early 1980s. The complex was the primary catalyst for this redevelopment and has stimulated new growth in the CBD.
- Generally, officials with the convention center complex have been pleased with the overall design and development of the facility.
- When the convention center opened, officials encouraged new hotel development to support the new center. This strategy was successful, and the number of hotel rooms in downtown Indianapolis is currently 3,667; citywide, there are 16,031 rooms. Two of the downtown hotels are connected to the complex by enclosed skywalks.

efforts has been rewarded handsomely: it has attracted an NFL franchise, hosted the Pan Am Games, and been selected as the location of numerous sports- and health-related conventions.

The facility, which is managed by the Capital Improvement Board (CIB), a municipal corporation, works closely with the Indianapolis Convention and Visitors' Association to market the convention center complex. It is much used by state and regional convention groups: in 1973, only 19 conventions were held in the center, but now, ten years after the addition of the dome and

ERNEST N. MORIAL CONVENTION CENTER

NEW ORLEANS, LOUISIANA

The Ernest N. Morial Convention Center was developed to meet the rapidly growing demand for convention and trade-show facilities in the Crescent City and to broaden the city's booming tourist industry. Since its opening in 1984, the center has accomplished these goals and more. Today, the center captures a sizable share of the nationwide convention market and influences every segment of the local hospitality and tourism industry. The convention center's reputation for spaciousness, flexibility, and extraordinary service continues to secure its position as one of the highest-attended facilities in the nation.

DEVELOPMENT STRATEGY

The center, originally named the New Orleans Convention Center, was first used as the Great Hall for the 1984 Louisiana World Exposition. Its creation came about when the Louisiana state legislature established the New Orleans Exhibition Hall Authority in 1978 to explore the feasibility of developing a modern convention cen-

ter. At that time, convention and trade-show demand was being served by the 137,000-square-foot Rivergate Center, built in 1962, and by convention facilities within the Superdome. By the mid-1970s, however, the city of New Orleans was becoming increasingly popular as a convention and trade-show destination, and existing facilities were no longer able to accommodate the rising demand.

When a feasibility study commissioned by the Exhibit Hall Authority determined that there was a need for a convention center, the authority developed a financing plan and selected a site in the downtown's warehouse district for the new center. Construction began in 1981, and the facility opened for the World Exposition in May 1984. The Exposition closed in November of that year, leaving center officials with the monumental task of repairing the wear and tear caused by millions of visitors in time for the center's first event in January 1985, the Helicopter Association International Exhibition. In total, 28 events were held at the center in its inaugural year.

The center's first expansion took place between 1989 and 1991 when a total of 800,000 square feet was added, including 340,000 square feet of exhibit space. Long before Phase II had been completed, the vision for Phase III was in place. While Phase II had answered the center's immediate needs, it was clear that future expansion would be necessary to keep the facility a competitive step ahead of other centers across the country.

In 1992, the New Orleans Convention Center was renamed the Ernest N. Morial Convention Center in honor of the city's mayor, a key supporter of the facility.

DESIGN AND SITE ISSUES

The Morial Center stands in the heart of New Orleans, within walking distance or trolley ride of the French Quarter, Jackson Square, the Aquarium of the Americas, and 16,000 hotel rooms.

The center's most marketable feature is its ability to offer meeting and trade-show managers 667,000 square feet of contiguous exhibit space on one level and in one building. This space can be divided into as many as seven separate exhibit halls.

Other components that distinguish the Morial Center include two spacious (36,000 square feet and 31,000 square feet) ballrooms; 83 upper-level meeting rooms; a 400-seat restaurant (the Atrium) and the La Maison restaurant for small-group fine dining; and two full-service production kitchens capable of serving 20,000 meals in a 24-hour period. The center also offers state-of-the-art, in-house technical services for show production, video

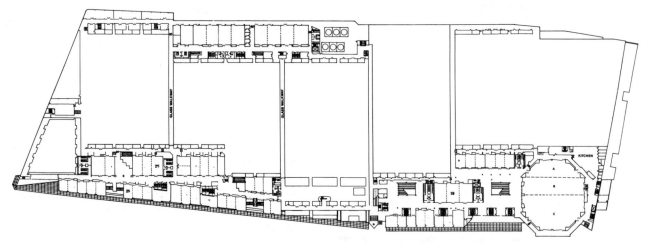

Second Level

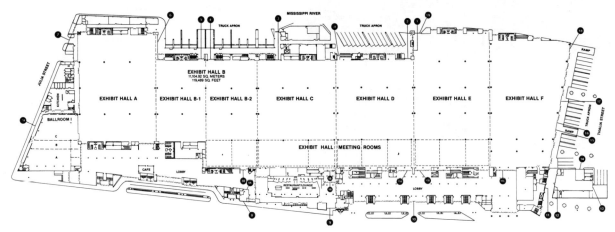

Ground Level

advertising, a complete television studio, and a fiber-optic network.

As the facility enters its second decade of operation, activity is underway to begin the Phase III expansion, targeted for completion in 1998, which will increase the center's contiguous exhibit space to 1.1 million square feet, all on ground level and under one roof. The total building space will increase from 1.7 million to more than 3 million square feet. The expansion will also add a conference theater with 4,000 permanent, tiered seats; this facility will be divisible into three acoustically separate smaller theaters of approximately 1,200 seats each. Additionally, Phase III will expand the upper-level meeting rooms to 156 and substantially increase truck docking and marshaling space.

Preliminary design work on Phase III is nearing completion. The project's architectural team is a joint partnership among three local firms: Cimini, Meric, Duplantier Architects/Planners; Billes/Manning Architects; and Hewitt-Washington & Associates. Demolition and preparation of the 23-acre expansion site, which is adjacent to the existing facility, was completed in early 1995, with actual construction expected to begin early in 1996 and a projected completion date in 1998.

FINANCING

The original center was built at a total cost of approximately $93 million. The state of Louisiana contributed

$30 million to the project because the facility was to be used as the state pavilion for the 1984 Louisiana World Exposition. Other funding sources included an urban development action grant and economic development grants for approximately $17.5 million. Hotel/motel taxes amounted to a $13 million revenue source throughout the three years of development. The first expansion of the Morial Convention Center, Phase II, was completed in 1991 at a construction cost of $95 million.

At a projected cost of $247 million, Phase III's financing plan received support and guidance from former Louisiana Governor Edwin W. Edwards, from the state legislature, and from New Orleans Mayor Marc Morial. In 1994, then-Governor Edwards signed legislation to pave the way for essential funding. Following the governor's action, the state bond commission extended a line of credit to allow the project to begin.

Phase III will be financed through $136 million in state general obligation bonds, $20 million from the city of New Orleans, and $91 million from the issuance of bonds by the Exhibition Hall Authority, to be supported by the taxes on hotels/motels, restaurants/lounges, tour buses, and service contractors. These dedicated tax increases are scheduled to expire after the bond debt has been repaid.

MARKET ORIENTATION

The Morial Center is managed by New Orleans Public Facility Management, Inc., a nonprofit corporation headed by Jimmie D. Fore. The in-house private management firm helps to insulate the facility's day-to-day operations from other distractions. The center's board members are appointed by both the governor and the mayor.

LESSONS LEARNED

■ Ernest N. Morial Convention Center has achieved extraordinary success through its unusual ability to attract both major trade shows and major conventions. This is a considerable accomplishment, given the limited population in the New Orleans metropolitan area and the city's comparatively modest level of air service.

■ This success may be largely a result of New Orleans's attractiveness as a destination, which is comparable to that of Orlando or Las Vegas, and may more than compensate for what the city lacks in regional population and air service, two criteria that are of paramount importance to trade-association event managers.

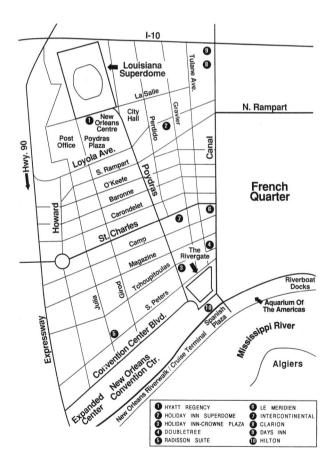

PROJECT DATA

ERNEST N. MORIAL CONVENTION CENTER
NEW ORLEANS, LA

Owner: Ernest N. Morial New Orleans Exhibition Hall
Authority
Developer/Builder: Algernon Blair, Montgomery, Alabama
Architects:
Phase I: Perez & Associates, New Orleans; Perkins &
James, New Orleans
Phase II: Perez & Associates, New Orleans; Billes/
Manning, Architects, New Orleans
Phase III: Cimini, Meric, Duplantier Architects/
Planners; Billes/Manning, Architects; Hewitt-
Washington & Associates, New Orleans
Year Construction Began:
Phase I: 1981
Phase II: 1989
Phase III: 1995
Year Construction Completed:
Phase I: 1984
Phase II: 1991
Phase III: 1998 (targeted)

PROJECT INFORMATION
Total Site Area: 46 acres
Total GBA: 1,746,859 square feet
Exhibit Space: 667,469 square feet
Meeting Space: 136,211 square feet
Ballroom Space: 67,000 square feet
Parking Spaces: 6,000[1]

ECONOMIC INFORMATION
Total Project Cost:
Phase I (1984 dollars): $93,000,000
Phase II (1991 dollars): $95,000,000
Phase III (1994 dollars): $126,000,000
Funding Sources, Phase I:
State of Louisiana: $30,000,000
Urban Development Action Grant: $17,500,000
Local Bond Issue:[2] $41,500,000
Funding Sources, Phase II:
State General Obligation Bonds: $55,000,000
State of Louisiana: $49,700,000
City of New Orleans: $1,500,000
Hotel/Restaurant Tax: $55,000,000
Additional Funding:[3] $15,100,000
Funding Sources, Phase III:
State General Obligation Bonds: $136,000,000
Local Bond Issue:[4] $91,000,000
City of New Orleans: $20,000,000

Notes:
[1]Four thousand spaces within walking distance; an additional
2,000 under construction.
[2]Debt service funded by hotel/motel taxes, which furnished $13
million during the three years of project development.
[3]Downtown development district's interest income on tax revenues; other sources.
[4]Debt service funded by hotel/motel, restaurant/lounge, tour bus,
and service contractor taxes.

JACOB K. JAVITS CONVENTION CENTER

NEW YORK, NEW YORK

The Jacob K. Javits Convention Center in New York City, which opened in April 1986, was designed by I.M. Pei & Partners and extends four city blocks along the Hudson River. The center contains 640,000 square feet of prime exhibition space. The focal point of the center is its 150-foot-high, glass-enclosed lobby. The size of the convention center, when originally planned in the late 1970s, was to have been the largest in the country. Today's finished convention center is still considered large by industry standards, but planning for the expansion to the originally intended size had to await the completion of an evaluation for doubling the size of the exhibition area.

In addition to its main exhibition space, the facility also has a special-events hall with a permanent stage and simultaneous language translation capabilities. The center features a 420-foot-long skylighted Galleria, with retail shops and small restaurants overlooking the exhibition hall.

DEVELOPMENT STRATEGY

The possibility of developing a convention center in New York City became likely in the late 1970s, under New York State's Urban Development Corporation

(UDC), which was established to finance, organize, and arrange tax subsidies primarily for the development of low-income housing. In the mid- to late 1970s, the UDC changed its emphasis to include residential and commercial development. The UDC took the original leadership and coordination role in developing the center. The entities that participated in the development of the Jacob K. Javits Convention Center included New York State, New York City, the UDC, the Triborough Bridge and Tunnel Authority (TBTA), the Convention Center Operating Corporation (CCOC), and the Convention Center Development Corporation (CCDC).

The stated twofold mission of the convention center was to provide for area redevelopment and to serve as a catalyst to provide significant economic and social benefits to New York City, the state, and the region. To these ends, the convention center was located in a former New York City railway yard. The state enacted legislation in 1979 to create the New York Convention Center (as it was first called) by bringing into existence two new entities, the development corporation (CCDC) and the operating corporation (CCOC).

The CCDC was responsible for the planning, design, construction, and development of the center. The CCOC—governed by four board members, two appointed by the UDC and two appointed by the TBTA—had the power to approve or disapprove the plans and designs of the CCDC.

The CCOC's main responsibility was to operate and maintain the convention center, although the private management firm of Ogden Allied was retained to conduct the day-to-day operation of the facility, and the CCOC primarily served as a liaison among Ogden, the state (UDC), and the CCDC. (The CCDC is still involved in the expansion and modification efforts associated with the center.)

The New York Convention Center Operating Corporation (CCOC) was created as a public benefit corporation. It has a 13-member appointed board: seven members appointed by the governor, two by the leader of the state senate, two by the speaker of the assembly, one by the senate minority leader, and one by the minority leader of the assembly. The governor selects the chairman of the board, and the board appoints an executive director.

DESIGN AND SITE ISSUES

The convention center is part of a major downtown renovation project. It stands between 34th and 39th

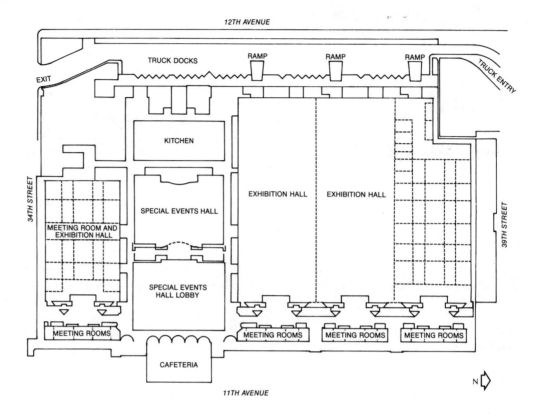

Streets and 11th and 12th Avenues. The architect selection committee produced the guidelines for the center's site, size, and construction budget, choosing the firm of I.M. Pei & Partners to design the facility. The original design featured a 150-foot Crystal Palace Lobby in what was then planned to be the largest convention center in the country. The convention center's design was unique in that the structure was to be built using a space frame rather than a beam frame to support the roof and exterior walls.

Construction ran into delays due to unanticipated rock beds, problems with infrastructure associated with the Lincoln Tunnel, and fabrication of essential elements of the space frame. The primary delay was caused by late delivery of the nodes used to support the roof structure for the atrium. These were manufactured abroad and fitted in the United States. As costs escalated with unforeseen problems, high inflation, and high interest rates, in 1981 the CCDC decided to reduce the size of the facility.

The convention center consists of 640,000 square feet of exhibition space divisible into a maximum of seven halls. The largest single exhibition area is 274,000 square feet. The center offers 81,000 square feet of meeting space with a maximum of 61 meeting rooms. As many

of the rooms must be configured out of the exhibition hall space, they reduce the hall's square footage when in use as meeting space.

The center site lies within a vast redevelopment area, and the convention center is the first component to be built. The dynamics of New York as a destination, its overall density, inner-city transit systems and supporting infrastructure, have allowed the center to operate in an environment that offers virtually no adjacent support facilities. The city's bus system offers a dedicated bus route linking the site to the balance of the downtown at frequent and regular intervals, making adjacent support development less necessary for the center's success as a trade-association venue.

The vicinity of the center has not experienced a high degree of private sector redevelopment and investment since the center's opening. Because the center borders the river, however, the potential likely exists for further development, especially if the city proceeds with upgrading the riverfront for pedestrians, as anticipated. Additionally, expansion of the center itself will use a large area of land identified for redevelopment purposes. The benefits from expansion have been questioned because of the perceived limited availability of hotel rooms in Manhattan.

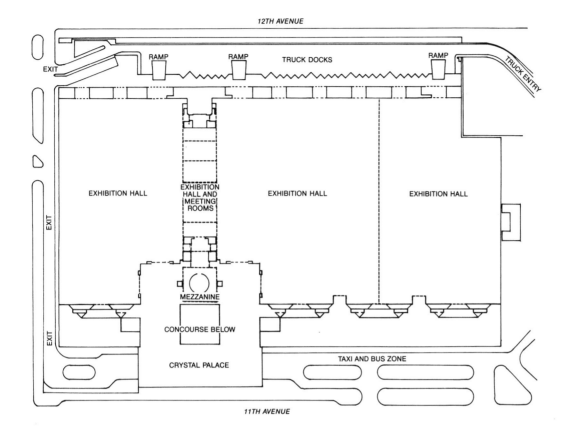

12TH AVENUE

EXIT

RAMP   RAMP   TRUCK DOCKS   RAMP   TRUCK ENTRY

EXIT

EXHIBITION HALL

EXHIBITION HALL AND MEETING ROOMS

EXHIBITION HALL

EXHIBITION HALL

EXIT

MEZZANINE

CONCOURSE BELOW

CRYSTAL PALACE

TAXI AND BUS ZONE

11TH AVENUE

FINANCING

The initial responsibility for financing the convention center project belonged to New York City and to the Triborough Bridge and Tunnel Authority (TBTA). The UDC became involved because the project entailed commercial development issues. The UDC, however, did not have the strength in the bond market that the TBTA did. Because the latter could issue bonds at lower interest rates, the convention center project became a joint UDC/TBTA project.

The original cost of the project in 1979 was to have been $375 million, financed through the issuance of TBTA bonds, and the center was to open in 1984. Construction began in spring 1980. Interest rates and inflation forced the TBTA to issue bonds with higher interest rates than expected. Escalating costs were a key factor in the financing from the initial phases of construction.

The convention center project was a year behind schedule primarily because of the problem with the nodes, and by 1983, the estimated cost for the center had risen to $450 million. By the end of 1983, in a UDC report to Governor Cuomo, the project cost estimates had risen to approximately $500 million, or 33 percent more than

the center's 1979 estimated cost of completion. By 1984, this estimate had decreased to slightly over $460 million. In 1986, the center opened at a cost of $486.2 million.

MARKET ORIENTATION

The main goal for the convention center from the outset was to attract large, high-quality conventions and trade shows. A second part of the goal was to attract new tourists to the city through national and international convention business. A lesser goal of the Jacob K. Javits Convention Center, as it was renamed before opening in 1986, is to maximize facility revenues without jeopardizing the economic benefits from convention and trade show events. At the April 1986 opening of the facility, the center president announced that the facility was 85 percent booked until 1990 and had events on the books as far ahead as the year 2010.

Notably, the center's opening coincided with the closing of the landmark New York Coliseum, which is planned to be demolished. Virtually every event that had occupied the 350,000-square-foot Coliseum transferred into the new center, and after having been constrained

for many years by the Coliseum's lack of space and obsolete configurations, these events were able to expand. This influx of events from the Coliseum, as well as pent-up demand for larger high-quality space, has resulted in a high level of occupancy, primarily by nonambulatory trade shows (95 percent).

LESSONS LEARNED

The Jacob K. Javits Convention Center is truly one of the most attractive convention facilities in the world, befitting a destination of New York's stature. The problems that plagued the development of the center, however, were many, including but not limited to the physical glitches that delayed construction:

- The facility opened two years behind schedule and ran more than $100 million (30 percent) over budget. By the time the center's construction finally got underway, cost escalations caused the budget for the facility to be inadequate, and square footage had to be cut. These delays and costs lessened public confidence in this high-profile venture.
- Once the facility opened, the transportation problems surrounding it surfaced. While bus lines were extended to reach it, there are no subway stations or nearby parking spaces. Exhibitors and visitors have had to park blocks away from the center and take taxis.

PROJECT DATA

JACOB K. JAVITS CONVENTION CENTER
NEW YORK, NY

Owner: State of New York
Developer: Convention Center Development Corporation, New York City
Architect: I.M. Pei & Partners, New York City
Year Construction Began: 1980
Year Construction Completed:[1] 1987

PROJECT INFORMATION

Site Area: 22 acres
Total GBA: 1,800,000 square feet
    Exhibition Space: 640,000 square feet
    Meeting Space: 81,000 square feet

ECONOMIC INFORMATION

Site Acquisition Cost: $22,700,000
Construction Costs: $273,800,000
Total Project Cost: $486,000,000
Funding Sources:
    Triborough Bridge Tunnel Authority Bonds: $392,000,000
    Interest on Unexpended Bond Proceeds: $34,000,000
    Municipal Assistance Corporation Surplus Funds: $60,000,000

Note:
[1]Building was occupied and operating in 1986.

- Although there are plans to rejuvenate the environment of the center, the neighborhood is still considered a warehouse district. The development of hotels, marinas, and high rises is still years away.
- The project experienced political, design, construction, financing, and operational problems. The development process points to an issue of major concern for any convention center's development, namely, the difficulty of building a center with a unique technology (the original design for a space frame) on time and on budget.

ORANGE COUNTY CONVENTION CENTER

ORLANDO, FLORIDA

Orange County Convention Center occupies a 115-acre site 15 miles from downtown Orlando. Phase I of the center's four planned phases opened in 1983 and provided 150,000 square feet of exhibition space and 30,000 square feet of meeting and banquet space. Upon completion of Phase IV, in 1998, the facility will provide over 1 million square feet of exhibition space and more than 350,000 square feet of meeting and banquet space, positioning the center among the largest in the country.

The area surrounding the convention center has become a complete support environment for the facility. New hotel, restaurant, and retail developments are taking advantage of the available mix of convention delegates and tourists.

DEVELOPMENT STRATEGY

Development of Orange County Convention Center (OCCC) resulted when Central Florida recognized the need for a large public assembly facility to accommodate national and regional conventions and trade shows. The county commissioned a feasibility study to determine the success that a convention center in Orange County could expect in attracting national and regional convention business. As a result of the study's recommendation, the county began to investigate financing for the first of the center's four phases.

DESIGN AND SITE ISSUES

Orange County viewed the convention-center project as an economic development tool. The project's initial design recognized the seasonality of the Orlando tourist market. Because of swings in tourist activity, the Orlando area experienced low hotel occupancy during some periods and high occupancy in others. Therefore, the center would target conventions during periods of low hotel occupancy and would seek civic and spectator events (which rely more on the resident market) when tourist levels were high.

The original center design included 5,200 telescopic seats that allowed the facility to function as a community arena; however, the Orlando Arena, home of the NBA Orlando Magic, opened in downtown Orlando in 1989 and now captures the demand for spectator events. Thus, the OCCC's strategy has changed to focus primarily on conventions, trade shows, and public shows. Since development of the OCCC, Orlando's hotel market has diversified greatly, meeting the need for a balance of convention, commercial, and tourist demands.

The convention center (after Phase II) consists of an exhibition hall of approximately 350,000 square feet, divisible into five halls. One hall offers 150,000 square

feet of exhibition space and was specially designed to accommodate the 5,200 telescopic seats mentioned above. A special steel beam was required to provide this feature in a clear-span design. Seventy thousand square feet of meeting space in 41 breakout rooms surrounds the exhibition halls.

Through 1992, the center offered more than 4,000 surface parking spaces, a significantly larger number than that typically offered by a downtown convention center. These spaces were needed to compensate for the lack of support parking nearby and to accommodate spectator events. Phase III construction began in 1993 and reduced parking by 50 percent. To offset this loss, 48 acres of adjacent land were purchased, and a 1,000-car parking structure was built. An additional 1,200 surface and 600 enclosed spaces were added to the inventory in October 1995. More than 4,000 spaces are available in 1996.

Phase III, which opened in January 1996, increased exhibit space to 733,400 square feet in two halls. Fourteen new meeting rooms have been added, encompassing an additional 178,518 square feet of meeting space, with a multipurpose function room of 60,000 gross square feet and a 2,800-seat auditorium. Phase III also includes two new lobbies and a registration concourse, as well as specialized technical capabilities such as four interpreters' booths, a sound room, a projection room, and a sound platform.

Phase IV—scheduled to open in 1998, coupled with a complete renovation of Phase I, slated to be completed in December 1997—will complete the OCCC's 1990 master plan. This expansion will add 367,200 gross square feet of exhibition space, bringing the center's total exhibit space to over 1 million square feet. Meeting space will increase to a total of 348,000 square feet in 49 meeting rooms, divisible into 149 rooms. The completed facility will contain the planned auditorium/performing arts center, a multipurpose ballroom that can seat 6,000, and four dedicated registration concourses.

Unlike many other convention centers, OCCC was not developed in a downtown location. Instead, the county chose to purchase land near the area's major tourist attractions to allow ample room for expansion and supporting development and, most importantly, to provide proximity to the area's concentration of hotel rooms. The county originally purchased 70 acres at the intersection of International Drive and the Bee Line Expressway and later bought an additional 45 acres. With such a large land parcel available to the Orange County government, county planners could build all expansions on one level and thus avoid problems associated with having center components on different levels, such as problems with crowd flow and orientation, as well as the costly problems of difficult loading and unloading.

The OCCC lies within an even larger (722-acre) master-planned development called Plaza International, (developed by a subsidiary of Martin Marietta Corporation) that lies adjacent to Martin Marietta's Orlando plant and its two master-planned corporate parks, Orlando Central Park and South Park. Plaza International, which is located between downtown Orlando and Disney World, capitalizes on regional convention and tourism development: It is an upscale, tourist-oriented project occupying a five-mile extension of International Drive linking the existing development with the Disney property and the northern end of International Drive. The convention district includes two major attractions as anchor tenants: Sea World and Universal Studios. Within Plaza International, more than 8,500 hotel rooms and a major specialty retail complex have been developed. Directly across from the OCCC stands the 850-room Peabody Orlando Hotel and the

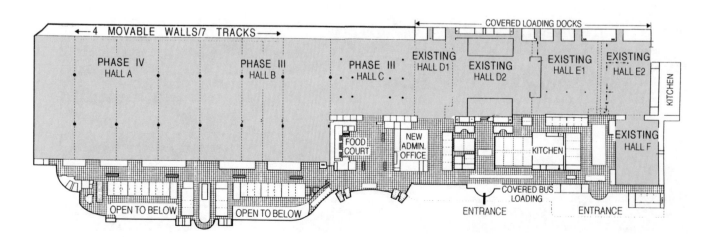

PROJECT DATA

ORANGE COUNTY CONVENTION CENTER
ORLANDO, FL

Owner: Orange County
Developer/Architect:
- Phase I: The Luckman Partnership, California, and Helman Hurley Charvat Peacock, Winter Park, Florida (joint venture)
- Phase II: Hellmuth, Obata & Kassabaum, Tampa
- Phase III: Thompson, Ventulett, Stainback & Associates, Inc., Atlanta, and Hunton Brady Pryor Maso Architects, Orlando (joint venture)
- Phase IV: Helman Hurley Charvat Peacock, Winter Park, Florida

Builder:
- Phase I: Great Southwest
- Phase II: Gilbane Building Company
- Phase III: CRSS Construction, Coral Gables, Florida; Hardin Construction, Atlanta; Kelsey Construction Company, Orlando (joint venture)
- Phase IV: CRSS Construction, Coral Gables, Florida; Hardin Construction, Atlanta; and Kelsey Construction Company, Orlando (joint venture)

Year Construction Began:
- Phase I: 1980
- Phase II: 1987

Year Construction Completed:
- Phase I: 1983
- Phase II: 1989
- Phase III: 1996
- Phase IV: 1998[1]

PROJECT INFORMATION

Site Area: 115 acres
Total GBA (Phases I–II): 1,000,000 square feet
    Exhibition Space: 350,000 square feet
    Meeting Space: 65,813 square feet
Total Projected Exhibition Space (Phases I–IV): 1,100,600 square feet
Total Gross Area (Phases I–IV): 4,100,000 square feet
Total Parking Spaces: 4,800

ECONOMIC INFORMATION

Total Project Cost:
- Phase I (1983 dollars): $54,000,000
- Phase II (1989 dollars): $96,000,000
- Phase III (1991 dollars): $205,000,000
- Phase IV[1] (1992 dollars): $210,000,000

Total Projected Cost (current '83–'92 dollars): $565,000,000
Total Projected Cost (1994 dollars): $633,000,000
Funding Sources: Including refinancing, there have been six bond issues backed exclusively by tourist development tax receipts.

Notes:
[1]Projected construction cost.

---

recently developed 1,334-room Omni Rosen Hotel. Owners of Plaza International are also researching what type of transportation system would best link Sea World, Plaza International, northern International Drive, and Universal Studios.

FINANCING

The OCCC was originally financed by long- and short-term revenue bonds guaranteed by a 2 percent county-wide hotel tax. The cost for Phase I was approximately $55 million. The state of Florida passed legislation allowing Orange County to increase its hotel tax from 2 percent to 4 percent to fund center expansion, the Orlando Arena, and Citrus Bowl improvements. Phase II was completed at a cost of $96 million, while Phase III cost $205 million, and Phase IV $210 million.

With more than 56,000 hotel rooms in Orange County and 82,000 hotel rooms in the Orlando metropolitan area, financing the project via a hotel tax was an obvious choice. The county now collects about $52 million annually from this comparatively modest 4 percent room tax.

MARKET ORIENTATION

The OCCC's original marketing plan targeted conventions and trade shows for two-thirds of the year and civic and spectator events for the remainder of the calendar. Due to the considerable demand by conventions and trade shows, as well as the opening of Orlando Arena, however, the center's market orientation has been revised to include only a limited number of spectator events. The facility now hosts a year-

round schedule of large national and regional conventions and trade shows.

Lessons Learned

The OCCC's high level of performance can be attributed to Central Florida's attractiveness as a tourist and convention destination and to the center's size and design.

OCCC development has enabled the county to diversify from its tourist-based economy and has added stability to the area's hotel market. The center has benefited the county economically and has enhanced Orlando's position as a national visitor destination. Some distinguishing aspects of the history of the center's development include:

- The county chose to build the convention center away from the downtown. At the time, this decision was highly controversial because several business leaders wanted the center placed in the downtown for traditional redevelopment reasons. Also, because the center's remote location had no support amenities, opponents thought that center performance would suffer. On the contrary, the location has allowed the county to control development surrounding the center and to make its land use complement convention business. Attesting to the success of this approach, the value of land surrounding the OCCC has risen from as little as $25,000 per acre in the 1970s to over $1 million per acre today.
- Phased development has allowed financing by means of the county's hotel tax. As convention business increases and more hotels are built to accommodate convention delegates and tourists, more money has become available for center expansion.

HENRY B. GONZALEZ CONVENTION CENTER

SAN ANTONIO, TEXAS

Located in HemisFair Park in downtown San Antonio, the Henry B. Gonzalez Convention Center reflects the color and culture of the city. This multipurpose complex, a permanent legacy of the 1968 San Antonio World's Fair, is one of the reasons why San Antonio attracts more than 300,000 delegates every year to conventions, business meetings, trade shows, and exhibitions.

DEVELOPMENT STRATEGY

The original convention center complex was built to help attract more out-of-town visitors and dollars to San Antonio by capitalizing on the city's tourism industry and its appeal as a tourist destination. In 1968, the convention center included over 92,000 square feet of exhibit-hall space, 29,000 square feet of banquet space, and 38,000 square feet of meeting-room space. In addition, a 2,700-seat theater and a 10,000-seat arena were included.

In 1974, due to the success of and anticipated demand for the convention center, the city council decided to expand the center. The expansion project was completed in 1977, increasing exhibit space by more than

40 percent, banquet space by 80 percent, and meeting-room space by nearly 20 percent. At that time, the center was renamed the Henry B. Gonzalez Convention Center (HBGCC), after the popular congressman from San Antonio.

The largest and most recent expansion of the HBGCC, which began in 1984 and was completed in January 1987, increased exhibit-hall space to more than 240,000 square feet, banquet space to over 51,000 square feet, and meeting-room space to 65,000 square feet.

Because of HBGCC's continued success, a citizens' committee was formed in 1990 to study further expansion of the convention center. The citizens' committee developed the following six expansion recommendations: 1) the convention center should be expanded to 500,000 square feet of contiguous exhibit space; 2) the Alamodome (San Antonio's 65,000-seat, multipurpose domed facility, completed in 1993) should be regarded as the first phase of the expansion; 3) center expansion should be accommodated on the existing site; 4) a master plan for the year 2020 should be adopted; 5) the facility should have state-of-the-art equipment; and 6) the cost of the expansion should be paid through a combination of an increased and dedicated hotel occupancy tax and increased facility rental charges.

In September 1994, the city retained the Urban Land Institute Advisory Panel Service to review the proposed expansion plans and to provide an independent analysis of alternative options. The ULI panel affirmed the need for contiguous exhibit-hall space and San Antonio's need to expand. In addition, ULI provided a number of innovative planning and design recommendations that will enhance the new and renovated convention center.

In October 1994, the San Antonio City Council authorized city staff and the design team to proceed with the design process for the projected $175 million expansion project. Expansion plans will increase the size of the exhibit hall to approximately 440,000 square feet of contiguous space and will provide proportionate increases in meeting-room and ballroom space. The design for the expansion of the convention center is expected to be completed in winter 1995, with construction slated to begin in late 1996. Upon completion of the new facilities in early 1999, renovation of the existing facilities will begin and should be completed in late January 2001.

DESIGN AND SITE ISSUES

The convention center's site lies on the northwest corner of HemisFair Park, bounded by Market Street to

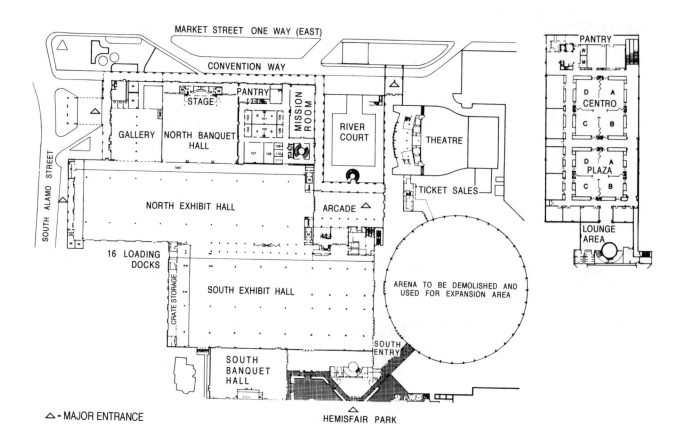

MARKET STREET ONE WAY (EAST)

CONVENTION WAY

SOUTH ALAMO STREET

STAGE

PANTRY

GALLERY NORTH BANQUET HALL

MISSION ROOM

RIVER COURT

THEATRE

TICKET SALES

NORTH EXHIBIT HALL

ARCADE

16 LOADING DOCKS

CRATE STORAGE

SOUTH EXHIBIT HALL

ARENA TO BE DEMOLISHED AND USED FOR EXPANSION AREA

SOUTH ENTRY

SOUTH BANQUET HALL

△ = MAJOR ENTRANCE

HEMISFAIR PARK

PANTRY

CENTRO

D A

C B

PLAZA

D A

C B

LOUNGE AREA

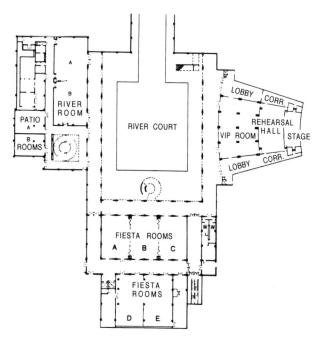

A

RIVER ROOM

B

PATIO A

B ROOMS

RIVER COURT

LOBBY CORR.

REHEARSAL HALL

VIP ROOM

STAGE

LOBBY CORR.

FIESTA ROOMS

A B C

FIESTA ROOMS

D E

the north, Alamo Street to the west, Durango Street to the south, and Bowie Street to the east. Development of the convention center has been instrumental to the growth and revitalization of the downtown. As the cen-

ter has expanded over the last three decades, the number of hotel rooms in the downtown has tripled. Included in this remarkable hotel growth is the Marriott Rivercenter project, which includes not only a 1,000-room hotel but also a 1,000,000-square-foot regional "River Center" shopping mall.

HBGCC offers two exhibit halls of 120,000 square feet each (or 240,000 square feet without partition) and 43 meeting rooms. The convention center is a three-level facility, with meeting rooms on the River (lower) Level. At street level are the two exhibit halls, additional meeting rooms, two banquet halls, and the 2,500-seat Lila Cockrell theater. The upper level consists of more meeting rooms.

FINANCING

The original convention center was funded through general obligation bonds issued by the city of San Antonio at a cost of $10.9 million (1968 dollars). Funding for subsequent center expansions has been provided by general obligation bonds and revenue bonds. For the current $175 million expansion, financing will take the form of a bond issue secured by receipts dedicated from a 2 per-

PROJECT DATA

HENRY B. GONZALEZ CONVENTION CENTER
SAN ANTONIO, TX

Owner: City of San Antonio
Architect:
    Phase I: Noonan & Krocker, San Antonio
    Phase II: Noonan, Krocker & Dockery, San Antonio
    Phase III: Cerna, Raba & Partners, San Antonio
Year Construction Completed:
    Phase I: 1968
    Phase II: 1977
    Phase III: 1987

PROJECT INFORMATION

Total Exhibition Space:
    Current: 242,000 square feet
    Projected: 440,000 square feet
Total Meeting and Ballroom Space:
    Current: 112,000 square feet
    Projected: 195,000 square feet
Seating Capacity:
    Lila C. Cockrell Theatre: 2,500 seats
    Alamodome: 65,000 seats

ECONOMIC INFORMATION

Total Project Cost (1968 dollars): $11,000,000
1995 Project Cost (projected): $175,000,000

cent increase in the hotel occupancy tax. In addition to the dedicated tax, revenues from convention-center facilities' increased rental rates may be used to service the debt incurred in with expansion.

MARKET ORIENTATION

As a convention, trade-show, and multipurpose facility, the San Antonio convention facilities serve the primary function of accommodating meetings, events, and activities that generate economic benefit to the city. Convention-center marketing is handled by the convention facilities staff and the San Antonio Convention and Visitors Bureau (both entities are city departments). The San Antonio Convention and Visitors Bureau is responsible for maximizing dates and for the use of all facilities for conventions and trade shows planned more than 24 months in advance. Local public shows and entertainment events can be confirmed by the facilities staff if the event will take place within 24 months of the request.

    Thanks to a number of factors—San Antonio's unique urban character, center expansions, downtown hotel development, aggressive marketing efforts, and solid facilities management—the convention center has a full calendar of events. For the past five years, both the number of convention and trade-show attendees using the convention center and the number of hotel room–nights generated by the facility have increased by nearly 20 percent annually.

SAN DIEGO CONVENTION CENTER

SAN DIEGO, CALIFORNIA

In November 1989, the San Diego Convention Center hosted its first convention. Situated on San Diego Bay, this state-of-the-art facility has made the city one of the nation's premier convention destinations. With 254,000 square feet of exhibit space, a spacious ballroom, and ample meeting rooms, the convention center augments the economic impact of the revitalized downtown by attracting national and international delegates to San Diego.

DEVELOPMENT STRATEGY

Since the early 1970s, San Diego officials had regarded the development of a convention center as the most important element in the city's downtown redevelopment efforts. Part of a comprehensive redevelopment plan, the convention center was conceived in concert with Horton Plaza, an entertainment and retail district located three blocks from the center site. City planners envisioned the development of a downtown meeting venue for convention delegates, along with a nearby entertainment area for delegate activities. The center stands near the marina, the Seaport Village themed retail area, and the Gaslamp Quarter historic district. Although conceived at about the same time, the center and Horton Plaza did not open simultaneously; as a result of development delays, the convention center opened approximately four years after Horton Plaza.

The delay in the completion of the convention center did not result from construction overruns but was primarily attributable to the facility's lengthy bidding process. Besieged by controversy, the proposed center remained "a plan" until bidding was opened on the project in early 1986. City officials stood fast following initial bids, all of which exceeded the original cost estimates by more than $24 million. After one year of value engineering, city officials' patience was rewarded when bidding was reopened and a joint partnership of Tutor-Saliba Corporation of Sylmar, California, and Perini Corporation of Massachusetts submitted the low bid of $110.9 million.

Delayed by more than a year after bids were first opened, construction of the San Diego Convention Center finally began in March 1987. By 1989, construction was complete, and the first convention was hosted. The center exceeded original attendance estimates, attracting more than 250,000 delegates in its first year. Not surprisingly, nearby retail areas have experienced an economic renaissance. Seaport Village, an adjacent ten-year-old shopping area with dozens of specialty retail stores and restaurants, has plans to develop entertainment facilities to coincide with currently planned expansion of the convention center. The Gaslamp Quarter, a nearby historic district featuring restaurants and retail shops, has enjoyed much higher traffic levels. According to city officials, many of the restaurants within the Gaslamp Quarter opened following construction of the convention center.

Other economic benefits of convention-center development have included the opening of several convention-quality hotel properties within the downtown. According to the San Diego Convention and Visitors Bureau, approximately 2,700 new hotel rooms opened in 1989, the year in which the convention center opened. By comparison, San Diego had had little increase in hotel room inventories in the late 1970s and early 1980s. Most important are the two hotels next to the center, a 1,355-room Marriott and a 875-room Hyatt, which together offer 2,230 rooms on site.

DESIGN AND SITE ISSUES

The architectural team faced two obstacles in designing the facility. First, while occupying 11 acres overlooking San Diego Bay, the site had limited building footprint space and close dimensions to nearby hotel towers. Second, the facility's exterior was subject to city policies on waterfront development. San Diego officials are protective of the waterfront, requiring that all bayside development "enhance" the bay's access and beauty. Challenged by these design constraints, the architects inserted an unusual element in the design that today is the facility's most celebrated feature: an open-air special-events hall on the center's top floor. This open-air terrace-pavilion, covered by a billowing, saillike roof (see Eb Zeidlers design for Vancouver CC), added some 100,000 extra square feet of reception and assembly space. This distinctive element also gave the center a nautical look that serves as an appropriate backdrop to the bay's coastline.

The other primary building components include 254,000 square feet of contiguous exhibit space, divisible into four sections; 100,000 square feet of flexible meeting space in 32 rooms; and a 40,000-square-foot ballroom.

Four miles from the city's airport, the convention center is easily accessible by taxi and airport shuttle. The San Diego Trolley, offering light-rail transit service from the San Diego Depot to the Tijuana border, has added the convention center to its destination list. This above-ground transport carries delegates from the convention center to many of the area's restaurants, shopping malls, and entertainment areas. Beginning every 15 minutes, a second, inner-core trolley ride carries visitors to shops and restaurants along the downtown loop. This ride costs 50 cents.

The San Diego Convention Center features two levels of underground parking, with space for approximately 2,000 cars. An agreement with the Marriott hotel requires that 700 spaces remain reserved for hotel guests; due to the cross-use of these facilities, however, many of the spaces are used by guests of both facilities. At present, additional parking for 1,750 cars is available in a paved surface lot adjacent to the center, though this area is the site of the Phase II expansion, to be funded by the city of San Diego and the San Diego Unified Port District and to be completed in time for the NFL Super Bowl in January 1998. The expansion will add about 300,000 square feet of exhibit space, increasing contiguous space to 546,500 square feet on the main floor. The upper level will be enhanced with two ball-

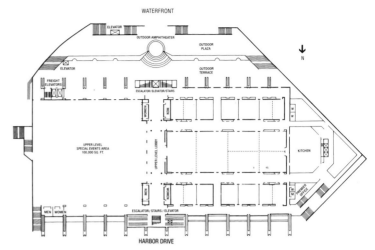

Upper Level

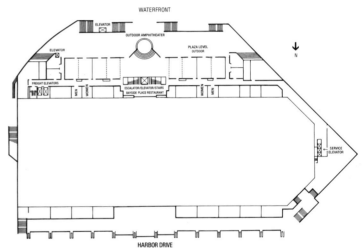

Mezzanine Level

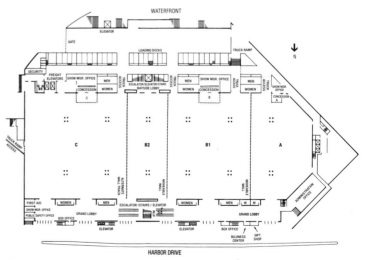

Ground Level

PROJECT DATA

SAN DIEGO CONVENTION CENTER
SAN DIEGO, CA

Owner: San Diego Unified Port District
Architects: Deems, Lewis & Partners, San Diego;
   Loschky, Marquardt & Nesholm, Architects, Seattle;
   and Arthur Erikson Associates, Vancouver
Year Construction Began: 1987
Year Construction Completed: 1989
Expansion to be Completed: 1998

PROJECT INFORMATION

Site Area: 11 acres
Total Space: 760,000 square feet
   Exhibition Space: 254,000 square feet contiguous,
      plus 100,000 square feet in a column-free pavilion[1]
   Meeting Space: 100,000 square feet
Total Parking: 3,750
   Underground: 2,000
   Adjacent: 1,750[2]

ECONOMIC INFORMATION

Site Acquisition Costs: Leased from Unified Port District
   at $1 per year
Construction Costs: $124,000,000
Site Preparation Costs: $20,000,000
Architecture, Engineering Fees: $20,000,000
Total Project Cost (1989 dollars): $164,000,000
Total Project Cost (1994 dollars):[3] $192,832,260[2]
Phase II Expansion (estimated): $170,800,000
Funding Sources: Unified Port District; San Diego's
   transient occupancy tax (TOT)

Notes:
[1]Does not include the open-air pavilion.
[2]Available until Phase II groundbreaking.
[3]Calculated based on the consumer price index.

rooms of 40,000 square feet and 40,000 to 50,000 square feet, respectively. After expansion, there will be 200,000 gross square feet of meeting space and over 100,000 square feet of lobby and ancillary space.

FINANCING

Funding for Phase I of the San Diego Convention Center was provided by the San Diego Unified Port District, the administrator of tideland properties surrounding San Diego Bay. By using a portion of its cash reserves, the port district was able, effectively, to fund the entire $164 million cost of the original facility. Because of the unique method by which this building was funded, the San Diego Unified Port District also retained ownership of the 11-acre site, leasing the property to the city at $1 a year for 20 years.

   The total cost of the Phase II expansion is estimated at $170.8 million for construction and related fees, with the Unified Port District providing $4.5 million toward the expansion and the city financing the difference through a 1.5-cent increase in the city of San Diego's transient occupancy (hotel) tax (TOT). One cent will be earmarked for the convention-center expansion and will provide $6 million to $8 million annually for debt service, while the remaining half-cent is earmarked for a downtown sports arena.

MARKET ORIENTATION

The primary objective of the San Diego Convention Center is to serve as a venue for large-scale private and public meeting events that will produce a positive identity for the city and that will generate substantial economic impacts for the entire community. To accomplish this end, a prioritized booking policy that grants favorable lead times for conventions and trade shows has been established.

   The San Diego Convention and Visitors Bureau (ConVis) is responsible for booking the facility in advance of 18 months. ConVis concentrates its marketing efforts primarily on the larger national and international conventions and trade shows. Regional consumer events, which typically draw attendance from surrounding communities, are given second-priority booking. These events, as well as local meetings, exhibitions, and social events, are scheduled by the San Diego Convention Center Corporation (SDCCC), a nonprofit organization created in December of 1984 by the San Diego City Council to

operate, maintain, manage, and market the convention center. The in-house SDCCC marketing department handles event scheduling for groups booking the facility within an 18-month time frame.

LESSONS LEARNED

- Access to the mezzanine-level meeting rooms must be gained either by going through the lobby to the back of the exhibit space on the ground level, or by ascending to the upper level and then maneuvering down to the mezzanine level. This arrangement may imply to most users that the meeting rooms on the mezzanine must be used in conjunction with the exhibit space, or that the exhibit space must not be rented if the mezzanine-level meeting rooms are being used.
- There is inadequate registration space in the lobby. Some of the current exhibit-hall space must be used for registration, thereby reducing the amount of exhibit space available for rental. Fortunately, Phase II expansion will increase the lobby from 40,000 square feet to over 100,000 square feet.

SANTA CLARA CONVENTION CENTER

SANTA CLARA, CALIFORNIA

The Santa Clara Convention Center stands in the heart of Silicon Valley, the center of the nation's computer industry and headquarters for many of its leading companies. Recognizing the need to diversify Santa Clara's economic base, representatives of the city's government and the chamber of commerce joined to develop a convention center. The resulting center is part of a $125 million complex (1985 dollars). Other components of the complex include a Westin hotel; Techmart, which houses sales offices and serves as the headquarters of the American Electronics Association; and the Santa Clara Golf and Tennis Club. An added attraction, Paramount's Great America®, a 100-acre family entertainment theme park, is located adjacent to the convention center.

DEVELOPMENT STRATEGY

The Santa Clara Convention Center was developed to diversify the community's economy by providing a means of attracting the convention and meeting industry. The planning and development process was initiated by the city's chamber of commerce in 1978, when it commissioned a convention-center feasibility study. The study concluded that a 100,000-square-foot exhibition hall was the appropriate size for Santa Clara to attract the medium-sized conventions and trade shows that were too large to fit into existing facilities. The chamber of commerce and the city then started a community awareness campaign to garner support for the convention center. The campaign proved successful when the citizens voted in favor of center development in a citywide advisory election.

The chamber and the city originally intended to develop the center through a public/private partnership. Although they attracted a developer for the hotel/trade mart portion of the complex, they did not succeed in finding a developer for the convention center. Thus, the city became its own developer, with the support of the public and the chamber to help ensure that few problems were encountered in the development process.

DESIGN AND SITE ISSUES

The size and configuration of the convention center were dictated in part by the triangular shape of the city-owned parcel set aside for it. The architects selected a pyramid design to fit 100,000 square feet of column-free exhibit space onto the site. The center's exhibition hall is located on the first floor, with the meeting rooms and prefunction space on the second level. The center is equipped with the latest computer technology and audiovisual services, including the capacity for telephone service at every exhibit booth and an interpreter's booth for language translation in the complex's 600-seat, multipurpose theater. In addition, the center has a computerized security system.

Adjacent to the convention center are the other components of the complex: a 500-room Westin hotel, which shares the convention center's 24,000-square-foot ballroom; a 100-acre theme park; a 1,500-car, on-site parking garage (2,000 spaces exist on site, with 9,000 additional parking spaces at the theme park); and a golf and tennis club with an 18-hole course.

In 1994, a 24,000-square-foot addition to the center was completed, providing another 11,150 square feet of flexible floor space (a 6,280-square-foot ballroom and a 4,870-square-foot meeting room) at a total cost of $5.5 million. This space enables the center to serve two events simultaneously and helps keep the facility competitive in the convention and trade-show markets.

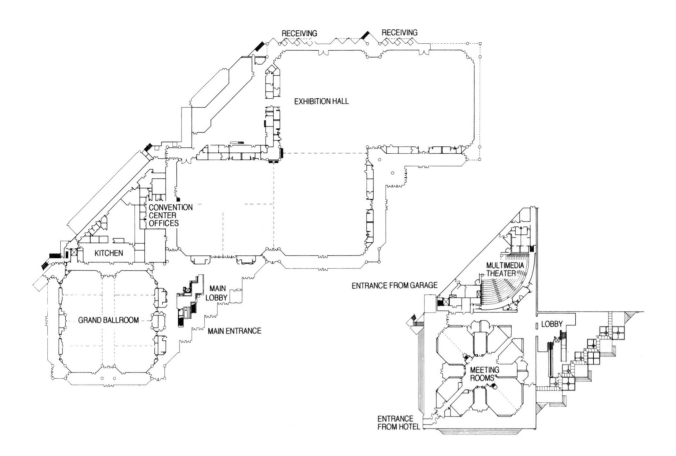

RECEIVING   RECEIVING

EXHIBITION HALL

CONVENTION
CENTER
OFFICES

KITCHEN

MAIN
LOBBY

GRAND BALLROOM

MAIN ENTRANCE

ENTRANCE FROM GARAGE

MULTIMEDIA
THEATER

LOBBY

MEETING
ROOMS

ENTRANCE
FROM HOTEL

FINANCING

The Santa Clara Convention Center's portion of the
$125 million complex cost the city $38.2 million. The
Westin hotel, which is connected to the convention center by a ground-floor walkway and a second-story skywalk, was developed by private investment interests.

The hotel operates under a land lease with the
city of Santa Clara, which retains the deed to the land.
Westin pays the city approximately 3.5 percent of gross
room revenue plus 3 percent of gross food and beverage
revenue. In addition, the hotel developer was offered
and accepted a number of attractive incentives, including use of one-half of the convention center's 25,000-
square-foot ballroom under a separate lease agreement.
In turn, the hotel pays the city the greater of 5 percent
of gross revenues from food and beverage sales or a lump
sum of $100,000 annually. The hotel also enjoys use of
the city-developed tennis, golf, and parking facilities.

Benefits of this arrangement are shared by the city
and Westin. The city benefits from increased room tax
revenues as a result of group meeting activity in the area
and uses land lease revenues to fund the project. The
hotel profits from increased group meeting occupancy

and from marketing cost savings because the convention and visitors' bureau sells the convention center to
groups that ultimately become hotel clients. The land
lease has also meant development cost savings for the
hotel because the city's parking facilities and ballroom,
used by the hotel, were both publicly funded.

The convention center opened on time and
within budget, though the hotel/trade mart portion of
the complex opened six months behind schedule. The
center's operating cost is funded by rentals at the facility
and through the city's general fund. Capital debt service
is paid from taxes collected by the city redevelopment
agency. The 1994 addition was financed from available
funds from surplus tax increment revenues paid to the
redevelopment agency.

MANAGEMENT AND MARKETING

The management structure at the convention center,
which opened on July 1, 1986, is unique in that the facility is city-owned but chamber-managed and -operated.
The city believed that the most efficient and least costly
option to operate the center was to allow the chamber

to manage it. To date, this arrangement has proved successful and is supported by all parties involved.

During the 1993/1994 fiscal year, the Santa Clara Convention Center hosted 309 events, including 31 conventions, 45 trade shows, 26 public shows, and 207 meetings and banquets. Many of the meetings are held in the theater, which also hosts a variety of musical performances such as ethnic concerts and dance recitals. The

facility places top priority on convention/trade-show events and subordinates consumer shows as a large, second-priority market. The facility is not equipped to host large concerts or entertainment events.

A light rail system between Santa Clara and San Jose, completed in 1989, connects the two convention centers, which are 30 minutes apart. The Santa Clara Convention Center competes with San Jose's center for some events, but overall there seems to be sufficient demand to support healthy occupancy rates at both centers. The first joint trade show using both centers via the light rail system will be held in 1997.

PROJECT DATA

SANTA CLARA CONVENTION CENTER
SANTA CLARA, CA

Owner: City Redevelopment Agency
Builder: Hansel Phelps, Santa Clara, California
Architect: Ellerbe Becket, Inc., Minneapolis, Minnesota
Year Construction Began: 1984
Year Construction Completed: 1986

PROJECT INFORMATION
Site Area (entire complex): 17 acres
Total GBA (convention center): 262,000 square feet
   Exhibition Space: 100,000 square feet
   Meeting Space: 16,500 square feet
Total Parking Spaces: 2,000 on site; 9,000 nearby

ECONOMIC INFORMATION
Total Project Cost (1985 dollars): $38,200,000
Total Project Cost (1994 dollars):[1] $51,761,710

Note:
[1]Calculated based on the consumer price index.

LESSONS LEARNED

The successful development and operation of the Santa Clara Convention Center can be attributed to several factors:

- The chamber and the city saw the importance of combining efforts to gain public and business support for the convention center at the project's inception. They joined to form a strong leadership force during the development phase of the project and were committed to a well-planned, market-oriented convention center.
- In addition, the city hired experienced, respected architects and builders. All participants in the process were experts in their fields.
- Few obstacles were encountered during the center's development, thanks to this detailed planning, strong leadership, and garnering of public support. This smooth development process and the center's high level of use are indicators of the Santa Clara Convention Center's success.

WASHINGTON STATE CONVENTION AND TRADE CENTER

SEATTLE, WASHINGTON

Since the 1970s, representatives of Washington's local and state governments and of its business community had tried to organize development of a convention center to diversify economic growth in the state. In 1981, a legislative joint select committee was appointed to research the issue. Several studies were conducted that indicated that Washington State could compete effectively in the convention and meetings industry if a suitable facility was available. Thus, in 1982 the committee introduced legislation designating Seattle as the site for the convention center and created the Washington State Convention and Trade Center Corporation (WSCTC) to design, build, and run the facility. The 726,800-square-foot Washington State Convention and Trade Center, which, through the purchase of air rights, is located above 12 lanes of Interstate 5 and over two city streets, opened in June 1988.

DEVELOPMENT STRATEGY

Washington House of Representatives Bill #1015 stated that the Washington State Convention and Trade Cen-ter was to "provide both direct and indirect civic and economic benefits to the people of the state of Washington." These benefits were expected to result from convention delegate spending, sales tax revenue, and increased state-wide tourism. Legislation specified the center's budget, size, location, and development approach and encouraged joint development of the center by the public and private sectors, in an effort to reduce costs and to contribute to Seattle's urban redevelopment.

The WSCTC, in compliance with the legislative intent to solicit private sector involvement, chose a site for the convention center that was located partially over Interstate 5 and partially on privately owned land. The convention center's nine-member board negotiated a lease for air rights with the Washington State Department of Transportation (DOT) and with CHG International, the owner of the air rights over the interstate highway as well as the holder of fee interests in adjacent parcels. The lease with the DOT was granted in exchange for private funding of costly highway improvements. CHG granted air rights and ground easements and agreed to develop retail and parking space to serve the center.

In 1984, however, CHG filed for financial protection under Chapter 11 of the federal bankruptcy laws. The lending institution, Westside Federal Savings & Loan, assumed CHG's obligations but later went into receivership as well. As a result of these two calamities, the WSCTC board members were forced to make a critical decision. Should they terminate the project and absorb the costs of site evaluation, design, and permit application, or should they continue the project by finding another developer or by developing the project without private sector involvement? The latter option meant resolving Westside's financial obligations in a way that would enable the board to obtain title to the center site.

The board decided to proceed with the project. Settling Westside's debts would require cooperative participation by the Federal Savings & Loan Insurance Corporation (FSLIC) and the Industrial Indemnity Corporation (IIC), the issuers of the performance bond behind Westside Federal's loan. This requirement delayed the project until June 1986, when a settlement agreement was reached among the board, the FSLIC, and the IIC, giving the WSCTC ownership control over the entire development site. The state, however, had not at that point chosen an ultimate development strategy. Negotiations were underway with a joint venture between the construction firm, Pachen Construction Company, and Tishman Midwest, but the state was weighing the option of eliminating private sector involvement. In the interim, the state provided resources to finance outstanding liabilities and thereby allowed development of the convention center to proceed.

DESIGN AND SITE ISSUES

Final site selection for the convention center began in July 1982. Three sites, all in or near downtown Seattle, were reviewed by the WSCTC's board of directors. Included was one site adjacent to Seattle Center, an arena and exhibition facility on the fringe of downtown. Its virtues included ample land and parking, but it was relatively distant from such essential support facilities as hotels and restaurants. Another site adjoined the Kingdome, Seattle's domed stadium. This site's assets and liabilities were virtually the same as those of Seattle Center's. Third was an air rights site over Interstate 5, next to the existing Freeway Park that had been built as a bridge over the interstate. This site was in the center of downtown Seattle and thus within walking distance of downtown hotel rooms. Another key promise offered

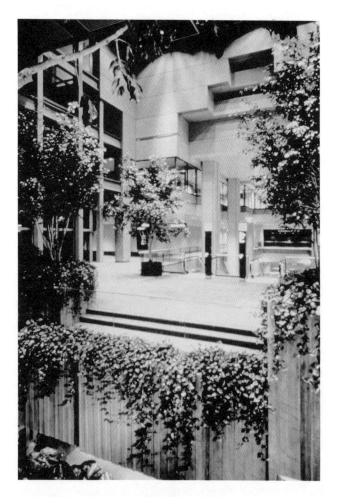

by this site was, as previously described, participation by the private sector in the development process, a prime goal for the project as specified by the legislature. Upon the completion of favorable environmental and financial analyses, in March 1983 the board adopted the freeway site as the future location of the convention center.

Situated atop the freeway, the convention center is a spectacular sight, adjacent to and extending the existing park. The convention center consists of six levels on which guests can find retail shops; 102,000 square feet of heavy-load exhibit space; 47,000 square feet of multipurpose banquet/exhibit space; 108,000 square feet of meeting space; and 1,035 covered parking spaces. Meeting space provides as many as 55 individual meeting rooms.

In 1988, the state legislature directed a program to improve and enlarge the convention center. Twenty-six million dollars was authorized to expand the sixth level of the existing facility and to develop an additional 76,300 square feet of meeting/ballroom space. Construction began in January 1990 and was completed in August 1991. The center is now better able to accommodate concurrent and consecutive conventions.

The 1994 legislature appropriated funds and directed the WSCTC, in collaboration with the city of Seattle, to prepare a development plan for a joint-use expansion project that would include up to 140,000 square feet of additional heavy-load exhibit space. An 11-member Convention Center Expansion and City Facilities Task Force was formed to consult with city and WSCTS officials to review and evaluate the expansion plan and to prepare a recommendation for the legislature. The task force recommended expansion, with the legislature having final approval.

Also in 1994, the 70-year-old Eagles Building next to the convention center was sold to A Contemporary Theater (ACT) and the Seattle Housing Resources Group (SHRG). ACT and SHRG will renovate this historic landmark, building two theaters and approximately 44 moderate-rent apartment units. The anticipated project completion date is fall 1996.

FINANCING

Construction of the $203 million convention center was funded by the sale of $158 million in state general obligation bonds, with the remaining $45 million coming from the city of Seattle, the state's department of transportation, private contributions, the sale of development rights, and settlement proceeds from the Industrial In-

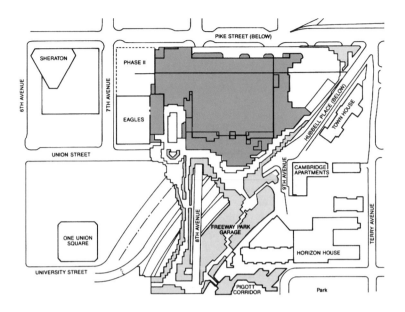

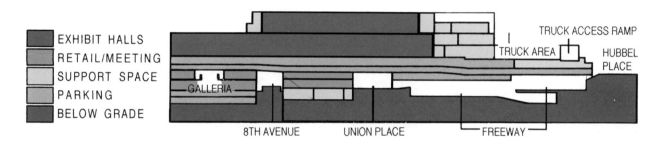

EXHIBIT HALLS
RETAIL/MEETING
SUPPORT SPACE
PARKING
BELOW GRADE

demnity Corporation (IIC). The cost of operating the facility is paid primarily by the county's special hotel/motel room tax.

It should be noted that the state became involved in financing the center primarily because most tax benefits, including those from the existing room tax on lodging units in Seattle and King County, accrue at the state level in Washington.

Market Orientation

In keeping with original project goals, the target markets for the convention center are regional, national, and international meetings ranging in size from 2,000 to 10,000 attendees. Seattle's location, which allows direct air routes to other major Pacific Rim destinations, enhances its potential competitive edge for international meetings.

National and international organizations have selected the convention center as the venue for their annual conventions and trade shows. The center hosts many medical, scientific, engineering, technology, legal, finan-

cial, and educational associations. Local and regional events are strong secondary markets for conventions and trade shows.

Some special features of the center include a public art program and participation in the development of low-income housing. The center's four-story Galleria, with its central escalator, offers a distinctive showcase for a rich and diverse cross section of art. It allows easy access for downtown residents, employees, shoppers, and meeting attendees. Museums, corporations, arts organizations, and art professionals display works on a rotating basis, creating a popular and highly accessible cultural attraction. Permanent and temporary works of art on display are valued at approximately $700,000.

The WSCTC board has been involved since the early days of construction in providing funding for low-income housing for downtown residents. The center has contributed $3.3 million toward a series of rehabilitation and new construction projects, which have achieved a net gain of 497 housing units in downtown Seattle. Restoration of the Eagles Building will boost that total by 44 additional units.

LESSONS LEARNED

- The Washington State Convention and Trade Center is one of the most attractive convention facilities in the United States. The determination of state leaders to place the center in the most beneficial location, from the standpoint of market appeal, has been rewarded. From a development standpoint, however, the state could not have chosen a more difficult site. Similarly, the state's insistence on participation by the private sector, which ultimately could not fulfill its commitments, resulted in a nightmarish start-stop development process for the project. The state has had to regroup, but its commitment to quality and marketability is obvious.

PROJECT DATA

WASHINGTON STATE CONVENTION AND TRADE CENTER SEATTLE, WA

Owner: State of Washington
Developer: CHG/Tishman, Seattle
Design Team: TRA, Seattle; Howard Needles Tammen & Begendorf (HNTB), Los Angeles; Danadjieva & Koenig Associates, Tiburon, California; Pietro Belluschi, Portland, Oregon; and Skilling Ward Magnusson Barkshire, Seattle
Year Planning Began: 1982
Year Construction Began: 1985
Year Construction Completed: 1988

PROJECT INFORMATION

Site Area:[1] 4 acres
Total GBA: 726,800 square feet
    Exhibition Space (heavy load): 102,000 square feet
    Meeting Space: 108,000 square feet
    Retail: 48,000 square feet
Total Parking Spaces: 1,035

ECONOMIC INFORMATION

Total Project Cost (1985 dollars): $203,000,000
Total Project Cost (1994 dollars):[2] $275,069,000
Funding Sources:
    State General Obligation Bonds: $158,000,000
        City of Seattle, State Department of Transportation, Private Contributions, Sale of Development Rights, and Proceeds from the Industrial Indemnity Corporation: $45,000,000
Total Funding: $203,000,000

Notes:
[1]Approximate acreage. Facility is located partially on air rights above Interstate 5.
[2]Calculated based on consumer price index.

- During the development phase, the WSCTC board was extremely sensitive to the surrounding environment. Citizens' task forces were set up to address safety, redevelopment, and neighborhood issues. Local community involvement amply aided local acceptance of the project.

WASHINGTON CONVENTION CENTER

WASHINGTON, D.C.

Located in the nation's third-largest convention city, the Washington Convention Center features state-of-the-art accommodations for large national and international conventions, trade shows, and other special events. The center opened in January 1983 after a 13-year planning period. This 800,000-square-foot facility benefits from its location near Mount Vernon Square in downtown Washington, the heart of the nation's association headquarters. Its locale helps it achieve nearly full operational capacity.

DEVELOPMENT STRATEGY

The history of the Washington Convention Center dates back to 1969, when the first development plans were commissioned by Washington, D.C.'s pre–home rule administration. The facility was then to be named the Eisenhower Civic Center and sited in the downtown business district.

In 1970, a campaign to build the center was developed, endorsed by economic consultants working for the city's downtown renewal program, and approved by the National Capital Planning Commission. In 1972, Congress authorized the District of Columbia to obtain plans for a facility that would be built by a private corporation and leased back to the city. By 1973, however, every plan submitted for the Eisenhower Civic Center had failed to win the approval of either potential backers or Congress. Eventually, the campaign lost momentum, and planning for the civic center was temporarily abandoned.

The center's development drive remained virtually dormant until 1976, when the District's first home rule administration, under Mayor Walter E. Washington, developed a top-level convention-center task force to study the merits of the proposed facility. An initial study and planning funds were provided by the U.S. Department of Commerce's Economic Development Administration. As a result, in April 1977 a public hearing was held regarding the proposed center, and by May the D.C. City Council had voted to allocate $27 million of its fiscal-year 1978 budget the center's development. Leaders of the Senate Subcommittee on District Appropriations were concerned, however, that the allocation was too large for D.C. taxpayers, and a lower amount was recommended. In November 1978, the city council and Congress approved a compromise that reduced the funds allocated to the center's initial development but called for a special hotel tax and secured development commitments for the rest of the needed funding. Congress then released funds for the center under D.C. Public Law 95-258.

On August 11, 1979, the city council passed the Washington Convention Center Management Act, which created a five-person board of directors for the center. On April 23, 1980, a ground-breaking ceremony was held on the site of the future Washington Convention Center, and construction of the facility began in August. Following a 500-person ribbon-cutting ceremony that included 300 top association executives, the Washington Convention Center officially opened on January 2, 1983. Only three days later, the National Capital Area International Auto Show became the center's first public show and attracted 249,000 people.

DESIGN AND SITE ISSUES

The Washington Convention Center site is located five blocks from the White House. It is bounded by New York Avenue, 9th Street, H Street, and 11th Street,

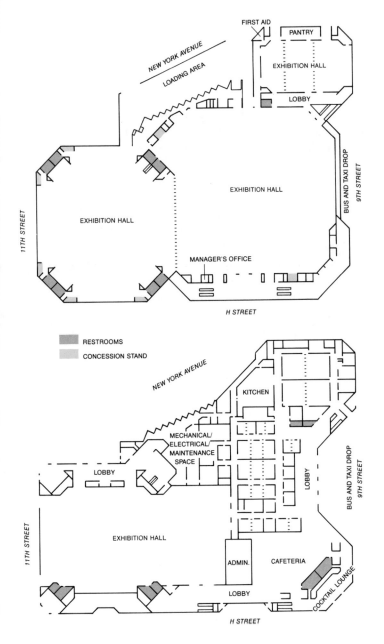

RESTROOMS

CONCESSION STAND

at attracting this portion of the market. Before construction of the center, no facility in the nation's capital was large enough to accommodate such events. The convention center is also flexible enough to accommodate local meetings, special events, and live entertainment.

The Washington Convention Center is a two-level facility with exhibition halls on both levels. On the lower level, there is a 105,000-square-foot exhibition hall, while on the upper level, there are three separate halls, two of which can be made into one large, 250,000-square-foot space. The additional upper-level exhibition hall contains 26,000 square feet. The center also offers some 70,000 square feet of meeting-room space. This design allows the facility to conduct multiple events at the same time with a minimal amount of group mixing.

FINANCING

Funding of the Washington Convention Center came from both District of Columbia and federal sources. Of the budgeted $98.7 million in center development costs, $77.3 million was funded from long-term U.S. Treasury loans to the District of Columbia, with annual debt service covered by the District's general revenue fund. The remaining $21.4 million, earmarked for site acquisition, relocation, and demolition costs, was borrowed from the U.S. Treasury by the District's capital projects fund and loaned to the convention center on a short-term basis. An additional $300,000 to cover principal and interest payments for the site acquisition loan was generated from a hotel occupancy tax (HOT), a surtax on the corporation franchise tax (CFT), and a surtax on the unincorporated business franchise tax (BFT). After repayment of the site acquisition loan, the hotel occupancy tax revenue is to be used for promoting conventions and tourism within the District of Columbia.

MARKET ORIENTATION

The key objective of the convention center is to serve as a generator of convention business in the community. The following considerations are taken into account when selecting potential users:
- Projected overall economic impact to the city.
- Number of hotel rooms required.
- Projected revenue to the facility from direct space rental and revenue from concessions and other building services.
- Time of year.
- Potential for repeat bookings.

Northwest. The convention center has sparked development in the surrounding area. Among the projects already completed or planned are a 950-room Grand Hyatt hotel, a Hecht's department store, and Techworld, which will ultimately contain 1.5 million square feet of office, convention, and hotel space. Naturally, this activity has boosted land prices and rental rates.

Initially, the primary goal of developing the center was to showcase national and international conventions, trade shows, meetings, and flat-floor exhibitions requiring more than 100,000 square feet of exhibition space. The center's design and booking policy are largely aimed

- Experience of potential users with respect to use of similar facilities.

Conventions, large meetings, trade shows, and flat-floor exhibitions are given specific priority over concerts, theater entertainment, or sporting events.

The Washington Convention Center's booking policy designates the Washington Convention and Visitors' Association (WCVA) as the official sales organization for the center. The WCVA is responsible for renting space and setting rental rates for events occurring more than 18 months into the future. The center's in-house marketing concentrates on filling in the center's schedule by attracting and booking events to be held within 18 months or sooner. The staff at the center works closely with the WCVA staff to develop all promotional materials and special sales efforts and to coordinate events.

The Washington Convention Center benefits from its location in a city that serves as the headquarters for hundreds of national associations that plan annual and semiannual meetings. In the first year of its operation, the facility hosted some 200 events, including seven major national conventions and trade shows and more than 30 multiple-day, public consumer shows. Since then, the number of national conventions and trade shows booked at the facility has been steadily rising and now accounts for a majority of the annual event days. After only a few years of operation, the center is virtually filled to capacity with high-priority events and has a waiting list of new national conventions and trade shows.

LESSONS LEARNED

The development of the Washington Convention Center was a long process, spanning 13 years from conception to reality. The success of the facility, and the economic benefits it provides to the community, can be attributed both to the facility's location in the heart of the nation's association headquarters and to its well-planned marketing and management policies. There are several design factors, however, that the convention center's management believes could have been improved, had the management team been in place and involved during the design process:

- Probably the most critical consideration is size. The center is too small to maintain its promising position in the national and international meetings industry.

PROJECT DATA
WASHINGTON CONVENTION CENTER
WASHINGTON, DC

Owner: District of Columbia
Builder: George A. Fuller & L.B. Griffin Construction, Washington, D.C.
Architect: Welton Beckett & Associates, Los Angeles
Year Planning Began: 1969
Year Construction Began: 1980
Year Construction Completed: 1983

PROJECT INFORMATION
Total GBA: 800,000 square feet
    Exhibition Space: 350,000 square feet
    Meeting Space: 70,000 square feet

ECONOMIC INFORMATION
Total Project Cost: $98,700,000
Funding Sources:
    Long-Term U.S. Treasury Bonds: $77,000,000
    Short-Term U.S. Treasury Bonds:[1] $21,400,000

Note:
[1] Earmarked for site acquisition, relocation, and demolition costs. Hotel occupancy tax, a corporation franchise tax surcharge, and a business franchise tax surcharge raised $300,000 to cover principal and interest payments on the site acquisition loans.

Currently, proposals are being discussed for an expansion that would provide at least 300,000 square feet of contiguous exhibition space. However, this space cannot be connected to the existing center because of the lack of available land around it.

- Another major design limitation has been the fact that the exhibition space is not contained on one level. This limits the ability of the center to compete for the rapidly growing market of large-scale events.
- The center lacks storage space for chairs and tables, which constantly forces management to move these items within the building or off the site.
- Loading-dock space comes only to half of what is needed. There are now 12 bays where 24 are needed.
- Finally, space for a management office was designed for a 40-person staff. The present management staff has 150 members.

ATLANTA-FULTON COUNTY STADIUM

ATLANTA, GEORGIA

Atlanta-Fulton County Stadium is located at the junction of Interstates 20, 75, and 85, offering excellent access from all parts of metropolitan Atlanta and the southeastern United States. The stadium is the regular-season home of major league baseball's Atlanta Braves.

DEVELOPMENT STRATEGY

Atlanta-Fulton County Stadium was developed to attract a major league franchise to the city of Atlanta. On March 5, 1964, Mayor Ivan Allen, Jr., announced that he had a verbal commitment from a major league baseball club to move to Atlanta if a stadium was available by 1966. Speculation focused on the Milwaukee Braves and the Philadelphia Phillies. The following day, the proposition was submitted to the board of aldermen,

which unanimously approved plans for a $19 million stadium complex.

The Fulton County Recreation Authority, created in 1961, was entrusted with the power to acquire land for, construct, equip, maintain, and operate an athletic stadium and to authorize the issuance of revenue bonds. This nine-member authority consists of six members appointed by the city and three members named by the county. Members serve four-year, staggered terms and may seek reappointment if they desire. The authority, which can issue bonds with the backing of the city and county, currently manages and operates the stadium.

The owners of the stadium are the city of Atlanta and Fulton County; the builder was Thompson & Street; and the architect was Heery & Heery.

The Milwaukee Braves became the Atlanta Braves in 1966. The stadium opened in April 1966, with the Braves playing the Pittsburgh Pirates before 50,000 fans.

DESIGN AND SITE ISSUES

The selected location for the stadium, an urban renewal area lying one-quarter mile from the state capitol and six miles from Atlanta's airport, was chosen because of its proximity to the downtown and the airport. The facility was designed and constructed in one year, with a $19 million budget.

The circular stadium's footprint is 750.5 feet in diameter and occupies 19.4 acres. The playing field, which lies 33 feet below the level of the 6,500-car parking area, initially measured 325 feet along the foul lines, 402 feet to the center-field fence, and 375 feet in the power alleys, but the power alleys were lengthened to 385 feet in the 1970s. The entire site, including parking, occupies 95 acres.

The lower level of the stadium consists of poured-in-place concrete, while the club and upper levels are of a basic steel construction with precast concrete in the seating areas. Originally, the seating capacity was 51,500 for baseball and 59,500 for football. Before the 1977 season, more seats were added, bringing the seating capacity of the three-tier structure to 52,785 for baseball and 60,748 for football. Thirty-three luxury suites rent for $45,000 to $87,500 per year on two- to three-year leases, and a stadium club offers seating for 325 people.

FINANCING

Atlanta-Fulton County Stadium was built in one year, with total site, construction, and development costs ap-

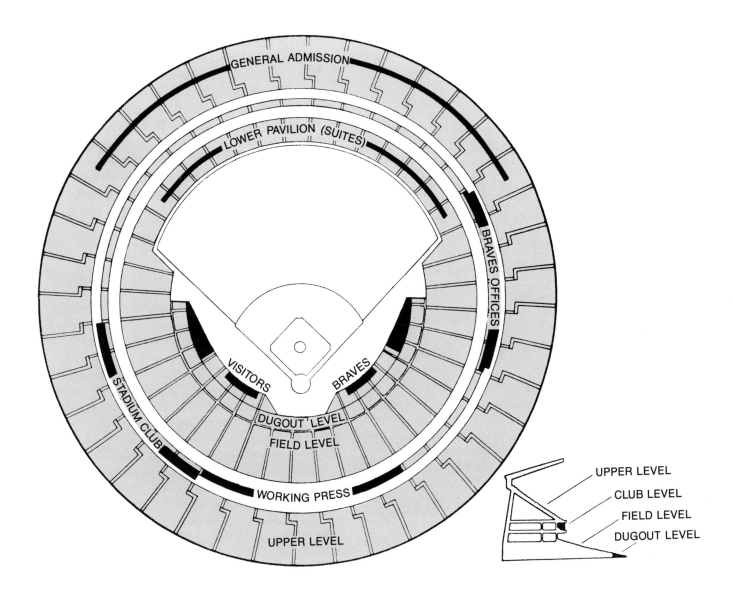

proximating $19.2 million. The stadium was financed through the sale of $16.5 million in revenue bonds issued by the city of Atlanta and the recreation authority. Postdevelopment financing also involved bond issues. In 1975, for example, the authority issued a second series of bonds in the amount of $1.5 million for the construction and installation of telescopic seats. A third series of revenue bonds was issued for $1.5 million in 1977 for the construction and installation of a video matrix sign to advertise sponsors and entertain fans during breaks in play. In 1982, the authority's fourth series of revenue bonds, for $1.3 million, resurfaced the existing parking areas. And in 1986, the authority's fifth series of bonds, which amounted to $13 million, funded a scoreboard, new natural athletic turf, waterproofing of the stadium's expansion joints, and renovation of the stadium's concrete surfacing.

MARKET ORIENTATION

Atlanta-Fulton County Stadium is home to the Atlanta Braves baseball team. In 1993, the Braves attracted nearly 4 million fans. The NFL Atlanta Falcons also played in the stadium from 1966 until 1992, when they moved to the new Georgia Dome. Other events hosted in the facility have included college football bowl games, concerts, and motor sports events.

LESSONS LEARNED

■ The stadium was built at a favorable location, easily accessible and highly visible from downtown Atlanta, the airport, and major highways. The seating configu-

PROJECT DATA

ATLANTA-FULTON COUNTY STADIUM
ATLANTA, GA

Owner: City of Atlanta and Fulton County
Builder: Thompson & Street
Architect: Heery & Heery (Atlanta)
Primary Users: Atlanta Braves (baseball)
Year Planning Began: 1964
Year Construction Began: 1964
Year Construction Completed: 1965

PROJECT INFORMATION
Site Area: 95 acres
Building Footprint: 19.4 acres
Total Seating Capacity: 52,785 (baseball), 60,748 (football)
Total Parking Spaces: 6,500

ECONOMIC INFORMATION
Site Acquisition Cost: $2,105,891
Site Impact Cost: $866,664
Construction Costs: $16,245,575
Total Project Cost: $19,200,000
Funding Source:
  City Revenue Bonds—1965 Issue: $16,500,000
  City Revenue Bonds—1975 Issue: $1,500,000
  City Revenue Bonds—1977 Issue: $1,500,000
  City Revenue Bonds—1982 Issue: $1,300,000
  City Revenue Bonds—1986 Issue: $13,000,000

ration at the stadium is adequate for baseball, and the 6,500 parking spaces surrounding the stadium are sufficient for most events. Several problems have arisen, however, regarding the stadium's design:

- Stadium concourses were not sealed during the original construction, causing a sometimes-unsightly appearance whose recurrence is difficult to prevent and allowing water leaks into offices and storage spaces.
- The stadium was built with an insufficient number of toilets for crowds of more than 35,000 people.
- The press area and lounge are too small, and there is insufficient storage space.
- The service tunnel is inadequate for servicing the stadium and the concession stands.
- With only one service elevator, the stadium needs a separate freight elevator.
- Concession stands are too small, increasing the time required to serve patrons.
- Playing field drainage is inadequate.

While these design/construction flaws are cause for many current complaints, it should be noted that:

- The facility was developed in record time (approximately 12 months) on a very limited budget of $16 million for "bricks and mortar."
- The facility is a tribute to the tenacious efforts of the city's mayor and key civic leaders, who succeeded in securing a team for the city on the condition that the stadium was ready for play within 12 months of a verbal agreement. While the two local governments, the city and county, cooperated to provide final financing for the stadium, initial funding for design was provided by local businesses, with no guarantee of repayment. Without this advance funding, the facility would not have been ready for play, and the Braves may have been lost to the city.

GEORGIA DOME

ATLANTA, GEORGIA

Situated in the heart of downtown Atlanta, the Georgia Dome is the largest cable-supported dome stadium in the world. It is home to the National Football League's Atlanta Falcons, host of the 1994 Super Bowl XXVIII, and site of the gymnastics and basketball events for the 1996 Olympic Games.

DEVELOPMENT STRATEGY

Business, civic, and government leaders began discussing the possibility of constructing a new stadium in Atlanta

as early as 1984, but the development process took more than eight years to complete. In 1985, Governor Joe Frank Harris, along with state, city, and county governments; the Atlanta Falcons; the Atlanta Chamber of Commerce; and Georgia Tech University formed a committee and contributed funds to study stadium options. A private firm was hired to conduct a feasibility study. The study and the committee concluded that a domed stadium would enjoy a high level of use.

It was proposed that the project be a public/private venture, with 30 percent of resources coming from public funds and 70 percent from private financing. In 1987, Governor Harris began planning the government's role in the financing process. Governor Harris, Mayor Andrew Young, and Fulton County Commissioner Michael Lomax reached a consensus on implementing an increase in the hotel/motel tax to finance the public portion of the project. Shortly thereafter, the Georgia house and senate approved the tax increase. Private financing was undertaken by the Georgia Stadium Corporation, a group of investors using $1 million in seed money to market club seats and executive suites. The corporation raised $55 million in pledged lease revenues for box suites, approximately one-half of the private sector financing needed to build the facility.

Ultimately, it became apparent that the 70 percent private financing share was unachievable as originally planned, and Governor Harris announced that the state of Georgia would construct the dome under an agreement with city and county governments, providing that they would also participate in the financing with an additional increase in the hotel/motel tax. The Georgia legislature gave its final approval of the project, and one-half of one cent of the existing hotel tax was allocated to it. Lastly, the Atlanta City Council and the Fulton County Commission gave their final approval, thus clearing the way for construction to begin.

A team of architectural and engineering firms was assembled: Heery Architects; Thompson, Ventulett, Stainback & Associates (also the designer of the Omni Arena, the adjacent Omni Hotel-Office-Retail complex, and all three phases of the Georgia World Congress Center); Rosser Fabrap International, Inc.; and Williams-Russell & Johnson, Inc. Beers, Inc., the firm chosen for construction management, compiled a team that included H.J. Russell & Company, the Holder Corporation, and Barton-Malow Company.

Construction of the primary structure began in mid-1990. Beers submitted a proposal of a guaranteed maximum price of $174.5 million for construction and other related costs. Two years later, the Georgia Dome celebrated its grand opening with an Atlanta Falcons exhibition game.

DESIGN AND SITE ISSUES

Consultants recommended that the Georgia Dome be constructed next to the Georgia World Congress Center (GWCC), so that it could be used for major convention assemblies and could share use of parking and the GWCC management team. The dome and convention center complex is located in downtown Atlanta, with accessibility to Hartsfield International Airport provided by the MARTA subway transit system.

Two parking decks offering a total of 1,260 spaces and two surface parking lots with a total of 2,600 spaces are located adjacent to the complex. More than 17,000 additional parking spaces are available within walking distance of the facility. The Atlanta metropolitan area offers more than 50,000 hotel rooms and a vast array of dining and entertainment options.

A cable-supported, Teflon-coated fiberglass roof filters natural light, producing an open-air atmosphere inside the dome. Beneath the roof, the Georgia Dome features a 102,000-square-foot, sealed concrete floor with a utility grid to service exhibit booths on 30-foot centers. The floor can accommodate a variety of configurations for sports and entertainment presentations, allowing it to host diverse spectator and exhibition events.

The Georgia Dome has a seating capacity of 71,500 for football. The dome floor seats up to 8,600 additional attendees, theater-style, and can host receptions of up to 10,000 people. Five additional meeting rooms can each accommodate 50 to 150 people.

The Georgia Dome offers 203 executive suites and 5,600 executive club seats that are leased on a ten-year basis. Both executive suite and club seat members receive Falcons season tickets, first option to buy tickets to public events, the option to purchase one parking pass for every four seats, and exclusive access to the Executive Concourse, which has specialty concessions and large-screen televisions. Club seats are leased for $1,000 to $1,800 per year and offer extrawide, cushioned armchairs with high backs; executive suites range in price from $20,000 to $120,000 per year and are equipped with custom furnishings, cable-ready television, wet bar, and private restroom.

FINANCING

Construction of the $214 million Georgia Dome was financed through revenue bonds issued by the Georgia World Congress Center Authority. Debt service is paid without taxpayer risk by dedicated hotel/motel tax and facility net revenue, guaranteed by a private letter of credit. Dedicated revenue was initially set up to be generated from stadium operations and from the leasing of executive suites, in addition to that portion of the hotel/motel tax pledged to the project. The sale of executive suites was boosted when the Georgia Dome was chosen to host 1994's Super Bowl XXVIII, as well as the gymnastic and basketball competitions for the 1996 Olympic Games. At present, a portion of the hotel/motel taxes collected in Atlanta and Fulton County are used to finance the dome.

Operating income is used to cover operating expenses and 50 percent of debt service, while the hotel/motel tax is used for the remaining 50 percent. As the hotel/motel tax grows, it must be allocated to debt service or early retirement of debt. Thus, as the tax covers more debt, a greater amount of operating income is available to the authority for other uses.

MARKETING AND MANAGEMENT

The Georgia Dome is owned by the state of Georgia and managed by the Georgia World Congress Center Authority, which also operates the GWCC. Coupled with the 2.5 million-square-foot GWCC, the two facilities constitute one of the largest sports, entertainment, and convention complexes in the world.

In addition to Atlanta Falcons football and the 1996 Olympic Games, the dome is and will be host to a vari-

PROJECT DATA

GEORGIA DOME
ATLANTA, GA

Owner: State of Georgia
Operator: Georgia World Congress Center Authority
Architect: Heery International, Atlanta; Thompson, Ventulett, Stainback & Associates (TVS), Rosser Fabrap, Atlanta
Builders: Beers, Inc., Atlanta; H.J. Russell & Co., Atlanta; Holder Corporation, Atlanta; Barton-Malow Company, Atlanta
Primary Users: Atlanta Falcons (football)
Year Planning Began: 1984
Year Construction Began: 1990
Year Construction Completed: 1992

PROJECT INFORMATION
Site Area: 42 acres
Exhibition Space: 102,000 square feet
Seating Capacity:
   Football: 71,500
   Maximum: 80,000
Total Parking Spaces: 3,860 on site

ECONOMIC INFORMATION
Site Acquisition Cost: $14,000,000
Construction Cost: $200,000,000
Total Project Cost (1992 dollars): $214,000,000
Total Project Cost (1994 dollars):[1] $222,500,000

Note:
[1]Calculated based on the consumer price index.

ety of sporting events, including the Peach Bowl, the SEC football championship, the NCAA Final Four basketball tournament in 2002, the SEC basketball championship tournament, and the USA/Mobil indoor track and field competition. The Georgia Dome also hosts major concerts, trade shows, and religious conventions such as that of the Southern Baptists. The dome's relationship, both physical and managerial, with the GWCC enables it to attract certain events with the unusual requirements for which these two facilities can jointly provide.

LESSONS LEARNED

The Georgia Dome was designed to be a multipurpose facility that would complement the GWCC. It was to be flexible enough to accommodate major sporting events, as well as spillover convention activity from the GWCC. The relationship between the Georgia Dome and the GWCC allows both facilities to achieve economies that lower their relative operating costs, giving the complex a competitive marketing advantage.

ORIOLE PARK AT CAMDEN YARDS AND PROPOSED FOOTBALL STADIUM

BALTIMORE, MARYLAND

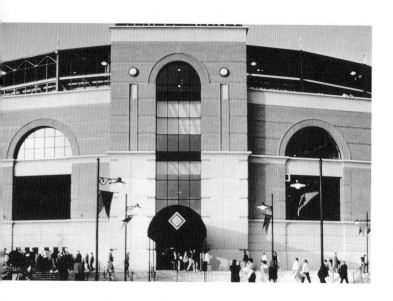

A new ballpark—Oriole Park at Camden Yards—has been completed in downtown Baltimore, and the state of Maryland has prepared a master plan for the site, where it hopes also to construct a football stadium. This location offers easy access via the interstate highway system (I-95, I-295, I-395), rail, subway, and an efficient bus system operating throughout the metropolitan area. The Camden Yards site was also appropriate because of its proximity to Baltimore's Inner Harbor (which features the National Aquarium, retail shops, hotels, and restaurants) and the downtown business district.

It was anticipated that the Camden Yards site would enhance the economic impact of the ballpark on the metropolitan area. The site offers appropriate field orientation

for both baseball and football. Abundant off-site parking is available within a comfortable walking distance, and the ballpark offers panoramic views of downtown Baltimore and the Inner Harbor.

DEVELOPMENT STRATEGY

The motivating force behind the state of Maryland's development of Oriole Park at Camden Yards was the desire to ensure that the major league baseball franchise for the Orioles remained in Baltimore under a long-term lease. Additionally, location of the ballpark in the downtown was seen as an opportunity to bring the economic benefits of baseball to the center city. Before their move to the Camden Yards ballpark, the Orioles had played since 1954 in Memorial Stadium, which was situated in a suburb and surrounded by residential development. Construction of the new ballpark began in July 1989 and was completed in April 1992.

Development of a new football stadium was proposed to provide Maryland with the best possible chance of regaining a National Football League expansion franchise or attracting an existing franchise to Baltimore. Baltimore has been without a professional football franchise since 1984, when the Colts moved to Indianapolis.

The Maryland Stadium Authority, an independent agency of the state government, oversaw the planning and construction of Oriole Park at Camden Yards and now owns and operates the ballpark. The architects—Hellmuth, Obata & Kassabaum (HOK)—worked closely with the Stadium Authority and the Orioles to design a traditional facility that offered modern amenities but that would recall a historic ballpark design and blend with Baltimore's existing design context.

DESIGN AND SITE ISSUES

Oriole Park at Camden Yards has a seating capacity of 48,262, including 72 private suites, three party suites, 3,757 club seats, and bleacher and standing-room-only accommodations. The ballpark is an open-air, natural-grass, baseball-only facility. There are more than 5,000 on-site parking spaces and more than 30,000 additional spaces within a comfortable walk of the ballpark.

The proposed football stadium will have a minimum seating capacity of 70,000 seats, with approximately 100 luxury suites and a stadium club that will accommodate 600. The football stadium will be an open-air structure with a natural-grass playing surface.

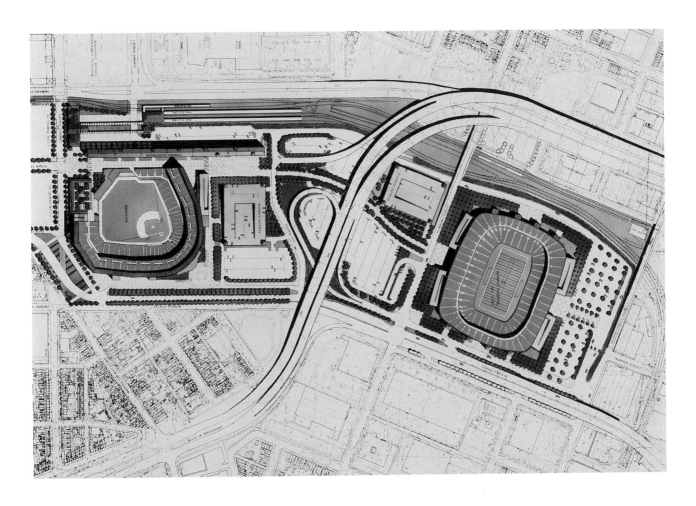

FINANCING

The Maryland Stadium Authority received approval from the state legislature to build the ballpark, proposed football stadium, and parking facilities on the 85-acre Camden Yards site. The legislature authorized the issuance of up to $235 million in revenue bonds for development costs; federal tax legislation, enacted in 1986, permitted up to $200 million of this bonding authorization to be tax-free. The authority's legislation imposed bond ceilings of $85 million for site acquisition and preparation, $70 million for the ballpark, and $80 million for the football stadium.

Annual principal and interest payments on the revenue bonds will be generated by revenues from periodic statewide sport lotteries, a grant from the city of Baltimore, and the pledge of rent, admissions tax, and revenues from parking and concession operations. The state's enabling legislation stipulates that the proposed football stadium cannot be finally designed or constructed without a long-term lease, as was the case for the ballpark.

In addition to the financing provided by revenue bonds, the Maryland General Assembly stipulated that private financing should be used to the maximum extent possible. The legislation states that the Maryland Stadium Authority shall solicit and evaluate proposals from private investors for financing structures that maximize use of private equity capital and privately secured debt. To this end, the Maryland Stadium Authority has been working to increase the use of The Warehouse at Camden Yards, and several tenants have signed leases or expressed an interest in locating their offices in this facility, a structure that was rehabilitated as part of the ballpark construction and that extends the entire length of the right-field side of the stadium.

MARKET ORIENTATION

A study completed in February 1987 estimated utilization and net operating profits for the then-proposed ballpark and football stadium. The ballpark was projected to be used by the Baltimore Orioles as the only tenant for 81

games per year, with annual attendance of approximately 2.4 million. In the first two years of operation, however, ballpark attendance exceeded 3.5 million per year. In fiscal 1994, operating revenues were $10.4 million and expenses $7.4 million, resulting in an operating profit of $3.0 million. This figure compares favorably with the $3.1 million net operating profit estimated by consultants.

The proposed football stadium will be used for ten professional football games per year, college events, concerts, family entertainments, and religious events. Operating revenues for the proposed stadium were estimated to be $4.0 million, with operating expenses projected at $1.6 million annually (paid by the team), resulting in an operating profit of $2.4 million a year before debt service.

PROJECT DATA

ORIOLE PARK AT CAMDEN YARDS AND PROPOSED FOOTBALL STADIUM
BALTIMORE, MD

Owner: State of Maryland
Construction Manager: Barton Malow/Sverdrup, Baltimore
Architect: Hellmuth, Obata & Kassabaum (HOK), Kansas City, Missouri
Primary Users: Baltimore Orioles (baseball)
Year Planning Began: 1986
Year Construction Began: 1989
Year Construction Completed: 1992

PROJECT INFORMATION
Site Area: 85 acres
Total Parking Spaces: 5,200[1]
Maximum Seating Capacity:
    Baseball: 48,262
    Football: 70,000

ECONOMIC INFORMATION

	Baseball	Football (proposed)[3]
Construction Costs:	$106,000,000	$164,000,000
Site Acquisition Costs:	100,000,000	10,000,000
Parking Facility:	4,000,000	
Infrastructure:[2]		1,000,000
Roadway Improvements:	27,000,000	
Sitework Costs:		5,000,000
Total (1989 dollars):	$237,000,000	N/A
Total (1994 dollars):[4]	$279,000,000	$180,000,000

Notes:
[1]All on site, with 30,000 additional spaces nearby.
[2]Proposed.
[3]Calculated using 1994 dollars.
[4]Calculated based on the consumer price index.

NORTH AMERICARE PARK

BUFFALO, NEW YORK

Situated in downtown Buffalo, North Americare Park (formerly Pilot Field) is distinctly reminiscent of old ballparks like Brooklyn's Ebbets Field. It has been designed to conform aesthetically with the surrounding neighborhoods.

DEVELOPMENT STRATEGY

The Downtown Buffalo Sports Complex was developed to aid revitalization of the downtown. Its objectives were to create employment opportunities and to provide a stimulus for economic development. City leaders thought that a suitable facility could attract a major league sports team, enhance the image of the Bisons AAA baseball team, and host other sporting events. The complex was also intended to host various special events, thereby complementing the Buffalo Convention Center, and to provide additional parking for the lower Main Street business community. North Americare Park has become the anchor of an extensive downtown revitalization program and has brought the flavor of old-time baseball back to Buffalo.

DESIGN AND SITE ISSUES

North Americare Park lies off Interstate 190, near lower Main Street in downtown Buffalo. The sports complex is a 21,050-seat, open-air facility designed primarily for baseball. If a major league team is secured, the stadium can expand to provide a total of 40,000 seats. It occupies a 12-acre site adjacent to the Joseph Ellicott Preservation District.

Phase I of the project was completed in April 1988 and included the 21,050-seat stadium and parking for 1,200 cars, while Phase II is the proposed expansion to 40,000 seats.

The appearance of North Americare Park was designed to blend well with nearby historic buildings and thus to contribute to the general revitalization of the downtown. The park has a natural turf playing surface.

In spring 1990, a $1.5 million renovation took place that entailed enlarging the bleacher section, expanding the picnic and tent facilities, creating an open area for catered parties, and updating mechanical equipment.

The stadium houses 15 full-service concession stands, several of which are unusual, e.g., a health-food stand, an Italian-theme stand, a charcoal-grilled hot-dog vendor, and barbecue concessions. Also, a restaurant on the mezzanine level can accommodate up to 300 people for dining with a view of the playing field. The restaurant is open year-round for lunch and dinner.

North Americare Park has four levels: the club, mezzanine, main concourse, and service levels. The club level contains 40 luxury suites, catered by a fully staffed kitchen. These suites, for which a waiting list exists, can accommodate eight, ten, or 12 people and cost $12,000, $14,000, or $16,000 per year, respectively, on a three-year lease. Broadcast booths are also located on the club level. The main level offers general seating, while the mezzanine contains both general seating and administrative offices. At the service level are locker rooms and an administration area.

A picnic area of about 20,000 square feet can be found behind the scoreboard and features shelter, concession stand, and restrooms. Downtown buses and shuttle trains schedule frequent stops in front of the stadium.

FINANCING

The total cost of North Americare Park was $54.7 million. The project was financed through the following sources: $22.5 million from the state; $6.4 million in federal funds; $8.7 million from city resources, includ-

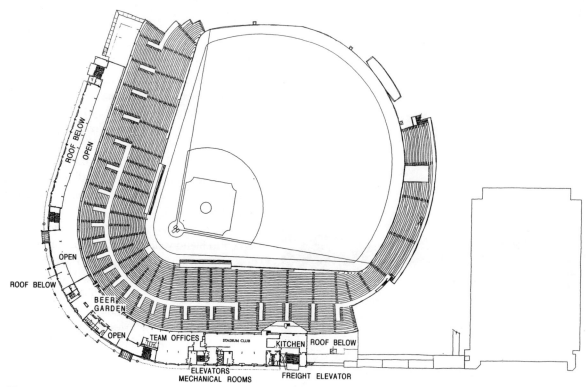

Mezzanine Level

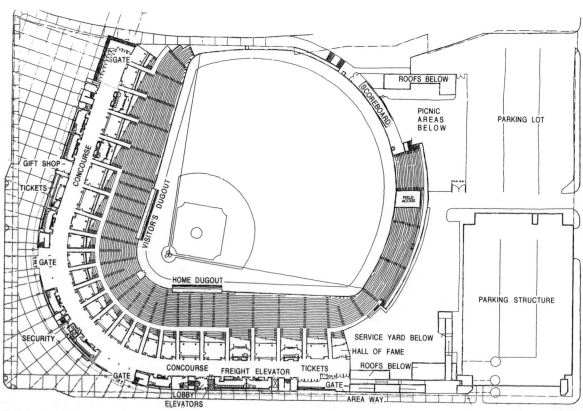

Main Concourse Level

232

PROJECT DATA

NORTH AMERICARE PARK
BUFFALO, NY

Owner: City of Buffalo
Operator: City of Buffalo Department of Stadium and
  Auditorium
Architect: Hellmuth, Obata & Kassabaum (HOK), Inc.,
  Kansas City, Missouri
Primary User: Buffalo Bisons (AAA baseball)
Year Planning Began: 1985
Year Construction Began: 1986
Year Construction Completed: 1988

PROJECT INFORMATION

Site Area: 12 acres
Total Seating Capacity: 21,050
Total Parking Spaces:
  On-Site: 1,200
  Nearby: 3,000

ECONOMIC INFORMATION

Total Construction Cost: $42,000,000
Total Soft Costs: $12,700,000
Total Project Cost (1986 Dollars): $54,700,000
Total Project Cost (1994 Dollars):[1] $72,367,883
Total Financing: $54,700,000
  State Funds: $22,500,000
  Federal Funds: $6,400,000
  City Funds: $8,700,000
  Private Funds: $17,100,000

Note:
[1]Calculated based on consumer price index.

ing $7.7 million in bonds; and $17.1 million in private funding. Thus, the union of the public and private sectors has made North Americare Park a reality.

MARKET ORIENTATION

North Americare Park is home to AAA baseball's Buffalo Bisons, and the city hopes someday to acquire a major league expansion team. In just over seven seasons, North Americare Park has broken all minor league attendance records by attracting more than 8 million fans. The ballpark draws many Canadian fans because of its proximity to the Canadian border.

LESSONS LEARNED

- After two years of drainage problems, a second irrigation system was installed, with marked improvement.
- Plans exist to expand the seating capacity if the city can acquire a major league expansion team.
- The stadium was developed as a component of Buffalo's downtown revitalization efforts, and the visual difference has been noticeable. The downtown is now filled with people on game days, and retail shops and restaurants benefit from this increase in attendee traffic.

CAROLINAS STADIUM

CHARLOTTE, NORTH CAROLINA

In October 1993, Charlotte city officials and football fans throughout the Carolinas celebrated the National Football League's decision to award Charlotte an expansion team, the Carolina Panthers, culminating six years of planning. By implementing an unusual ticket and seat marketing campaign, the owners—Richardson Sports—convinced the NFL that a state-of-the-art stadium could be built with private funds provided in large part by the fans themselves.

DEVELOPMENT STRATEGY

Planning for Carolinas Stadium began in 1987, when Richardson Sports officially announced an NFL franchise bid and a stadium plan to serve North and South Carolina. A 15-member partnership, the Carolinas Stadium Corporation, was formed to sponsor the expansion effort. In 1989, the site in "uptown" Charlotte (the CBD) was selected as the proposed location for the new stadium. A joint-venture group comprising F.N. Thompson of Charlotte and Turner Construction Company of New York was selected to build the stadium. Construction

began on March 3, 1994, and was completed on schedule in June 1996.

SITE ANALYSIS

With approximately 72,500 seats, the open-air, natural-turf Carolinas Stadium was designed specifically for football. The stadium and adjacent practice fields occupy 33 acres of land in uptown Charlotte. This location is conveniently near hotels and restaurants and takes advantage of 37,500 existing parking spaces that now serve office buildings in the central core, the headquarters of NationsBank, First Union, Wachovia, Duke Power, and other corporations. A minimal number of parking spaces will be available on-site for staff and players. Immediate interstate access allows for easy entry to and exit from the parking areas. The stadium design will consist of more than 23,000 seats and 10,000 club seats in the lower deck, more than 36,000 seats in the upper deck, and some 2,000 suite seats in 135 luxury suites on two levels along stadium sidelines. Seating capacity of a luxury suite ranges from ten to 40 persons.

Each individually climate-controlled luxury suite is fully enclosed with an operable glass window along its front to provide an unobstructed view of the gridiron. Suite furnishings include carpeting and wall covering, upholstered spectator chairs, conversational seating arrangements, a serving counter, and a wet bar with a built-in sink, refrigerator, and ice cabinet. Suites are also equipped with private restrooms. Closed-circuit TV monitors hang above the service counter and in front of the viewing seats, and a choice of audio options is afforded.

The club seating section features a fully furnished lobby/lounge where food and beverages are served and sit-down dining is available. Closed-circuit TV also services this enclosed, climate-controlled club concourse.

The approximate total number of point-of-sale concession areas is 425.

FINANCING

The financing plan was based on the sale, beginning in July 1993, of permanent seat licenses (PSLs), which provide the buyer with a right to purchase season tickets; luxury suites; and club seats. By the end of the first day of sales, all 8,314 club seats had sold out, at rental rates of $975 to $2,975 per year, and all 104 luxury suites available at that time had been leased, at $40,000 to $296,000

PROJECT DATA

CAROLINAS STADIUM
CHARLOTTE, NC

Owner: Carolinas Stadium Corporation
Architects: Hellmuth, Obata & Kassabaum (HOK), Inc.,
  Kansas City, Missouri
Primary Users: Carolina Panthers (football)
Year Construction Began: 1994
Projected Year of Completion: 1996

PROJECT INFORMATION
Site Area: 33 acres
Total Seating Capacity: 72,500 (approximately)
Total Parking: 37,500 in the vicinity

ECONOMIC INFORMATION
Total Project Cost (1994 dollars)[1]: $160,000,000

FINANCING
Total Financing: $160,000,000
  Permanent Seat Licenses: $142,700,000
  Richardson Sports: $20,000,000
  Less Taxes on PSLs: $50,000,000

Note:
[1]Projected.

©Les Duggins

MARKET ORIENTATION

On October 26, 1993, NFL owners unanimously selected the Carolina Panthers as the 29th NFL franchise and the first NFL expansion team since 1976. Richardson Sports has succeeded in large part because of its unique financing plan and its recognition of the chance to house a home team for both Carolinas. The Carolina Panthers and the Jacksonville Jaguars, the 30th NFL expansion team, opposed each other in the inaugural season opener, the 1995 Hall of Fame Game.

LESSONS LEARNED

- Thanks to the overwhelming support of the fans and to the stadium's flexible design, more club seats and 56 more luxury suites could be added to the premium seating areas.
- The sale of permanent seat licenses, luxury suites, and club seats was both a unique and a successful way of financing the project. In a sense, the plan combined the concept of premium-seat revenue financing, as pioneered by Joe Robbie Stadium and Texas Stadium, with the sale of rights to seats in a specific location, as proposed earlier for a domed stadium in New York City.

per year. Later, 31 more luxury suites and 2,400 more club suites were added to the stadium plans. More than 49,000 PSLs were reserved, representing a total pledge of $112.7 million. In addition to annual rental fees, PSLs are assessed a one-time charge of $600 to $5,400, depending on a seat's desirability. NationsBank and Wachovia have posted a $30 million guarantee to purchase the unsold PSLs, bringing the total pledged to $142.7 million. The remainder will be provided by Richardson Sports.

RIVERFRONT STADIUM

CINCINNATI, OHIO

The 55,000-seat Riverfront Stadium, adjacent to the central business district of Cincinnati, has been the anchor of redevelopment along the Ohio River and a major stimulus to the economic health of the CBD. Home of the Cincinnati Reds major league baseball team and Cincinnati Bengals National Football League team, the stadium was built during the flurry of construction of round, multipurpose stadiums that occurred during the late 1960s and early 1970s.

DEVELOPMENT STRATEGY

Riverfront Stadium, which opened in 1970, culminated many years' work toward bringing a facility of this type to Cincinnati. As early as 1948, a stadium had been proposed for Cincinnati's riverbank. However, the idea remained dormant until 1957, when the Cincinnati Reds threatened to move because of the existing Crosley Field's poor condition. Although a new stadium was not built

at that time, the threat did prompt the state legislature to enact laws permitting the county to issue either mortgage revenue bonds or revenue and general obligation bonds to finance such a structure.

In 1965, at a time when many National League teams were planning new baseball stadiums, Cincinnati's business and political communities combined their efforts to bring a new facility to the city. An eight-member steering committee was formed to oversee the feasibility study, site selection, design, and construction processes.

The city of Cincinnati and Hamilton County, through a cooperative agreement signed in 1967, joined to provide the construction, acquisition, improvement, management, occupancy, maintenance, and repair of the stadium. Among other terms of the agreement was the conveyance of the site from the city to the county for the sum of $3,245,996. Air rights were retained by the city, which had responsibility for all details of construction. Currently, the county owns the improvements and the land, and the city operates the stadium. In 1967, the year of the cooperative agreement, an American Football League franchise was brought to Cincinnati by its new owner and coach, Paul Brown. The team began playing in 1968 at Nippert Field, home stadium of the University of Cincinnati, but the commitment of a professional football team intensified the drive to build a stadium and enhanced the ability to obtain financing.

DESIGN AND SITE ISSUES

More than one-half dozen sites were considered for stadium development. The 48-acre riverfront site that was eventually selected offered less land than the others and was in the Ohio River's floodplain. This location was chosen despite these limitations because of its potential as a symbol for downtown revitalization. Furthermore, federal aid could be used to clear the site because of its designation for urban renewal. After the city had acquired the land necessary to assemble the entire parcel, the city demolished the vacant warehouses and industrial buildings standing on it.

The facility was designed by Heery & Heery; engineered by Finch, Alexander, Barnes, Rothschild & Paschal; and built by Huber, Hunt & Nichols. The stadium is circular, with one section of movable seats that enables adaptation for either football or baseball. Stadium parking is located around the facility. Because of its location within the floodplain, the facility was built to be safe from water levels of up to 80 feet, the height of Cincinnati's great flood of 1937. Placement of the garage around the field and provision of a sealable entrance protect the stadium's interior space from flood damage.

Seating capacity at the stadium totals approximately 55,000 for baseball and 60,000 for football, on four levels. On-site parking totals 5,000 spaces, 3,200 of which are housed in the structured parking and 1,800 in lots surrounding the stadium. Additional parking is available on downtown streets and garages connected via skywalks to the stadium. These skywalks extend from the stadium into the core of the central business district, adjacent to the Lytle Park Historic District. Thanks to this feature, fans enjoy convenient access to retail shops, hotels, and eating and drinking establishments before and after games. Thus, the downtown parking facilities for the stadium have generated significant downtown economic activity.

Long-range plans for the vicinity now call for an upgrading of the Riverfront West area. At present, the area west of the stadium is the site of large produce distribution sheds. The city envisions developing a waterfront park bordered by residential and retail space, with recreational amenities farther inland. Proposed additions to the skywalk system would connect the stadium with this new development.

FINANCING

During the preliminary stage, financing for the proposed facility was provided through $44 million in stadium revenue bonds issued in 1967 by Hamilton County and backed by the city of Cincinnati's credit. To overcome the professional football and baseball owners' reluctance to commit themselves fully to Cincinnati's new stadium, the business community and the chamber of commerce worked together to raise money to continue design work while the financing was being obtained. For example, the city sought to allay controversy over possible traffic problems by financing new roadways to alleviate traffic congestion arising from the use of the stadium. Furthermore, Francis Dale, owner of the local newspaper, purchased the Cincinnati Reds and subsequently signed a 40-year lease agreement for the team. In the same year, the Cincinnati Bengals also signed a 40-year lease.

MARKETING AND MANAGEMENT

The facility's primary use is as the home field for the Cincinnati Reds and Bengals. It occasionally hosts other events. In a typical year, Riverfront Stadium hosts 81 Reds home games, eight regular-season and two preseason Bengals games, and five to eight other events, in-

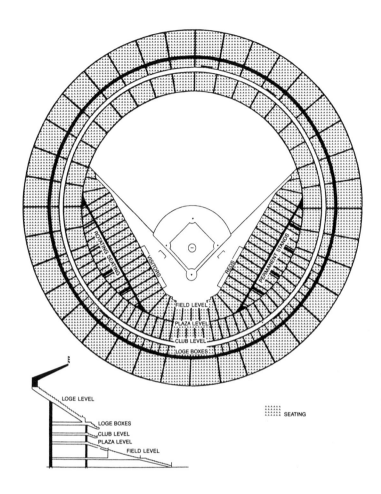

cluding the Kool Jazz Festival and several amateur football games.

The city's department of public utilities undertakes the management and upkeep of the facility, which is leased to the city by Hamilton County. Lease payments from the city to the county must cover the repayment of the bond issue. If the revenue from stadium operations cannot adequately cover this debt service, the city must provide the shortfall. In 1967, the city signed the 40-year leases with the Reds and Bengals mentioned above. Leases were to begin when each team occupied the stadium. Rent paid by the Reds is 7.5 percent of baseball gate receipts—excluding taxes and visiting team and league shares—with a yearly minimum of $175,000. Similarly, rent paid by the Bengals is 10 percent of football gate receipts, excluding taxes, with a minimum rent of $100,000.

LESSONS LEARNED

Riverfront Stadium offers valuable lessons in stadium development, particularly in its siting and construction:

- With regard to siting issues, the venue exemplifies the use of a public assembly facility for downtown revitalization. Located in what was once a dying industrial riverfront, the stadium has brought activity back to this district, connecting it with the heart of downtown through the use of skywalks. These skywalks not only provide access to additional parking but also increase the possibility of fans' using city restaurants and retail shops both before and after games, producing demand for downtown establishments beyond the work week and boosting the potential downtown economic impact.

- In general, use of the downtown beyond the workday has increased due to stadium usage. Further investment is now being made in the area that will encompass retail, residential, commercial, and park development. These projects, through the skywalks, will tie into the stadium, which was once the catalyst and now is a major anchor for upgrading the banks of the Ohio River.

- Another feature in which Riverfront Stadium offers a valuable lesson is parking. The innovative placement of a parking structure so that it adjoins and partially encircles the stadium solved the dual problem of the site's location within the river's floodplain and the limited amount of available land. Parking, used both on game days and leased for downtown employee parking during the work week, provides an extra source of revenue to the stadium, which receives a percentage of this income. In addition to being a revenue source, structured parking around the stadium reduces damage to the stadium from major floods and uses a minimal amount of space.

- The stadium and the surrounding development it has encouraged are very successful. The stadium design is ideal for neither baseball nor football, however, and despite measures to counteract this limitation, the facility still does not offer fans the sightlines and proximity to the field of play that contemporary standards demand.

PROJECT DATA

RIVERFRONT STADIUM
CINCINNATI, OH

Owner: Hamilton County
Builder: Huber, Hunt & Nichols, Inc., Indianapolis
Architect: Heery & Heery, Atlanta
Primary Users: Cincinnati Reds (baseball), Cincinnati Bengals (football)
Year Planning Began: 1967
Year Construction Began: 1968
Year Construction Completed: 1970

PROJECT INFORMATION
Site Area: 48 acres
Total Seating Capacity:
    Football: 60,000
    Baseball: 55,000
Total Parking Spaces: 5,000

ECONOMIC INFORMATION
Site Acquisition Cost: $3,245,996
Construction Costs: $32,693,136
Total Hard Costs (including site acquisition, site improvements, construction, and amenities): $35,939,132
Total Soft Costs: $8,060,868
Total Project Cost (1970 dollars): $44,000,000
Total Project Cost (1994 dollars):[1] $165,000,000
Funding Sources:
    Revenue Bonds (1970 dollars): $44,000,000

Note:
[1] Calculated based on consumer price index.

FARGODOME

FARGO, NORTH DAKOTA

When the FARGODOME opened in 1992, its opening marked the culmination of five years of work and a massive community effort led by Fargo Parks Superintendent Bob Johnson. Johnson had seen domes in other, comparable cities and thought that such a facility might benefit both the city of Fargo and North Dakota State University. He then spent six months presenting his concept to local service organizations and obtained the support needed to proceed with a financing plan. In 1988, voters approved a sales tax to fund the dome, and just short of four years later, the Fargodome opened its doors.

DEVELOPMENT STRATEGY

The dome's initial plan included an agricultural mall, plus a combination of fine arts center and swimming facility. Eventually, the plan was simplified into a dome in which football and other events could be held. Once the dome's location had been chosen, a steering committee was formed to begin a petition for a half-cent sales tax to finance the project. The committee, basing its plans on the Tacoma Dome near Seattle, proposed a 20,000-seat dome at a cost of $25 million. It was suggested that the construction be financed by the sales tax over a 20-year period.

In December 1988, voters approved what was actually an amendment to the city's home rule charter allowing the tax. In March 1989, the city commission created the Fargo Dome Authority to carry out the project. Wayne Bradley was chosen president of the authority. Sink Combs Dethlefs of Denver was hired as the administrative architect, to represent the city during construction.

Construction began with groundbreaking on April 26, 1990. A management contract with Ogden Allied Leisure Services of New York was approved soon after. Five Fargo firms were awarded the dome's construction contracts. By November 1990, officials had put the dome's price tag at $44 million. Later in the month, Roger Newton from Huntsville, Alabama, was hired as the Fargodome's first executive director.

DESIGN AND SITE ISSUES

The design of the dome was the joint effort of Sink Combs Dethlefs, Architects, and Triebwasser Helenske & Associates, Architects, as well as seven engineering groups, including Houston Engineering, Martin/Martin, and Hurst & Henrichs.

PROJECT DATA

FARGODOME
FARGO, ND

Owner: City of Fargo
Builder: Industrial Builders, Inc., Fargo
Architects: Sink Combs Dethlefs, PC, Architects, Denver;
   Triebwasser Helenske & Associates, Ltd., Architects,
   Fargo
Engineering: Houston Engineering, Fargo; Martin/Martin,
   Fargo; Hurst & Henrichs, Ltd., Fargo
Primary Users: North Dakota State University Bison
   (football), other college sports, concerts, family shows
Year Planning Began: 1988
Year Construction Began: 1990
Year Construction Completed: 1992

PROJECT INFORMATION

Site Area: 50 acres
Total GBA: 470,000 square feet
   Exhibition Space: 100,000 square feet
Seating Capacity:
   Football: 19,129
   Basketball: 8,600
Total Parking Spaces: 4,000

ECONOMIC INFORMATION

Site Acquisition Cost: $300,000
Construction Costs: $48,000,000
Total Project Cost (1992 dollars): $48,300,000
Total Project Cost (1994 dollars):[1] $50,200,000
Funding Sources: Half-cent sales tax on first $2,500 of
   any purchase, excluding food and food products;
   leases of ten private suites.
Amount Collected in Sales Taxes as of 1994: $22,000,000

Note:
[1] Calculated based on consumer price index.

Despite Johnson's original concept and despite its
name, the Fargodome does not have a domed roof. The
first major design change in the dome took place in June
1989, when the administrative architects recommended
that, rather than build a round, domed stadium, the city
erect a rectangular stadium with a Quonset roof (a semicircular, arching roof of corrugated metal insulated with
wood fiber). The Dome Authority approved the new
roof design in October. A construction milestone was
marked in December 1991 when the roof, which had
been built just above ground level, was lifted into place
by four hydraulic jacks.

The Fargo-Moorhead area sits on the bed of what
was once Lake Agassiz. Because this glacial lake bed is
too soft to bear the weight of the dome, supports were
dug 120 feet below the floor. This subsurface glacial drift
layer can withstand 12 tons of weight per square foot,
whereas the surface is limited to one ton per square foot.

A 50-acre location on the campus of North Dakota
State University (NDSU) was chosen, to combine the
business benefits of a stadium with the advantages of a
college campus. The dome is situated east of Interstate
29 and south of Hector International Airport. This site
provides access to existing hotels, restaurants, road systems, transportation, and utilities. Parking is available
for approximately 4,000 vehicles in six surrounding lots;
overflow for larger events is directed to NDSU campus
lots and adjacent streets, with traffic support provided
by the staff of the dome, NDSU, or the Fargo Police
Department, depending on the event.

The facility has 19,000 permanent seats and ten
private suites, each seating 16 people. Individual suites
are leased for five years at $20,000 per year. Two press
boxes can accommodate up to 240 media personnel. The
east-side box, which is a bi-level structure enclosed by
glass that can be opened and closed, is used primarily
for football, while the north-side booth will be used for
basketball and hockey. Live broadcasts are also made
possible by the ability to uplink to satellites. In addition,
there is a press lounge, darkroom, and meeting room one
level below the press boxes.

The style of the stadium is modeled on NFL standards, rather than on a collegiate design. Fans have access
to 13 concession stands on the concourse level and two
on the field level. Portable concession units are also used
when necessary.

FINANCING

After dropping the circular design, architects estimated
the stadium's cost at $32.8 million, nearly 10 percent
more than initial estimates. The city and architects later
reached an agreement under which the building would
cost $35.7 million because of a 5.5 percent administra-
tive architect's fee and $1 million in project add-ons. The
final development cost was actually $48 million. The city
of Fargo agreed to pay NDSU $301,000 upfront and
$1 per year to lease the site from January 1, 1990, to
December 31, 2089.

The half-cent sales tax went into effect on April 1,
1989, and will be collected through December 31, 2009.
More than $22 million had been collected as of Septem-

ber 1994. Other financing comes from the lease of the ten private suites.

MARKET ORIENTATION

The dome's target markets include events such as concerts, family shows, flat shows, and professional and amateur sports. In the first two years of operations, the facility hosted NDSU football, the Ice Capades, rodeos, trade shows, concerts, and an annual indoor fair. The dome's parking lots have been used by Ford and Pontiac for test drives, as well as by local car shows.

The dome became the new home of the NDSU Bison, winners of five NCAA Division II national football championships. This relationship is beneficial both for the Fargodome and for NDSU. The 1993–1994 contract between NDSU and the Dome Authority totaled $105,500, plus event-related expenses; the subsequent year's base increased to $147,500. The university is guaranteed access to the dome for 40 events per year, with football accounting for five to eight of these events. NDSU also uses the dome for graduation ceremonies.

The North Central Conference held its postseason basketball tournament in the dome in 1994.

LESSONS LEARNED

- The location choice for the dome was well planned. Its college campus setting has provided NDSU with a larger home stadium for its football team, thus affording the dome an anchor tenant. It is also conveniently situated just off the interstate near the area's international airport, which gives the dome access to existing hotels and restaurants, making it more attractive to out-of-town patrons.
- Traffic congestion occurs through the NDSU campus before and after events due to the high volume in peak periods. A new access road through the university was proposed in 1994 to alleviate this problem.
- The original lobby design did not take into account winter weather conditions. At present, spectators have to stand in line outside in inclement weather. A larger foyer is proposed to accommodate more patrons waiting to enter the dome.

HOUSTON ASTRODOME

HOUSTON, TEXAS

Opened in 1965, the Houston Astrodome represents the first enclosed, multipurpose stadium to be built in the United States. Originally conceived by Judge Roy Hofheinz, president of Houston's professional baseball team and former mayor of the city, the Astrodome was intended to accommodate the city's professional sports teams while protecting them and their fans from the area's seasonally hot and rainy weather conditions. Judge Hofheinz formed the Houston Sports Association (HSA) to manage the Astrodomain Complex, which consists of the Astrodome Stadium, the Astroarena Complex (8,000-seat arena and 150,000-square-foot exhibition hall), and the Astrohall Complex (550,000-square-foot exhibition hall and 75,000 square feet of meeting space). Located on 260 acres near the downtown, the Astrodomain Complex enjoys a prominent status among Houston's major developments.

DEVELOPMENT STRATEGY

The goal of the principals involved in developing the concept for the Astrodome was to provide a facility for professional teams that would "combat heat, cold, rain, and mosquitos," according to George Kirksey, vice president of the Houston Astros.[1] As mentioned above, Judge

Roy Hofheinz formed the HSA in the early 1960s and owned both the professional baseball team (Houston Astros) and the HSA until the late 1960s, when he sold both entities to the Ford Motor Credit Company. In 1979, the Ford Motor Credit Company sold the team and the HSA to John J. McMullan. The HSA has operated the stadium, exhibition hall, and baseball team since the Astrodome was completed in 1965 though Drayton McLane, Jr., purchased the HSA and the baseball team in November 1992 and the name of the company operating the Astrodome has been changed to Astrodome USA.

DESIGN AND SITE ISSUES

Because the Astrodome was the first enclosed stadium ever built, its designers had no prior experience to guide their efforts. The size of the facility and the unique development concept proved a challenge to the design team assembled for the project. Indeed, as construction proceeded, several problems arose with the design and the site. First, hinges connected to the columns supporting the dome's roof structure were adjusted due to the unforeseen forces of wind and temperature. Because of these forces, which cause expansion and contraction of the building, the dome roof is never actually hemispherical. Adjustments were required to diminish the effects of these forces on the stability of the structure.

The site, purchased by Harris County for $3 million, presented problems relating to soil consistency and drainage. Because the soil was not accommodating to the paving process, a new technique called lime stabilization was used. This lime surface treatment enabled the completion of the parking lot paving. Stormwater drainage problems were remedied by using additional pumps during construction.

The site's location, too, presented general problems for the development team. For instance, the area surrounding the site lacked an adequate road network to support the increased levels of traffic; the city and state joined efforts to remedy the problem. Also, the site was not connected to the city's sewer system, so holding tanks had to be built for use until the site could be connected. Although the construction process required such special solutions as these, the facility was completed nearly six months ahead of schedule.

Designed primarily to serve the needs of the city's professional baseball (Astros) and football (Oilers) teams, the Astrodome has a permanent seating capacity of some 55,000 for baseball, 62,000 for football, and 66,000 for concerts. The entire Astrodomain Complex covers 260 acres and includes 25,000 on-site parking spaces.

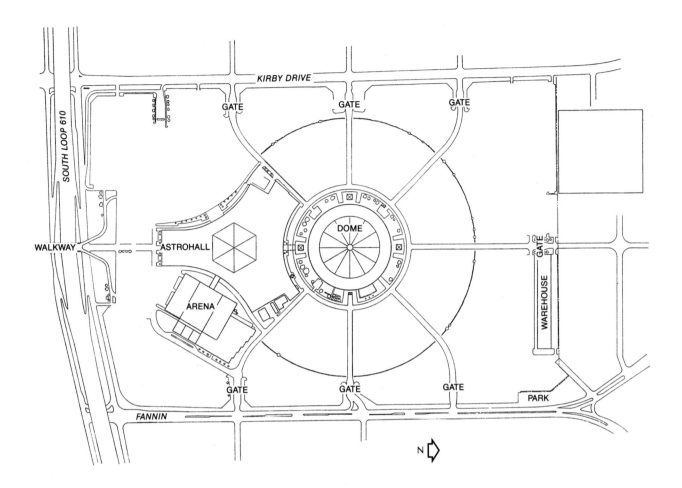

Several functional problems that first appeared after completion of the facility affected the performance of participants in sporting events. For example, the facility's transparent roof allowed sunlight into the building. Sunlight was necessary to allow a special variety of Bermuda grass to grow, but the glare of the light inhibited outfielders' vision while they were attempting to catch fly balls. After experimenting with sunglasses and orange baseballs, several coats of paint were applied to the skylights on the homeplate side of the dome. While this solved the glare problem, the grass began to die. In 1966, the Astrodome introduced an artificial turf developed by Monsanto Corporation, named AstroTurf, to replace the natural grass. Today, the stadium provides two separate turfs, one for baseball and one for football.

Financing

The Houston Astrodome was completed in April 1965, at a cost of approximately $35 million. Additionally, property owners contributed some $4 million in rights-of-way for roadways and a freeway, and the HSA spent $6 million for restaurants, skybox suites, a scoreboard, and the like. The total cost for all development expenses was slightly greater than $45 million.

There were four bond issues made to finance the stadium. The first, in the amount of $15 million, a second for $3 million, and a third for $4 million were issued in 1961. The fourth issue, of $9.6 million, was made in 1963. Thus, in total, the bond issues came to $31.6 million. Almost $1.4 million was accumulated through interest payments received while the bond funds were on deposit. Thus, the total available funds approximated $33 million. Additional expenses relating to off-site improvements were absorbed by the city and state.

The original rental agreement between the Astrodomain Corporation and Harris County was set at $750,000 per year for 20 years, with the rental figures reportedly based on 5 percent of the initial 1961 bonds issued ($15 million). Harris County is paying the debt service and costs on the other bonds.

The Houston Oilers committed to a ten-year lease arrangement with the HSA ending in 1997. Terms of the lease include agreements by HSA to increase the stadium's regular seating capacity by 10,000 and to build 72 luxury box suites, with 100 percent of HSA's lease revenues accruing to the team.

MARKET ORIENTATION

The Astrodome's current professional tenants include the Houston Oilers NFL franchise, the Houston Astros major league baseball team, and the Houston Livestock Show and Rodeo. The University of Houston football team plays home games in the facility as well.

In a typical year, the Astrodome accommodates nearly 200 events, including some 105 sporting events, five concerts, 20 family events, 35 conventions and trade shows, and 35 consumer/public shows. Before 1985, the Astrodome hosted the Blue Bonnet Bowl for college football. In August 1992, the Republican National Convention was held at the Astrodome.

LESSONS LEARNED

Architects, engineers, and contractors involved in the design and construction of the Astrodome have indicated that the development process went very smoothly, considering that this was the first structure of its type ever built. Each firm stated that the major reason for the project's success was the ability of several highly talented firms, in conjunction with the city and county, to work successfully together.

---

[1]"Take Me Out to the Ballpark," *Sporting News* (June 1985), p. 122.

PROJECT DATA
HOUSTON ASTRODOME[1]
HOUSTON, TX

Lessee: Astrodome USA
Developer: City of Houston and Harris County
Architect: Lloyd & Morgan, Houston; Wilson, Morris, Crain & Anderson, Houston
Primary Users: Houston Astros (baseball), Houston Oilers (football), Houston Livestock Show and Rodeo, University of Houston (football)
Year Planning Began: 1960
Year Construction Completed: 1965

PROJECT INFORMATION
Site Area: 260 acres[2]
Total Seating Capacity:
  Concerts: 66,000
  Football: 62,000
  Baseball: 55,000
Total Parking Spaces: 25,000

ECONOMIC INFORMATION
Site Acquisition Cost: $3,000,000
Total Hard Costs (including site acquisition, site improvements, construction, and amenities): $35,000,000
Total Project Cost (1960 dollars): $45,000,000
Total Project Cost (1994 dollars):[3] $221,655,000
Funding Sources:
  Bond Issue: $15,000,000
  Bond Issue (1961): $3,000,000
  Bond Issue (1961): $4,000,000
  Bond Issue (1963): $9,600,000
  Interest: $1,400,000
Total Bond Issues: $33,000,000

Notes:
[1]Part of the Astrodome Complex, which includes the Astrodome, the Astroarena, and Astrohall.
[2]Astrodome Complex.
[3]Calculated based on the consumer price index.

HARRY S TRUMAN SPORTS COMPLEX

ARROWHEAD AND KAUFFMAN STADIUMS

KANSAS CITY, MISSOURI

Arrowhead Stadium, with 79,000 seats, and Kauffman Stadium (formerly Royals Stadium), with 41,000 seats, form the Harry S Truman Sports Complex and are home to the NFL Kansas City Chiefs and the Kansas City Royals major league baseball team. Located southeast of downtown Kansas City, the complex is readily accessible via Interstates 70 and 435. The stadiums were built in the early 1970s, a period noted for the rapid growth in the number of sports facilities nationwide.

DEVELOPMENT STRATEGY

Before construction of the Truman Sports Complex, Kansas City's Municipal Stadium was the home of the Kansas City Athletics major league baseball team. Originally built in the 1920s with a capacity of 17,500, Mu-

nicipal Stadium was expanded in 1955 to 30,000 seats. The Dallas Texans, who became the Kansas City Chiefs, joined the Athletics at Municipal Stadium in 1963. The next year, however, the Athletics hesitated to renew their lease at Municipal Stadium, although they eventually signed a four-year lease after pressure from the league office.

Partly because of these lease negotiations, the Capital Improvements Commission, composed of local citizens, was recognized by Jackson County to identify capital improvement needs and costs for sports facilities in the county. It was this commission that first suggested the need for a new stadium. A feasibility study confirmed the desirability of a new stadium, though at that time a single, multipurpose stadium was envisioned.

In 1965, Maurice Dubiner (Jackson County Commissioner) succeeded in convincing Missouri's state legislature to create the Jackson County Sports Authority. This authority consists of five members nominated by the state legislature (three nominees for each position) and appointed by the governor. Each member serves a five-year term and can be renominated for a second term. Renomination is uncommon, however, because of the legislature's and governor's desire to maintain the authority as a vital and dynamic entity. The terms are staggered, so that one appointment is made annually. The authority, funded by Jackson County, was formed to oversee the site selection, design, construction, and leasing of the stadium and was empowered to issue bonds.

In 1967, the county issued voter-approved general obligation bonds that would, among other functions, provide financing for a new stadium. Despite this commitment to a new sports complex, at the end of the 1967 season the Athletics left Kansas City for Oakland, California.

Without a baseball team, Kansas City proceeded with its plans to build the sports complex. The lack of team input complicated the ballpark design process. In 1969, however, an expansion team was formed that would eventually use the baseball component of the complex. Named the Royals, this team also began play at the old Municipal Stadium, along with the Chiefs, who had continued to use that facility.

In 1970, the Jackson County Sports Authority issued revenue bonds, providing additional funding for the complex. The two teams were intimately involved in the development of their respective facilities and also participated in the financing. Through the combined efforts of the county, the authority, and the two tenant teams, the Harry S Truman Sports Complex became a reality. What had originally been conceived as one stadium evolved into two facilities, one for football and

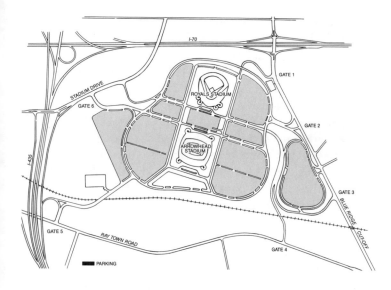

Parking

one for baseball; Arrowhead Stadium opened in 1972, and Royals (now Kauffman) Stadium opened in 1973.

DESIGN AND SITE ISSUES

The complex was designed by Charles Deaton, in conjunction with Kivett & Myers, and was built by a group headed by Sharp Kidd Webb. Arrowhead Stadium was the first professional facility designed exclusively for football. The complex's original design included a sliding roof that could be opened and closed over both stadiums. Because of construction and weather delays, however, cost overruns eliminated this feature.

The two stadiums, covering 12 acres each, were situated next to each other so that they could share common loading, infrastructure, and parking facilities, thus minimizing the cost of these to either stadium. The loading and infrastructure area is located between the two stadiums so that both have ready access to it. Surface parking surrounds the stadiums and provides spaces for 24,000 cars and 300 buses.

Those responsible for site selection considered a downtown site, as well as the current location at the intersection of Interstate 70 and the Blue Ridge Extension Road. The current site was selected for its excellent road access and for the amount of undeveloped land available for infrastructure and parking at a lower cost per acre than it would be on a downtown site. This site originally totaled 270 acres. Additional land has been purchased to bring the current acreage to approximately 500 acres.

Arrowhead Stadium has a seating capacity of some 79,000, including 80 luxury suites, which lease on a four-year basis for $18,000 to $55,000 annually, and 2,000

club seats. Kauffman Stadium seats about 41,000 fans. The stadium has 19 suites, which lease at $30,000 to $40,000 per year, and 200 club seats.

FINANCING

In 1967, a general obligation bond issue was approved by Jackson County voters in the amount of $102 million. Of this amount, $43 million was assigned to the construction of the sports complex. An additional $13 million revenue bond issue was produced by the Jackson County Sports Authority in 1970 and combined with the general obligation bond funds. These were secured by revenue from the lease of the facilities to the Chiefs and the Royals. Lamar Hunt, owner of the Chiefs, guaranteed a portion of the Chiefs' minimal annual lease payments.

The $14 million balance of the approximately $70 million total project cost was provided by the teams in the form of improvements to their individual stadiums. These improvements included the scoreboards and much of the finishing, such as box suites and a large, elaborate fountain at Kauffman Stadium.

MARKET ORIENTATION

The two facilities exist primarily for the use of their professional team tenants. The Kansas City Chiefs first used Arrowhead Stadium in 1972, the year of its opening, and the Royals began playing in their stadium a year later. In addition to their regular eight-game seasons, plus two preseason home games for the Chiefs and 81 regular-season home games for the Royals, the complex hosts

additional sports and entertainment events. These events are held primarily at Arrowhead Stadium and include concerts, motorcross, tractor pulls, industrial shows, and college and high-school football games.

The teams pay the authority a percentage of gross receipts plus a base rent. All expenses resulting from operations are paid by the Chiefs and/or the Royals; each team manages its respective stadium. Structural repairs are undertaken by the authority.

LESSONS LEARNED

- Arrowhead Stadium, as the first professional venue designed specifically for football, offered optimal sightlines, seating arrangements, and overall stadium configurations that have greatly enhanced the fans' experience.
- A roof, originally planned to cover both stadiums, is now considered impractical. A rolling roof is not feasible and could not adequately contain cooled or heated air.
- The positioning of the football stadium next to the baseball stadium allowed the sharing of some improvements, such as loading areas and parking. The costs of these improvements, therefore, were borne by both stadiums, reducing the cost of the infrastructure to each.
- The parking, which is shared by both facilities, has proved limited for large crowds. Arrowhead Stadium's manager recommends that it would have been appropriate to count on a ratio of one car per 2.5 to 3.0 spectators. Based on this ratio, the now-available space is slightly less than sufficient for Arrowhead.
- Another important decision in the development process allowed the teams to manage their own stadiums. The concept of a joint effort between a public entity—in this case, the owner, Jackson County—and a team or teams was a departure from the more traditional arrangement at the time, in which the owner and operator of a given stadium were one and the same.

PROJECT DATA

HARRY S TRUMAN SPORTS COMPLEX
ARROWHEAD AND KAUFFMAN STADIUMS
KANSAS CITY, MISSOURI

Owner: Jackson County Sports Authority, Jackson County, Missouri
Developer/Builder: Sharp Kidd Webb, Kansas City, Missouri
Architects: Charles Deaton, Golden, Colorado, with Kivett & Myers (merged with HNTB), Kansas City, Missouri
Primary Users: Kansas City Chiefs (football), Kansas City Royals (baseball)
Year Planning Began: 1965
Year Construction Began: 1967
Year Construction Completed:
    Arrowhead Stadium: 1972
    Kauffman Stadium: 1973

PROJECT INFORMATION
Site Area: 500 acres[1]
Total Seating Capacities:
    Arrowhead Stadium: 79,000
    Kauffman Stadium: 41,000
Parking Spaces:
    Cars: 24,000
    Buses: 300 buses

ECONOMIC INFORMATION
Site Acquisition Cost: $9,567,000
Construction Costs: $35,115,000
Total Hard Costs (including site acquisition, site improvements, construction, and amenities): $44,682,000
Total Soft Costs: $11,318,000
Total Project Costs: $70,000,000
Funding Sources:
    General Obligation Bonds (1967): $43,000,000
    Revenue Bonds (1970): $13,000,000
    Contributions from Royals and Chiefs: $14,000,000

Note:
[1] Each stadium covers 12 acres.

LOS ANGELES COLISEUM

LOS ANGELES, CALIFORNIA

For more than 70 years, the Los Angeles Coliseum has been the site of major sports and cultural events. Home to the University of Southern California Trojans (football), this 93,000-seat stadium is located west of Interstate 110, adjacent to the USC campus. Designated a state and federal historic landmark, the Coliseum has helped shape the sports and cultural history of southern California and has played an important role in the history of spectator entertainment in the United States.

DEVELOPMENT STRATEGY

The Los Angeles Coliseum site was originally dedicated for public use in the 1870s. First named Exposition Park, the site was later developed as a horse racetrack. The track proved to be so popular with students at the University of Southern California that a USC law professor and a city councilman joined forces to close the track, arguing

that it was an undesirable influence upon the young men of USC. City Councilman William Bowen believed that the 90-acre site should instead be available for use by the general public. In 1908, the city, county, and state joined in the commitment to develop the property. Although specific types of development were not identified, a stadium had been suggested. The president of USC asserted that if a stadium were built, the USC team would play there.

In 1919, the movement to build a stadium in Los Angeles gained momentum when the California Fiesta Association, a public group formed to revive the old Spanish atmosphere of Los Angeles, agreed upon the importance of building a city stadium. To be called the Los Angeles Memorial Colosseum (later changed to Coliseum) and located in Exposition Park, the stadium was to be a factor in the City Beautiful movement popular in Los Angeles at the time. Part of the nationwide City Beautiful movement stimulated by the World's Columbian Exposition of 1893, Los Angeles's City Beautiful movement prompted the beginning of urban planning here. Later in 1919, John Parkinson, a key figure in the movement, began preliminary design work on the stadium, providing his first year of services at no charge.

By 1921, financing for the Coliseum had been obtained by the Community Development Association (CDA), a nonprofit group formed to oversee the construction and management of the facility. During the same year, the municipal art commission approved Parkinson's design for the Coliseum, and a construction agreement was signed that involved the city, county, state, lending banks, architects, and contractors. A lease was also signed for 17 acres in an abandoned gravel pit at the south end of Exposition Park, and construction of the Los Angeles Coliseum began on December 21, 1921.

The Coliseum was completed in May 1923. During the same year, it was selected to host the 1932 Olympic Games and as a result was enlarged from its original 76,000 seats to 105,000, in an expansion made between February 1930 and May 1931.

By the 1970s, the Coliseum's capacity had been reduced to 93,000 because of a change from the original bench-style seating to individual seats in all locations except the east end zone and the peristyle.

DESIGN AND SITE ISSUES

Exposition Park had been a focus of Los Angeles entertainment activity since before the turn of the century. Because of its location next to USC, the stadium had the commitment of the university to use its field for Trojan football games, a promise that proved crucial to the CDA's ability to obtain financing for construction. In keeping with the City Beautiful movement, the site was also planned to include a museum and exposition hall that would expand its use to include a recreational and cultural center. Today, in addition to the Coliseum, Exposition Park is composed of the Los Angeles Sports Arena, California Museum of Science and Industry, Los Angeles County Natural History Museum, California Afro-American Museum, and Exposition Park Rose Garden.

The Coliseum was built by Edwards, Widley & Dixon Company. The original elevation contained a triumphal arch surrounded by seven smaller arches at the east peristyle. The remainder of the building's exterior consists of a series of panels and pilasters on an earth-berm base. This berm, the result of the stadium's placement within a gravel pit, helped lower costs. Shaped as an ellipse, the Coliseum was formed with cast-in-place reinforced concrete. Some modifications to the original design have been made in adapting the venue for the two Olympiads (1932 and 1984) and for NFL football.

The facility's original structure was built at a cost of some $955,000. The 1931 expansion, also designed by the Parkinson team, cost $950,000. With the addition of a scoreboard, theater-type seats, remodeled concession stands, and other modernizations, the cost of the facility through 1979 had approached $9.5 million. Additional improvements to the concession areas for the 1984 Olympics increased the total construction costs to $11.1 million.

Former tenants, the NFL Raiders, had negotiated a loan agreement with the Los Angeles Memorial Coliseum Commission construct box suites at the facility. Construction began but was stopped, pending litigation between the Raiders and the Coliseum commission and pending the Raiders' proposed move from the Coliseum to Irwindale. Suggestions were also made to reduce the number of seats and to make seating more appropriate

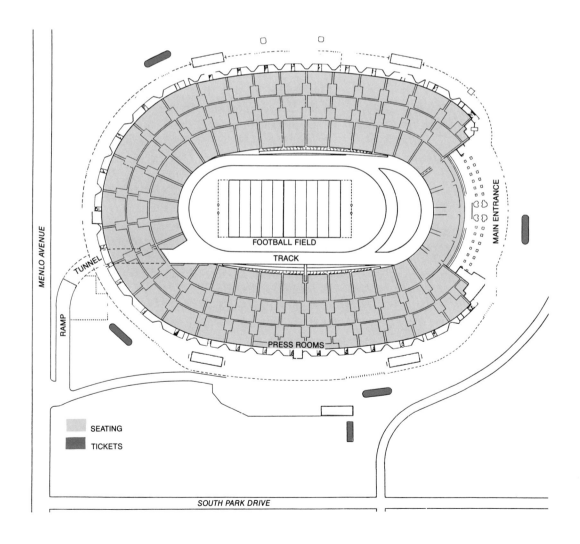

SEATING

TICKETS

MENLO AVENUE

RAMP

TUNNEL

FOOTBALL FIELD

TRACK

MAIN ENTRANCE

PRESS ROOMS

SOUTH PARK DRIVE

for football viewing by providing two levels of seats, the second cantilevered over the first. These design changes would have reduced the distance between the field and the upper rows of seating, thereby improving spectator sightlines. Additionally, by reducing its seating capacity, the Coliseum would have been easier to sell out for professional football thereby increasing television revenues from local broadcasts. These improvements have not been made because the Raiders have relocated to Oakland.

FINANCING

The Coliseum's original construction was financed through private funding provided by 14 banks. A loan of $800,000 was obtained at a rate of 6 percent, 1 percent below what was then the market rate. Financing and miscellaneous

expenses brought the total cost to some $955,000. Expansion of the facility for the 1932 Olympics was financed through a $1 million bond issued in 1927 and through aid from the city and county of Los Angeles. Throughout the years, financing for additional construction has been obtained from a variety of sources. For instance, the scoreboard, added in 1972, was sponsored by American Airlines and ARCO. Improvements and expansion of the Coliseum's concession facilities, ownership of which eventually reverts to the Coliseum, were financed partly by the concessionaires.

Operations are currently overseen by the Los Angeles Memorial Coliseum Commission, which was formed in 1955 and which also supervises the operations of the Los Angeles Sports Arena. Both facilities lease land from the California Museum of Science and Industry for $80,000 annually on a lease that runs through the year 2006. At that time, a new lease may be negotiated based upon the relative property value in the year 2003 compared with that of 1956, the year in which the commission's first lease was originated.

MARKET ORIENTATION

On October 6, 1923, the first football game was played at the Coliseum between the University of Southern California and Pomona College. Although the stadium's capacity was approximately 76,000 at the time, the crowd only approached 13,000. This was the beginning of a longstanding relationship between the Trojans and the Coliseum.

In 1946, the Cleveland Rams moved to Los Angeles, heralding the advent of professional football at the Coliseum. The first of a series of professional sports teams to move to southern California, the Rams were followed by the Dodgers (baseball), who played at the Coliseum for their first four years in Los Angeles before moving to Dodger Stadium in 1962. In 1960, the Coliseum was home to the newly formed American Football League's Chargers before their move to San Diego in the following year. The Rams moved to Anaheim Stadium in 1979—a move that made room for the Raiders, who came from Oakland to the Coliseum in 1982. The Raiders moved back to Oakland in 1995.

Today, the Coliseum is home to the USC football team. The facility has been host to myriad football-related events, among them Super Bowls, NFL conference championships, and NFL championships (before the merger of the National Football League with the American Football League). For 22 years, the Coliseum

PROJECT DATA

LOS ANGELES COLISEUM
LOS ANGELES, CA

Owner: City of Los Angeles
Developer/Builder: Edwards, Widley & Dixon Company, Los Angeles
Architect: John & Donald Parkinson, Los Angeles
Primary Users: University of Southern California Trojans (football)
Year Planning Began: 1919
Year Construction Began: 1921
Year Construction Completed: 1923
Year Expansion Completed: 1931

PROJECT INFORMATION
Site Area: 17 acres
Total Seating Capacity: 93,000
Total Parking Spaces:
  On-Site: 6,000
  Nearby: 10,000

ECONOMIC INFORMATION
Site Acquisition Cost: $80,000 annually[1]
Construction Costs:
  Original Facility: $955,000
  Expansion: $950,000
Funding Sources:
  Bank Loan (1921): $800,000
  Bond Issue (1927): $1,000,000

Note:
[1]Leased from the California Museum of Science and Industry.

was also the host of the NFL's Pro Bowl. In addition to football, the Coliseum has accommodated a variety of other events, many of which have figured among the 20th century's major sports and cultural events, including two Olympic Games and a papal mass.

Facility operations are financed through rent paid by the Trojans and special events.

LESSONS LEARNED

Enduring since the 1920s, the Los Angeles Coliseum is an example of a facility that has adapted and continues to adapt to the changing needs of its tenants and fans. The stadium has the distinction of being the only facility in America to host two Olympiads, in addition to hosting professional and collegiate football, baseball, motocross, concerts, soccer, and other sports. The seating arrangement has been changed, concession stands renovated, and scoreboards added in efforts to maintain the facility as a modern venue. Following are some instructive points that can be made regarding the Coliseum's long history:

■ A joint venture among municipal, county, and state entities, each with representatives on the commis-

sion, oversaw the building of the Coliseum and still runs it. This venture exemplifies a successful coordination of government bodies for the benefit of the general public.

■ The joint effort, however, limits the flexibility of management with regard to operations and capital improvements. No single government is accountable; hence, the essential maintenance of the facility is hindered.

■ The commission has no fundraising power to finance major improvements. Because the facility is self-supporting, however, some improvements can be funded by stadium management.

LOUISIANA SUPERDOME

NEW ORLEANS, LOUISIANA

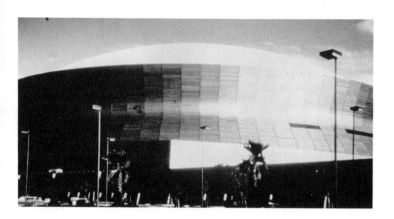

The Louisiana Superdome is the largest enclosed multipurpose facility for mass-audience events in the world. Sited in downtown New Orleans, the 76,000-seat, enclosed stadium opened in 1975. David Dixon, a New Orleans businessman, is credited with conceiving the idea for the Superdome to entice professional football to New Orleans. Former Governor John McKeithen supported Dixon's proposal, and in November 1966, the voters of Louisiana passed a constitutional amendment to build the Superdome.

DEVELOPMENT STRATEGY

As a result of the stadium issue's success at the polls, the state formed the Louisiana Stadium and Exposition District to develop the project, and David Dixon was named its executive director. To assist in the development process, an advisory committee composed of the deans of the Tulane University Architectural School, the Louisiana State University (LSU) Engineering School, and the LSU School of Environmental Studies was established. The Gulf South Research Institute prepared a feasibility study that recommended specific building program requirements, such as sizing, configuration, and ancillary support services, and that specified the preferred location of the facility, namely, downtown New Orleans.

DESIGN AND SITE ISSUES

The Superdome's design was indeed a challenge to the architects, engineers, and development team, a joint venture among principal designers Curtis & Davis Associates, Architects; Edward B. Silverstein & Associates, Architects; Norman, Nolan & Nolan, Architects; and Sverdrup & Parcel Associates, Engineers. The facility has a 13-acre building footprint. Construction required 169,000 cubic yards of concrete, 20,000 tons of structural steel, 15,200 lighting fixtures, 400 miles of interior wiring, and 9,000 tons of HVAC equipment.

Because of the high water table in New Orleans, just five feet below grade, the foundation and structural supports for the dome required innovative design techniques. The playing field could not be located below street level, as in many stadiums, so pedestrian ramps were needed for fans to use in entering the stadium. Rainwater drainage proved to be a problem as well. The Superdome's 9.7-acre roof is washed with an enormous amount of rainwater during periods of heavy rain. The large runoff from the roof was a flooding problem for the site, but designers solved it with a system of gutter tubs positioned on the roof's edge; the tubs have a 345,000-gallon capacity, so that stormwater can drain gradually.

The Superdome's roof is the largest clear-span steel structure in the world. Its construction required the use of 37 scaffolds in concentric circles, along with mobile cranes. Structurally, the roof is vital to the Superdome's design, as it quite simply holds the building together. The walls of the building literally hang from the roof, with the force vectors at the foundation level pointing away from the center. A 75-ton gondola with a 124-foot diameter hangs from the center of the roof, strategically placed to provide stability against upward forces.

Most of the steel roof deck was lifted into place by helicopter, in a process considered unique at the time. The roof is covered with an inch-thick layer of polyurethane topped by a layer of hypalon, a synthetic waterproofing substance that was applied using a special procedure that protected the spraying process from the wind and sun. The roof coating process took 162 days.

Flexibility is one of the distinctive characteristics that allows the Superdome to accommodate a variety of events. In an arena configuration, its seating capacity ranges from 10,000 to 40,000. As a stadium, the Super-

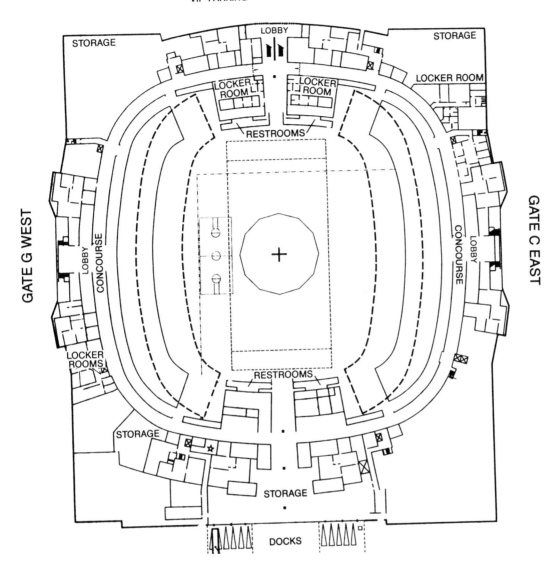

VIP PARKING

STORAGE

LOBBY

STORAGE

LOCKER ROOM

LOCKER ROOM

LOCKER ROOM

RESTROOMS

GATE G WEST

LOBBY

CONCOURSE

CONCOURSE

LOBBY

GATE C EAST

LOCKER ROOMS

RESTROOMS

STORAGE

STORAGE

DOCKS

dome has three seating capacities: 69,971 (regular football); 72,582 (expanded football); and 63,515 (baseball). Maximum capacity for general assemblies (i.e., political conventions) is 85,000 seats, including temporary seating on the main floor. The facility contains 77,000 square feet of meeting space as well. The total area it traditionally uses for exhibitions and consumer shows is some 166,000 square feet, comprising the stadium-floor level.

After several available sites had been reviewed, a 52-acre downtown location was selected. A primary reason for the selection of the downtown site was the lower cost of the land, which had only a deteriorating freight yard on it at the time. Also, the infrastructure necessary to support the Superdome was already in place at this location. The site within the central business district gave access to existing major hotels, restaurants, road systems, communication networks, public transit systems, and utilities. Development of 5,000 on-site parking spaces became an asset to the downtown by providing daily parking for office employees. The Superdome's garages are available on weekdays as part of the CBD shuttle bus system, which links downtown retail and tourism areas to most of New Orleans's major hotels.

FINANCING

The Superdome was financed with a $163 million package of private bonds offered by the state of Louisiana in three original phases totaling $137.5 million. A $16.5

on rooms in Orleans Parish and a 2 percent hotel/motel tax in Jefferson Parish supported the bond issue.

In 1976, Louisiana's legislature authorized a reissue of $134 million to pay the balance on the original issues at a lower interest rate. The remaining outstanding bonds, amounting to $50 million, were again refinanced in April 1994. At the same time, Louisiana's legislature also approved $150 million for new facilities to be financed through hotel taxes, much as the Superdome was. Of this amount, $20 million is reserved for dome renovations. Various improvements will be made, including refurbishment of present seating, concessions, and restrooms, plus additional amenities and access for disabled patrons.

MARKET ORIENTATION

The Superdome's major sports tenants include the New Orleans Saints (NFL) and Tulane University's football and basketball teams (NCAA). The dome was home court to the NBA's New Orleans Jazz until the team's move to Utah. The Superdome has hosted three Super Bowls (it will host Super Bowl XXXI in 1997) and three NCAA Division I Final Four basketball championships. Each year, the Nokia Sugar Bowl Classic and Bayou Classic college football games are held at the Superdome.

In a typical year, the Superdome attracts about 100 spectator events, including some 35 sporting events, five concerts, ten family shows, 45 large assemblies and trade shows, and 15 consumer/public shows. Large gatherings have included the 1987 papal visit, which was attended by 80,000 people, and the 1988 Republican National Convention.

Twice, the Superdome has set all-time attendance records, for the NCAA Division I Final Four championships in 1982 and 1987. Other records held by the Superdome include the world's largest one-night indoor concert crowd (87,500 for a Rolling Stones concert in 1981) and the most tickets sold for a college basketball game (68,112 for an LSU game against Notre Dame in 1990).

Although owned by the state, the Superdome is operated through a private management contract with Spectacor Management Group (SMG). The dome was the first public facility to be operated by private management.

LESSONS LEARNED

Key individuals involved in the development of the Superdome attribute its success to two crucial factors, timing and strong political support:

million bond issue was sold on May 5, 1970, to defray the costs of preparing plans and specifications for the site and project, the site costs, and land preparation expenses. A second issue for $113 million was authorized by a district resolution in March 1971, and a final issue for $8 million was sold in February 1974. Additional financing was derived from interest on the bond issue during the construction period. A 4 percent hotel/motel tax levied

- The movement to develop the Superdome benefited from the healthy economic conditions in New Orleans and Louisiana that ensued from the oil boom of the early 1970s. Because Louisiana's economy was surging, an aggressively prodevelopment attitude arose among its constituents.
- Additionally, the city and state provided vigorous support for the project. The governor of Louisiana backed the project's concept immediately, and his leadership enabled the developers to gather the political support needed for a project of this magnitude.

PROJECT DATA

LOUISIANA SUPERDOME
NEW ORLEANS, LA

Owner: Louisiana Stadium and Exposition District
Builder: Huber, Hunt & Nichols, Inc., Indianapolis; Blount Brothers, Birmingham
Architects: Curtis & Davis Associates, Architects, New Orleans; Edward B. Silverstein & Associates, Architects, New Orleans; Norman, Nolan & Nolan, Architects, New Orleans; Sverdrup & Parcel Associates, Engineers, St. Louis
Primary Users: New Orleans Saints (football), Tulane University (football and basketball), Nokia Sugar Bowl Classic, Bayou Classic, Super Bowl, Final Four (basketball), other college sports, family shows, concerts, trade shows, consumer shows, and conventions
Year Planning Began: 1966
Year Construction Began: 1971
Year Construction Completed: 1975

PROJECT INFORMATION

Site Area: 52 acres
Total GBA: 13 acres (566,280 square feet)
    Exhibition Space: 166,000 square feet
    Meeting Space: 77,000 square feet
Seating Capacity:
    Sports Events: 72,582
    General Assemblies: 85,000
Total Parking Spaces: 5,000

ECONOMIC INFORMATION

Site Acquisition Cost: $2,400,000
Construction Costs:[1] $107,000,000
Total Soft Costs:[2] $54,000,000
Total Project Cost (1975 dollars): $163,000,000
Total Project Cost (1994 dollars): $448,979,032
Funding Sources (1975 dollars): $137,500,000
    Bond Issue (1970): $16,500,000
    Bond Issue (1971): $113,000,000
    Bond Issue (1974):[3] $8,000,000
Funding Sources for Renovations:
    Bond Issue (1994)[3]: $20,000,000

Notes:
[1]Includes general contract, $98 million; seating, $5 million; scoreboards, etc., $2.5 million; and miscellaneous, $1.5 million.
[2]Includes architectural/engineering fees, $10 million; and financing, legal fees, FFE, and contingencies, $44 million.
[3]Supported by a 4 percent hotel/motel tax.

JOE ROBBIE STADIUM

DADE COUNTY, FLORIDA

Joe Robbie Stadium, situated on the northern edge of Dade County, Florida, is the home of the Miami Dolphins National Football League and Florida Marlins major league baseball teams. The 75,000-seat, open-air stadium opened in August 1987. Joe Robbie, the Dolphins' original owner, privately financed the construction of the stadium on land leased from Dade County. The stadium features 216 executive suites, more than 61,000 general seats, and 10,209 club seats. Successful preselling of the suites and club seats enabled Robbie to convince lenders to back the project. Robbie also equipped the stadium with 40 permanent concession stands, eight ramps for patron access, ten elevators (five for club seats and executive suites only, with more planned), and two Sony JumboTron giant video boards for instant replay and advertising.

DEVELOPMENT STRATEGY

Ever since the Dolphins began as a new franchise in 1965, Miami's Orange Bowl had served as the team's home stadium. During the 1970s, Robbie became increasingly dissatisfied with the physical condition of the Orange

Bowl and with the city's efforts to refurbish and renovate the 75,000-seat stadium, which was built in 1937.

Joe Robbie retained the architectural firm of Hellmuth, Obata & Kassabaum (HOK) to design a new $115-million stadium, which has since been characterized as the prototype for future stadium projects in terms of design features and financing techniques. Groundbreaking for the facility took place in 1985.

On March 7, 1990, H. Wayne Huizenga, chairman of the board and chief executive officer of Blockbuster Video and Huizenga Holdings, Inc., agreed to purchase 50 percent of Joe Robbie Stadium and became the main sponsor in the drive to bring major league baseball to Florida. That effort was rewarded in July 1991, when southern Florida was awarded a major league baseball franchise.

DESIGN

The introduction of the Florida Marlins in 1993 created the need to install movable seats to reconfigure the stadium for baseball. Huizenga provided the capital for the needed changes. Although the stadium was designed to be adaptable for baseball, the extra cost for the movable seats was not incurred at the time of the original construction. Mechanisms include a section of 6,400 seats that fold away to become the backdrop for a manually operated baseball scoreboard, covering 5,500 square feet; a hydraulically controlled pitcher's mound that lowers under the football field; and a baseball bull pen and dugout that were developed in the corner of a football end zone. Conversion of the Dolphins' stadium into the Marlins' ballpark requires a 12-hour changeover time.

On January 24, 1994, Huizenga acquired a controlling interest in the Dolphins and the remaining 50 percent of Joe Robbie Stadium, to give him 100 percent ownership. Under his direction, the stadium is now in the final stages of an $18 million facelift that will further enhance the experience of stadium guests.

The emphasis of the stadium design is on fan comfort. Each seat is a self-rising theater-style chair with arm rests, a back, and a cupholder. Executive suites, built for $7 million, feature seating for ten, 12, or 16 persons. Leasing a suite for the football season costs from $30,000 to $80,000 per year on a ten-year lease.

SITE ANALYSIS

The stadium occupies a 143-acre parcel in northern Dade County, one mile south of the Broward County

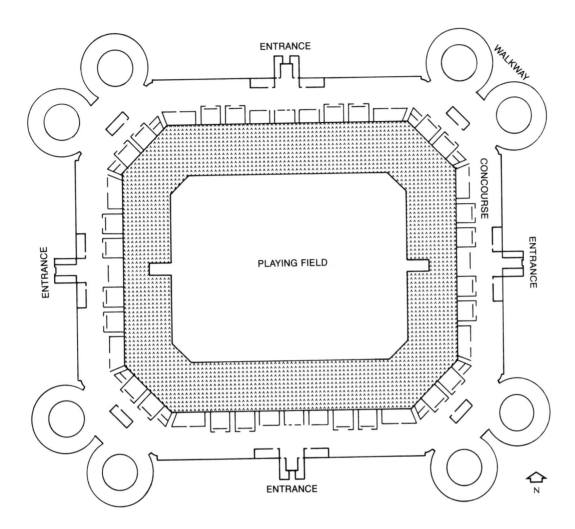

line. The site was owned by Miami Beach developers Emil and Laurence Morton, who diverted the property to Dade County, which in turn declared it park property. The county then leased the parcel to Joe Robbie for $1 per year on a 99-year lease. Although the site's position north of the Dolphins' former home, the Orange Bowl, might have seemed a drawback, the majority of Dolphins season-ticket holders live in north Dade or south Broward County.

FINANCING

The most significant element in the development of Joe Robbie Stadium was the method of financing used to construct it. No public monies were used; the facility and site improvements were completed with private funds alone. Robbie, using deposits for executive and club seats totaling $9 million as collateral, attempted to entice a consortium of banks to back his project. He was not entirely

successful, however, until he pledged the Dolphins franchise as security for the completion of construction. With the banks' backing, $83 million was raised through a 30-year issue of industrial revenue bonds.

MARKET ORIENTATION

Joe Robbie Stadium is scheduled to host all ten Dolphins regular-season home games and all 81 Florida Marlins regular-season home games. The stadium was the site of Super Bowl XXIII in 1989 and Super Bowl XXIX in 1995. The Carquest Bowl, an NCAA-sanctioned football game, is also played at Joe Robbie Stadium. The Orange Bowl game will move to Joe Robbie Stadium in January 1997, leaving the University of Miami Hurricanes as the last football tenant in the older venue.

Three locker rooms were included in the stadium design to accommodate the University of Miami football team, should it decide to leave the Orange Bowl. The

PROJECT DATA

JOE ROBBIE STADIUM
DADE COUNTY, FL

Owner: Robbie Stadium Corporation
Developer: Joe Robbie
Architect: Hellmuth, Obata & Kassabaum (HOK),
    Kansas City, Missouri
Primary User: Miami Dolphins (football), Florida
    Marlins (baseball)
Period When Planning Began: 1970s
Year Construction Began: 1985
Year Construction Completed: 1987

PROJECT INFORMATION
Site Area: 143 acres
Total Seating Capacity:
    Football: 74,916
    Baseball: 47,662
Total Parking Spaces: 20,000

ECONOMIC INFORMATION
Total Project Cost (1987 dollars): $115,000,000[1]
Total Project Cost (1994 dollars):[2] $147,600,000

Notes:
[1]Not including the 1992 refurbishment in preparation for the
Marlins.
[2]Calculated based on the consumer price index.

stadium has accommodated soccer, motor-sport races, NCAA games, and major concerts. In addition to these events, the stadium hosts trade shows and community-based events, including the largest scout show in the country, sponsored by the South Florida Council of the Boy Scouts of America. One of the stadium's most memorable events was a 15-hour entertainment marathon, "Comic Relief," in 1992. During that event, headlined by singer Gloria Estefan, over $2 million was raised for southern Florida residents whose homes had been destroyed by Hurricane Andrew.

LESSONS LEARNED

Joe Robbie demonstrated that a stadium could be built and financed completely with private funds, though it is unlikely that many other franchise owners will be willing to forgo the public subsidies available for new venues. Nonetheless, Robbie's project set the standard for premium seating as the cornerstone of the sports stadiums and arenas built after 1987.

The items that the stadium's owners list under the heading "if we had it to do over again" include the following:

- There are only 14,970 reserved parking spaces on the site, a considerable amount of on-site capacity compared with other stadiums around the league. However, unlike the situation of most other stadiums, off-site parking is limited, and fans without reserved spaces have had problems. Two auxiliary lots to the east and west have been added that can accommodate 5,000 cars. Also, two more sites to the south are being acquired.
- Traffic jams have developed at Dolphins games because of limited access roads to the stadium. To lessen parking problems and traffic congestion, stadium officials have urged fans to use public transportation to and from stadium events. At present, both Broward County and Metro Dade transit agencies provide shuttle bus service from local park-and-ride facilities to the stadium. The stadium has also enlisted the services of traffic consultants to make further improvements in the traffic flow.

HUBERT H. HUMPHREY METRODOME

MINNEAPOLIS, MINNESOTA

The Hubert H. Humphrey Metrodome, named after the former U.S. senator and vice president, stands in downtown Minneapolis. The Metrodome, with a total area of 470,840 square feet, is the largest air-supported, multiple-use stadium in the world. It is also the first nearly rectangular domed stadium and features movable seating to provide sightlines for both football and baseball. The stadium is the regular-season home of the Minnesota Twins major league baseball team, the National Football League's Minnesota Vikings, and the University of Minnesota's Big Ten football team, the Golden Gophers.

DEVELOPMENT STRATEGY

The motivating force behind the development of this facility was the fact that, when the Minnesota Twins' and Vikings' leases expired in 1975, franchise management stated that the teams would leave Minnesota if a domed stadium was not provided. Both the Twins and the Vikings had to agree to a 30-year lease renewal if a domed facility was built.

When the state legislature authorized the construction of a new stadium in 1977, its mandate called for a reasonably priced, multipurpose, domed facility flexible enough to accommodate virtually every type of sporting event. The Minnesota legislature also established the Metropolitan Sports Commission in 1977 to oversee the development of the new facility and to serve as the owner and operator of the new stadium. The commission was made up of seven people representing the state of Minnesota and appointed by the governor.

The state of Minnesota conducted a study to determine the dome's monetary impact and to examine suitable development sites. The study concluded that the downtown site had the most to offer with regard to shopping, restaurants, and hotel accommodations. Also, the downtown site was expected to incur much lower construction costs because the water table was located well below the surface, as opposed to only 20 feet below ground level at the site of the existing stadium in Bloomington. After considering additional sites, the commission voted 4 to 3 to build the stadium in downtown Minneapolis.

Groundbreaking took place on December 20, 1979, and the dome opened on April 3, 1982, with an exhibition game between the Twins and the Philadelphia Phillies.

DESIGN AND SITE ISSUES

The stadium was designed and built with a $75 million budget. The total playing field encompasses 142,515 square feet, and the facility has a seating capacity of 63,000 for football and 55,000 for baseball. One of the commission's prime objectives in developing the Metrodome was to maintain the facility's flexibility to host a variety of events. One step in that direction was the purchase of portable seating, enabling the stadium to convert from a 63,000-seat football stadium into a 36,000-seat arena for events such as basketball, wrestling, and concerts.

The dome, at its peak, is 195 feet (16 stories) from the AstroTurf floor, compared with 208 feet in Houston's Astrodome and 250 feet in Seattle's Kingdome. Like other domes built in the early 1980s, the Metrodome features an air-supported, translucent fiberglass-fabric roof equipped with snow-melting ducts to prevent collapse from excess weight. Thanks to supporting steel cables, however, even if the roof should deflate, it would settle 100 feet above the floor, well above the heads of spectators.

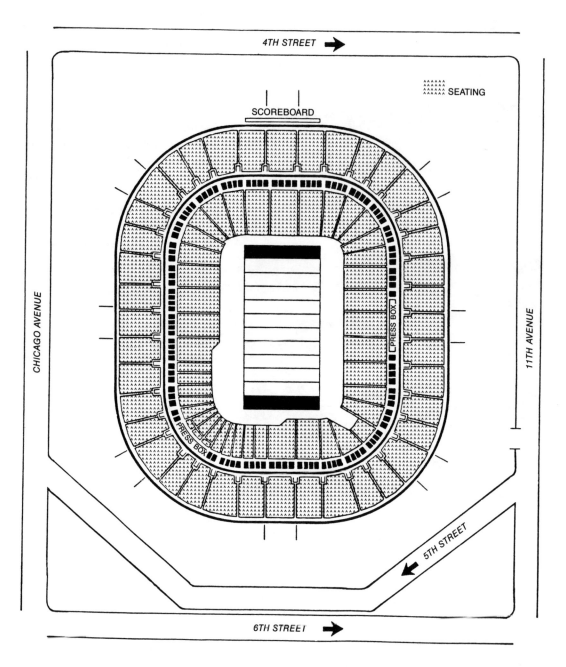

4TH STREET →

SEATING

SCOREBOARD

CHICAGO AVENUE

PRESS BOX

PRESS BOX

11TH AVENUE

5TH STREET ←

6TH STREET →

Although parking on the stadium site is limited to some 500 spaces, there are another 23,500 spaces located in the adjacent downtown area, within a 20-minute walk of the stadium.

FINANCING

Perhaps the most remarkable aspect of the Metrodome was that it was built on time and approximately $2 million under budget, during a period of high inflation. Total construction and development costs were about $75 million, excluding land and relocation costs for streets, services, and existing buildings. The project was financed in part through the sale of $55 million in revenue bonds issued by the city of Minneapolis. The remaining costs were financed with $13 million in interest earned on the revenue bonds and $7 million from the Minnesota Vikings and Twins for ancillary stadium facilities (including $5 million for luxury box suites). The stadium site, then valued at approximately $9 million, was donated by a group of Minneapolis businessmen in return for development rights around the facility.

The stadium operator, the Minneapolis Metropolitan Sports Commission, entered into an agreement with the metropolitan council of the city of Minneapolis to provide revenues, as needed, from the city's hotel/motel and liquor tax. On or before October 15 of each year, the metropolitan council is required to establish the city tax requirement for the next calendar year. This figure is the amount of revenue determined by the council to be required, together with all other revenues available to the commission, to pay all debt service on bonds and operating expenses at the Metrodome. Once the dollar amount of the city tax is determined, the city must set the rates of the liquor tax and/or the hotel motel tax so that the estimated net tax proceeds from the taxes will equal the commission's revenue requirement.

In addition, the commission imposes a 10 percent admission tax on tickets to all events held at the Metrodome. this tax is dedicated to pay current operating expenses and, to the extent possible, debt service.

MARKET ORIENTATION

In 1993, the Metrodome hosted more than 100 events, which attracted more than 3 million people. Major league baseball continues to be the largest attendanced of any type of event in the dome, with 81 games annually and a 1993 attendance of 2.5 million fans. In 1993, more than 600,000 fans attended the Minnesota Vikings football games. In addition to University of Minnesota college football games, other events hosted at the Metrodome include NCAA basketball championship games, professional wrestling, concerts, motor sports events, amateur baseball games, corporate conferences, and high-school sports activities. The Metrodome also hosts a limited number of consumer shows, such as exhibitions of automobiles and recreational vehicles.

The stadium receives 9.5 percent of the gross ticket revenues from the Vikings under the terms of a 30-year lease. Under similar arrangements, the Twins and the Golden Gophers each pay 7.5 percent of their gross gate proceeds in exchange for the use of the facilities.

LESSONS LEARNED

- The successful development and operations of the Hubert H. Humphrey Metrodome can be credited to two major factors: (1) the cooperation and support of the downtown Minneapolis business community, and (2) the cooperation and support of the three major

PROJECT DATA
HUBERT H. HUMPHREY METRODOME
MINNEAPOLIS, MN

Owner: Minneapolis Metropolitan Sports Commission
Developer/Builder: Minneapolis Metropolitan Sports Commission
Architect: Skidmore, Owings & Merrill, Chicago
Primary Users: Minnesota Twins (baseball), Minnesota Vikings (football), University of Minnesota (football)
Year Planning Began: 1977
Year Construction Began: 1979
Year Construction Completed: 1982

PROJECT INFORMATION
Site Area: 20 acres
Total GBA: 470,840 square feet
Total Seating Capacity:
  Football: 63,000
  Baseball: 55,000
  Concerts: 50,000
  Basketball: 36,000
Total Parking Spaces: 500[1]

ECONOMIC INFORMATION
Total Project Cost:[2] $75,000,000
Funding Sources:
  City Revenue Bonds: $55,000,000
  Bond Interest Earnings: $13,000,000
  Team Payments:[3] $7,000,000

Notes:
[1]An additional 23,500 spaces exist within a 20-minute walk of the stadium.
[2]Excluding land and relocation costs for streets, services, and existing buildings.
[3]From the Vikings and Twins, to cover ancillary stadium facilities.

tenants. The downtown business community assisted in the development of the Metrodome when it donated the land for the site and when five companies purchased the $55 million in revenue bonds. Such cooperation contributed to the timely completion of this stadium and to the below-budget construction cost.

- The local liquor industry vehemently opposed the contingent liquor tax established to provide revenues for debt service. Implementation of this tax, however, has not been necessary because the stadium's operating revenues and ticket tax have historically generated sufficient revenues to cover debt service.

OSCEOLA COUNTY STADIUM

KISSIMMEE, FLORIDA

Osceola County Stadium in Kissimmee, Florida, is the spring training facility for the Houston Astros major league baseball team and home to the Astros' minor league team, the Osceola Astros. The complex contains a 5,200-seat exhibition stadium, four full-size practice fields, and a 21,000-square-foot clubhouse equipped with a catering kitchen.

DEVELOPMENT STRATEGY

Development of Osceola Stadium began in April 1976, when Florida's legislature passed a bill allowing counties to impose a local-option sales tax on rentals of hotel rooms and campground sites to provide communities with additional funds to attract tourists. Funds were to be spent either on advertising or on building tourist information centers, stadiums, or civic centers. A county commission was formed to determine how the tourist development tax could best be used in Osceola County.

The committee decided to earmark 50 percent of the tax for advertising and administrative costs and to set aside the remaining funds for building a facility in the future.

Many proposals for sports complexes were presented, but these plans were criticized by leaders of the hotel/motel industry, who questioned spending county promotional dollars on a sports complex. There was also considerable doubt that the county could legally be allowed to spend tourist development funds on tennis courts, a swimming pool, and parks, as these were all considered primarily local (community) facilities.

When county officials requested an opinion from the state attorney general's office, the reply stated that facilities could be financed with tourist development tax revenues as long as the facilities were built for the advancement, generation, growth, and promotion of tourism in the area.

Earl Palmer, former city manager of Kissimmee, and Tom Brandt of Orlando are credited with conceiving the idea of developing a baseball facility that would support major league spring training and minor league baseball while serving the local community. Osceola County Stadium opened in 1985.

DESIGN AND SITE ISSUES

The facility was designed by Hellmuth, Obata & Kassabaum (HOK) of Kansas City, Missouri, with the Astros organization providing input on the baseball aspect of the complex. The county commission also had a significant amount of input into the stadium's design process. The commission requested that, in addition to concession stands at the stadium, there should also be a stand at the clubhouse because the practice fields would be used extensively during the summer months for little league baseball. Also, the commission anticipated moderate crowds during the Astros' practice sessions. Graham Contracting, Inc., was awarded a contract to build a stadium and training club facilities.

The 87-acre site on which the complex stands was originally bought to construct a tourist information center. While the information center required only five acres, the price of the entire site, $6,000 per acre, was hard to pass up. The county would then have another 82 acres to use for future development projects. This site was considered appropriate for the tourist information center because of its proximity to a Florida Turnpike exit, its location between the cities of Kissimmee and St. Cloud, and its adjacency to the Silver Spurs

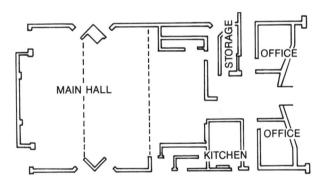

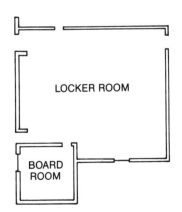

rodeo stadium, which allowed for sharing of parking between the two venues.

The Osceola stadium, upon its opening in March 1985, was considered by many to be the ultimate in major league spring training facilities. It provides all the space necessary for the Astros' operation and much more room than is typically available.

FINANCING

The preliminary budget allocated to building a minor league stadium was $3.2 million, but with the signing of the Astros organization to bring major league spring training to the stadium, that figure was increased to $5.5 million. Since the inception of the room tax in 1976, half of the collected funds had been put aside for the development of such a facility. By the time development was to begin, the total savings had reached over $2 million. To cover the remaining costs of the project, the county had the option of issuing bonds or using a commercial lender. While, in other cases, a bond issue might have been considered the ideal way to finance such a project, in this case three banks approached the county with terms that were financially more attractive than a public bond offering.

MARKET ORIENTATION

Osceola County Stadium was built to attract major league spring training baseball to the Kissimmee/St. Cloud resort area. The facility's primary operating revenue source has always been ticket sales for major league spring training. Marketing is intense for the spring training season; newspaper and radio advertisements are run statewide, and billboards are used throughout central Florida. Many Astros fans plan their vacations around spring training. The stadium also advertises in national publications to attract college teams and tournaments. The facility manager and his assistant handle all marketing functions.

Other events held at the stadium and practice fields include high-school and little league baseball, major league oldtimers' games, baseball camps, soccer tournaments, concerts, and the circus.

Marketing of meeting facilities at the stadium clubhouse is generally targeted to local events, such as wedding receptions, meetings, class reunions, parties, trade shows, and seminars.

PROJECT DATA

OSCEOLA COUNTY STADIUM
KISSIMMEE, FL

Owner: Osceola County
Builder: Graham Contracting, Inc., Orlando
Architect: Hellmuth, Obata & Kassabaum, Kansas City, Missouri
Primary User: Houston Astros (baseball spring training)
Year Planning Began: 1976
Year Construction Completed: 1985

PROJECT INFORMATION
Site Area: 87 acres
Total GBA Clubhouse:[1] 21,000 square feet
Total Seating Capacity: 5,200
Total Parking Spaces:[2] 1,000 on site

ECONOMIC INFORMATION
Site Acquisition Cost: $522,000
Total Project Cost: $5,500,000
Funding Sources:
    Resort Tax Revenues: $2,000,000
    Bank Loans: $3,500,000

Notes:
[1]Includes a 324-square-foot boardroom and a 2,760-square-foot main hall.
[2]Some 650 spaces are paved, 350 unpaved.

LESSONS LEARNED

- Osceola County Stadium's success can be attributed to excellent community support and an effective management and marketing team.
- Batting-tunnel covers were originally made of canvas and collapsed during the first spring of heavy rains, bringing down the surrounding tunnels as well. The canvas covers were replaced by sheet metal.
- Drainage under the field is excellent, and no problems were anticipated with drainage from the bleachers beyond the warning track. Because the track was made of a clay mixture, however, the water was retained on the surface. This problem was resolved by replacing the track with a sand/gravel mixture that absorbed excess rainwater.

THUNDERDOME

ST. PETERSBURG, FLORIDA

The ThunderDome is a 43,000-seat, domed baseball stadium in St. Petersburg, Florida. Completed in 1990, it was the first tension-ring, cable-supported, domed baseball stadium built in the United States and is one of the largest of its type in the world. The dome was designed for efficiency and flexibility. Although originally intended for baseball, the ThunderDome hosts a variety of events, including hockey, basketball, football, tennis, auto and motorcycle racing, concerts, equestrian events, ice shows, consumer/trade shows, and community festivals.

The ThunderDome was originally named the Florida Suncoast Dome. The name changed to the Thunder-Dome in August 1993, when the Tampa Bay Storm arena football league and the Tampa Bay Lightning National Hockey League teams began playing in the facility.

DEVELOPMENT STRATEGY

The ThunderDome is owned by the city of St. Petersburg and managed by the city's downtown facilities department. The motivation behind development of the

ThunderDome was the hope of offering a state-of-the-art venue as an incentive for major league baseball to locate in St. Petersburg.

DESIGN AND SITE ISSUES

Movable grandstands in various seating configurations accommodate a wide spectrum of events. An 80-foot-high, customized curtaining system that is used to downsize the building surrounds the fixed seating and creates the ThunderDome arena configuration. A customized "scrim" curtain system conceals the upper deck, thereby providing additional intimacy for smaller arena events.

A $1.5-million system of overhead concert rigging was specially designed for the dome to hold more than 70,000 pounds of sound and light equipment. In addition, there are 2,200 amps of three-phase power adjacent to the stage to drive concert amplifiers and lights. Spotlight locations were built for six Xenon-bulb Gladiator III event spotlights. And 152,000 square feet of unobstructed stadium or floor space accommodates trade and consumer shows; floor boxes on 30-foot centers provide power, water, and telephone capacity. The facility has more than 6,000 on-site parking spaces.

The roof design of the ThunderDome was the largest of its kind. The concept is similar to that of an open umbrella. Steel cables connected by struts support the roof, which is made of six acres of translucent, Teflon-coated fiberglass. The lightweight structure is self-supporting and, unlike earlier fabric roof systems, does not require internal air pressure (fans) for support. The roof allows natural light to shine in.

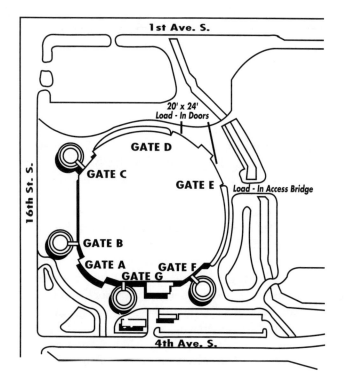

More than a design feature, the distinctive 6.5-degree slope of the dome's roof cuts off 16.8 million cubic feet of interior space that would otherwise require climate control. The roof rises 225 feet above the floor.

Additional features will be added to accommodate major league baseball, such as additional field-level seating; a stadium-club restaurant and lounge; a custom-designed, 9,000-square-foot home-team clubhouse; team offices; 50 luxury skybox suites; an outfield scoreboard and video board; artificial turf; and in-house TV production facilities. Other features being considered are a wellness center, outfield restaurant, expanded lobbies with food courts, and family picnic grounds.

The ThunderDome has become a model for other major cable-supported, domed facilities in the United States, which now feature some of the same elements originally designed into the ThunderDome, including the arena curtains and overhead rigging grids.

FINANCING

In addition to $13 million in federal and state grants and money from the city of St. Petersburg for land acquisition and related costs, ThunderDome financing involved the sale of two bond issues. The first issue was an $85 million Pinellas Sports Authority (PSA) excise-tax revenue bond secured by a triparty agreement among the PSA, the city, and Pinellas County. The second issue was a $22.5 million public-improvement revenue bond secured solely by payments from the city of St. Petersburg.

Additional costs of $8,385,000, including demolition, acquiring additional adjacent land, and remediation of the site, were financed through other sources. Some $30 million in funding is anticipated from state sales taxes when baseball is brought to the dome. The additional money will be used to complete the stadium for baseball use.

MARKET ORIENTATION

The ThunderDome stands in the city of St. Petersburg, approximately one mile from the downtown. The dome is bordered by an interstate highway loop system involving I-275, I-375, and I-175. The Pinellas Suncoast Transit Authority provides bus service.

The ThunderDome has been named as the site of the 1999 NCAA Final Four men's basketball championship. The ThunderDome, the city of St. Petersburg, and the University of South Florida hosted the first and sec-

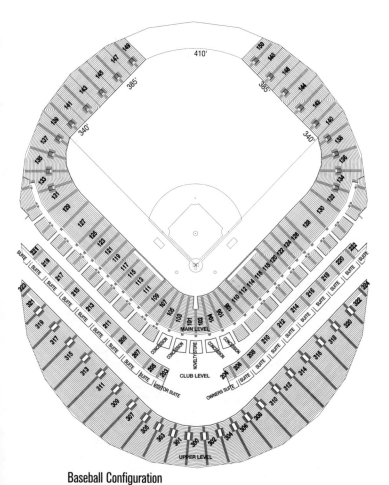

Baseball Configuration

PROJECT DATA

THUNDERDOME
ST. PETERSBURG, FL

Owner: City of St. Petersburg
Developer: St. Petersburg City Council
Architect: Hellmuth, Obata & Kassabaum (HOK), Kansas City, Missouri
Primary Users: Tampa Bay Lightning (hockey), Devil Rays (baseball), Tampa Bay Storm (arena football)
Period When Planning Began: mid-1980s
Year Construction Began: 1987
Year Construction Completed: 1990

PROJECT INFORMATION

Site Area: 65 acres
Seating Capacity:
  Baseball: 43,000
  Arena Football: 37,000
  Hockey and Basketball: 28,000
  Concerts: 8,000–50,000
Exhibition Space: 152,000 square feet
Parking Spaces: 6,000 on site

ECONOMIC INFORMATION

Site Acquisition Cost: $13,000,000
Development and Construction Costs: $97,000,000
Total Project Cost (1990 dollars): $110,000,000[1]
Total Project Cost (1994 dollars):[2] $122,708,490
Funding Sources:
  PSA Excise-Tax Bond Issue: $85,000,000
  Public-Improvement Revenue Bonds: $22,500,000
  Federal and State Grants and City Monies: $13,000,000
Gross Funding: $120,500,000
Debt Reserves and Capitalized Interest: $10,500,000
Net Funding: $110,000,000

Notes:
[1]Does not include $8,385,000 for demolition, remediation of the site, and acquisition of adjacent land for parking in anticipation of baseball.
[2]Calculated based on the consumer price index.

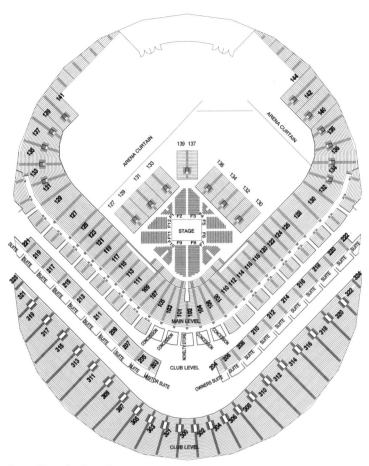

Center Stage Configuration

ond rounds of the 1994 NCAA men's basketball championships. The dome is the temporary home of the Tampa Bay Lightning hockey team and home to the Tampa Bay Storm, an arena football team. It was the site of the 1990 World Group Finals of the USTA Davis Cup.

In March 1995, Tampa Bay was awarded a major league baseball franchise. The Tampa Bay Devil Rays will play their inaugural season in the ThunderDome in 1998.

LESSONS LEARNED

- The city and the local newspaper were unable to convince the voters to accept the financial risk of building the dome without the guarantee of a baseball franchise.
- The height of the roof was reduced on one side to obtain a savings in construction costs and in heating and air conditioning. Because the slanted part of the roof is located above homeplate when the dome is configured for baseball, the slant does not interfere with viewing the game. For some other events, sight lines are obscured in these seats.
- The arena configuration proved cost-beneficial. In the last reporting year, fiscal 1994, the dome generated in excess of $18 million in gross ticket sales and $7 million in gross ancillary revenues.
- The dome has been selected for 5 or 6 superstar concert performances each year that have required more seats than are available at the 11,000-seat Sun Dome in Tampa but fewer seats (or more weather protection) than at the 74,000-seat Tampa Stadium.

CARRIER DOME

SYRACUSE, NEW YORK

The Carrier Dome is located on the campus of Syracuse University, approximately one-and-one-half miles from downtown Syracuse. Construction began in April 1979 and reached completion in time for the kickoff of the Orangemen's football season in September 1980. Named after the Carrier Corporation, which donated $2.75 million to help finance the stadium, this 50,000-seat spectator sports and entertainment facility replaced the 25,000-seat, open-air Archbold Stadium, home of Syracuse University's football games for 75 years.

DEVELOPMENT STRATEGY

The Carrier Dome was developed to attract events such as Division IA football and basketball games, concerts, and other indoor events, which Archbold Stadium could not accommodate. Forty sites were considered as potential Carrier Dome locations. Strong opposition to many of the sites by local residents, however, caused the university to select an on-campus locale. Because the site was already owned by the university, services such as ground maintenance and custodial work could be performed under existing university service contracts or by college personnel. These cost-cutting efficiencies have contributed to the facility's successful operation.

DESIGN AND SITE ISSUES

The Carrier Dome's 50,000 seats are arranged on three levels encircling the facility's main playing surface. Thirty-eight luxury boxes, each containing 18 permanent and six additional seats, are available for prices that range from $15,000 to $25,000 for a one-year lease, excluding tickets and varying with location. In addition, the Carrier Dome has complete press, radio, and television facilities.

The dome has a translucent, air-supported roof equipped with special lighting for night events and television broadcasts. The dome floor is covered by an artificial athletic turf for football, soccer, and lacrosse that is removable and underlaid with a 200-meter, eight-lane oval track with accommodations for field events. Seats surrounding a wooden basketball court assembled at one end of the field can accommodate more than 32,000 fans if the bleachers are moved down the field. This seating arrangement is also appropriate for events such as academic ceremonies, concerts, and family shows.

The location of the $28 million facility caused significant problems during its construction period. The Carrier Dome was built on the Archbold Stadium site, which meant that the old stadium had to be demolished before construction could begin on the new one. This site was built into a hill, with a narrow tunnel providing the only entrance. All construction materials, including concrete columns, had to be transported through the tunnel using the site's only access road. In addition, general contractors Huber, Hunt & Nichols had to develop a new construction technique to assemble the roof from the inside out. Despite these obstacles, the Carrier Dome was completed in time for the first game of Syracuse University's 1980 football season, just two years after demolition of Archbold Stadium and about one year after construction had begun on the new facility.

FINANCING

The Carrier Dome was partly funded by a $15 million grant from the state of New York. The remaining $13 million was raised through private donations to Syracuse University, including $2.75 million from the Carrier Corporation for naming rights.

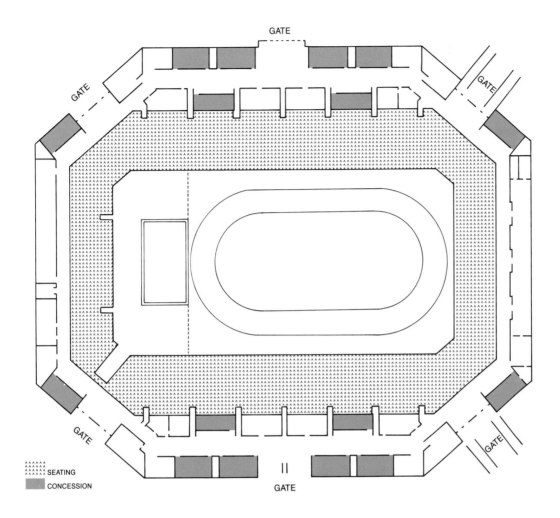

GATE

GATE

GATE

GATE

GATE

GATE

^^^^^^
^^^^^^ SEATING

CONCESSION

MARKET ORIENTATION

The Carrier Dome is used primarily for spectator and entertainment events oriented toward the student, local, and regional populations. Marketing efforts have occasionally included radio and newspaper advertisements and mailers. Even without these promotions, the Carrier Dome hosts between 90 and 100 events in a typical year, including six college football games, 18 college basketball games, seven soccer games, two track meets, six to eight lacrosse games, two to three major concerts, 12 to 14 days of high-school athletic championships, the Empire State Games, university graduation ceremonies, career days, and other college-oriented events.

The dome hosts very few nonuniversity events and must turn away many promoters. All events must be approved by the University Senate, which limits nonuniversity events in an effort to prevent the facility from becoming "another Madison Square Garden." There is

no set rent structure for nonuniversity events, but the university tries at least to recover its daily operating costs.

LESSONS LEARNED

- Successful development of the Carrier Dome can be attributed to the financial support of both the public and private sectors and to the selection of an excellent contractor. Thanks to the generosity of private patrons and corporations and the professional efforts of Huber, Hunt & Nichols, the Carrier Dome overcame many obstacles to reach completion on time and within budget.
- The passage of time has exposed a few flaws that have caused unforeseen problems and inconveniences:
  - One flaw, later corrected, was the limited seating available for the disabled. The Carrier Dome underwent renovations from 1985 to 1989 to increase space for the handicapped significantly. This move

provided greater accommodation for people in wheelchairs, as new platforms were installed on the first and second seating levels.

- A low-quality sound system, mounted at the center of the dome, placed unforeseen stress on the structure at this critical point. Also, lighting was not uniform across the playing field, causing problems during television broadcasts. Both of these design flaws were corrected in 1991 with more suitable equipment. The new sound system features speakers distributed in smaller clusters, closer to the seating area; new lighting provides a uniform 200 foot-candle illumination on the playing surface.

PROJECT DATA

CARRIER DOME
SYRACUSE, NY

Owner: Syracuse University
Builder: Huber, Hunt & Nichols, Inc., Indianapolis
Primary Users: Syracuse University (football, lacrosse, men's basketball, soccer), other university events, spectator events
Year Construction Began: 1979
Year Construction Completed: 1980

PROJECT INFORMATION
Site Area: 7.7 acres
Seating Capacity: 50,000

ECONOMIC INFORMATION
Site Acquisition Cost: Site owned by Syracuse University
Total Project Cost (1980 dollars): $28,000,000
Total Project Cost (1994 dollars):[1] $49,500,000
Funding Sources:
   State of New York Grant: $15,000,000
   Private Donations:[2] $13,000,000

Notes:
[1]Calculated based on the consumer price index.
[2]Includes a $2.75 million payment from the Carrier Corporation.

- The original scoreboard was replaced in 1993 with a state-of-the-art model with greater computer-based graphics capabilities.
- A major drawback of the dome's air-supported roof is that it does not allow for a strong system of overhead rigging. For this reason, the facility is unable to host some major concerts and circuses.

UB STADIUM STATE UNIVERSITY OF NEW YORK AT BUFFALO

BUFFALO, NEW YORK

In 1990, the State University of New York (SUNY) at Buffalo was chosen as the site of the 1993 World University Games. For this reason, the university proposed the construction of a new stadium in which to hold the event. When the state-of-the-art track and field, football, and soccer complex opened in 1993, it became Buffalo's third-largest sports facility.

DEVELOPMENT STRATEGY

Hellmuth, Obata & Kassabaum (HOK), Inc., of Kansas City, Missouri, was retained to provide environmental analysis, facilities programming, site analysis, conceptual design alternatives, cost estimates, schematic design, and implementation planning for the new facility. Ultimately, HOK was also selected by the state of New York, the University of Buffalo, and the World University Games Committee to provide full architec-

tural services for the project. Because the structure's long-term use would be as a football stadium, HOK's design provided a complex yet efficient strategy to convert the space designed for the World University Games into a venue more suited to support its permanent users. For example, the spacious international press lounge was converted into the athletic department's administrative offices, and the athletes' registration center became the strength training quarters for the university's football team.

Stadium construction began in 1991 and was completed in spring 1993. The construction team was managed by Lehrer, McGovern & Bovis in Ithaca, New York.

DESIGN AND SITE ISSUES

The stadium is located on the campus of SUNY at Buffalo. It provides seating for 16,300 spectators on three levels, with room for an additional 9,000 in temporary bleachers. Two suites were included in the original construction: one seating 45 and one seating 14. Space is provided for 38 additional private donor suites with 14 seats each. The space used for timing control and results/data management during the World University Games was converted into a press box with 75 seats and several broadcast booths.

The stadium features an eight-lane, 400-meter synthetic track with a Spurtan surface and a natural grass infield. The field's subsurface drainage and irrigation system is comparable to that of Joe Robbie Stadium in Miami and Ben Hill Griffin Stadium at the University of Florida in Gainesville. The stadium configuration allows all field events to be staged on the infield, which is equipped with subsurface conduits and boxes for event timing and measurement.

Stadium illumination is provided by four light standards, which, at 186 feet high, are the tallest free-standing light standards in North America. They are engineered to prevail against 100-mile-per-hour winds. The stadium also features a large-screen scoreboard capable of displaying computerized graphics and a world-class Finish Lynx timing system for track and field competition.

The site development plan integrated the new stadium complex into the university's existing athletic, recreational, and physical education fields and facilities. The comprehensive site plan for the World University Games included entry plazas and ticket pavilions lined with 140 flags of the nations and festive VIP and sponsor tents surrounding the stadium.

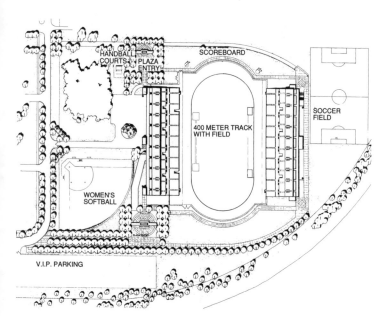

FINANCING

The stadium was financed by bonds sold through the New York State Dormitory Authority. Total construction cost came to $17.6 million.

MARKETING AND MANAGEMENT

The stadium is home to the university's NCAA Division I football and track and field teams. Although the facility was originally built to host the 1993 World University Games, it has also hosted the U.S. junior track and field team warm-ups for the World Junior Championships. Within the next three years, the facility is scheduled to host the World Veterans' Games, New York State's high-school championships, the Empire State Games, the NCAA Men's and Women's Division I Outdoor Track and Field national championships, and the Mobil Games.

LESSONS LEARNED

- In designing the field's drainage system, the approach taken for infield communications/power handholes and manholes does not allow adequate drainage. The initial approach, percolation through the bottom of the box, has resulted in the accumulation of water during heavy rains. To modify the present system, a drain would need to be tied to the underfield drainage system for relief.
- The use of tighter tolerances for the cast-in-place and precast concrete elements would have provided improved performance over that of the standard tolerances originally used.
- The long-jump/triple-jump areas were originally designed with one combined landing pit. Two divided landing pits would have been more desirable.

PROJECT DATA

UB STADIUM
STATE UNIVERSITY OF NEW YORK AT BUFFALO
BUFFALO, NY

Owner: State University of New York at Buffalo
Architect: Hellmuth, Obata & Kassabaum (HOK), Kansas City, Missouri
Construction Manager: Lehrer, McGovern & Bovis, Ithaca, New York
Primary Users: SUNY at Buffalo Division I football and track and field
Year Planning Began: 1990
Year Construction Began: 1991
Year Construction Completed: 1993

PROJECT INFORMATION
Seating Capacity: 16,300
Total Parking Spaces at Stadium: 540

ECONOMIC INFORMATION
Total Project Cost (1993 dollars): $22,500,000
Total Project Cost (1994 dollars):[1] $23,085,000
Funding Source:
    SUNY Dormitory Revenue Bond Issue: $22,500,000

Note:
[1] Calculated based on the consumer price index.

FARMINGTON AQUATIC CENTER

FARMINGTON, NEW MEXICO

The Farmington Aquatic Center is a natatorium designed to provide recreation, competition, and instruction for swimmers and divers of all skill and age levels.

DEVELOPMENT STRATEGY

The Farmington Aquatic Center was built as part of a package of five recreational facilities financed through voter approval of a .25 percent gross receipts tax. Before the center's construction, the only local indoor swimming pool was a small (35- by 75-foot) municipal pool with five lanes, much too small a facility to fulfill the aquatic needs of a growing community. A task force was formed to study the issue and determined that a new pool was needed. The funding would be provided by a sales tax increase, which was approved by local residents by a three-to-one margin.

DESIGN AND SITE ISSUES

The center occupies an eight-acre site, adjacent to a baseball park and city recreational complex. The building encompasses a total of 44,000 square feet and contains four pools: one for competition, one for multiple uses, a splash-down pool, and a children's play facility.

The 50-meter by 25-yard competitive pool has eight lanes and can be divided into two 25-meter race areas through the use of a movable bulkhead. The pool's 14-foot deep end has three diving boards ranging from one to three meters in height. Next to the pool is a deck that can accommodate 500 spectators in portable bleachers.

The leisure area contains three freeform pools. A 65-foot (three- to four-foot-deep) multiuse pool affords space for aquacise sessions, swimming lessons, and recreation. It can be heated to 90 degrees and used as a therapy pool for arthritis patients. A splash-down pool measuring 25 feet in diameter and three feet in depth is located at the bottom of a triple-turn, 20-foot-high, pretzel-shaped, spiraling, 150-foot waterslide. And the children's play pool, which is approximately 50 feet wide and slopes from the deck to a maximum depth of 20 inches, features a playscape fountain with play equipment including water valves and nozzles, a mini-waterslide, and waterfalls. All pools have stairs or ramps for getting into and out of the water.

Other center features include an outdoor sundeck and family locker rooms to accommodate single parents with opposite-gender children. The entire center has skylights and glass panels on the sides to admit natural light and reduce heating costs. Three Pool-Pak units

PROJECT DATA

FARMINGTON AQUATIC CENTER
FARMINGTON, NM

Owner: City of Farmington
Architect: William Freimuth Architecture, PC, Farmington, New Mexico
Aquatics Consultant: Councilman/Hunsaker & Associates, St. Louis, Missouri
Primary Users: General public
Year Construction Began: 1993
Year Construction Completed: 1994

PROJECT INFORMATION
Site Area: 8 acres
Total GBA: 44,000 square feet
Pool Capacity: 400
Spectator Capacity: 500
Total Parking Spaces: 134

ECONOMIC INFORMATION
Site Preparation Cost: $300,000[1]
Construction Cost: $4,900,000
Architectural and Engineering Fees: $300,000
Construction Products and Services (Gross Receipts Tax): $300,000[2]
Total Project Cost (1994 dollars): $5,800,000

Notes:
[1]Includes $220,000 for land acquisition.
[2]Paid to construction contractor.

dehumidify the air and return byproduct heat and water to the pools.

FINANCING

In March 1987 voters approved a 5-year increase in the sales tax to finance the capital costs. The site was purchased in 1993 by the city of Farmington for $220,000. Also in 1993, the city council authorized $5.8 million for the project: $4.9 million for construction, $300,000 for site preparation, $300,000 in architectural and engineering fees, and $300,000 (in gross receipts taxes) paid to the construction contractor for fees and services.

To help finance operating costs by attracting more users, an emphasis was placed on recreational use of the pool. Attendance averages 100 per day when only the 50-meter pool is open and can rise to more than 500 per day when all pools are open. Daily passes range in price from $1.75 for children to $5.00 for adults. Annual passes are available, and swimming lessons are offered at $20 for ten hours of instruction.

MARKET ORIENTATION

The Farmington Aquatic Center is open to the public. Its emphasis is on instruction and recreation, but it also meets the needs of competitive swimmers and divers. Many high-school swimming and diving competitions,

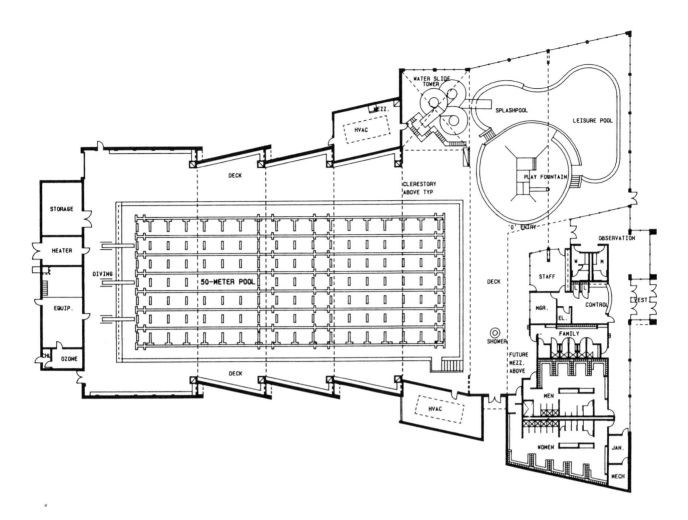

as well as state and regional water polo games, have been held at the center. In 1995, the New Mexico Swimming State Championship short-course and long-course meets were held at the facility.

LESSONS LEARNED

The waterslide and children's play pool are the overwhelming favorites at the center, and their public use generates the majority of center revenue. Although there are no immediate plans to enlarge these pools, if they were larger the center could be more profitable.

MAJOR TAYLOR VELODROME

INDIANAPOLIS, INDIANA

Considered by many to be the finest facility of its type in the country, the Major Taylor Velodrome was officially dedicated at ceremonies held at the track on July 15, 1982. Located in Indianapolis, Indiana, the velodrome is a $2.6 million facility that brings the sport of cycling to Indianapolis and the Midwest. The track was built to accommodate all classes of riders from the most inexperienced recreational class to the Olympic or professional class. Programs held at the velodrome, which has a permanent seating capacity of 3,000, provide opportunities for recreational riding, bicycle education programs, rider development, athletic training, and regional, national, and international cycling competitions. The facility, sited at the Lake Sullivan Sport Complex, is owned and operated by the Indianapolis Department of Parks and Recreation.

Development programs include cycling classes, intramural and stock bike racing, and special group riding programs. In addition, the velodrome is available for rent by groups for profit and nonprofit activities, including the United States Cycling Federation's district championships, concerts, parties, and fundraisers.

The EDS National Cycling Championships were held at the velodrome in August 1995, receiving major cable television coverage. The EDS championships have been held at the velodrome for the last three years and are scheduled to remain in Indianapolis until the 1996 Summer Olympics in Atlanta.

DEVELOPMENT STRATEGY

Original planning for the velodrome began in the 1970s, in the hope that the facility might be completed in time to help promote Indianapolis for the site of the National Sports Festival, slated for 1982. It should be noted, however, that one of the primary reasons for building such a facility was to accommodate public recreation.

Franz Arthur Strong, former director of the city's department of parks and recreation, was the driving force behind the development of the Major Taylor Velodrome. He headed the committee, which looked at eight or ten possible sites in Marion County. The site that was chosen, lying some three miles northwest of downtown Indianapolis, was picked because it was owned by the city and would save acquisition costs.

The namesake of the facility is former world champion racer Marshall "Major" Taylor. In 1899 and 1900, Taylor was the undisputed American champion and won two world titles at a meet in Montreal. But the fact that Taylor was African American caused his career to be plagued with difficulties: riders "drawing the color line" refused to race against him, tracks banned him from riding, and during actual races physical and tactical moves were made against him by other riders. All of this led to his retirement in 1910 at the age of 32. His racing career was often more successful in Europe and Australia than at home.

The Friends of the Major Taylor Velodrome is a recently created advisory group of local individuals from the private sector who are interested in the maximum use of the facility for all types of community recreation and entertainment, encompassing such activities as cycling, go-karting, concerts, in-line skating, corporate events, and private parties. Founded in 1993, this organization is still in its early growth stages but is already proving a most valuable asset.

DESIGN AND SITE ISSUES

The velodrome was designed by the firm of Howard, Needles, Tammen & Bergendoff and built by the Tousley-

Bixler Construction Company. There were no site acquisition–related problems encountered during development because the land was city-owned. The community was supportive of the project, as were city officials, who wanted a facility designed for public recreational purposes. Some unique aspects of the Major Taylor Velodrome include its tunnel leading to the infield and its full-time, year-round staff.

In addition to its permanent seating capacity of 3,000, the velodrome can seat an additional 2,000 spectators around the perimeter of the 333.3-meter track. A tunnel to the infield ensures spectators a view of the track not obstructed by a bridge. The precise engineering of the 28-degree banked turns and smooth transitions were other innovations at the time of its design. The setting of the facility is a pleasing one, with a view of the downtown skyline.

Fastmasters, Inc., invested $250,000 to add a new, widened concrete apron (a flat transitional area inside the banked bicycle track) to accommodate the Saturday Night Lightning racing series for ESPN2 cable television. This series consists of 15 races that include go-karts, motorcycles, Winston Mini-Cup cars, and other motor sport entertainment.

The Central Indiana Bicycling Association, in association with the Friday Night Tornado race series, hosts an annual family-fun event. Known as the N.I.T.E. (Navigate Indianapolis This Evening) Ride, the event allows spectators who come to watch the races to ride leisurely to downtown Indianapolis and back to the velodrome, a 20-mile trek. Music and food are provided at the velodrome to create a party atmosphere for the participants.

FINANCING

Of the $2.6 million needed for construction of the facility, $802,400 was provided by private donors such as the Krannert Charitable Trust, the Lilly Endowment, and the Jaycees. The remainder of the construction funding came from a $475,000 federal grant; $100,000 of state funds, as reimbursement for damage caused by Interstate 65 construction; and $1,223,174 in city funding, 48 percent of which represented the value of the donated land, 29 percent monies from the general fund, and 23 percent ($280,748) bond sales proceeds. Members of the community had petitioned for a bond issue to construct the velodrome, and because there was no counterpetition filed, as would have been routine in funding procedures of this type, there was no public forum called; the issue passed.

In 1994, total revenue generated from the velodrome was $41,277. Major sources of income included $12,000

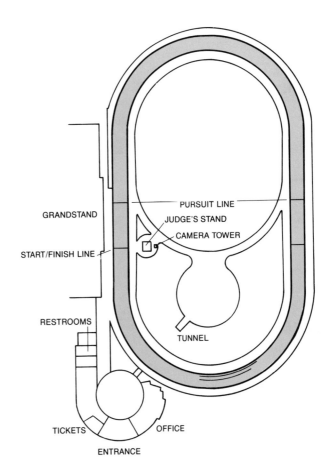

from sponsors and facility rental of about $16,000. Sponsorship funds are generally used as prizes for races. Total expenses for 1994 were $130,000. The difference in operating expenses and operating revenues is funded by city taxes. For 1995, $125,000 has been budgeted for operating expenses.

MARKET ORIENTATION

Primary marketing tools for the velodrome include mailings of promotional/solicitation material to past and potential sponsors and press kits to members of the local and national media. Velodrome officials claim that while they do have a few local corporate sponsors in Indianapolis, they lack the time for travel that they believe is required to obtain national sponsorships. The facility obtains leads from a sports marketing newsletter, and the staff also contacts the advertising agencies of companies, such as Michelob and Subaru, that might be interested in sponsoring velodrome events. There is now only one staff marketing person, who devotes 25 to 30 hours a week to promotional activities.

PROJECT DATA

MAJOR TAYLOR VELODROME
INDIANAPOLIS, IN

Owner: Indianapolis Department of Parks and Recreation
Builder: Tousley-Bixler Construction Company
Architect: Howard, Needles, Tammen & Bergendoff
  (HNTB), Kansas City, Missouri
Primary Users: Recreational riders and regional, national,
  and international competitions
Period When Planning Began: Early 1970s
Year Construction Completed: 1982

PROJECT INFORMATION
Total Seating Capacity: 3,000 permanent; 2,000 perimeter

ECONOMIC INFORMATION
Site Acquisition Cost: None[1]
Total Project Costs (1982 dollars): $2,600,000
Total Project Costs (1994 dollars):[2] $3,790,800
Funding Sources:
  Private Donations: $802,000[3]
  Federal Monies: $475,000
  State Funds: $100,000
  Local Funds: $1,223,000
Total: $2,600,000

Notes:
[1]The site was city-owned, with a land value of $587,123.
[2]Calculated based on the consumer price index.
[3]From the Krannert Charitable Trust, the Lilly Endowment,
and the Jaycees, among others.

LESSONS LEARNED

Velodrome officials believe they have a high-quality facility. Some things that they would do in the same way,
and some things that they would do differently, if they
had the chance to do them over again, include:

- Although the developer and design team decided to
  make the track's turns less banked than those of a 35-
  degree Olympic facility, the riders seem to like the
  track as it is and can still take the turns at full speed.
  This allows the track to be friendly to the novice as
  well as to professional cyclists.

- Originally, the velodrome staff concentrated too heavily
  on marketing the facility, rather than on events programming, but that has changed. Officials believe
  that there are too many diverse activities taking place
  in Indianapolis for the velodrome to survive by attracting only a narrow following. Consequently, they
  continue to focus on providing a broad spectrum of
  event programming.

- A major reason for the comparatively low number of
  spectators, on average 100 per event, is the simple fact
  that bicycle racing in the United States, unlike arena
  or stadium events, is perceived as more of a participant activity than a spectator sport.

- Other problems mentioned by officials include: government restrictions that prohibit the approval of multi-
  year sponsorship agreements; the impossibility of marketing the facility as a professional sports/entertainment
  venue because the local government lacks sufficient
  funds for television and radio publicity; the fact that
  beer and cigarette sponsorships are not considered
  politically correct for this facility; budget cuts prompted
  by the city's decreasing tax/revenue base; and insufficient support for velodromes by the United States
  Cycling Federation.

KENTUCKY HORSE PARK

LEXINGTON, KENTUCKY

At the time of its opening in 1978, Kentucky Horse Park was the only equestrian park in the world that combined championship equestrian facilities with a variety of tourist amenities.

DEVELOPMENT STRATEGY

The history of the land on which Kentucky Horse Park stands dates back to 1777, when Patrick Henry, then governor of Virginia, granted 9,000 acres in the Kentucky Territory to his brother-in-law, William Christian. Christian moved his family to Kentucky in 1785 and established a farm on Bear Grass Creek, near Louisville. Upon Christian's death, his daughter inherited 3,000 acres in Scott and Fayette counties. The land was sold and resold until December 1972, when a portion of the property was purchased by the commonwealth of Kentucky in the hope of creating an equestrian attraction that would help revitalize Kentucky's tourism industry. In 1978, after more than seven years of planning and development, Kentucky Horse Park opened to the public.

The impetus behind the development of Kentucky Horse Park was the wish to create an attraction that would symbolize Kentucky's horse-industry tradition and help maintain the state's inflow of tourist dollars. These dollars, which had primarily been generated by Kentucky's privately owned but open-to-the-public horse farms, were in jeopardy because vandalism, labor costs, and inflation had made it too expensive for private farms to remain open. (The number of farms opening their doors to the public had declined from 100 in 1970 to one or two at the time of the opening of Kentucky Horse Park in 1978.) In addition, the park was also to be Kentucky's contribution to the Bicentennial project.

John Gaines of Gaines Dog Food and Gainesway Farm was the principal individual spurring the movement to build Kentucky Horse Park. William Kenton, then Kentucky's speaker of the house, was also a prime mover.

The project's first hurdle came in determining its scope. An advisory committee consisting of leaders in the horse industry, representatives of local and state government, and area businessmen was formed by the governor's office to formulate the initial project concept and report to Governor Louie B. Nunn. The task force's study, presented in 1971, concluded that the park should be designed both for educational and for recreational purposes and should serve Kentuckians and the touring public alike.

Although defining the project's scope was the park's first hurdle, its biggest problem occurred during the construction phase, when construction had to be stopped to obtain an interpretive design team. Although the original architectural team was said to have done a fine job in designing the facility, a separate team was needed to determine the actual functionality of the design. The cost of stopping construction was estimated at between $5 million and $7 million. However, the development team believed that, had they not replaced the original interpretive design team, major facility problems would have ensued.

This unexpected cost overrun resulted in a scaling-down of amenities. The main effects were the elimination of additional exhibits along the horse-drawn tours and the walking farm tours and the replacement of a proposed tramway transport system for visitors with a less elaborate, motorized shuttle.

DESIGN AND SITE ISSUES

In addition to hosting some of the world's finest equestrian events, such as steeplechase racing and polo matches, the 1,000-acre park also contains the Man o'War Memorial; the 360-seat Clubhouse Restaurant; a 260-site resort RV campground; a visitor information center with

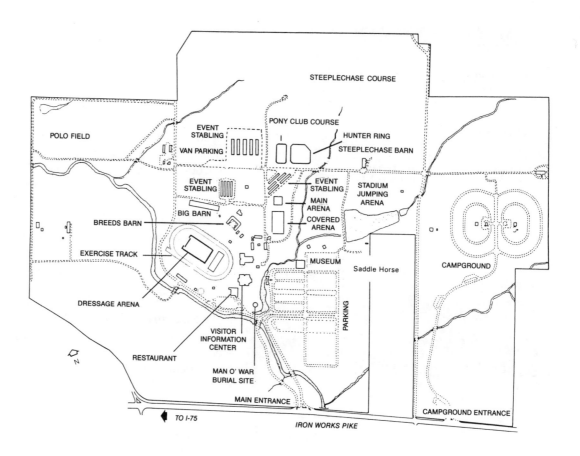

two 210-seat movie theaters; the International Museum of the Horse, which includes 35,000 square feet of exhibition space; a 3,100-square-foot gallery for changing exhibitions, a 4,600-square-foot gift shop, and picnic grounds. Equestrian facilities consist of an indoor arena with a seating capacity of 5,500, multiple barns with a total of 1,095 stalls, a 1.5-acre jumping stadium with a 6,800-person seating capacity, a steeplechase course, a half-mile exercise track, and several show rings.

The facility occupies land formerly known as Walnut Hall Stud Farm. The land was sold to the commonwealth of Kentucky in 1972, after plans had begun for the development of the horse park and the project's site selection committee had concluded that the site was the most appropriate one for the attraction, which was initially to be called Thoroughbred State Park. The site lies off Interstate 75, minutes from downtown Lexington, and offers excellent accessibility.

The appraised value of the 963 acres was about $3 million. Remaining infrastructure and interstate highway access ramps were constructed at a cost of approximately $2.4 million.

FINANCING

The total cost of Kentucky Horse Park, excluding interstate access ramps, was $27 million. Approximately $13 million of this cost was financed by a bond issue. The remaining cost was covered by general state funds. The park was not financially supported by the local community; however, the state of Kentucky realized the importance of the park to state tourism and provided its full support.

Jim Durham

MARKET ORIENTATION

The Kentucky Horse Park was built to be the world's definitive equestrian facility, dedicated to all breeds of horses; to provide show facilities capable of hosting national and international equestrian events; and to exert a positive economic impact on both the local and state economies by establishing itself as a nationally recognized tourist attraction.

Today, the Kentucky Horse Park's primary market is tourists from Kentucky and states to the north via Interstate 75 corridor. Another major group of visitors consists of Canadians traveling to Florida for the winter season. This element represents an expanded market orientation for the park, which during its first six years of operation attracted mainly visitors from Kentucky and Ohio. All marketing and advertising work is completed in house.

Peak season is June through August. Operations are significantly reduced during the winter months, when the park closes on Mondays and Tuesdays. Horse operations are also minimal in the winter, generally causing a reduction of staff.

LESSONS LEARNED

In retrospect, among the insights gained since the inception of Kentucky Horse Park are the following:

- The existence and success of the park can be attributed to the foresight of concerned citizens and state and local governments in recognizing the need for such a facility when privately owned farms closed. Had the facility not been built, the state likely would have suffered a major decrease in the inflow of tourist dollars, according to projections.
- The primary lesson learned from this project was the importance of hiring an experienced interpretive design team. For Kentucky Horse Park and the state of Kentucky, this lesson cost between $5 million and $7 million.

PROJECT DATA
KENTUCKY HORSE PARK
LEXINGTON, KY

Owner: State of Kentucky
Developer: State of Kentucky
Architect: Chrisman, Miller & Wallace, Lexington
Primary Users: Equestrian events, steeplechase races, polo, horse shows, merchandise marts, art exhibitions
Year Planning Began: 1970
Year Construction Completed: 1978

PROJECT INFORMATION
Site Area: 963 acres
Exhibit Area:
  Exhibition Space (in museum): 35,000 square feet
  Exercise Track Infield: 427,500 square feet
Total Seating Capacity:
  Indoor Arena: 5,500
  Jumping Stadium: 6,800
  Movie Theaters (two): 420

ECONOMIC INFORMATION
Site Acquisition Cost: $3,000,000
Site Improvement Costs: $2,400,000
Construction Costs: $24,000,000
Total Project Cost: $29,400,000[1]
Funding Sources:
  General State Funds: $16,400,000
  Mortgage Bond Issue: $13,000,000

Note:
[1]Includes cost of access ramp.

PETTIT NATIONAL ICE CENTER

MILWAUKEE, WISCONSIN

Pettit National Ice Center is the only facility of its kind in the United States and one of only a few in the world. It features an enclosed ice training and competition center for speedskating, hockey, and figure skating. The center is located in Milwaukee, just ten minutes west of the downtown.

DEVELOPMENT STRATEGY

Pettit National Ice Center, a nonprofit corporation, was built to retain Wisconsin's and Milwaukee's status as the speedskating capital of the United States. The Olympic outdoor speedskating rink that then existed had been built in 1966 and was in dire need of repair. It was suggested that a new indoor facility be constructed so that athletes could train year-round; at the time, they had to train in Europe in the off-season.

The Pettit Center offers Olympic training facilities for speedskating, figure skating, and hockey and hosts competitive skating events. It was named after Milwau-kee philanthropists Jane and Lloyd Pettit in recognition of their contributions to the center.

Construction of the Pettit Center began in January 1992 and was completed in December of the same year. Designated an Olympic training center, it opened in time to be used as a training facility for the 1994 Winter Olympics.

SITE ANALYSIS

The Pettit Center has three floors, the upper one containing the Hall of Fame Room, a kitchen, a media room, and the control room. On the main floor are the box office, a pro shop, the ice rink, and the main seating area. The lower floor has eight team locker rooms, two referee rooms, the Competitive Edge sports medicine clinic, facilities for skate rental and skate changing, concessions, competitors' warm-up area, and access to the ice, gained through a tunnel from the lower floor.

The arena is 155,000 square feet in size. A total of 97,000 square feet of ice comprise a 400-meter speedskating oval with two international-size ice rinks in the center for hockey, figure skating, and short-track speedskating. Bleachers on the north side of the oval accommodate up to 2,000 spectators for speedskating events, and there is also seating for some 1,000 people on the infield (the space between the oval and the two rinks) for hockey, figure skating, and short-track speedskating. Seating for hockey events can be increased by extending the bleachers onto the oval, to accommodate as many as 3,000 people.

A glass-walled meeting room on the upper floor overlooking the ice, the Hall of Fame Room can accommodate up to 200 people seated and 250 standing at re-

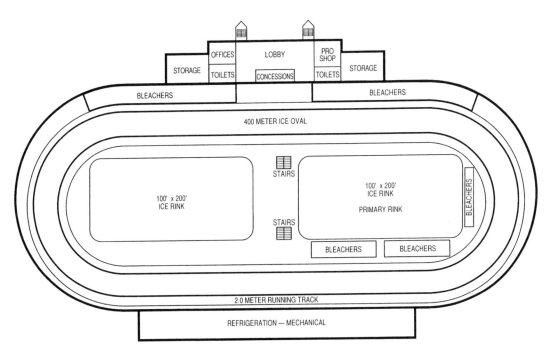

PETTIT NATIONAL ICE CENTER
MAIN FLOOR

ceptions. This room can be rented for private use, with catering available.

FINANCING

The state of Wisconsin contributed a total of $9.3 million in revenue bonds to help finance the Pettit Center, whose total project cost was $13.3 million. Local and private funds of $2 million were raised through private corporations, foundations, and individuals; Jane and Lloyd Pettit donated an additional $2 million. To date, the Pettits have donated more than $6 million to the fa-

cility and have established an annual endowment fund for operations.

Operating costs are funded mainly through fees charged for public skating sessions and training sessions for amateur athletes.

MARKET ORIENTATION

The Pettit Center is the home training ground of the U.S. speedskating team, and well-known athletes like Bonnie Blair and Dan Jansen are familiar faces there. The center, which is open to skaters from Wisconsin,

PROJECT DATA

PETTIT NATIONAL ICE CENTER
MILWAUKEE, WI

Owner: State of Wisconsin
Operator: Pettit National Ice Center, Inc.
Architects: Venture Architects
Primary User: Speedskating, figure skating, and hockey
Period When Planning Began: 1991
Year Construction Began: January 1992
Year Construction Completed: December 1992

PROJECT INFORMATION

Site Area: 200,000 square feet
Total Seating Capacity: 3,000
Total Parking Spaces: 500+

ECONOMIC INFORMATION

Total Project Cost (1992 Dollars): $13,300,000
Total Project Cost (1994 Dollars):[1] $13,821,383
Financing:
    Revenue Bonds: $9,300,000
    Private Funds: $4,000,000
Total Financing: $13,300,000

Note:
[1]Calculated based on the consumer price index.

the United States, and the world, hosts world-class competitions that include some of the best athletes from around the world.

The Pettit Center supports and encourages ice skating as healthy, wholesome, and relatively inexpensive recreation. Public skating sessions run twice a day; rental skates are available. At Learn to Skate sessions, participants can obtain instruction at all levels in hockey, figure skating, and speedskating, while Kids on Ice is a daily field-trip program for area grade schools.

The Pettit Center can be rented in whole or in part for corporate meetings or private group parties such as birthdays, holiday gatherings, and other special occasions. Concessions and catering are available. Also, the Pettit Center conducts tours for grade-school children, as well as for the general public. The facility now operates year-round, except for the oval, which is open from September through June.

The Pettit Center was awarded the 1995 World Sprint Speedskating Championships by the International Skating Union. This competition took place in February on the center's 400-meter oval.

LESSONS LEARNED

- The Pettit Center has incurred more operating costs than were expected. Marketing of the public skating sessions generates enough revenue to fund these costs.
- Ironically, the center sometimes loses money when hosting events because it was not designed as a spectator facility, and seating is limited. Also, if public skating sessions must be canceled to host an event, that revenue is lost.

TACOMA DOME

TACOMA, WASHINGTON

When the Tacoma Dome opened its doors to the public on April 21, 1983, it was one of the largest wood-domed structures in the world. Consisting of a 130,000-square-foot stadium and a 30,000-square-foot exhibition hall, the dome is a multipurpose entertainment facility. It hosts football, soccer, basketball, hockey, wrestling, ice skating, and gymnastics. Its ability to accommodate audiences of up to 23,000, combined with its 150,000 square feet of exhibition space, allows the facility to host family shows, concerts, merchandise marts, conventions, and exhibitions (in one of the largest exhibition halls in the Northwest). The Tacoma Dome is owned by the city of Tacoma and operated through an enterprise fund under the city's department of public assembly facilities, which also operates the dome's exhibition hall and Cheney Baseball Stadium.

The Tacoma Dome is the site of a new sports museum, which houses the Washington State Sports Hall of Fame.

DEVELOPMENT STRATEGY

The Tacoma Dome was funded through a city bond issue that received voter approval in March 1980. Although

attempts to fund a public facility had been made sporadically for years before this approval, in 1980 the city had yet to select a site, prepare the necessary environmental impact statements, or settle the design and construction issues and contracts. These tasks had to be completed quickly, before the high inflation and interest rates of that time ate away at the project budget.

In July 1980, the city issued requests for proposals for the design/building team. To find the team, the city launched a nationwide advertising campaign requesting proposals for a preliminary design concept. Of the submitting teams, three finalists were selected to provide final design plans. It was decided that the city would pay the winning finalists $100,000 as the first payment on what would be a $1 million contract. The remaining two finalists would each receive $50,000.

The responsibility for choosing the three design finalists was given to a seven-member citizen jury appointed by the city council. The creation of a citizen jury, besides opening the proposal presentations to the public, also assured community involvement in selecting a final design concept. By November 1980, the three design finalists had been selected.

The finalists' three project designs consisted of a wooden dome similar to the Ensphere in Flagstaff, Arizona; a cable-suspended dome similar to the Forum in Los Angeles; and an air-supported fabric dome similar to the Carrier Dome in Syracuse. In May 1981, the city council chose the wooden dome design, primarily for its heating efficiency. At that time, a wooden dome cost some $90,000 per year to heat; to heat a structure made of other materials would cost several times that amount. The wooden dome was also considered stronger and more aesthetically pleasing than the other designs.

The project was completed one month ahead of schedule.

DESIGN AND SITE ISSUES

The Tacoma Dome's market orientation is mainly attributable to its flexible seating design, which allows the facility to convert easily from stadium to arena events. Seating schemes can be as intimate as 8,000 in an auditorium configuration, expandable to 12,000, or as capacious as the arena and stadium configurations of 16,000 and 23,000 seats, respectively.

Use of the facility by various sports groups is maximized by the dome's permanently set and insulated ice sheet. Events can be held over the ice sheet, so that a hockey game, a football game, and a soccer match can

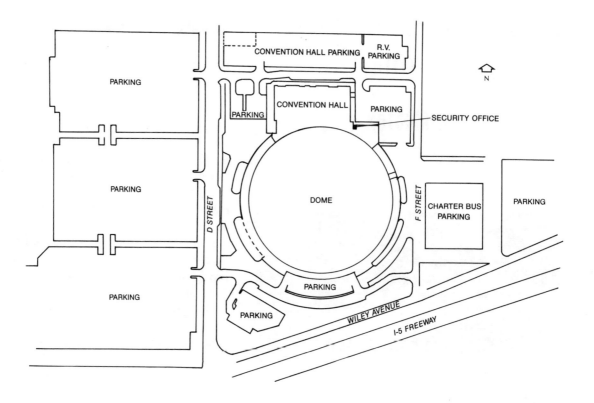

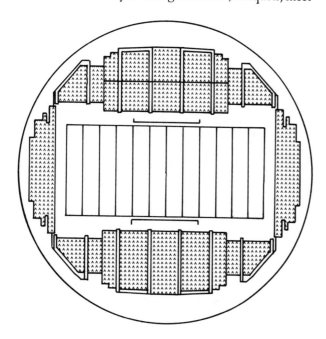

be held on consecutive nights without removing the sheet. This feature saves many event days that would normally be lost in rink conversion. Typically, rink conversion requires ten hours to remove an ice sheet and an additional 20 hours to rebuild it.

The Tacoma Dome's 30,000-square-foot exhibition hall allows the facility to host graduations, banquets, meet-

ings, dances, and merchandise marts. The exhibition hall can be used in conjunction with the arena or separately, for small events. The hall can be subdivided into six sound-proof rooms. A total of 150,000 square feet of exhibition space is provided by combining the two facilities.

The well-known Tacoma Dome roof is made up of 288 triangular sections. The geodetic "blue diamond" pattern of the roof is recognizable for miles on Interstate 5.

The city considered eight potential sites for the proposed facility, and the consulting firm of Kramer, Chen & Mayo of Seattle was chosen to prepare an environmental impact statement for the three best sites. Selection of the three sites was made by a team consisting of representatives of Kramer, Chen & Mayo and of various city government departments.

The city then hired two appraisers to determine the expected costs of acquiring each of the three sites. Two appraisal firms were picked because it had been determined that one firm alone could not complete the work within the established cost of $37,000. By conducting appraisals concurrently with the preparation of the environmental impact statement, however, the city could save approximately five months in the project schedule, compared with starting the appraisals after the site had been chosen.

The site ultimately acquired for the Tacoma Dome was a 6.1-acre parcel near Interstate 5. This site won by a narrow margin over a site within Tacoma's central business district. Although one group of supporters believed that development on the downtown site would be a stronger catalyst for economic revitalization, an opposing group argued that the downtown's constrained parking situation and traffic congestion were major drawbacks of the CBD site. If this site had been selected, parking would have had to consist of existing parking garages and available curbside parking.

The selected site encompassed 155 separate parcels on which 376 residents in 131 households, one business, and a school were located. Federal relocation assistance laws guaranteed that, in these situations, displaced residents would be relocated to comparable or better housing in other neighborhoods within the city or adjacent to the county, without suffering financial hardship. Because the city of Tacoma was funding the project, these laws did not apply. To minimize public opposition and avoid lawsuits, however, the city passed a relocation assistance ordinance patterned after the federal relocation laws, and the city ultimately spent $1.1 million to move the residents. The existing structures on the site, which were acquired through eminent domain, were either demolished or sold. Sale of these structures netted the city $384,500.

Dome renovations were conducted over a three-year period, from 1989 through 1991. The $1.6 million improvements included restroom expansion, stadium seats, a permanent rigging grid, a multiple curtain system, and seat covers.

Professional staff, called the "Dome Team," provide on-site services such as ticketing, security, ushering, and concessions. The dome also provides catering services and houses the Gallery Restaurant, which is open to the public during major events.

FINANCING

Throughout the 1970s, in a number of elections, bond issues were defeated that would have funded a facility similar to the Tacoma Dome. In 1979, a bond issue was voted on in a countywide election and again failed, but an analysis of election returns by precinct revealed that, had the election been held citywide, the bond issue probably would have passed. On March 18, 1980, city of Tacoma voters passed, with 70 percent support, a $27,950,000 bond issue to build a multipurpose sports and convention center. In order to pay for additional project amenities, the city council was forced to pass an internal bond issue of $8,130,600. Another $1 million was derived from other sources.

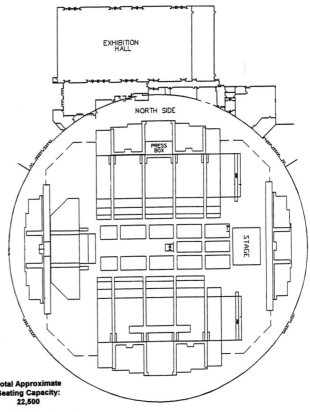

Total Approximate Seating Capacity: 22,500

End Stage Layout

The city of Tacoma sold the initial bonds within six months of voter approval. This was ultimately a good move because high interest rates following the bond sale brought in an additional $7,467,000 in interest earnings for the project.

MARKET ORIENTATION

The Tacoma Dome is home to the Tacoma Stars major league soccer franchise and to the new expansion team of the Western Hockey League, the Tacoma Rockets. The venue is oriented primarily toward sports events, including football, basketball, boxing, and tennis, and secondarily to conventions, trade shows, and local events. It hosts about 350 events per year.

Because a long-term proactive marketing plan was developed to maintain a competitive edge, the dome's marketing department has expanded its programs to include an extensive public information network to spread the word about dome events and a sponsorship and advertising program to build relationships with the business community.

LESSONS LEARNED

- The city of Tacoma overcame several major obstacles in the Tacoma Dome's development by attaching great importance to the needs and involvement of the community. Residents displaced by the city's eminent domain action filed for injunctions against the project in several courts. However, the city's decision to pass a relocation assistance ordinance and its community-oriented approach to project decisions helped overcome the legal challenges.
- The city's efficient development plan, which was essentially geared toward timely project completion, also led to the project's success. The Tacoma Dome opened one month ahead of schedule, only 37 months after approval of the project's authorizing bond issue.
- Some deficiencies that became clear after the development of the Tacoma Dome, and that would be changed in the city's approach to a similar structure today, include: the installation of all-bench seating, rather than seats with backs, in order to save money; the shortage of parking spaces; the difficulty of access to the rigging, which requires that a crane be used at the promoters' expense; and the problematical outside surface of the dome, which, at a total cost of $500,000, has been repainted three times due to fading.

PROJECT DATA

TACOMA DOME
TACOMA, WA

Owner: City of Tacoma
Builder: Tacoma Dome Associates, with Merit Construction as general contractor
Architect: McGranahan, Messenger Associates
Primary Users: Sports events, conventions, trade shows, and local events
Year Planning Began: 1980
Year Construction Began: 1981
Year Construction Completed: 1983

PROJECT INFORMATION
Site Area: 6.1 acres
Total GBA: 434,699 square feet
    Convention Hall: 30,000 square feet
    Exhibition Space: 150,000 square feet
Total Seating Capacity: 23,000
Total Parking Spaces: 2,953

ECONOMIC INFORMATION
Site Acquisition and Relocation[1] *Costs:* $1,500,000
Construction Costs: $42,000,000
Consulting Fees: $1,047,000
Total Project Costs (1981 dollars): $44,547,000
Total Project Costs (1994 dollars):[2] $71,451,624
Renovations (1989–1991): $1,600,000
Funding Sources:
    Original Bond Issue: $27,950,000
    Internal Issue: $8,130,000
    Other Sources: $1,000,000
    Interest Earnings: $7,467,000
Total Financing: $44,547,000

Notes:
[1] Relocation of the site's former tenants.
[2] Calculated based on the consumer price index.

PART III
INTERNATIONAL CASE STUDIES

SEIDENSTICKER HALL

BIELEFELD, GERMANY

Seidensticker Hall was completed in March 1993 after many years of planning and decision making. It is a multipurpose facility capable of hosting school and club sports, as well as large, ticketed sporting and nonsporting events. Ravensberg Park encompasses the Seidensticker Hall as well as Rochdale Park, Wiesenbad (a natatorium), the Delius Ice Rink, an adult education school, and a historical museum; together, these facilities form a center for leisure, sport, and recreation.

DEVELOPMENT STRATEGY

The city of Bielefeld sponsored a competition for the design of a multipurpose sporting facility in 1979. The selected site was a cleared area in Ravensberg Park, part of the city's urban renewal project. The original intention was to build a six-sport facility consisting of three gymnasiums and a competitive arena with seating for 2,500 spectators.

The city's office of structural engineering reworked the plan proposed by the winning architects, Friedrich Pramann and Friedrich Kuhn. The revised concept of-

fered seating for 5,000 people and a 200-meter (656-foot) circular running track. Actual construction of the facility began in 1990 and was completed in 1993.

DESIGN AND SITE ISSUES

Because of German reunification, Bielefeld's location has worked in its favor. Bielefeld is centrally located in the Federal Republic, at the crossroads of main traffic arteries. Public transportation is available by bus line. Also, a bus shuttle runs between Seidensticker Hall and remote parking when larger events are held. Approximately 1,500 parking spaces lie within 500 meters (1,640 feet) of the arena. Within 1,000 meters' walking distance (3,280 feet), there is sufficient parking for 3,000 cars.

Seidensticker Hall contains more than 8,000 square meters (86,000 square feet) in total building area. The arena offers the capacity for two to six gymnasiums (separated by sliding partitions), track and field athletics, all disciplines of ball sports, and nonsporting events. For track and field events, the entire hall is used, but because the track is partially covered by the telescopic seats, the seats must be retracted for such events.

There are eight dressing rooms, and three rooms are available for teaching in the facility. Also, a physical therapy area is provided, offering weight training, physician services, massages, and a sauna.

The seating capacity of the arena depends upon its configuration for the sporting event being held. For instance, for ice shows the capacity is 4,200, whereas for center-stage and ringside events, seating is available for 7,500 and 7,000, respectively.

FINANCING

Construction of the hall was made possible by the cooperation and support of the state of North-Rhine/Westphalia, the Seidensticker Company (a generous sponsor), the Development Association, and many firms and individuals. The facility was financed by the city government, the taxpayers of Bielefeld, and the state of North-Rhine/Westphalia, as well as by the Seidensticker Company.

The entire cost of the facility amounted to 35 million Deutschmarks ($21,169,526). During the planning and construction phase, construction costs rose by 30 percent, primarily because of construction price increases, difficulties with the foundation, and the need to upgrade the furnishings. Facility construction cost approximately 336 DM per cubic meter ($155 per cubic yard) of enclosed space.

The Seidensticker Company donated 10 percent of the cost for the building of the arena: the city of Bielefeld contributed 75 percent, and the remaining 10 percent came from the state of North-Rhine/Westphalia.

MARKET ORIENTATION

Three Bielefeld schools that border the inner city have access to the arena for school sports and are permitted to use the facility year-round for track and field athletics.

The entire spectrum of club sports can be played in the hall: competitions, sports for the handicapped, and

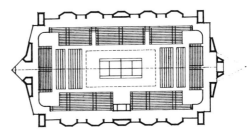

Tennis

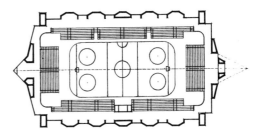

Ice Hockey

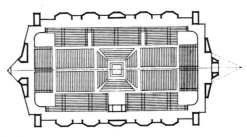

Boxing

therapeutic athletics. Clubs united in the City Sports Federation, as well as the organized groups formed by educational entities, are all eligible to use the arena.

The hall's flexibility makes possible an optimal mix of many sports disciplines, with up to 7,500 spectators for any one event. At present, approximately 30 large events per year are planned for the hall. Staged events held in the facility include concerts and plays. Ice hockey and figure skating can be held in the facility, as can ringside events such as boxing and wrestling.

LESSONS LEARNED

■ Some roads and streets were improved and connected to allow greater accessibility and smoother traffic flow to and from the hall.
■ The building enjoys some economic advantages because the same management organization operates three public assembly facilities within the city of Bielefeld—Seidensticker Hall, Bielefeld Convention Centre and the Arts Hall.

PROJECT DATA

SEIDENSTICKER HALL
BIELEFELD, GERMANY

Owner: City of Bielefeld
Operator: Stadthalle Bielefeld Betriebs
Architects: Friedrich Pramann, Bielefeld, and Friedrich Kuhn, Braunschweig
Primary Users: Area schools and sporting clubs
Year Planning Began: 1979
Year Construction Began: 1990
Year Construction Completed: 1993

PROJECT INFORMATION
Site Area: 5 acres
Total GBA: 86,000 square feet
    Arena: 43,000 square feet
Total Seating Capacity:
    Staged Performances: 7,500
    Ice Shows: 4,200
    Ringside Events: 7,000
Total Parking Spaces: 1,500 within 500 meters
    3,000 within 1,000 meters

ECONOMIC INFORMATION
Site Acquisition Cost: DM 384,000
Development Cost: DM 26,826,000
Building, Equipment, Grounds Installations, Additional Measures: DM 29,706,000
Additional Construction Cost:[1] DM 4,910,000
Total Project Cost (1993 DM): DM 35,000,000
Total Project Cost (1993 U.S. dollars):[2] $21,169,526

Notes:
[1]Costs due to construction price increases, difficulties with the foundation, and upgrading of the furnishings.
[2]Calculated based on the 1993 exchange rate (annual average).

NATIONAL INDOOR ARENA

BIRMINGHAM, ENGLAND

Birmingham's National Indoor Arena (NIA) opened in October 1991 near the city's center. The venue positions Birmingham as a primary provider of Britain's major indoor events. The NIA is a multipurpose facility with superb potential for other entertainment events, such as concerts, and capacity for large assemblies of up to 12,000 delegates.

DEVELOPMENT STRATEGY

The city of Birmingham initially decided to build the NIA to benefit both the region and the nation. The Sports Council—an independent group financed by a grant from the central government and dedicated to increasing the quantity and quality of sports facilities and sports participation—determined that the arena would be a nationally important venue.

DESIGN AND SITE ISSUES

The NIA offers many features that are new to the United Kingdom. A six-lane, 200-meter (656-foot) indoor track is the first of its kind in the country. Demountable, the track can be stored to allow the arena floor to be used for other sports.

Spectator capacities can accommodate 8,000 persons for track, 10,000 for tennis, 11,000 for gymnastics, and up to 13,000 for boxing. There is a portable ice mat for staging various types of ice events.

Audience accommodation was taken into account in the design of the NIA by Hellmuth, Obata & Kassabaum, a U.S. architectural firm. In addition, ten hospitality boxes offer event viewing for suiteholders.

The design also includes full ancillary facilities for warming up, a medical station, dressing rooms, and office space. Catering service for spectators and visiting teams features a range of choices from fast-food outlets and cafeteria dining to banqueting and hospitality services. Media facilities—with television-quality lighting available—enable worldwide event coverage, placing Birmingham potentially in the sporting spotlight. The NIA has two multistory parking structures, on the north and south corners, with a total capacity of 2,500 cars, plus an additional VIP parking area with an exclusive entrance into the arena.

The NIA's location, alongside the International Convention Centre (ICC) and close to the core of the city, offers important road, rail, and air links. It also enables the NIA and ICC to be used in conjunction, providing a total sport, entertainment, and convention package.

FINANCING

The NIA's total cost of £51 million was partially funded by a generous grant of £3 million from the Sports Council. The remaining £48 million was funded by the Birmingham City Council.

MARKET ORIENTATION

The Sports Council has expressed confidence that the building and its management team will continue to attract and stage successful sporting events. A specialist team brings together the experience and expertise of the National Exhibition Center (NEC), Ltd., and of the Birmingham City Council Recreation and Community

Services Department to market and manage the arena. The partnership is unique, and the team's professionalism and talent in the marketing and staging of events have proven to be strong assets. NEC also manages Birmingham's other arena, the NEC Arena, which is well known in the U.K. entertainment industry and has been open since 1980.

The sports world is supportive of the NIA. Four world championships have already been staged or confirmed at the venue: badminton (1993), netball lacrosse (1995), archery (1995), and powerlifting (1992). European championship table tennis (1994), karate (1994), and judo (1995) have also appeared on the event calendar. The NIA now has its own resident basketball team, the Birmingham Bullets, who play more than 20 games per season at
the facility.

NIA management has targeted a balanced program of sports and entertainment. In addition to sports, the arena stages top entertainment, including concerts, grand opera, ice spectaculars, and the British *Gladiators* television show.

LESSONS LEARNED

■ The NIA was designed with numerous glass doors, both as entrances and as emergency exits. Despite appropriate signage, the building still appears to have many more entrances than needed, causing difficulty in controlling public access and contributing to increased security and staff costs. The size of the building and the distance between doors cause some confusion for the public, particularly in bad weather. Various solutions have been implemented to indicate correct entry routes,

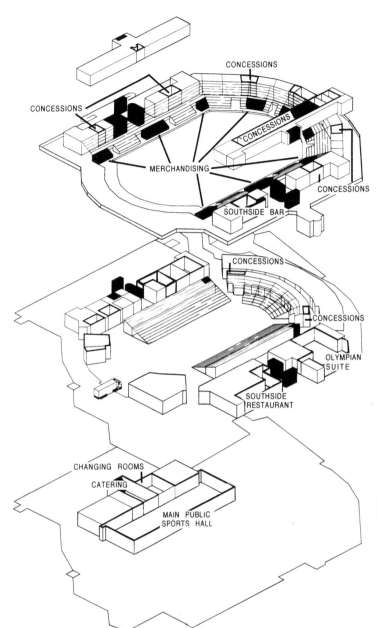

and opaque film will be applied to exit doors in 1995 to counteract the impression that they are entryways.
■ The NIA suffers operational difficulties as a result of its center-city location. The facility is surrounded by roads on two sides and by the city's canal network and footbridges on the other two sides. The local road network and the speed with which the multistory parking structures can be filled and emptied create local traffic problems that have called for substantial traffic control efforts during high-capacity events.

Soon, the NIA will have its own station on the adjoining suburban rail network. Also, the site is part

of an urban renewal project that will provide further traffic-support infrastructure.

- Family shows seem to attract a large number of buses. Lack of suitable parking has made it necessary to allow buses to park on the street adjoining the arena. As a result, audiences arriving by bus are much closer to the arena entrance than they are at other large-capacity arenas and stadiums.

- A permanent ice floor was deliberately omitted in the design of the facility, to allow as many seating configurations as possible. The omission has not been a drawback because visiting ice shows either bring their own ice or use one of the two temporary pads owned by the NEC Group.

PROJECT DATA
NATIONAL INDOOR ARENA
BIRMINGHAM, ENGLAND

Owner: City of Birmingham
Architects: Hellmuth, Obata & Kassabaum, Inc., Kansas City, Missouri
Year Construction Completed: 1991

PROJECT INFORMATION
Seating Capacity: 13,000
Exhibition Space: 5,500 square meters (59,140 square feet)
Parking Spaces: 2,500

ECONOMIC INFORMATION
Total Project Cost (1991 pounds sterling): £51,000,000
Total Project Cost (1991 U.S. dollars):[1] $89,943,917
Total Project Cost (1994 U.S. dollars):[2] $96,283,576
Funding:
    United Kingdom Sports Council: £3,000,000
    Birmingham City Council: £48,000,000

Notes:
[1]Calculated based on the 1991 exchange rate (annual average).
[2]Calculated based on Consumer Price Index.

AUSTRIA CENTER VIENNA

VIENNA, AUSTRIA

Vienna has long been a popular conference destination. The city became a focus of international attention more than 25 years ago, when the United Nations chose it as its third headquarters, after New York and Geneva. Later, construction of the Austria Center Vienna (ACV)—a world-class conference complex—ensured that the Austrian capital would remain a meeting place for the world. The ACV is crucial to this role.

DEVELOPMENT STRATEGY

In 1967, the Austrian federal government decided to build permanent headquarters for two Vienna-based international organizations, the United Nations Industrial Development Organization (UNIDO) and the Inter-national Atomic Energy Agency (IAEA). A national conference center was also envisioned in connection with the project.

An international architectural competition, launched in 1970, specified a complex to accommodate the secre-

tariats of UNIDO and the IAEA, ancillary service installations, and meeting space, as well as a large conference center. Ultimately, the competition was won by an Austrian, Johann Staber.

In 1971 the federal government and the city of Vienna established the Internationales Amtssitz- und Konferenzzentrum Wien, Aktiengesellschaft (IAKW-AG). This company was charged with the planning, construction, maintenance, administration, and financing of the Vienna International Centre (VIC) project. Construction of VIC's first stage began in April 1973, and in August 1979, the building was handed over to the international organizations.

Construction of the Austria Center Vienna itself began in 1982. In 1985, the IAKW-AG was entrusted with the center's marketing and operation, but in July of that year, all tasks relating to the ACV were transferred to the Austrian Conference Center PLC. This company in turn charged the IAKW-AG with the planning, construction, and all preparations for the ACV. The center officially opened on April 22, 1987.

DESIGN AND SITE ISSUES

With the opening of the Austria Center Vienna, the city added to its existing conference venues a facility with the necessary capacity and technical systems for large international events. The layout of the halls enables a number of events to be held simultaneously.

The building has a net floor area of 90,000 square meters (967,742 square feet) and contains 14 conference halls on four levels, with a combined space of 9,500 square meters (102,150 square feet). Each hall has its own conference rooms, offices, and foyer with catering areas. In addition, some halls can be divided by using flexible partition walls, thus permitting optimal use of the building for events with related seminars, workshops, and specialized exhibitions.

All halls are fitted with full convention equipment, including simultaneous interpreting systems for up to nine languages, audiovisual equipment, and closed-circuit television. The larger halls are equipped with stages of variable dimensions. The center's restaurant seats approximately 750, and its movable walls make it possible for part of the restaurant to operate as a self-service facility.

In May 1993, the ACV's exhibition space was expanded by the addition of a new hall. This hall has a gross exhibition area of 3,252 square meters (34,968 square feet).

The ACV's location enjoys excellent transportation links to points throughout Vienna. The center is just a

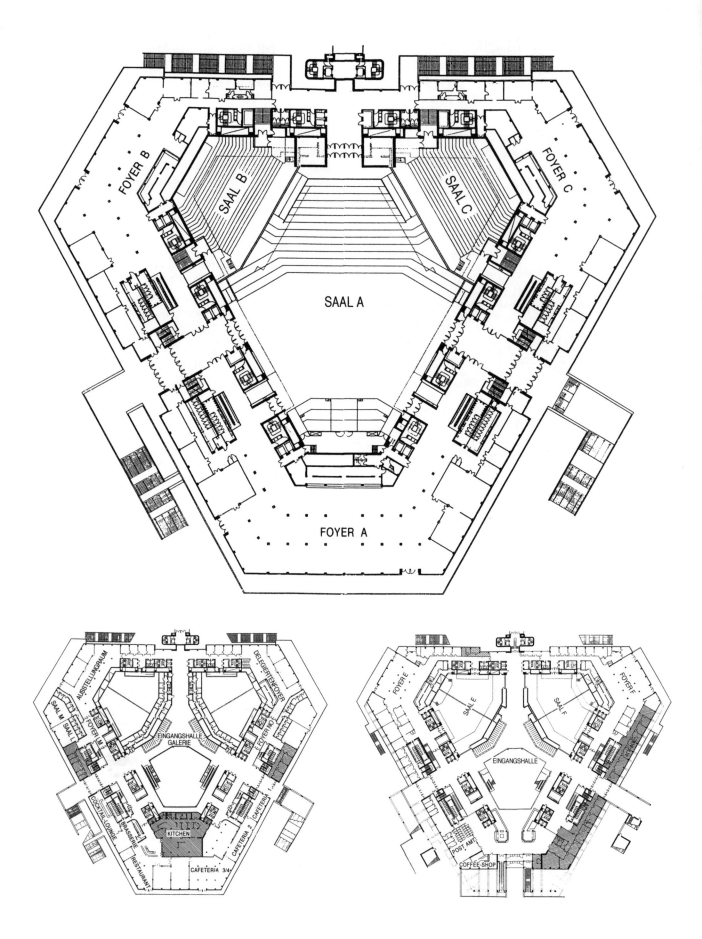

FOYER B

SAAL B

FOYER C

SAAL C

SAAL A

FOYER A

AUSSTELLUNGRAUM

SAAL M

FOYER M

SAAL

DELEGIERTENFOYER

FOYER D

EINGANGSHALLE
GALERIE

COCKTAIL-LOUNGE

BRASSERIE

RESTAURANT

KITCHEN

CAFETERIA 2

CAFETERIA 1

CAFETERIA 3/4

FOYER E

SAAL

SAAL E

SAAL F

FOYER F

EINGANGSHALLE

POST AMT

COFFEE-SHOP

20-minute drive from the airport and 12 minutes by taxi from the State Opera. Also, the Vienna Fairgrounds exhibition center is only five minutes away, enabling events to be held concurrently at two locations. Hotel accommodations include some 5,300 beds at 13 five-star hotels, 15,000 beds at 95 four-star hotels, and 9,000 beds at 114 three-star hotels.

FINANCING

In 1971, the Austrian federal government and the city of Vienna jointly founded the IAKW-AG, a stock corporation entrusted with the planning, construction, maintenance, administration, financing, and later the operation of the VIC and ACV. Other sources of capital for the ACV included Saudi Arabia, Kuwait, and Abu Dhabi.

MARKET ORIENTATION

IAKW-AG is responsible for managing the ACV. Events held at the center include major international conferences, such as the European Council summit and the UN Conference on Human Rights. Conventions with related exhibitions include those of medical and technical associations, such as the Central European Anaesthesia Congress and the American Association of Petroleum Geologists. Product launches at the facility have included events staged by Coca-Cola, Ford, IBM, and Mercedes Benz. Concerts hosted by the ACV range from classical to jazz. The complex has hosted such artists as Al Jarreau, Miles Davis, and the Vienna Philharmonic Orchestra.

Today's tighter corporate budgets mean that meeting managers are becoming increasingly cost-conscious. To keep expenditure to a minimum, conference venues are being retained in lieu of developing and operating "in-house" facilities. In turn, for convention facilities, repeat business is of vital importance.

The ACV's efforts to meet customer requirements and to keep in close touch with regular clients have been rewarded by growing numbers of follow-up events. In 1995, the ACV launched an important marketing initiative in the United States: the center joined forces with Austrian Airlines, other conference facilities, and the Vienna Convention Bureau in establishing the Vienna Destination Group, whose purpose is to promote Vienna as a conference destination by undertaking combined sales and marketing activities aimed at attracting more American meetings and incentives to Vienna.

PROJECT DATA

AUSTRIA CENTER VIENNA
VIENNA, AUSTRIA

Owner: Österreichisches Konferenzzentrum Wien, AG (ACC)
Developer: Internationales Amtssitz- und Konferenzzentrum Wien, AG (IAKW-AG)
Architect: Johann Staber
Primary Users: National and international meetings, concerts
Year Construction Began: 1982
Year Construction Completed: 1987

PROJECT INFORMATION
Building Volume: 506,000 cubic meters (661,342 cubic yards)
Total GBA: 90,000 square meters (967,742 square feet)
   Exhibition Space: 13,200 square meters (142,000 square feet)[1]
   Meeting Space: 9,500 square meters (102,150 square feet)
Total Seating Capacity: 9,750
Total Parking Spaces: 1,000

ECONOMIC INFORMATION
Total Project Cost (1987 Austrian schillings): ATS 3,300,000,000
Share Capital of ACC (Austrian schillings):
   Republic of Austria: ATS 1,500,000,000
   Kingdom of Saudi Arabia: ATS 775,000,000
   State of Kuwait: ATS 500,000,000
   Abu Dhabi: ATS 225,000,000

Note:
[1]Without meeting halls.

Other high-priority markets include Germany, the United Kingdom, Belgium, France, the Netherlands, and Scandinavia.

LESSONS LEARNED

- Expansion of the exhibition facilities has been proposed in order to meet the rising demand for this type of space.
- The center's location is excellent, thanks to nearby public transportation and new infrastructure planned in the immediate vicinity. More hotels within walking distance, however, would be advantageous.
- Redesigning the entrance hall to allow for a dedicated registration area and cloakrooms on each of the four levels would be beneficial.

HONG KONG CONVENTION AND EXHIBITION CENTRE

WANCHAI, HONG KONG

Just as Hong Kong is a place where the ultimate in modern technology coexists comfortably with exotic age-old traditions, the Hong Kong Convention and Exhibition Centre is a sophisticated, state-of-the-art facility that interweaves ultramodern technology with the Chinese tradition of fine service.

DEVELOPMENT STRATEGY

For many years, the Hong Kong Trade Development Council and the organizers of exhibitions and meetings in Hong Kong had been interested in securing a purpose-built convention and exhibition facility. In February 1985, the Hong Kong government deeded a 7.7-acre plot of Victoria Harbour to the Hong Kong Trade Development Council (TDC) for a new world-class convention and exhibition centre. Polytown Company, Ltd.—a subsidiary of New World Development Company, Ltd., a large Hong Kong–based multinational—was contracted to design, build, market, and eventually operate the Hong Kong Convention and Exhibition Centre (HKCEC) after its opening in 1988.

DESIGN AND SITE ISSUES

The entire complex, which has an area of about 4.4 million square feet, consists of a podium that contains the HKCEC and ancillary supporting areas. Towers, standing at each corner of the podium, house the Grand Hyatt and New World Harbour View hotels, office space, a trade mart, and apartments.

HKCEC constitutes most of the complex's podium. From the lower levels upward, the center consists of automobile parking and storage at the basement level; ground-level loading and unloading areas, registration area, and pedestrian promenade; and a conference level composed of exhibition, meeting, and banquet space, plus a restaurant, cafe, and lounges.

A total of 194,000 square feet (18,000 square meters) of exhibition space is offered in two exhibition halls, each of which can be subdivided with operable acoustic walls to create flexible spaces as small as 43,000 square feet (4,000 square meters). The halls are serviced by ten freight elevators, two of which are capable of carrying fully loaded, 40-foot-long container trucks.

The convention hall provides 19,400 square feet (1,800 square meters) of multipurpose space to accommodate conferences, gala performances, light exhibitions, receptions, and large banquets. The hall can be subdi-

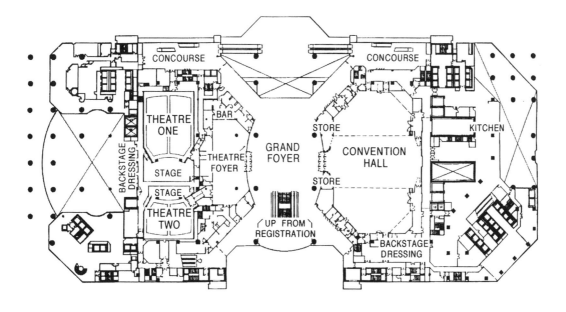

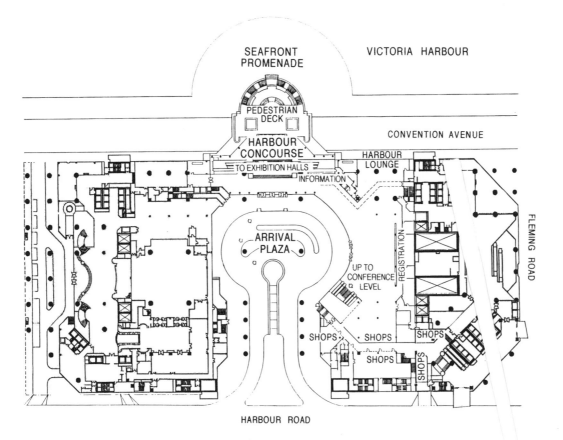

vided into three smaller ones and is equipped with theatrical lighting and sound systems; facilities for projection, audiovisual, and central recording; and language interpretation for up to eight languages. VIP suites, a press area, and backstage facilities are included, as well as an in-house teleconferencing system linking the hall to the center's two theaters to accommodate larger meetings of up to 3,500 delegates.

HKCEC's two theaters are designed for international conferences, with seating for 634 and 636 persons.

Interpretation for up to eight languages is provided in the larger theater and up to four languages in the smaller one. Connecting the theater and the convention hall are the theater foyer and grand foyer.

Twenty-four meeting rooms containing a total of 36,000 square feet (3,427 square meters) are located on three levels to serve the conference facilities and exhibition halls.

HKCEC functions are supported by two international hotels, the Grand Hyatt and the New World Harbour View, which offer a total of 1,464 rooms. Both hotels are connected directly to the HKCEC arrival area. A 38-story office and trade mart tower stands on the southeast corner of the podium and provides about 12,500 square feet (1,170 square meters) of net usable office space on each floor. On the southwest corner, a 35-story apartment tower houses 630 fully furnished apartments. A three-level parking garage with 1,070 parking spaces is located within the complex. Enclosed footbridges link the complex to surrounding areas and provide easy access for pedestrians.

HKCEC is currently undergoing an expansion that will increase its available exhibition space to a total of 539,000 square feet (50,000 square meters). The expansion will include three exhibition halls, a convention hall, and additional meeting space. Other features will include an international business centre and more restaurants. The new space will be linked to the existing building by a three-story, glass atrium and foyer.

FINANCING

Financing for the existing center (Phase I) was provided by New World Development, Co., Ltd., at a total cost of 3.8 billion Hong Kong dollars. When completed, the HKCEC portion of the complex was given to the Hong Kong Government/TDC.

The center is privately funded. Totally self-supporting, it receives no funding from the government. HKCEC Management, Ltd., pays the TDC 5 percent of the center's annual gross income for the right to manage.

MARKET ORIENTATION

Though HKCEC finished its first year with just 24 bookings, since 1988 that number has increased to 1,472 in 1995. HKCEC's marketing strategy is to position the center among the top international venues by offering the highest-quality service. The center's location, design, and surrounding amenities make it a highly regarded meeting and convention destination.

Members of the center management staff strongly believe that the facility should also should serve the local community. They have been very successful in attracting large local receptions, corporate receptions, and social functions. They also work with local media, schools, and charitable organizations on a variety of joint promotions to improve life in Hong Kong.

PROJECT DATA

HONG KONG CONVENTION AND EXHIBITION CENTRE WANCHAI, HONG KONG

Owner: Hong Kong Trade Development Council
Developer: Hong Kong Trade Development Council
Architects: Polytown Company, Ltd.
Year Planning Began: 1985
Year Construction Completed: 1988

PROJECT INFORMATION

Site Area: 4.4 million square feet (entire complex)
    Exhibition Space: 194,000 square feet
    Conference Space: 19,400 square feet
    Meeting Space: 36,900 square feet
Total Parking Spaces: 1,070

ECONOMIC INFORMATION

Construction Costs: HK$1,100,000,000
Total Project Cost (1988 Hong Kong dollars):
    HK$3,800,000,000
Total Project Cost (approximate U.S. dollars):
    $490,618,000[1]

Note:
[1]Calculated based on the exchange rate of 0.12911.

LESSONS LEARNED

- The success of the HKCEC can be attributed to the partnership between the HKCEC, the TDC, the hotels, and Hong Kong's convention bureau.
- The vertical design of the complex and of HKCEC does not provide for smooth pedestrian traffic flow between function areas. Phase II will improve multi-use capability and the flow of people by changing the placement of function areas.

KYOTO INTERNATIONAL CONFERENCE HALL

KYOTO, JAPAN

Though Kyoto International Conference Hall is situated on the shore of Lake Takaraga-ike, with a backdrop of rolling green hills, it is only ten minutes from downtown Kyoto. The hall is a modern, fully equipped international convention center. Its outstanding architecture, comprehensive facilities, and service have drawn high praise from congress and trade-show organizers since its opening in 1966. The rich opportunities for sightseeing and recreation in this historic and cultural city help to distinguish the conventions held there.

DEVELOPMENT STRATEGY

Kyoto International Conference Hall is owned by the government of Japan and operated by a nonprofit organization called the Statutory Foundation. After gaining membership in the United Nations in 1956, the Japa-

nese government decided that building an international conference center would further enhance and confirm Japan's new position in the world. Under the auspices of the Ministry of Construction, the central government sponsored an open contest soliciting designs for the new center, which should synthesize the best of contemporary design and traditional architecture. The winning design was submitted by Sachio Otani, professor emeritus at Tokyo University.

Construction began in November 1962, and the building opened its doors on May 21, 1966. The land and building are the property of the Ministry of Finance.

After the center had hosted several intergovernmental conferences, management acknowledged a shortage of space for press conferences and banquets. To correct this deficiency, a ¥1.02 billion expansion began in 1970 and was completed in 1973.

In 1985, the event hall was built at a cost of ¥3.03 billion to meet client needs for exhibition space for trade shows and conventions with exhibitions. The event hall is connected to the main building by a roofed passageway.

DESIGN AND SITE ISSUES

Kyoto International Conference Hall is composed of the main building and the event hall/lodgings facility. The main building has seven major rooms, 13 meeting rooms, 47 general-purpose rooms, and two banquet halls (Swan and Sakura); the event hall/lodging facility

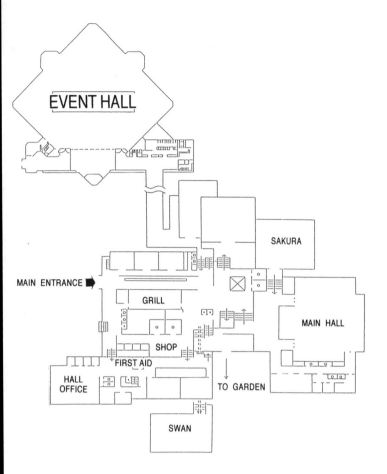

EVENT HALL

MAIN ENTRANCE ▶

SAKURA

GRILL

MAIN HALL

SHOP

FIRST AID

HALL OFFICE

TO GARDEN

SWAN

PROJECT DATA
KYOTO INTERNATIONAL CONFERENCE HALL
KYOTO, JAPAN

Owner: Government of Japan
Operator: Statutory Foundation
Architect: Sachio Otani
Primary Users: Government, international organizations, and medical, scientific, and academic associations
Period When Planning Began: 1956
Year First Construction Began: 1962
Year First Construction Completed: 1966
Second Construction Completed: 1973
Third Construction Completed: 1985

PROJECT INFORMATION
Site Area: 157,100 square meters (1,688,200 square feet)
Total Floor Space: 42,008 square meters (451,700 square feet)
Total Seating Capacity: 9,000
Total Parking Spaces: 600

ECONOMIC INFORMATION
First Construction Cost (1966 yen): ¥3.66 billion
Second Construction Cost (1973 yen): ¥1.02 billion
Third Construction Cost (1985 yen): ¥3.03 billion
Total Project Cost: ¥7.71 billion

includes 3,000 square meters (32,300 square feet) of multipurpose space and 30 sleeping rooms (28 western-style twin bedrooms and two Japanese-style bedrooms). The Hoshoan Tea Ceremony House, designed in the traditional sukiya style and standing in the gardens, was designed by Soshitsu Sen, Grand Master XV of the Urasenke School of Tea.

The total site area is over 157,000 square meters (1,688,200 square feet), while the center contains a total floor space of 42,008 square meters (451,700 square feet). Overall, there are 600 on-site parking spaces and nearly 100 meeting rooms that can accommodate 10 to 3,000 people. Seven rooms are equipped for simultaneous interpretation into six to eight languages. There is a teleconferencing room, a fiber-optic communication network, and a LAN system wired throughout the entire hall. A new subway station will open in 1997 next to the facility.

MARKET ORIENTATION

Kyoto International Conference Hall focuses on attracting conferences of international organizations, intergovernmental and corporate/industrial conferences, and meetings associated with incentive travel activities. The hall also hosts official receptions, concerts, banquets, and exhibitions, such as those of the Nishijin textile industry, auto shows, Buddhist altars, furniture exhibitions, fashion shows, banquets, and ceremonies.

LESSONS LEARNED

- The conference hall was designed more than 30 years ago. Today, international organizations are larger and have different space requirements than were provided for in the original building. To meet the changing needs of potential clients, the facility requires an expansion of this building.
- In 1966, the conference hall was the first such purpose-built congress facility in Japan. It provided a stimulus to the Japanese convention industry and continues to fuel the growth of that industry.

THE QUEEN ELIZABETH II CONFERENCE CENTRE

LONDON, ENGLAND

Before 1974, government conferences held in central London relied on inefficient and outdated facilities. Commercial facilities available at that time lacked roundtable seating, secretariat and delegation offices, high-quality simultaneous interpretation capabilities, media facilities, and security. Government-owned facilities such as Lancaster House and Marlborough House, while beautiful historic buildings, were unsuitable for high-level government conferences. It was then that U.K. government officials determined that a purpose-built conference center was needed in central London. In 1975, architects Powell Moya Partners were commissioned to carry out a feasibility study on developing a new conference facility in London for the government of the United Kingdom.

DEVELOPMENT STRATEGY

Although there was common agreement that a purpose-built government conference facility was required in central London, its location, size, and financing arrangements were by no means certain. In 1978, then–Prime Minister James Callaghan gave approval for the project to begin, but it was not until June 1986 that Her Majesty officially opened the Queen Elizabeth II Conference Centre (QEIICC).

DESIGN AND SITE ISSUES

Several central London sites were considered, but ultimately the government-owned Broad Sanctuary site was selected. The land had been unoccupied for some time, as government officials believed that it was too important a location to be used for offices and should therefore be reserved for a building of national significance. Opposite Westminster Abbey and within sight of the Houses of Parliament, the site presented the design team with both aesthetic and practical problems. It involved strict regulations on building and street construction, which put severe limitations on the architects who designed the center.

The QEIICC can accommodate meetings of 300 to 1,000 delegates and small exhibitions. The center's Churchill Auditorium is equipped with full audiovisual capabilities and can provide simultaneous interpretation for up to nine languages. Building and delegate security

was of primary importance throughout all stages of the design and construction process.

FINANCING

The project was originally intended to be privately financed; by 1982, however, it became apparent that construction would need to be funded by the central government. Development began in April 1982 and was planned to be completed in 45 months, aiming for a January 1986 opening. In mid-1983, the government began to explore the commercial viability of the conference center. The result was a change in policy regarding future use, to allow commercial conferences to take place when government conferences were not using the center, without compromising government security. This decision was to have a profound effect on future center operations.

MARKET ORIENTATION

It was originally thought that, apart from government and quasi-government organizations, there would be only limited use of the facility by the private sector. This misperception was reinforced when the UK held the presidency of the European Community and during the cen-

ter's first six months of operations the center was used almost exclusively to support that activity. The view of many practitioners in the conference industry was that QEIICC security restrictions would discourage use by commercial groups. This expectation turned out to be unwarranted: clients, particularly those seeking confidentiality or guaranteed privacy, use the center because of its security. Center users include international, national, and regional medical, financial, and legal groups and associations, in addition to the high-level government groups for which the facility was designed. Functions have included economic summits, NATO summits, and major intergovernmental conferences.

The QEIICC's location in central London—an international, financial, and cultural center—is well served by international airlines and the rail link to Europe.

LESSONS LEARNED

- The center design team clearly met its goals by producing an architecturally pleasing building that fits comfortably into its beautiful, historic surroundings.
- The QEIICC's roles are "to provide and manage fully secure conference facilities for national and international government meetings up to the highest level, and to market its facilities commercially as a high-

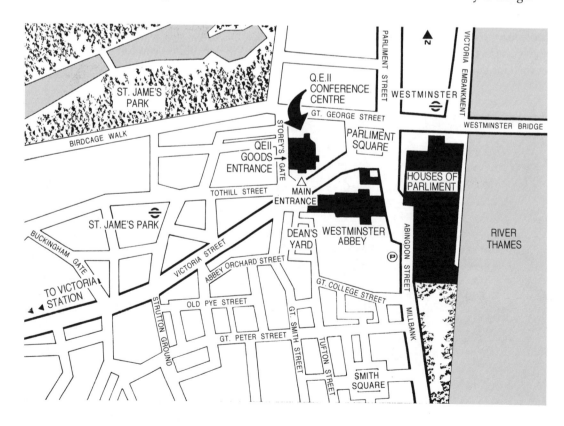

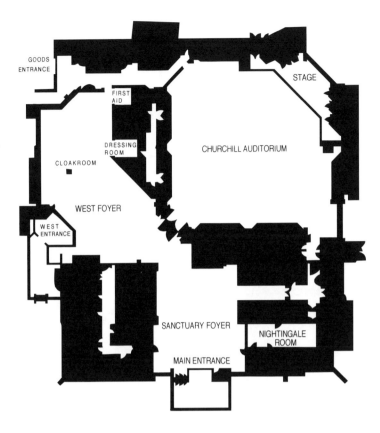

quality venue for government and private sector use."
If these roles had been identified before the design
work had commenced, the facility would certainly be
different today.

The private sector requires catering and banqueting
facilities not normally needed by government groups.
Exhibition space is limited, and loading dock access
and capacity are restricted. Catering requirements
have, to a large extent, been met by adapting existing
space for banqueting and providing satellite facilities
when needed. The loading-in and loading-out problems are being ameliorated by the construction of a
large freight elevator on the outside of the building.

- Despite the apparent difficulties associated with operating within both the government and private sectors,
the access problems on site, and the challenge of managing a facility designed for government conferences
only, the QEIICC has made its mark as a high-quality

venue for international conferences. By 1993, the center had been voted the U.K.'s best conference venue
for six consecutive years by the meetings industry and
had been awarded a national Citizens' Charter Mark
in recognition of the outstanding quality of service it
has given to the public.

- The QEIICC, by making a virtue out of a necessity,
has gained a worldwide reputation for its emphasis on
delegate safety and security. Through this reputation,
the center has unintentionally gained a marketing
advantage. Evidence includes the growing number of
corporate clients that have perceived the benefits of
holding trouble-free stockholders' meetings in a secure environment.

Additionally, the unrivaled safety and security
expertise that exists at the QEIICC has been made
available on a consulting basis to conference and exhibition facilities internationally. Security director David
Reilly, who served on the project's steering committee,
is in regular demand as a speaker at international conferences and seminars.

MONTRÉAL CONVENTION CENTER

MONTRÉAL, QUEBEC, CANADA

Montréal has historically been a preferred destination for convention organizers, but not until 1983 did the city have the proper facilities to accommodate these events. Since Montréal Convention Center opened, the city has typically ranked in the top five meeting destinations in North America. Essentially, construction of the convention center was a need whose time had come because it was essential to retaining the city's share of the North American market.

DEVELOPMENT STRATEGY

Planning for Montréal Convention Center began over 150 years ago. When the city was planning its 1842 bicentennial, officials of the day talked about building a "municipal center." Enthusiasm for the idea came and went well into the next century, and by the 1930s, a few proposals seemed to sustain interest, including one to build a civic center above Central Station in the downtown. Unfortunately, the outbreak of World War II shelved this plan indefinitely.

Recommendations for a center regained momentum in the late 1940s and early 50s, but to no avail. Finally,

in 1977, it appeared that years of perseverance would bear fruit. The Quebec Cabinet, acting on the recommendations of a study on the project's economic, social, and political advantages that had been conducted by an engineering consulting firm, approved development of the convention center, which would be built on the very location first proposed—a few steps from Bleury Street, halfway between Viger Square and Central Station.

The government's decision to proceed with construction came on the heels of the 1976 Summer Olympic Games. In the wake of that celebration, and coupled with the worldwide kudos the city had received for Expo '67 World's Fair, Montréal was establishing itself as a widely respected host to international events. Members of Montréal's business and tourism communities recognized the need for an added drawing card to maintain the accustomed volume of visitors to this cosmopolitan and historically rich city.

The city was also looking for new ways to raise its international profile and enhance its drawing power, and the creation of a convention center would enhance its attractiveness.

Groundbreaking took place in 1979, and after more than three years of construction, the official inauguration was held on May 27, 1983. Since that time, the Société du Palais de Congrès de Montréal has been responsible for the center's administration and promotion.

In its first ten months of operation, the Montréal Convention Center hosted 74 events, bringing 350,000 visitors to the city and exerting an estimated $14.5 million impact on Quebec's tourism industry. Montréal Convention Center was well on its way to fulfilling its twofold mandate: to attract delegates and visitors from outside Quebec and to stimulate tourism development within the province.

By its tenth anniversary in 1993, Montréal Convention Center had hosted 1,551 events, which drew the participation of 5.4 million visitors, generating an added value estimated at $1.6 billion for the city and province.

DESIGN AND SITE ISSUES

The decision to locate the convention center on Viger Avenue responded ideally to the perceived needs of delegates and tourists. The property purchased for the convention center by the Quebec Ministry of Supply and Public Works in 1977 challenged architectural and engineering firms literally to build over one of the city's main expressways, the Ville-Marie. As the location was studied in greater depth, the functional, architectural,

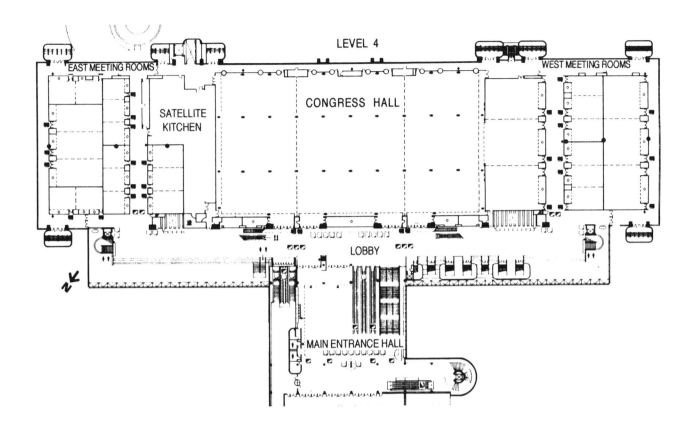

LEVEL 4

EAST MEETING ROOMS

SATELLITE KITCHEN

CONGRESS HALL

WEST MEETING ROOMS

LOBBY

MAIN ENTRANCE HALL

N

and aesthetic considerations also became opportunities for innovation.

The expressway, a modern symbol of accelerated communication, would form the foundation for the center and act as a bridge between the city's venerable past—Old Montréal—and its future—the expanding landscape of a new, internationally oriented business district uptown. This conjunction would effectively place the center at the heart of the city's social, cultural, and business activity. Thus, the structure itself had to reflect not only the unique allure of the city but also the most innovative architectural thinking of the day. (Montréal's buildings, from Victorian gray stone structures to post-modern office towers, reflect just about every major movement in architecture since the 17th century.)

From a practical standpoint, the site met every location criterion as well: proximity to a burgeoning number of hotels, shops, restaurants, and tourist attractions; accessibility to the subway system, or Metro; and convenient access to a growing network of shopping complexes that link the north and south axes of the city.

In 1978, the Quebec government launched an official design competition. This type of selection process was a first for Quebec and inspired a high level of creativity in the design proposals. The winning submission, chosen primarily for its originality, engineering, and use of space, was produced by a team of urban architects headed by Victor Prus. Integration with the environment, energy conservation, and the selection of building materials native to Quebec were important judging criteria as well.

Construction began in 1979 and would be completed in five phases, starting with the parking levels on the north side, followed by the foundation work and infrastructure, the underground parking on the south side of the expressway, the superstructure, and finally the tunnel linking the center with shopping complexes and cultural centers.

Designed as a small to mid-sized facility by today's standards, Montréal Convention Center has been hailed as a harmonious blend of concrete, steel, and glass, combining the power and solidity of the bridge engineering employed in its expressway facades with the more ethereal and open atrium effect of its sloping glass wall, or north facade. The interior is the primary beneficiary of this concept, with its easy circulation of visitors, a sense of space produced by the absence of columns, and an abundance of natural light.

The convention center offers a total of 180,000 square feet of available public area: about 100,000 square feet for exhibition space and 80,000 square feet for meetings and food functions. The building houses six floors, with Levels 1 and 4 devoted to convention facilities. The exhibition hall on Level 1 has an area of 102,450 square feet, with room for 520 display booths, and can be divided to accommodate smaller exhibits simultaneously. An outdoor plaza, the Esplanade, located off the main entrance, offers 29,280 square feet of additional event space.

On the Convention Level is a 45,280-square-foot congress hall with seating for 6,030 people in theater style or 4,620 people for a banquet. Thirty-one meeting rooms are also available for other functions in this level's east and west wings.

FINANCING

In 1977, the project cost was estimated at $60 million, but the final tally was $81.5 million. Fortunately, project planners were prepared to handle the overrun. According to the Quebec Ministry of Supply and Public Works, which relied on Statistics Canada for its budget data, the rate of cost escalation closely mimicked the inflationary scale for nonresidential construction costs.

The Canadian government invested $24 million in the project, while the provincial government assumed the balance of $57 million. This joint venture demonstrated the will of both governments to make Montréal and the province key players on the North American and international markets.

MARKET ORIENTATION

From the outset, marketing efforts were targeted at professional associations in international and North American (U.S. and Canadian) markets. Research suggested that convention center sales representation in Washington and Paris would expand the center's reach to meeting planners in these markets, so offices in Paris and Washington were opened in 1985 and 1991, respectively. And it was thought that events should be solicited according to their potential for economic spinoffs: delegate spending, hotel nights, and the like. This strategy has remained intact since the beginning.

The main focus is on North American associations or organizations because 90 percent of their headquarters are located in Washington, while 70 percent of the head offices of international associations are located in Europe. Approximately 25 percent of the events staged at the center today (events of 1,500 delegates and up, primarily medical and scientific congresses and professional and trade exhibitions) draw participation from outside the province. National or continental outreach, coupled with a wide range of local and regional activities, enables the center to adhere to its dual mandate of developing tourism and contributing to the economic and cultural life of Montréal.

In 1985, the center began a strategy of expanding its representation to international markets with the found-

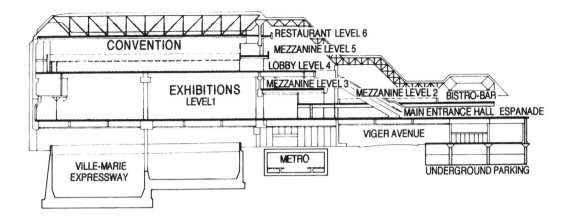

ing of the Ambassadors' Club, which recruits prominent members of the Montréal community, whose professional status in certain fields helps to bring about the staging of major international events at the convention center.

LESSONS LEARNED

Montréal Convention Center has exceeded its original occupancy estimates. Because of this success, limited space is a problem faced by the center today. Occupancy levels have consistently ranged close to the practical maximum, or about 70 to 75 percent. The increased popularity of Montréal as an international destination, along with the globalization of markets, has spurred a demand that the convention center is now struggling to accommodate. To stay competitive and responsive to its clientele, the center will need to double its current exhibition and convention space. And to meet that objective, it is estimated that government financing of $150 million will be required.

The first step has been taken, however, with the addition of a $5 million banquet room, which will increase the center's available rental space by 15 percent. The open-air rooftop terrace on the center's west wing has been converted into an enclosed panoramic room with a capacity of 1,800 people at a seated meal or 2,700 people at a reception. This initiative, financed through the center's existing budget, has already proved helpful in securing future bookings.

PROJECT DATA
MONTRÉAL CONVENTION CENTER
MONTRÉAL, QUEBEC, CANADA

Owner: Government of Quebec
Developer: Ministry of Supply and Public Works
Design Team:
    Architecture: Victor Prus, urban architect, Montréal; Lemoyne et Associes, urban architects, Montréal; Labelle, Marchand, Geoffroy, architects, Montréal; Hebert & Lalonde, architect and designer, Montréal
    Structure: Martineau, Vallee & Associes, Montréal; Deslauriers, Mercier & Associes, Montréal; Dr. Jules Houde and Pierre Sibille, engineers, Montréal
    Mechanical and Electrical Engineering: Pageau, Morel & Associes, Montréal
Year Planning Began: 1977
Year Construction Began: 1979
Year Construction Completed: 1983

PROJECT INFORMATION
Exhibition Space: 100,000 square feet
Meeting Space: 80,000 square feet
Total Parking Spaces: 434

ECONOMIC INFORMATION
Total Project Cost (Canadian dollars): $81,560,907
Funding Sources (Canadian dollars):
    Government of Canada: $24,000,000
    Government of Quebec: $57,000,000

NICE ACROPOLIS CONVENTION CENTRE

NICE, FRANCE

The Nice Acropolis Convention Centre in Nice, France, has established itself as one of the most popular meeting and exhibition facilities in Europe. With over 50,000 square meters (537,600 square feet) of flexible space, the center can adapt to meet the needs of both large and small groups. Its location on the French Riviera and its proximity to France's second-largest airport makes it an ideal destination for national and international meetings and trade shows.

DEVELOPMENT STRATEGY

The idea of building the Acropolis was introduced by the city of Nice, which already had an exhibition center and all the other amenities required for meetings and conventions: hotels, restaurants, shopping, attractions, and air service. It was therefore a natural progression to develop appropriate meeting facilities, and Nice authorities

began planning the convention center in 1979. The center was built adjacent to the existing exhibition center and named the Acropolis out of respect for Nice's ancestry. Originally, Nice was a colony of Greece, where the word "acropolis" meant the highest place in the city.

DESIGN AND SITE ISSUES

The concept and design of the center were entrusted to a group of architects and to the members of a local research unit, who were instructed to pay special attention to two factors: color and light. The sky and the city are visible through the glass walls of the Agora, the atrium that links the center's three levels and serves as a focal point and reception area.

The center's flexibility is enhanced by a system of movable walls allowing for the creation of large or small meeting spaces. Advanced acoustical engineering prevents the transmission of unwanted noise throughout the facility. With closed-circuit technology, all rooms can be electronically linked. The Acropolis was designed for conventions and professional exhibitions, but superior acoustics in the main auditorium (Apollon) make it useful as the city's second opera house.

The Nice Acropolis Convention Centre contains 50,000 square meters of meeting and exhibition space on three levels, including a main hall (Agora); four auditoriums (Hermes, Apollon, Athena, and Iris); two multipurpose/exhibition areas (Mediterranee and Rhodes); and banquet rooms (Les Muses). This makes the center suitable for events of 50 to 5,000 people.

The Apollon auditorium, which spans all three levels, seats 2,500 or 3,400 by special arrangement. Its orchestra pit has a capacity of 120 musicians, and some of the world's most famous opera companies have performed here.

The Mediterranée, a multipurpose room of 1,800 square meters (19,350 square feet), is found on the first level and has movable partitions to accommodate more than 100 booths. The Rhodes, a hall on the second level, is accessible from the Mediterranée and can be used in combination to provide a total of 4,300 square meters (46,225 square feet) of exhibit space. The Iris amphitheater is located next to the Mediterranée and is fully equipped for conferences.

The Acropolis' second level is unique because of its spatial design. The Rhodes hall can be used in combination not only with the Mediterranée, as mentioned, but also with the 300-seat Hermes and 750-seat Athena auditoriums to accommodate conferences with exhibitions.

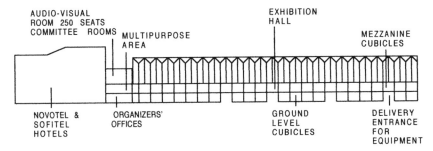

Acropolis Expositions

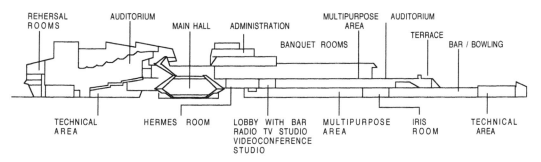

Acropolis Congress

The third level features the Les Muses banquet rooms, with a total of 2,600 square meters (27,950 square feet). Les Muses can accommodate 2,000 for banquets and up to 4,000 for receptions. A 1,500-square-meter (16,125-square-foot) terrace also situated on this level is used for outdoor receptions.

The Acropolis, which stands in the city center, is accessible from nearby hotels by foot or public transportation and is about ten minutes' drive from the Nice Côte d'Azur international airport, the second-busiest airfield in France. Facilities adjacent to the center include restaurants, a post office, a bank, and two hotels, one on each side of the entrance to the exhibition center.

Financing

Center construction was financed entirely by the city of Nice, which also provides operating subsidies.

Market Orientation

The Acropolis was chosen as the winner of the Best Convention Center Award in the meetings category for three consecutive years—1991, 1992, and 1993—by the London magazine *Meetings and Incentives*. It has captured

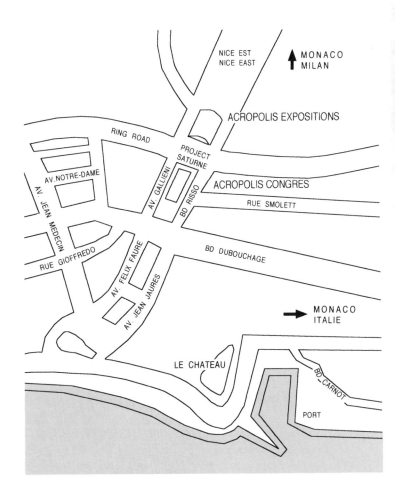

a share of the highly competitive medical and scientific conference market and is one of the leaders in new car shows. The facility is one of the few in France with a full range of capabilities for holding conventions with more than 1,000 participants.

The center's primary users are international association conferences and exhibitions, corporate meetings, and national and international professional trade shows. More than 100 conferences are held at the Acropolis annually, attracting upwards of 85,000 participants, over half of whom come from other countries.

LESSONS LEARNED

- Underground parking would have been a desirable feature, but it was not feasible, given the geology of the site. The building is constructed on the "vaults" of an ancient underground river, standing on the land above the river bank; therefore, underground parking was impossible. Nonetheless, parking facilities for 2,000 cars are available nearby.
- More exhibition space and larger storage areas would have been preferred.
- The possibility of on-site specialty retail shops needs to be explored.
- The center's success is dependent on the city's keeping the facility equipped with the latest in technological developments.
- Transforming the center's immediate surroundings into a pedestrian zone and diverting auto traffic would be beneficial.

PROJECT DATA

NICE ACROPOLIS CONVENTION CENTRE
NICE, FRANCE

Owner: City of Nice
Architect: Georges Buzzi, Pierre Baptiste, and Pierre Bernasconi, Nice
Primary Users: Conferences, trade shows, concerts, opera, and ballet
Year Planning Began: 1979
Year Construction Began: 1981
Year Construction Completed: 1985

PROJECT INFORMATION
Site Area: 7.9 acres
Meeting and Exhibit Space: 50,000 square meters (537,600 square feet)
Total Parking Spaces: 2,000 nearby

ECONOMIC INFORMATION
Total Project Cost (1985 French francs):[1] Fr625,000,000
Total Project Cost (1985 U.S. dollars):[2] $82,700,000
Total Project Cost (1994 U.S. dollars):[3] $112,060,037

Notes:
[1]Financed by the city of Nice.
[2]Calculated based on the exchange rate on December 31, 1985.
[3]Calculated based on the consumer price index.

LE PALAIS DES CONGRÈS DE PARIS

PARIS, FRANCE

Before 1974, Paris lacked a modern facility to accommodate meetings and international conferences. The city and chamber of commerce helped to fill this void by building a center that reflects the trends and personality of the city, Le Palais des Congrès de Paris (Paris Congress Center). In the heart of Paris, this "city within a city" is well placed to offer high-quality facilities to groups of all sizes.

DEVELOPMENT STRATEGY

The Paris Congress Center is owned by the Société Immobilière du Palais des Congrès and operated by the Société d'Exploitation du Palais des Congrès de Paris (SEPCP); both are private corporations. When the city of Paris promoted the center's development and searched for a partner to share the risk, Paris' chamber of commerce responded to this request by entering into a joint venture with the city to build the center. The design was provided by the French architectural firm of Guibout, Maloletenkov, Gillet.

SITE ANALYSIS

The center stands on the Champs-Elysées between the Arc de Triomphe and the town of Neuilly. Its features include three auditoriums, an exhibition hall, and 50 conference (meeting) rooms. The center is connected to the 990-room Hotel Concorde Lafayette and is directly across the street from the 1,027-room Hotel Meridien.

Built on seven levels, the Paris Congress Center was constructed around a 3,700-seat auditorium that accommodates major assembly sessions. The auditorium's design allows it to downsize to 1,800 seats for smaller assemblies. It is equipped with state-of-the-art audiovisual technology and can provide simultaneous interpretation in six languages. Two smaller theaters, Salle Bleue (Blue Room) and Salle Havane (Brown Room), provide seating for 826 and 400, respectively.

The center's 8,000 square meters (86,000 square feet) of exhibit space offers the flexibility to accommodate groups requiring as little as ten square meters to those with up to 500 exhibitors. Each of the facility's 50 conference rooms is provided with its own entrance and cloakroom. A 2,000-square-meter (21,500-square-foot) banquet hall on the seventh level can be transformed into private lounges or opened to accommodate up to 2,000 diners seated or 4,000 at a reception; the adjacent Hotel Concorde Lafayette and the center have an agreement that grants the hotel exclusive use of the seventh level for banqueting.

The Paris Congress Center promotes itself as "a city within a city." The center's first three levels afford underground parking and access to public transportation and contain a post office, a travel agency, and 80 boutiques, restaurants, and nightclubs.

FINANCING

The Paris Congress Center was built in 1974 at a cost of 250 million francs. The chamber of commerce obtained a bank loan to finance the project, whose total cost, including the hotel and parking, was some 500 million francs.

MARKET ORIENTATION

The Paris Congress Center hosts local, national, and international meetings of groups as small as 300 or as large as 10,000 people, with an average of approximately 875,000 attendees per year. Primary users include international associations, medical exhibitions, and new prod-

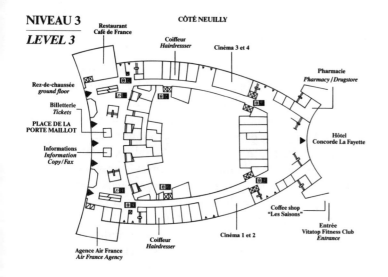

NIVEAU 3
LEVEL 3

CÔTÉ NEUILLY

Restaurant
Café de France

Coiffeur
Hairdresser

Cinéma 3 et 4

Pharmacie
Pharmacy/Drugstore

Rez-de-chaussée
ground floor

Billetterie
Tickets

PLACE DE LA
PORTE MAILLOT

Informations
Information
Copy/Fax

Hôtel
Concorde La Fayette

Coffee shop
"Les Saisons"

Entrée
Vitatop Fitness Club
Entrance

Coiffeur
Hairdresser

Cinéma 1 et 2

Agence Air France
Air France Agency

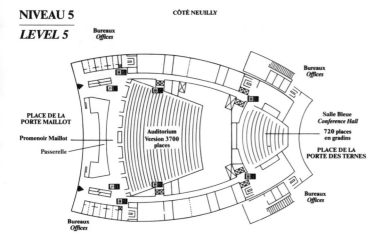

NIVEAU 5
LEVEL 5

CÔTÉ NEUILLY

Bureaux
Offices

Bureaux
Offices

PLACE DE LA
PORTE MAILLOT

Promenoir Maillot

Passerelle

Auditorium
Version 3700
places

Salle Bleue
Conference Hall

720 places
en gradins

PLACE DE LA
PORTE DES TERNES

Bureaux
Offices

Bureaux
Offices

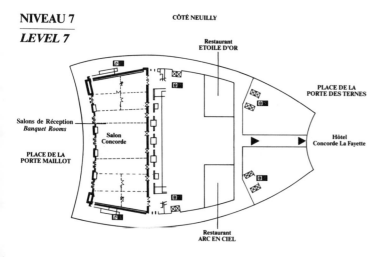

NIVEAU 7
LEVEL 7

CÔTÉ NEUILLY

Restaurant
ETOILE D'OR

PLACE DE LA
PORTE DES TERNES

Salons de Réception
Banquet Rooms

Salon
Concorde

PLACE DE LA
PORTE MAILLOT

Hôtel
Concorde La Fayette

Restaurant
ARC EN CIEL

PROJECT DATA

LE PALAIS DES CONGRÈS DE PARIS
PARIS, FRANCE

Owner: Société Immobilière du Palais des Congrès
Developer: Paris Chamber of Commerce and Industry
Architect: Guibout, Maloletenkov, Gillet
Manager: Société d'Exploitation du Palais des Congrès de Paris (SEPCP)
Year Planning Began: 1968
Year Construction Began: 1972
Year Construction Completed: 1974

PROJECT INFORMATION
Total GBA: 90,000 square meters (970,000 square feet)
  Exhibition Space: 8,000 square meters/86,000 square feet
  Conference Space: 50 rooms
  Banquet Space: 2,000 square meters/21,500 square feet
Auditorium Seating Capacity: 3,700
Total Parking Spaces: 1,500

ECONOMIC INFORMATION
Total Project Cost (1974 francs): 250,000,000

uct demonstrations. In addition to conferences, the auditorium hosts international ballets, concerts, operas, and theatrical productions.

The Paris Congress Center is accessible from the airport via shuttle bus, the metro, or the new "fast subway" (the RER), which serves Paris and the outlying metropolitan area.

LESSONS LEARNED

- Many Paris Congress Center clients have outgrown its exhibition space. The original developers did not anticipate the rate at which demand for exhibition space would increase. Also, the availability of additional banquet facilities at the center would increase its marketability and usage.
- The center's success can be attributed to its location near the center of the city, its accessibility via public transportation, and its excellent management organization. Past users attest to the efficiency and cordiality of its service staff for professional events and of its well-trained event coordinators. Professional staff have been trained and supervised by Mme. Laure Mouton, executive director for congresses and exhibitions. She has served in this capacity since the center opened.

KOREA EXHIBITION CENTER

SEOUL, SOUTH KOREA

The year 1994 marked the sixth centennial of the city of Seoul, the capital of the Republic of South Korea. Seoul was founded in 1394 during the Yi Dynasty, when the "seat of the throne" was moved there from Kaesong. Seoul, which is located in the middle of the Korean Peninsula on the northern banks of the Han River, has served for generations and continues to serve as the political, cultural, educational, and financial center for the Republic.

With its strategic location at the crossroads of transportation and commerce in Northeast Asia, Seoul offers promising business opportunities for both Korean and foreign enterprises. As Korea Exhibition Center, Inc. is the largest and most comprehensive full-service exhibition and convention facility and trade show organizer in Korea, the center provides a good setting for companies seeking to establish or expand their market presence.

DEVELOPMENT STRATEGY

The Korea Exhibition Center is better known worldwide by its acronym, KOEX. The original KOEX was built in 1979 and was owned by the Korea Foreign Trade Association (KFTA). In August 1984, a master plan to build the Korea World Trade Center on the site of the existing KOEX was endorsed by KFTA and approved by the government. Construction of the Korea World Trade Center, including a new exhibition complex, began in March 1985.

In May 1986, Korea Exhibition Center, Inc., was formed to manage and operate the new exhibition complex. The Korea World Trade Center, which is also part of the KOEX complex, opened in September 1988, just in time for the Summer Olympic Games.

The Korea World Trade Center is a completely integrated facility. Its components include a trade tower, an exhibition complex, convention facilities, a world-class hotel, a shopping mall, and a public transportation terminal. As a member of the global network of world trade centers, it is designed to provide service for resident exporters, importers, and visiting international businesspersons.

DESIGN AND SITE ISSUES

KOEX is located south of the Han River at the center of the Youngdong Area, a fast-growing business district and second downtown for Seoul. The center provides versatile, world-class exhibition space to meet the needs of exhibition and meeting planners now and into the 21st century. The KOEX design offers functional integration, with its related facilities and state-of-the-art energy conservation equipment and a floor plan that enables efficient intrabuilding crowd flow and minimizes the time needed for set-up and removal of exhibits.

KOEX has three soccer field–size exhibition halls. The Pacific Hall and Atlantic Hall are located in the Main Building, and the Continental Hall is found in the Annex. Each hall is capable of being subdivided to meet various requirements. In addition, Atlantic Hall can be transformed into multipurpose, column-free Olympia Hall which can seat up to 5,300 persons, making it ideal for conventions, conferences, and special events.

The KOEX Main Building contains large display halls designed to function as an international merchandise mart for year-round display of export and import products. These display halls are divided into the Trade Mart, Furniture Mart, and Sample Showcases. Items on display range from light- to heavy-industrial and high-tech products. The rental fee for this display space is paid by the manufacturer of the product on display.

In addition to Olympia Hall, KOEX contains conference rooms of various sizes, all with state-of-the-art equipment and first-class finishes. The Trade Tower and the Hotel Inter-Continental offer several conference rooms as well. Currently, an average of 1,000 events, including conferences, seminars, and fashion shows, are being held at KOEX annually.

FINANCING

KOEX is a wholly owned subsidiary of the Korea Foreign Trade Association. Therefore, it is a 100 percent private, profit-making corporation and is not subsidized by the government. The construction of the $126 million (1988 dollars) new KOEX was financed by the Korea Foreign Trade Association.

MARKET ORIENTATION

The center s key objective is to promote international commerce through trade shows and conventions. Exhibitions aimed at trade promotion, new product development, and exchange of technologies are given priority over general exhibitions targeted at the domestic market. Also, exhibitions organized by government and public organizations are given specific priority.

The KOEX staff also produces and organizes its own international trade shows. The proportion of trade shows organized by KOEX has grown to 35 percent annually.

To attract foreign exhibitors, KOEX maintains overseas representatives in Germany, the United States, Italy, Taiwan, and Japan.

KOEX hosted the 19th World Congress of the Societé Internationale de Chirurgie Orthopédique et de Traumatologie and the 21st Universal Postal Union World Congress Seoul '94, establishing itself not only as a leading international trade-show organizer but also as an international congress organizer.

LESSONS LEARNED

- The international trade-show industry is a relatively new and fast-growing market segment in South Korea. The number of trade shows held at KOEX grew from

37 in 1988 to 103 in 1994. It is projected that five new shows will be added each year.

- The establishment of the World Trade Organization in 1994, following the successful conclusion of the Uruguay Round of the GATT talks, widens opportunities for entirely new market strategies for product sales and services.

- As Korea accelerates the pace of its trade liberalization, many foreign firms are eager to enter the market. KOEX is proud of having promoted trade and tech-

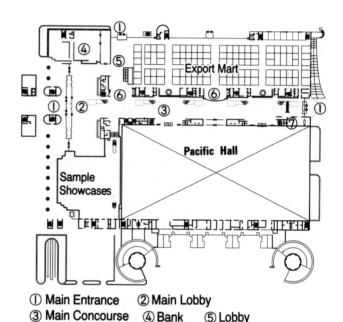

① Main Entrance ② Main Lobby
③ Main Concourse ④ Bank ⑤ Lobby
⑥ Elevator ⑦ Telephone Office

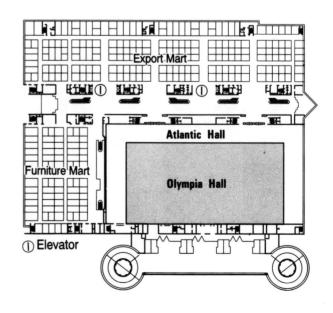

① Elevator

nology exchange between domestic and foreign companies through high-quality exhibitions and events.

■ At present, KOEX has the capacity to meet exhibition demands; should the need for more space arise, however, expansion of existing facilities may be considered.

PROJECT DATA

KOREA EXHIBITION CENTER
SEOUL, SOUTH KOREA

Owner: Subsidiary of the Korea Foreign Trade Association
Developer: Korea Foreign Trade Association
Year Planning Began: 1984
Year Completed: 1988

PROJECT INFORMATION

Site Area: 122,658 square meters (1,318,903 square feet)
Total Exhibition Space: 72,621 square meters (780,871 square feet)
Total Meeting Space: 41,167 square meters (442,656 square feet)
Total Parking: 2,500 spaces

ECONOMIC INFORMATION

Total Project Cost (1988 U.S. dollars): $126,000,000[1]
Total Project Cost (1994 U.S. dollars): $155,289,940[2]

Notes:
[1] All privately financed.
[2] Calculated based on the consumer price index.

SINGAPORE INTERNATIONAL CONVENTION AND EXHIBITION CENTRE

SINGAPORE

The city-state of Singapore, located just one degree north of the equator, is among the world's top convention and incentive travel destinations. One of the leading meeting, convention, and exhibition centers in Asia, Singapore is now enjoying one of the fastest-growing economies in the world, and its seaport is ranked among the world's busiest. The city-state has advanced as an international business center incorporating a network of telecommunications and banking services. This network has elevated its status as a financial center, attracting multinational corporations to make Singapore their regional headquarters. With the opening of Singapore International Convention and Exhibition Centre (SICEC), Singapore further enhances its reputation.

SICEC is part of the giant Suntec City Development at Marina Centre near the heart of the city. Suntec City Development Pte., Ltd., incorporated in 1988, was selected by the Urban Redevelopment Authority (URA) in late 1988 to build a billion-dollar complex comprising convention and exhibition facilities, office towers, and a retail component. Situated on some 30 acres of prime land, Suntec City is the largest privately owned commercial development in Singapore. It will include SICEC, an 18-story office block, four 45-story office towers, and a three-story retail and entertainment mall. When the futuristic Suntec City is fully completed in 1997, it will be one of Singapore's most prominent landmarks and a one-stop business hub.

DEVELOPMENT STRATEGY

Singapore and Hong Kong have long enjoyed close trade and investment relations, but it was not until 1988 that a project of such magnitude and long-term commitment to the Republic of Singapore was undertaken by Hong Kong investors.

A group of Hong Kong businessmen incorporated as Suntec City Development Pte., Ltd., (Suntec Ltd.) in August 1988 for the sole purpose of developing and owning this mixed-use complex. In December of the same year, Suntec Ltd. won the government's authorization to build the convention-exhibition project with the highest bid of S$208 million (US$142 million) for the 30-acre parcel at Marina Centre, near the civic and financial districts of Singapore. Suntec Ltd. was credited with submitting the best design largely because it had sized the height and mass of its buildings to those of the neighboring developments. The award was a watershed in Singapore's history of public land sales by the URA because it inaugurated the first major investment by Hong Kong businessmen. When completed, the S$2.2 billion (US$1.57 billion) project will house 490,000 square meters (5.2 million square feet) of convention, exhibition, office, and retail space.

The design was the effort of Tsao & McKown, a design consulting company from New York. The large scale and scope of the project necessitated the establishment of a Singapore office for the firm. Local collaboration with Tsao & McKown is provided by DP Architects, a well-established firm in Singapore. Having a local partner on the team has eased the negotiations with government and professional bodies and the resolution of design issues.

The main building contract for the first and second phases, worth S$1.03 billion (US$700 million), was awarded to the Korean Hyundai-Ssangyong Consortium. Construction of Suntec City began in December 1989 and will continue until 1997. The development is to be completed in three phases. The first phase, completed at the end of 1994, comprises SICEC, the 18-story office block, and the adjoining retail podium. Construction of the second phase will include two of the four 45-story office towers, the central fountain area, and the adjoining retail area and was projected to be completed by mid-1996. The final phase, consisting of the last two 45-story towers and the remaining retail area, is planned for completion in 1997.

DESIGN AND SITE ISSUES

SICEC is situated in the heart of Singapore, making it easily accessible by Mass Rapid Transit (MRT), public bus, taxi, or private auto. The center is within seven minutes' walking distance of 5,000 deluxe hotel rooms, most of which are accessible via pedestrian link and underpass. Approximately 12,000 additional hotel rooms are available in nearby Orchard Road, only a few minutes' drive away. And SICEC is only 20 minutes from the Singapore Changi International Airport.

The center's most impressive features are its separate convention and exhibition halls, with a combined area of 22,600 square meters (243,000 square feet). The column-free convention hall can seat 12,000 guests, giving every attendee an unobstructed view through the use of its fully automated portable telescopic seating system, which includes 7,560 of the 12,000 seats.

In addition, SICEC has 26 meeting rooms, an auditorium, a multipurpose ballroom, and a 3,300-square-meter (35,500-square-foot) gallery. It also houses a retail arcade and 12 food and beverage outlets. When completed in 1995, the center offered over 100,000 square meters (1 million square feet) of space.

SICEC's first level includes the main entrance and registration area, information and reception desks, shops, a restaurant, and two lounges. The ballroom and auditorium are to be found on the second level above grade. The multipurpose ballroom can be subdivided into three sections to accommodate lightweight exhibitions, performances, seminars, and banquet functions. An auditorium, fitted with state-of-the-art video and audio equipment, accommodates 600 people in fixed seating on a sloped floor. Ten of the 26 meeting rooms of various sizes are also located on this second level, as is the 1,400-square-meter (15,000-square-foot) main kitchen, capable of handling banquet functions for 4,000 to 5,000 people.

Three other satellite kitchens dotted throughout the center provide additional food and beverage support.

The third level includes the upper sections of the ballroom and auditorium, 16 meeting rooms, a gallery for long-term exhibitions, and a restaurant seating 304 people with its own private dining rooms.

Levels four and five house the exhibition hall, which can be subdivided into four sections and which is equipped with built-in floor ports and conduits (pits and trenches) to allow easy access to utilities and data communication services.

The column-free convention hall is located on the sixth level, and can be subdivided into three sections.

Vehicular access ramps capable of handling 40-foot container trucks provide two-way access to all center levels. Each hall has ten loading bays, material handling areas, storage facilities, and cargo lifts. Two basements provide 3,200 underground parking spaces.

Linked to the center will be the 18-story Suntec City Tower and four 45-story office towers. When completed, they will offer 2,292,240 square feet of space for multinational and blue-chip companies. The office towers will be a self-contained, one-stop business complex. When these towers are fully occupied, the daily working population in them is estimated to be more than 22,000 people.

The three-story retail and entertainment mall is distributed over two arms that wrap around the five office towers. Beginning on the ground floor of the SICEC, the mall is connected to the five office towers.

Outdoors is a spacious sunken plaza and a ring of restaurants serving Asian and western cuisine surrounding it, with the whole to be framed by the four high-rise towers. This is the setting for a spectacular water feature. Rising almost three levels above the first basement, Suntec City's central fountain consists of an elevated bronze ring from which thousands of gallons of water cascade to a receiving pool at the center of the fountain terrace. The terrace has been designed to create a focal point for social interaction among visitors and Singaporeans and to forge a distinctive identity for Suntec City.

FINANCING

The Project Finance Facility, as the financing plan is termed, has been jointly arranged by the United Overseas Bank (UOB), Ltd., and its joint-venture merchant bank in Hong Kong, United IBV, Ltd. This is the largest financial package assembled in Singapore. Total financing for Phases I and II approximated S$850 million

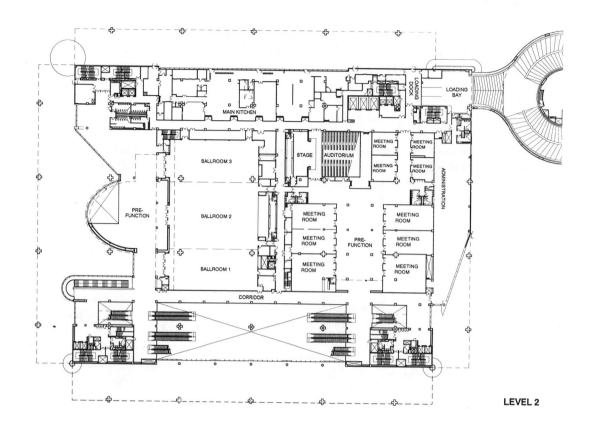

LEVEL 2

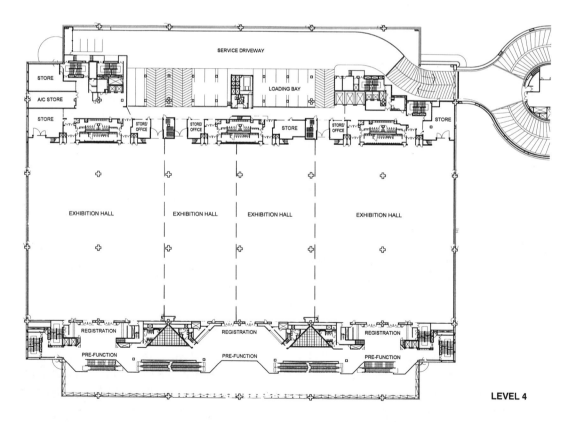

LEVEL 4

(US$578 million). Proceeds of the loans, as well as S$430 million (US$293 million) in shareholders' equity, are being used to finance construction of Suntec City.

The loan structure comprises various borrowings to be drawn in a number of currencies, thus giving Suntec City Development some flexibility. Principal banks participating in the financing include UOB, Ltd., Oversea-Chinese Banking Corporation, Ltd., and The Development Bank of Singapore, Ltd.

In mid-1994, Suntec City Development signed a S$550 million (US$374 million) plan known as the Additional Project Finance Facility. This addition was arranged by UOB, Ltd., to finance the balance of the construction cost of the development. Most of this sum will go toward financing the third phase of the project.

The total cost of Suntec City is estimated to be S$2.2 billion (US$1.57 billion). SICEC accounts for about S$750 million (US$536 million) of this amount.

MARKETING ORIENTATION

An aggressive marketing drive, started three years before the opening of the center, has proven beneficial. Mega-events that have previously bypassed Singapore due to a lack of space may now consider Singapore with the opening of SICEC.

The existence of the center was one factor contributing to Singapore's successful bid for the 1999 Rotary International Convention, which is expecting 25,000 delegates. At its peak, the center will have a staff of 550, including personnel in food and beverage service, operations, sales, marketing, and administration.

LESSONS LEARNED

- Suntec City will be quite "green" when completed, as about 900 trees are scheduled to be planted in the project. A drainage system has been designed to enable the roof to collect water from the abundant annual rainfall, to be used for irrigation purposes.
- Unlike centers in the United States and Europe, where the largest exhibit halls are located on the ground level for the convenience of freight move-in and move-out, Singapore's center does not have the luxury of accommodating single-story halls on grade. Located on limited prime land, the center has to build in a vertical direction. Studies were conducted on several convention centers, and SICEC tried to learn from their experiences and to improve on aspects that were deemed

PROJECT DATA

SINGAPORE INTERNATIONAL CONVENTION AND EXHIBITION CENTRE SINGAPORE

Owners/Developers: Suntec City Development Pte., Ltd.
Architects: Tsao & McKown, New York and Singapore; DP Architects, Singapore
Structure: Hyundai-Ssangyong Consortium, South Korea
Year Planning Began: 1988
Year Construction Began: 1989
Year Construction Completed:
  Phase I: 1994
  Phase II: 1995
  Phase III: 1997

PROJECT INFORMATION

Site Area: 30 acres
Total GBA: 1,000,000 square feet
  Exhibition Space: 254,693 square feet
  Meeting Space: 195,742 square feet
  Total Parking Spaces: 3,200

ECONOMIC INFORMATION

Total SICEC Project Cost (1995 U.S. dollars): $536,000,000
Total Suntec City Project Cost (1995 U.S. dollars): $1,571,000,000
Funding Sources for Suntec City (U.S. dollars):[1]
  Shareholders' Equity: $293,000,000
  Project Finance Facility: $578,000,000
  Project Finance Facility: $374,000,000

Note:
[1]Includes funding for SICEC, amounting to US$536 million.

inefficient. Centers with halls above grade usually rely on freight and cargo elevators to transport exhibits. SICEC, however, has addressed this need by building a spiral vehicular access ramp for two-way, 40-foot container traffic. With each lane six meters wide, the ramp serves all building levels and was constructed at a cost of S$10 million.
- SICEC halls have a floor load capacity of 17.65 kilonewtons per square meter, or 350 pounds per square foot. This means that most commercial exhibitions can be held there. However, heavy machinery/equipment-type shows cannot be scheduled at the center.
- SICEC lacks the capability to host outdoor exhibitions, which some shows require.

HONG KONG STADIUM

SO KON PO, HONG KONG

Hong Kong Stadium, which was conceived and developed to replace the city's aging Government Stadium, has hosted a wide variety of sporting and leisure events since its completion in 1994.

DEVELOPMENT STRATEGY

The Royal Hong Kong Jockey Club, a nonprofit organization, recognized the need for a stadium to host international sporting events and cultural activities, as a means to further promote Hong Kong's image as a world-class city. The 28,000-seat Government Stadium, built in 1952, offered inadequate seating capacity and little spectator comfort. For this reason, the Jockey Club, along with the Urban Council, chose to replace the stadium with a new facility designed to accommodate both local and international sports competitions and entertainment. The new Hong Kong Stadium (HKS) was completed in March 1994 and transferred to the Urban Council for management.

DESIGN AND SITE ISSUES

At the north end of the HKS are the entrance and box offices; the south side offers end-zone seating, the scoreboard, and the Diamond Vision screen, which is capable of delivering live telecasts of action on the field. The majority of the seats are located on the east and west sides of the oval-shaped structure. In total, the stadium contains four levels: service, main, executive, and upper.

The service level houses the box office, locker rooms, and administrative offices, while the main level seats 18,240 persons along the full perimeter of the stadium. Ten concession areas on the main level offer a variety of fast-food options, such as McDonald's, Häagen-Dazs, and Kentucky Fried Chicken. Four souvenir shops and a hospitality suite are also found on this level.

The executive level offers seating for 3,153 people. There are also 50 suites, each comprising a kitchen, toilet, and lounge. Although there are no concessions on this level, spectators are served by four lounges and four bars along the east and west sides of the stadium. On the north side of the executive level is Jimmy's Sports Bar and Grill, a two-tier restaurant offering both Asian and western cuisine. The restaurant is open to the public every day and offers views of the stadium and the surrounding neighborhood.

The stadium's upper level seats 18,647 spectators along the east and west sides. Eight concession areas and four souvenir shops are situated on this level as well.

Ramps, elevators, and escalators convey spectators to their desired levels. Maximum seating capacity at the HKS is 46,088, with 40,088 permanent seats and an additional 6,000 temporary chairs on the field for concerts. Seventy-five percent of the permanent stadium seating is covered by a Teflon-coated fiberglass roof.

Security is taken seriously at the stadium. If a capacity crowd is expected for an event, at least 400 stewards are employed to assist patrons and to monitor crowd behavior. Closed-circuit television cameras also survey the crowd, both within the stadium and from peripheral roads, and a public address system is available to relay announcements and instructions in case of emergency. At full capacity, evacuation of the stadium would take about 11 minutes.

FINANCING

The capital cost of HK$850 million was provided by the Royal Hong Kong Jockey Club, with the Urban Council of Hong Kong funding the fitting-out cost of HK$150 million, for a total project cost of HK$1 billion (approximately US$129 million).

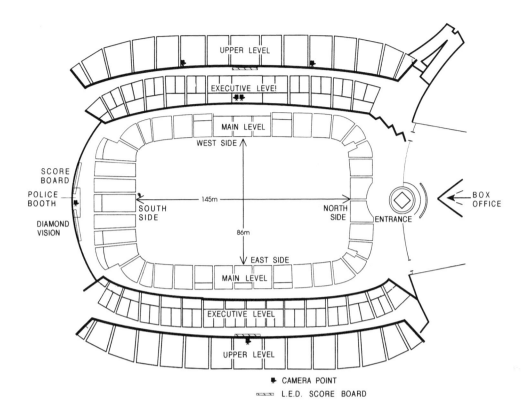

UPPER LEVEL

EXECUTIVE LEVEl

MAIN LEVEL

WEST SIDE ↑

SCORE BOARD

POLICE BOOTH

DIAMOND VISION

SOUTH SIDE

←— 145m —→

NORTH SIDE

86m

ENTRANCE

→| BOX OFFICE

↓ EAST SIDE

MAIN LEVEL

EXECUTIVE LEVEL

UPPER LEVEL

♦ CAMERA POINT

▭▭▭ L.E.D. SCORE BOARD

Market orientation

Though the stadium's primary user is the Hong Kong Football Association, as a multiuse facility it hosted 51 events in its first year of operations, including football (soccer), rugby, family fun fairs, charity carnivals, and graduation ceremonies, attracting more than 1 million visitors. Although parking is reserved exclusively for promoters, convenient public access is gained by taxi, bus, or subway.

Lessons learned

- Hong Kong is a densly populated city. When the original Government Stadium was built in the same district in 1952, the area was somewhat isolated. Since that time, however, the vicinity has become crowded with high-rise apartments, and noise from stadium concerts has often disturbed local residents. If funds were available, the HKS would add a retractable roof and use it during concerts to alleviate the problem. Meanwhile, the noise problem is being mitigated through the use of high-tech sound systems.
- Because of the heavy rainfall in Hong Kong's tropical climate, a 100 percent sand mesh pitch (or playing field) was installed. Management is still evaluating the advantages and disadvantages of this system.

Project data

HONG KONG STADIUM
HONG KONG

Owner: The Urban Council of Hong Kong
Operator: Wembley International (HK), Ltd.
Architects: Hellmuth, Obata & Kassabaum International (Asia/Pacific)
Primary User: Hong Kong Football Association
Year Completed: 1994

PROJECT INFORMATION
Site Area: 37,120 square meters (9 acres)
Seating Capacity:
　　Football: 40,088
　　Concerts: 46,088
Total Parking Spaces: Limited to promoters' use only

ECONOMIC INFORMATION
Construction Costs (Hong Kong dollars):
　　HK$850,000,000
Total Project Cost (Hong Kong dollars):
　　HK$1,000,000,000
Total Project Cost (U.S. dollars): $129,110,000

EARLS COURT OLYMPIA

LONDON, ENGLAND

Olympia Grand Hall

Olympia opened in 1886, accommodating the Paris Hippodrome Circus, and for many years it housed themed spectacles, Edwardian roller skating, and boxing. For its part, Earls Court began its association with exhibitions and entertainment in 1887, with Buffalo Bill Cody's Wild West Show and a pleasure garden and fun fair. The two adjacent rival venues joined forces in 1973 to form what is now known as Earls Court Olympia.

DEVELOPMENT STRATEGY

Olympia's Grand Hall, originally called the Great Hall, was conceived by a General Burnaby, who, along with other senior army officers, wanted to build a bigger venue than the existing Agricultural Hall in Islington in which to house the Royal Military Tournament. This new venue was financed by the National Agricultural Hall Company, Ltd., and designed by architect Henry E. Coe. Set in five-and-a-half acres of gardens and completed in 1886, the building was given the name the "New Agricultural Hall." However, it quickly became known as Olympia.

Earls Court, a district of London, got its name from the Earl of Zetland, who owned the site on which the arena now stands. Originally, the building's site was an awkward triangle of railway tracks, siding, and depots, all of which rendered it hopeless for residential development. Businessman John Robinson Whitley conceived the idea of using it for exhibitions. His open-air arena, which held covered seating for 25,000 spectators, opened in 1887.

Whitley retired in 1891 and was replaced by Imre Kiralfy, whose theatrical extravaganzas were well known. Kiralfy negotiated a 21-year lease on the Earls Court site; during those years, he opened the 5,000-seat Empress Theatre and staged exhibitions and lavish productions in the arena until World War I, when the grounds were used as a Belgian refugee camp. In 1935, with Kiralfy's lease at its end and Earls Court in decline, the facility was reborn. The new freeholders of the site, the London Passenger Transport Board, promised a new lease to a revived Earls Court, Ltd., controlled largely by American shareholders. The company began by renovating the Empress Theater, which reopened as an ice skating rink seating 7,000 in 1935 and was renamed the Empress Hall.

The 12 remaining acres of the Earls Court site were used to locate the present exhibition hall. Designed by Chicago architect Howard Crane and originally managed by the firm Hegemon-Harris of New York, the building was constructed in 1936 and 1937 at a cost of £1.5 million. It was one of the largest reinforced concrete structures of its day.

DESIGN AND SITE ISSUES

Olympia's first expansion came in the form of a small annex to the Grand Hall ten years after the latter had been built. In 1923, the New Hall, or National Hall, opened and was closely followed by the construction of the Empire Hall. Designed by Joseph Emberton, the Empire Hall was prompted by the Department of Overseas Trade's decision that its British Industries Fair, previously held in White City, would require an extra 500,000 square feet of floor space, roughly the total space of the two halls already at Olympia. The result, Empire Hall, was refurbished and enlarged in 1984 and is now known as Olympia 2. It caters specifically to the needs of small and medium-sized exhibitions and is able to host three exhibitions simultaneously.

Offering hotel-standard levels of comfort and substantial conference facilities, the Olympia Conference Center at Olympia 2 was added in 1987.

The Grand Hall (part of Olympia 1) cost £140,000 in 1886 (equivalent to more than £5 million today) and featured seating for 7,000. Its roof, however, was really its most amazing feature. Built of glass, zinc, and iron, the massive, glazed barrel vault soared to over 100 feet at its highest point and covered an area of more than three-and-a-half acres. Ball bearings, mounted inside the hall's fluted columns, enabled the entire structure to move during extremely strong winds.

Earls Court is a triangular building covering nearly 42,000 square meters (almost 450,000 square feet). The upper floor is divisible into three sections so that four exhibitions can be shown simultaneously. The venue seats 18,500, making Earls Court the largest covered auditorium in Europe. It also contains an enormous swimming pool holding two-and-a-quarter million gallons of water. Tiered seating has been built in three sections, which can be raised or lowered by hydraulic jacks.

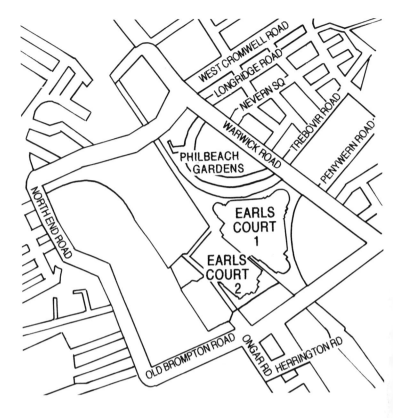

Earls Court

Earls Court 2, with an additional 17,000 square meters (182,796 square feet) of space, opened in 1991 at a cost of £100 million. This new hall has hosted events such as the world championships of boxing and wrestling and a celebration of Her Majesty the Queen's 40-year reign.

The Brompton Conference Suite, a conference and multipurpose center, opened in 1994 on Level 3 of Earls Court. It is composed of a flat-floor auditorium that can seat 500 delegates or can be divided into two 250-seat rooms by a retractable acoustic wall. Demountable seating and staging capable of displaying products as large as cars make the space highly adaptable. A 180-delegate breakout room can be used alongside the main auditorium for a variety of purposes.

MARKETING ORIENTATION

West Kensington's Olympia opened its doors to the public on Boxing Day 1886, with the Paris Hippodrome Circus. Many circuses have been held there over the last century, as well as lavish extravaganzas such as "Venice," an event for which the building underwent a transformation to become a vision of that city. Other events have included the International Horse Show, boxing and wres-

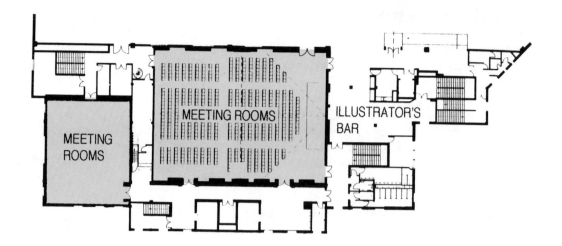

tling matches, and trade exhibitions. These trade exhibitions have since become the lifeblood of Olympia.

Olympia played host to the Royal Tournament for 40 years, until that event moved to Earls Court. The tournament's early displays involved horsemanship, driving, drill, and weapon fighting. In more recent years, Earls Court Olympia has hosted operas; popular music concerts such as U2, Pink Floyd, and Dire Straits; boxing; and banquets. The complex hosts most of the nation's key information technology shows as well.

LESSONS LEARNED

Renovations have become a priority recently at Earls Court Olympia, to make the complex more efficient and user-friendly:

- Improvements now underway include clearer signage at the Earls Court Olympia underground stations; a glazed, covered walkway, and a new escalator for the Grand Hall entrance.
- The Grand Hall's vast, glazed barrel-vault roof caused cooling problems in the summer months. It was reglazed with solar-protective laminated glass that allows light in while keeping the heat out.

PROJECT DATA
EARLS COURT OLYMPIA
LONDON, ENGLAND

Owner: Earls Court Olympia, Ltd.
Manager: Douglas Littlejohns, managing director of the halls
Architects:
  Earls Court: C. Howard Crane, Chicago
  Olympia: Henry E. Coe (Grand Hall); Joseph Emberton (Empire Hall)
Primary Users: Trade shows, family shows, concerts

PROJECT INFORMATION
Site Area:
  Earls Court: 27 acres
  Olympia: 10 acres
Exhibition Space: 450,000 square feet
Total Seating Capacity:
  Earls Court: 18,500
  Earls Court 2: 10,250
  Olympia Grand Hall: 8,500
  Olympia National Hall: 4,500
Total Parking Spaces: 2,100

FLINDERS PARK

MELBOURNE, AUSTRALIA

Flinders Park in Melbourne, Australia, was designed and built to accomplish two goals. First was to provide a world-class tennis facility in which to host the Australian Open Tennis Championship and thereby to retain the city's international reputation as the site of one of the four Grand Slam championship tournaments. (The others are the U.S. Open in New York, the French Open in Paris, and Wimbledon in England.) The second goal was to provide a high-quality entertainment facility for the city of Melbourne. A revolutionary design solution for a movable roof enabled both of these goals to be satisfied in one facility.

DEVELOPMENT STRATEGY

In June 1984, the Lawn Tennis Association of Australia (Tennis Australia) and the State Government of Victoria agreed to plan Flinders Park as a joint initiative. The decision to construct the venue was made by the state government in 1985.

DESIGN AND SITE ISSUES

Flinders Park encompasses an area of 60,000 square meters (645,161 square feet) on the banks of the Yarra River and within walking distance of the heart of Melbourne. The site was controversial because it was designated as public parkland. The architectural design was completed by the team of Peddle Thorp Learmonth and Phillip Cox. Construction began in March 1986 and, using a fast-track design/build method, was completed in time for the Australian Open in January 1988.

Flinders Park has a total of 21 match courts: Match Court One (6,000 seats), Match Court Two (3,000 seats), Center Court/Auditorium (15,000 seats, including 26 "superboxes"), five indoor practice courts, and 13 outdoor match courts. The facility also houses a pro shop, dining rooms, and function rooms.

A second stage of development completed in 1995 includes Match Court Three (3,000 seats), Match Court Four (2,000 seats), eight additional outdoor match courts, and one clay court. A 1,800-seat function center capable of hosting banquets, a garden square, and 500 additional parking spaces are also included in Stage Two.

Flinders Park has won 12 major international and national design and construction awards, including the United Kingdom's Institution of Structural Engineers' Special Award for 1988, in recognition of physical achievement in engineering, in particular for the movable roof concept. The movable roof enables tennis to be played in the open air on Center Court by moving two 350-ton sections of the roof along rails to positions over the fixed roof. This process takes only 20 minutes.

FINANCING

Initial construction costs totaled A$85 million. Management reported (1994) an annual operating surplus of A$5 million.

Flinders Park is controlled by a state government–appointed trust. When the financial structure was altered in 1993 by the state government, this state-appointed trust was left with a debt to be serviced and allowed funds for the second stage of development. In 1994, the trust approved Stage Two development at an estimated A$23 million, including site preparation.

Stage Two is aimed at maintaining the competitive position of Flinders Park in relation to other Grand Slam facilities also undergoing redevelopment or expansion. The Australian Open produces approximately 75 percent of the total revenue generated by the facility. In the last six years, this event has attracted more than 300,000 spectators annually, with a worldwide television audience of 500 million.

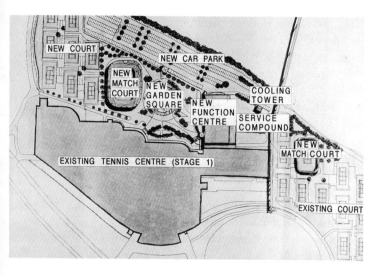

MARKETING

Throughout January of each year, Flinders Park is reserved exclusively for the Australian Open. In addition to tennis, however, the venue hosts professional basketball, boxing, supercross motorcycling, all-star basketball, and rodeo exhibitions. Major musical events have included concerts by Neil Diamond, Phil Collins, Elton John, Billy Joel, U2, Jose Carreras, Placido Domingo, and Luciano Pavarotti, plus operas and other musical productions. The facility is also available for meetings, conventions, and exhibitions. Usage increased to approximately 115 events, attracting more than 1 million patrons annually.

The state government–appointed trust delegates the day-to-day management of the facility to Tennis Australia. This unusual management arrangement is the result of a revenue-sharing agreement that ensures that the Grand Slam remains at Flinders Park for the next 25 years.

Staff specialists manage the facility, their duties including event administration, marketing, building and court rentals, merchandise, and coaching services. A separate team is dedicated to preparing for the Australian Open each year. Catering, cleaning, security, ticketing, and many building maintenance services are subcontracted.

LESSONS LEARNED

- During the construction phase, an A$8 million restaurant was eliminated to contain the overall cost of the project. As a result, Flinders Park realizes less than its full potential in catering revenue. The new function

PROJECT DATA
FLINDERS PARK
MELBOURNE, AUSTRALIA

Owner: State Government of Victoria
Operator: Tennis Australia
Architect: Peddle Thorp Learmonth, Melbourne; Phillip Cox, Melbourne
Primary Users: Australian Open tennis, basketball, concerts
Year Planning Began: 1984
Year Construction Began: 1986
Year Construction Completed:
　　Stage One: 1988
　　Stage Two: 1995

PROJECT INFORMATION
Total Site Area: 115,000 square meters (1,236,559 square feet)
　　Stage One: 60,000 square meters (645,161 square feet)
　　Stage Two: 55,000 square meters (591,398 square feet)
Seating Capacity:
　　Center Court: 15,000
　　Match Court One: 6,000
　　Match Court Two: 3,000
　　Match Court Three: 3,000
　　Match Court Four: 2,000
Total Parking Spaces: 825
　　Stage One: 325
　　Stage Two: 500

ECONOMIC INFORMATION
Total Project Costs (1986 Australian dollars): A$85,000,000
Total Project Costs (1986 U.S. dollars):[1] $56,542,274
Total Project Costs (1994 U.S. dollars):[2] $75,217,733
Stage Two Development (1994 Australian dollars): A$23,000,000
Stage Two Development (1994 U.S. dollars):[3] $19,420,040
Funding Source: State Government of Victoria

Notes:
[1]Calculated based on the 1986 year-end exchange rate.
[2]Calculated based on the consumer price index.
[3]Calculated based on the 1994 year-end exchange rate.

center will help overcome this problem when Stage Two development has been completed.

- Private and public transportation access to the facility is inadequate. A study is currently underway to improve the railway infrastructure and scheduling of services, and the addition of 500 parking spaces in Stage Two will boost the parking capacity of the venue significantly.

SKYDOME

TORONTO, ONTARIO, CANADA

SkyDome is located in downtown Toronto, Ontario, adjacent to the CN Tower. It is home to major league baseball's Blue Jays, the National Basketball Association's Raptors, and the Canadian Football League's Argonauts. This extraordinary domed stadium features a retractable roof, enabling it to be an enclosed stadium for fall and winter events and an open-air facility during the summer months. In its first five years of operations, SkyDome has accommodated 35 million people and hosted more than 1,500 events and exhibitions.

DEVELOPMENT STRATEGY

In 1982, Bill Davis, the premier of Ontario, and Paul Godfrey, Toronto's metropolitan chairman (regional "mayor"), attended the CFL Championship Grey Cup game at Toronto's old Exhibition Stadium. The game was poorly attended because of cold weather, leading Davis and Godfrey to resolve to build a new stadium. They began looking for a site, and by 1985 they had obtained authorization from the provincial and metropolitan government legislatures to build the facility. Rod Robbie of Toronto was the architect initially employed to design SkyDome.

DESIGN AND SITE ISSUES

The stadium has a number of interesting design characteristics. The entire development, which is located on a 12.7-acre site and has a building footprint of eight acres, is linked to its neighbors by SkyWalk, a climate-controlled, indoor pedestrian walkway connecting Union Station to SkyDome and the downtown underground walkway system. (The adjacent CN Tower is the world's tallest freestanding structure and includes an observation area and revolving restaurant.) The facility is also accessible via subway, bus, streetcar, or commuter train. Parking is available for 14,500 vehicles in various lots nearby, though only 600 spaces exist on site.

SkyDome is the first domed sports and entertainment facility to contain a fully integrated hotel, the SkyDome Hotel, which is operated by Canadian Pacific Hotels and Resorts. It is built into the northern end of the dome and offers 348 rooms, 70 of which overlook the playing field. Four private SkyBoxes are available for events and meetings and can accommodate up to 25 people each.

SkyDome has the world's first fully retractable stadium roof. Covering eight acres and rising 282 feet at its highest inside point, the roof has four telescoping panels that slide along tracks similar to railway tracks, powered by 54 drive mechanisms called "bogies." Opening or closing the roof takes only 20 minutes, and energy consumption for the entire process is estimated to cost $10. The entire field (baseball or football) is uncovered when the roof is open, as are 91 percent of the seats.

SkyDome's maximum seating capacity is 53,000. The Level 100 (first-level) seating is built on 1,400 precast concrete bleachers that also move on a system of railway tracks, to reconfigure the field from baseball to football or vice versa. Astroturf is used for both sports.

The pitcher's mound is constructed on a fiberglass "dish" 18 feet in diameter that was built by Ontario Yachts. The dish is permanently stored beneath the field in a holding chamber. As the chamber is filled with water, the mound rises to field level, where it is locked into place.

SkyDome provides a total of 161 private suites: 60 SkyBoxes on Level 300, and 101 on Level 400. The boxes are priced according to size and location and range from $100,000 to $225,000[1] per year with ten-year leases. Box capacity varies from 16 to 40 people, and each box is unique in design and decor. A number of SkyBoxes are also available for rent on a per-event basis.

There are 5,700 club seats located on Level 200. These extrawide, upholstered seats are available on ten-year leases and are priced according to location. Club seat holders pay a one-time subscription fee of $2,000 or $4,000 and annual dues of $250 a year for the first five years, then $350 a year for the remaining five years. The cost of tickets is not included in this fee structure; holders of club seats are required to purchase Blue Jays season tickets.

SkyDome uses a unique video screen for advertising and instant replay. The $17 million Sony JumboTron is one of the largest video display boards in the world. Indeed, the single-sided screen is three stories high by nine stories wide and measures one-twelfth of an acre. A full production control facility with a five-

camera input and a crew of 11 to 26 people is required to operate the video display.

Another SkyDome feature is the SkyTent, a large acoustical curtain that completely encloses one section of SkyDome to create SkyBowl, which accommodates 10,000 to 30,000 spectators for arena-sized events.

SkyDome is one of the first accessible, barrier-free facilities in Canada. To gain a better understanding of the needs of its guests with disabilities, SkyDome formed its own Accessibility Council in 1991, which meets twice a year to discuss issues of seating, sightlines, parking, elevators, entrances, exits, and signage. Since the council was formed, the dome has made additional modifications and improvements costing nearly $300,000, including a new elevator, an automatic door at the hotel entrance, improved signage, and a TDD (telecommunications device for the deaf) telephone.

FINANCING

Financing for the $570 million SkyDome was a joint effort of public and private parties. The province of Ontario and metropolitan Toronto each provided $30 million, and 30 corporations contributed $5 million each, for a total of $150 million. These contributing corporations received certain rights. McDonald's, for example, was granted catering rights, while Labatt and Molson breweries were granted pouring rights for alcoholic beverages.

Subscription fees for leasing the 5,700 club seats generated $20 million. SkyBox buyers were required to pay a first- and last-year deposit on each ten-year subscription. SkyBoxes generated a total of $40 million, which was applied to the development cost of the dome. The remaining $300 million was financed by the government of the province of Ontario.

In March 1994, seven corporations purchased the dome for $151 million. The new owners include Labatt, Coca-Cola, the Ford Motor Company, the *Toronto Sun*, and others.

MARKET ORIENTATION

Since its opening in 1989, SkyDome has achieved several honors: *Performance* magazine's Best New Venue (1989) and Stadium of the Year (1990 to 1993). The dome also has set all-time American League baseball attendance records for four years in a row, from 1990 through 1993. The dome is a versatile facility, capable of hosting baseball, football, family shows, concerts, trade and consumer shows, and corporate events, such

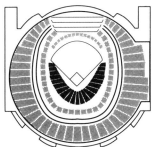
Baseball Mode

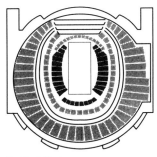
Football Mode

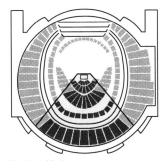
SkyTent Mode

as new product introductions or "rollouts" and company sales meetings.

Open-air stadium events include Toronto Blue Jays baseball, Toronto Argonauts football, and Ribfest,

PROJECT DATA

SKYDOME
TORONTO, ONTARIO, CANADA

Owner and Operator: Stadium Corporation
Builder: Ellis Don, Toronto
Architect: Rod Robbie, Toronto
Primary Users: Toronto Blue Jays (baseball), Toronto Argonauts (football), concerts, family shows
Year Planning Began: 1984
Year Construction Began: 1986
Year Construction Completed: 1989

PROJECT INFORMATION
Site Area: 12.7 acres
Building Footprint: 8 acres
Exhibition Space: 150,000 square feet
Maximum Seating Capacity: 53,000
Total Parking Spaces: 15,100
    On Site: 600
    Nearby: 14,500

ECONOMIC INFORMATION
Total Project Cost (1989 Canadian dollars): $570,000,000
Total Project Cost (1989 U.S. dollars):[1] $492,227,979
Total Project Cost (1994 U.S. dollars):[2] $578,764,833
Funding Sources (Canadian dollars):
    Province of Ontario: $330,000,000
    Metropolitan Toronto: $30,000,000
    Private Corporations: $150,000,000
    SkyBox Leases: $40,000,000
    Club Seat Subscriptions: $20,000,000

Notes:
[1]Calculated based on the 1989 year-end exchange rate.
[2]Calculated based on the consumer price index.

an outdoor food festival. The domed stadium is home to Raptors basketball and has hosted two baseball World Series, the Rolling Stones, and religious events. For instance, Billy Graham's June 1995 Crusade boasted an all-time attendance record of 68,500 people. SkyTent events have included Madonna, Disney on Ice, and Depeche Mode. The Sony JumboTron telecasts out-of-town World Series games and Stanley Cup hockey.

Event service companies within SkyDome contract with the facility to provide a range of services, from audiovisual and electrical supply to food services and merchandising. Controlled Media Communications (CMC), which is one of the new owners of SkyDome, acts as its exclusive advertising sales agent, having been closely involved with the facility since its inception.

LESSONS LEARNED

- SkyDome was built with the intention that it would be able to pay for itself. Operating revenue has not been meeting costs, however, leaving the owners responsible for the shortfall, despite the fact that the dome is used 261 times per year.
- Two drawbacks of the facility are the limited number of parking spaces on site and the lack of a drainage system inside the stadium. When the stadium was built, it was thought that the enclosed area would not be susceptible to rain, as the roof could be closed during inclement weather. Drainage problems do exist, however, because the seating areas are washed down regularly.
- SkyDome's limited capacity of 53,000 has not caused it to lose events to nearby NFL venues with more seating, thanks to SkyDome's location and its ability to convert to an indoor stadium. The closest NFL facility, Rich Stadium in Buffalo, New York, is an outdoor open venue.

---

[1]All dollars are in Canadian currency except as noted in Data Box.